THE UNIVERSITY OF NORTH CAROLINA
SESQUICENTENNIAL PUBLICATIONS

IN SEARCH OF
THE REGIONAL BALANCE
OF AMERICA

THE UNIVERSITY OF NORTH CAROLINA
SESQUICENTENNIAL PUBLICATIONS

Louis R. Wilson, DIRECTOR

———————◆———————

CHRONICLES OF THE SESQUICENTENNIAL

THE UNIVERSITY OF NORTH CAROLINA, 1789–1835:
A Documentary History

THE CAMPUS OF THE FIRST STATE UNIVERSITY

THE GRADUATE SCHOOL: RESEARCH AND PUBLICATIONS

THE GRADUATE SCHOOL: DISSERTATIONS AND THESES

STUDIES IN SCIENCE

STUDIES IN LANGUAGE AND LITERATURE

A HUNDRED YEARS OF LEGAL EDUCATION

A STATE UNIVERSITY SURVEYS THE HUMANITIES

SECONDARY EDUCATION IN THE SOUTH

IN SEARCH OF THE REGIONAL BALANCE OF AMERICA

STUDIES IN HISTORY AND POLITICAL SCIENCE

LIBRARY RESOURCES OF THE UNIVERSITY OF NORTH CAROLINA

RESEARCH AND REGIONAL WELFARE

PIONEERING A PEOPLE'S THEATER

UNIVERSITY EXTENSION IN ACTION

BOOKS FROM CHAPEL HILL

IN SEARCH
OF THE
REGIONAL BALANCE
OF AMERICA

Edited with a foreword

BY

HOWARD W. ODUM

Kenan Professor of Sociology

AND

KATHARINE JOCHER

Professor of Sociology and
Assistant Director of the Institute for
Research in Social Science

CHAPEL HILL
THE UNIVERSITY OF NORTH CAROLINA PRESS
1945

EDITORS' FOREWORD

THE TITLE FOR THIS VOLUME is one that has grown cumulatively from the first quarter century's work of the Institute for Research in Social Science of the University of North Carolina and SOCIAL FORCES. It reflects the persistent attempt to contribute sound theory which has developed out of empirical research that can also be applied to practical social study and direction. From the beginning SOCIAL FORCES has featured its area of work as "a medium for social study and interpretation" and the Institute early characterized its task as social study which sought the materials of social science as well as social research itself which, in turn, sought to make contributions of scientific value. From the materials and researches, contributions of value follow logically in the wake of continued analysis and use. The conclusion that the most dynamic problem in postwar America, namely, the achievement of the regional quality and balance of America, is of one part with the search for a better regional balance of people and resources everywhere. This fact adds strength to our premises of American regionalism and new purpose to continued research and planning in this field.

The editors wish to express appreciation for the extraordinary support which has been given to both SOCIAL FORCES and the Institute for Research in Social Science from within and without the University and from within and without the region which is called South. If this volume (which also appeared as No. 3 of Vol. XXIII of SOCIAL FORCES) falls short of being fully representative of other authors and fields of interest which might have been included, it may be said also that neither is it possible in this space to comprehend all that should be included in the areas which we have selected. A later issue of SOCIAL FORCES will continue certain features of regional development which could not be incorporated in the present volume. In choosing a theme and area in which a consistent thread may be said to run through the total fabric rather than selecting wider samplings of a variegated total, the editors hope for a sympathetic understanding of and by those who follow this attempt to approximate as nearly as possible the spirit and letter of the University's one hundred and fiftieth anniversary program of which this volume forms a part.

H. W. O.
K. J.

Chapel Hill, N. C.
March 1945

CONTENTS

PART I

FROM EMPIRICAL STUDIES
TO REGIONALISM

FROM
COMMUNITY STUDIES
TO REGIONALISM

I

THIS paper indicates something of the way in which certain theoretical aspects of regionalism and folk sociology in the early 1940's have developed from beginnings in community studies of race and folk culture in the early 1900's. In so far as they have a bearing upon social research and planning, as applied to the regional quality and balance of America, there are a number of assumptions. One is that responsible social theory grows naturally out of the synthesis of results of practical empirical studies and, therefore, is basic to planning which is essentially the bridging of the distance between science and knowledge on the one hand and practical problems on the other. Another is that in the social sciences, as in the natural sciences, there is needed the living laboratory for research and planning where the people live and that the smallest and basic unit for the complete scientific study of society is found in the region embodying all the elements of time, of spatial relationships, and of total cultural environment.

The definitive culture to be studied through the region is the folk-regional society, in the study of which folk sociology may assume the new dynamics of a functional sociology as a natural-cultural science which combines the cultural and statistical methods of study. In the folk-regional society, moreover, may be found the laboratory for contrasting the folkways and mores with the stateways and technicways, basic to differentiating the folk society and culture from the state society and civilization now so tragically destructive in contemporary society. In the technicways, as it were, newly discovered through the inquiries of folk sociology, may be found objective ways not only of measuring change but of describing the processes of change basic to an understanding of what is the definitive, enduring human society in a new equilibrium between culture and civiliza-

tion. The particular application of this theory is to American society, and more particularly the southern regions of the United States, which have constituted the several laboratories for study. Still more specifically the Institute for Research in Social Science, the Department of Sociology, and SOCIAL FORCES have constituted the later media through which studies have been made and theory developed.

While the emphasis here is primarily upon the theoretical, the assumption is always that sound theory which grows out of "the day's work" is the most practical thing in the world and is basic to all enduring programs of societal development. Such theory is peculiarly essential in contemporary society when, as is commonly assumed, the foundations of society are being shaken and "fundamentals" are being questioned. Such sound organic theory is essential to the redefining of many of our assumptions of democracy, equality, opportunity, "Americanism," and of developing sound programs of security, defense, and public welfare. Both the need and the effectiveness of such theory perhaps may best be reflected in the postulates of social planning, the essence of which may be found in the search for balance and equilibrium between and among conflicting and complex forces and processes. The more detailed specifications and implications of the evolving theory of regionalism and folk sociology are stated subsequently as growing out of the several stages of inquiry and records.

Now we come to answer the questions as to how the concept of regionalism and the search for the regional balance of America ever evolved through the southern regional studies made at the University of North Carolina during the last twenty-five years. How did we come upon the concept of regionalism as sociological theory inherent in the larger application of ecology to human society? How did we come to the concept of folk sociology

3

and the folk society as a general sociology studying the definitive society? How did we come to assume the relatively new phenomena, the technicways, as ways of explaining and also of directing the rapidly changing society which is contemporary technological civilization?

The answers to these questions given here in the nature of a special twentieth and twenty-fifth anniversary of SOCIAL FORCES, and the Institute for Research in Social Science, and the Department of Sociology at the University of North Carolina must be partly a rationalization of one author's interpretation reflected first in his own work, and second in the cooperative efforts of his colleagues. This rationalization is essentially of two sorts. One is found in the earlier beginnings and backgrounds in the concrete study of the Negro and of folk culture in Mississippi and Georgia in the first decade of 1900. The other is the gradual expansion of folk studies and regional research at the University of North Carolina from 1920 to 1945. In the years covering these periods there were firsthand studies and observations in all the major regions of America set in the framework of current sociological theory and trends.

II

The earlier community inquiries into race relations, to which we refer, were concrete studies of Negroes in southern towns, begun in Mississippi and Georgia in 1905. These studies grew out of the observation that there had been practically no scientific studies of the Negro in the South; that the South itself was amazingly ignorant about the Negro; that practically no one was interested in the subject; and that nevertheless this was the distinctive field of inquiry where knowledge must be had before progress in other respects could be made. In the wake of the community studies themselves it soon became evident that in the folk character of the Negroes and their relationship with the whites, in their folk songs and sayings, their folk beliefs and folk culture were to be found an extraordinary untapped mine of information that was not only essential to the understanding of the Negro and the South but which would soon be passing beyond the point where it could be recovered. To the community studies, therefore, were added the subsidiary inquiries into the folk society of the Negro which existed and has always existed within the white "state society" and which has been responsible for much of the vitality

and surviving powers and progress of the Negro in the United States.

The first of the background community inquiries was a concrete study of the Negroes of Oxford, Mississippi. This was followed by a similar study of Covington, Georgia, in order to begin comparative studies of relatively similar communities. Each of these southern towns had a population of less than three thousand. Each was neighbor to a college, the one the University of Mississippi and the other, Emory College, at Oxford, Georgia, one mile from Covington. Each had about the same ratio of Negroes to whites, and as towns in the lower South reflected much similarity in segregation patterns and racial folkways. Other points of resemblance in economy and culture were sufficiently numerous to establish a satisfactory homogeneity index.

Having made these concrete studies and summarized their findings, the effort was made to set up a continuing frame of inquiry to test the findings in other similar communities. First, some fifty towns through the Southeast, with population under ten thousand, were checked through the questionnaire and schedule method, some by mail, some through assignment to individuals known to the author. Following this, then, other still more general inquiries were made in some twenty-five other towns in the Southeast. The results were published in 1909.[1]

It was emphasized that the study was "of town life rather than city or rural; is further a study of community relationship, showing something of Negro life as it is related to the whites ... its purpose is to get at a proper beginning rather than to generalize on ultimate solutions." Again, the purpose of the work, as published, was stated as "an effort to contribute something toward a scientific knowledge of the Negro ... to describe the conditions of Negro life in southern communities ... not as a final treatment of the entire subject but as a beginning, along with other special studies, for a scientific but practical study of the Negro in the South."[2]

[1] Howard W. Odum, *Social and Mental Traits of the Negro.* Research into the Conditions of the Negro Race in Southern Towns. A Study in Race Traits, Tendencies and Prospects. Columbia University Studies in History, Economics and Public Law, V. 37 (New York: Longmans, Green & Co., 1910), pp. 305–606.

[2] *Ibid.*, especially pp. 5 and 18.

In the prosecution of these studies, it early became clear that much of the realistic situation was not to be measured in terms of socio-economic data, both because the records were not there and because they failed to measure the attitudes, folkways, and institutional character of the people. Studies were begun then and continued for a number of years, especially into the folk songs and folk beliefs of the southern Negro. In the first publication in this series, *Religious Folk-Songs of the Southern Negroes*, the first sentence was: "To know the soul of a people and to find the source from which flows the expression of folk-thought is to comprehend in a large measure the capabilities of that people."[3]

The general framework of the study was expressed in the following quotations: "To preserve and interpret the contributions of a people to civilization is to add to the science of folk-history. Posterity has often judged peoples without having so much as a passing knowledge of their inner life, while treasures of folk-lore and song, the psychic, religious, and social expression of the race, have been permitted to remain in complete obscurity. Likewise peoples have lived contemporaneously side by side, but ignorant of the treasures of folk-gems that lay hidden and wasting all about them. The heart and soul of the real people are unknown, science is deprived of a needed contribution, and the world is hindered in its effort to discover the full significance of the psychological, religious, social, and political history of mankind. That which is distinctly the product of racial life and development deserves a better fate than to be blown away with changing environment and not even remain to enrich the soil from which it sprang. Justice to the race and the scientific spirit demand the preservation of all interesting and valuable additions to the knowledge of folk-life. . . . The exact form of expression itself constitutes a contribution to knowledge and literature.[4]

The next publications in the series were two articles in the *Journal of American Folk Lore* in July–September and October–December, 1911, under the general title "Folk-Song and Folk-Poetry as Found in the Secular Songs of the Southern Negroes: A Study in Folk-Thought and Folk-

Ways." In these articles it was pointed out that the collection of secular folk songs among the Negroes had been permitted to lapse; that the supply seemed almost inexhaustible; and that the current Negro folk songs were no less distinctive than the earlier slave songs.[5] The conclusion was that "they are most valuable to the student of sociology and anthropology as well as the student of literature and the ballad."[6] These studies of southern communities and of folk life were made from the University of Mississippi, where the author was instructor from 1905–1908. Parts of the material on the folk songs and folk thought were used for the doctor's dissertation at Clark University and parts of the community studies for the doctor's dissertation at Columbia.[7]

The next studies, again comparative studies of Negro communities, were made in Philadelphia from 1910–1913,[8] under the auspices of the Philadelphia Bureau of Municipal Research. These studies followed two general patterns of approach. One was the application of intelligence and learning tests to Negro children in the schools alongside white children in the same schools, together with the subsequent study of the community environment of each group. The other was comparative reference to W. E. B. DuBois' notable study of the Philadelphia Negro to indicate certain trends in the decade between the time of his study and the present author's. The study was divided into three main divisions. "The first was a brief study of the Negro population of Philadelphia; the second was a study of the school status, schools, progress and education of Negro children in the public schools of Philadelphia; the third embodied the results of more detailed studies of school children, including educational and psychological tests, anthropometric measurements, and research into related facts concerning Negro children."

A summary of this study was published in the

[5] Howard W. Odum, "Folk-Song and Folk Poetry as Found in the Secular Songs of the Southern Negroes: A Study in Folk Thought and Folk-Ways," *Journal of American Folk Lore* (July–September 1911; Part II, October–December, 1911).

[6] *Ibid.*, (July–September, 1911), p. 1.

[7] *Social and Mental Traits of the Negro.*

[8] These studies were made under the auspices of the Bureau of Municipal Research in direct cooperation with Martin G. Brumbaugh, then superintendent of the Philadelphia public schools and later Governor of Pennsylvania.

[3] Howard W. Odum. "Religious Folk-Songs of the Southern Negroes," *American Journal of Religious Psychology and Education*, 3 (July 1909), p. 265.

[4] *Ibid.*, p. 266.

Annals of the American Academy, in 1913.[9] A few general preliminary conclusions were ventured as a result of these studies, but presented primarily as assumptions to be rechecked. With reference to the results of the tests, which were made in consultation with Professor Thorndike of Columbia University, it was suggested that the efficiency of the Negro children varied inversely with age and with the complexity of the process. This followed the pattern of extraordinary age retardation in the school grades. Immediately, however, it was clear that these general conclusions meant little until the home life and community relationships had been compared. A distinguished and able Negro nurse was, therefore, employed to work with other investigators to check upon the home and community conditions. The result of this indicated that other things being equal it seemed quite likely the home and community environment, including bio-chemical factors of diet and social conditioning factors of segregation, were sufficiently different to account for most of the differences in achievement. These studies later became the basis for the conclusions drawn from subsequent folk-regional studies that, in the scientific sense, the distinction between race differences and race differentials is a fundamental one and assumes that races instead of being inherently different are group products of differentials due to the cumulative power of the physical and folk-regional cultural environment.[10]

From these studies it was increasingly apparent that at most they were "materials of science" rather than scientific studies, and that perhaps their chief value was to indicate the need for more generic and inductive studies. In an article in *The Journal of Race Development*, in 1915, the statement of this need was ventured in the continuation of this interest from the University of Georgia. In substance, this article held that "there is a decided tendency on the part of both individuals and communities to reduce any and all problems that arise because of the presence of the Negroes in the United States to one commonly accepted composite 'The Negro Problem.' It matters little whether the question considered be one of race development, admixture, or race adjustment on the one hand, or whether it be one of concrete and specific detail of study, philanthropy or public policy on the other, the usual mode of thought tends to be essentially the same. ... Hence, arises an increasing realization of the need for scientific study of the several problems of the Negro. ... Most of the local problems of the Negro are local in name only. A fundamental step of one community is of basic importance to a whole group of communities, which find it necessary to deal with the same question. The community relation to the problem is representative of the total national problem, and any step in the study of public policy for one community may mean much to the nation at large. For, after all, the basis for practical measures can be had only through extensive and thorough study, in which the most effective results will be accomplished through the most scientific methods, provided such study is properly correlated with the problems at hand. On the other hand, from the viewpoint of academic and scientific work including the departments of education, sociology, anthropology, and psychology, it is embarrassing to find few facts concerning innate race qualities, and to find that little attempt has been made to ascertain by objective methods the genesis and evolution of such qualities."[11]

III

When the Institute for Research in Social Science was established at the University of North Carolina, with the specific keystone of its program that of Regional Research and Study, immediately the Negro and the folk life became a first unit. One of the first steps was to rework and publish some of the earlier collections of Negro folk songs and to recapture as much as possible of their vividness and appeal at that time as well as to revive the interest in the older Negro songs and to introduce the Negro workaday song. They were projected not as primarily folklore or folk song or literary study, but as materials for the study of folk culture.

[9] Howard W. Odum, "Negro Children in the Public Schools of Philadelphia," The *Annals* of the American Academy of Political and Social Science (September, 1913).

[10] Howard W. Odum. "The Position of the Negro in the American Social Order in 1950," *Journal of Negro Education*, VIII (July 1939), 589. See also, *Race and Rumors of Race* (Chapel Hill: University of North Carolina Press, 1943).

[11] Howard W. Odum, "Some Studies in the Negro Problems of the Southern States." *The Journal of Race Development*, 6 (October 1915), pp. 185–186.

The first volume was published in 1925 under the title of *The Negro and His Songs* and was presented as a unit in this field. "This volume," so the preface began, "is presented simply as a part of the story of the Negro. Other volumes are planned to follow: another collection of songs brought more nearly up to date; a presentation of song and story centered around case studies; a series of efforts to portray objectively the story of race progress in the United States in the last half dozen decades."[12] Furthermore, the volume was presented as "a part of the story; a small part, it is true, but nevertheless a very real and vivid part, rich in examples of the Negro's creative effort within the limitations of the collection, vivid in the visualization of his imaginings and the technique of his song."[13]

In beginning the new studies it was suggested that a desirable attainment would be to get the South to "look at" instead of to "feel about" the Negro. In this exercise it was recalled that the Negro's singing had universal appeal and always reflected much of the personal and cultural situation in which the Negro common man found himself.

In 1926, *Negro Workaday Songs* was published with the following note: "*Negro Workaday Songs* is the third volume of a series of folk background studies of which *The Negro and His Songs* was the first and *Folkbeliefs of the Southern Negro* was the second. The series will include a number of other volumes on the Negro and likewise a number presenting folk aspects of other groups. The reception which the first volumes have received gives evidence that the plan of the series to present scientific, descriptive, and objective studies in as interesting and readable form as possible may be successful in a substantial way. Since the data for background studies are, for the time being, practically unlimited, it is hoped that other volumes, appearing as they become available and timely, may glimpse the whole range."[14] And again it was pointed out that "here is important material for the newer scientific interest which is taking the place of the old sentimental viewpoint.

And here is a mine of descriptive and objective data to substitute for the emotional and subjective attitudes of the older days.

"It is a day of great promise in the United States when both races, North and South, enter upon a new era of the rediscovery of the Negro and face the future with an enthusiasm for facts, concerning both the newer creative urge and the earlier background sources."[15]

Other regional studies of the Negro followed, some published in books, some in a varied series of articles, and some remaining in the catalogue of the Institute's unpublished studies. Of the books, the following are illustrative: *Folkbeliefs of the Southern Negro* by Newbell N. Puckett, *Phonophotography in Folk Music* by Milton Metfessel, *Rainbow Round My Shoulder* by Howard W. Odum, *John Henry: Tracking Down a Negro Legend* by Guy B. Johnson, *Wings on My Feet* by Howard W. Odum, *The Negro Sings a New Heaven* by Mary A. Grissom, *Folk Culture on St. Helena Island* by Guy B. Johnson, *Black Yeomanry* by T. J. Woofter, Jr., *Cold Blue Moon* by Howard W. Odum, *Negro Child Welfare in North Carolina* by Wiley B. Sanders, *The Tragedy of Lynching* and *Preface to Peasantry* by Arthur F. Raper, *Race and Rumors of Race* by Howard W. Odum. In addition to these Guy B. Johnson directed the sociological inquiries of the Myrdal study and contributed the first part to Klineberg's *Characteristics of the American Negro*.[16]

As in the earlier studies of the Negro, so again it was very clear that it was the region and the folk that constituted the field of inquiry, and that the whole regional culture was the basis upon which realistic studies must be made. As a medium of social interpretation, THE JOURNAL OF SOCIAL FORCES was founded in 1922, and during its first few years, prior to becoming SOCIAL FORCES, its editorial and workshop notes were often devoted to a critical appraisal of southern culture and economy. From these critical inquiries grew other publications and research projects. In *Southern Pioneers in Social Interpretation* the keynote was stated somewhat in terms of deficiencies, which were later to be measured in more scientific terms. In the meantime, the process of regional exploration was continued.

[12] Howard W. Odum and Guy B. Johnson, *The Negro and His Songs* (Chapel Hill: University of North Carolina Press, 1925), p. v.

[13] *Ibid.*, p. 2.

[14] Howard W. Odum and Guy B. Johnson, *Negro Workaday Songs* (Chapel Hill: University of North Carolina Press, 1926), p. ix.

[15] *Ibid.*, p. 1.

[16] See Gunnar Myrdal, *An American Dilemma*, 2 vols. (New York: Harper and Brothers, 1944). Also Otto Klineberg, *The Characteristics of the American Negro*, (New York: Harper and Brothers, 1944).

These exploratory efforts have been described on various occasions and have been partially summarized from time to time. Four types of studies in the southern regional group were listed as illustrations of regional and folk portraiture, as materials for social science, and as illustrating the development of methodology and personnel in social research within a given area.[17] The first of these has to do with studies of folk culture which emphasize primarily the more primitive elements of society. From these studies come materials and methods which throw light upon social capacities, racial capacities, the development of culture patterns and areas.

Samplings of these notes, taken from southern regional studies include Milton Metfessel's *Phonophotography in Folk Music*, a cooperative effort between psychologists and sociologists, through an exhaustive analysis involving more than sixty thousand computations, throws much light on the mooted question and qualities of folk music of modern, cultured peoples. Guy B. Johnson's *Folk Culture on St. Helena Island* and other studies throw new light upon the relation of the Negro spirituals to old New England and southern church hymns, and in showing that the Gulla language, commonly assumed to be of foreign imprint, to be primarily English throws considerable new light upon the Negro's patterns of adaptation. Newbell N. Puckett's *Folkbeliefs of the Southern Negro* provides similar fundamental materials for the comparison of Negro and white cultures and for the study of adaptation. Other portraitures which enrich the social materials for the study of cultures are found in T. J. Woofter's *Black Yeomanry: Life on St. Helena Island*, Guion Griffis Johnson's *Social History of the Sea Islands*, Guy B. Johnson's *John Henry: Tracking Down a Negro Legend*, Mary Grissom's *The Negro Sings a New Heaven*, Howard W. Odum's *Rainbow Round My Shoulder, Wings on My Feet, Cold Blue Moon*, Howard W. Odum and Guy B. Johnson's *The Negro and His Songs* and *Negro Workaday Songs*, George Pullen Jackson's *White Spirituals in the Southern Uplands*, and other studies of mountain folk song and culture now under way. Other studies illustrating this type of material of science may be found in Lee M. Brooks' "The New Mobility and the Coastal Islands," and Rupert B. Vance's "The Concept of the Region."

The second type of regional portraiture was concerned more nearly with materials for the study of that sort of folk society which, comprehending the

whole culture life of the region, reflects the peculiar civilization which still transcends the stateways of government. To use again an illustration from the southern region, the folk society following the Civil War was more powerful and effective than the combined bayonets and governmental routine of the whole Nation. The study of such a society has been illuminating not only to sociologists and historians but to political scientists, and provides much data for the scientific study of democratic government. It is generally admitted by the historians that scientific study of such folk society would have avoided many blunders both North and South. It is possible to study in that region four generations of Americans whose changing cultures provided the most dramatic episodes in the American scene and comprehended every known element in the architecture of modern civilization. Manifestly, this was not merely a local problem but one of national importance, which could be attacked through regional analysis. Manifestly, also, such portraiture suggests many other illustrations from other regions.

Samplings from southern regional studies of this sort include Rupert B. Vance's *Human Factors in Cotton Culture* and *Human Geography of the South*, Broadus Mitchell's *William Gregg: Factory Master of the Old South*, Howard W. Odum's *An American Epoch: Southern Portraiture in the National Picture* and *Southern Pioneers in Social Interpretation*, F. M. Green's *Constitutional Development in the South Atlantic States, 1776–1860*, Guion Griffis Johnson's *Social History of North Carolina*, William S. Jenkins' *Political Theories of the Slave Holder*, Julia C. Spruill's *Women's Life and Work in the Southern Colonies*, Guion Griffis Johnson's *Ante-Bellum North Carolina*, Benjamin B. Kendrick and Alex M. Arnett's *The South Looks at Its Past;* and the larger compendium, Howard W. Odum's *Southern Regions of the United States* and its interpretation by Gerald W. Johnson, *The Wasted Land*.

The third type of regional portraiture is concerned more nearly with materials for the study of practical social problems of economic or social policy, or of social planning, whether of local or national import.

Samplings from southern regional studies of problems include Clarence Heer's *Wages and Income in the South*, J. J. Rhyne's *Some Southern Cotton Mill Workers and Their Villages*, Claudius Murchison's *King Cotton Is Sick*, Harriet L. Herring's *Welfare Work in*

[17] Howard W. Odum, "Notes on the Study of Regional and Folk Society," *Social Forces*, X (December 1931), 164–175.

Mill Villages, George Mitchell's *Labor Unionism in the South*, T. J. Woofter's *The Plight of Cigarette Tobacco*, J. F. Steiner and Roy M. Brown's *North Carolina Chain Gang*, Paul W. Wager's *County Government in North Carolina*, C. K. Brown's *State Movement in Railroad Development* and *The State Highway System of North Carolina*, Roy M. Brown's *Public Poor Relief in North Carolina*, H. C. Brearley's *Homicide in South Carolina*, Harriet L. Herring's *Southern Industry and Regional Development*, Howard W. Odum's *Southern Regions of the United States*, and Arthur Raper's *Tragedy of Lynching* and *Sharecroppers All*. The long list of unpublished studies is catalogued in a separate bibliography.

A fourth type of regional effort has tended to emphasize cooperative, methodological, and theoretical studies, partly incidental to the regional portraiture of the special studies and partly as an objective in the development of social science, social research, and personnel within the given region. An illustration of cooperative efforts is that in which the Social Science Research Council cooperated in making possible a two-year study of St. Helena Island. The three published studies, *Black Yeomanry, Social History of the Sea Islands*, and *Folk Culture on St. Helena Island*, already listed, resulted from cooperative study—anthropological, economic, historical, psychological, sociological. The field work was done by representatives of Harvard, Columbia, George Peabody College for Teachers, together with certain specialists from State departments, in addition to the staff from the University of North Carolina. *Southern Regions of the United States* was done under the auspices of the Social Science Research Council as were parts of *Recent Social Trends*.[18]

The development of more critical analyses, better methods of research, practical avenues for presenting results and for increasing resources are all important problems in such regional study. Efforts toward these objectives included early round tables by visiting specialists, such as Charles E. Merriam, Clark Wissler, Ulrich B. Phillips, Walton Hale Hamilton, and the series of regional conferences on teaching and research in the social sciences. A first regional conference on local government was held in the early 1920's and the Institute has had the cooperation of the Southern Regional Committee of the Social Science Research Council. A number of regional cooperative institutes have been held, notably the one in the

summer of 1936 on "Social Science and Regional Development," and in the spring of 1940, one on "Population Research, Regional Research, and the Measurement of Regional Development."

Finally there were the later efforts toward both synchronizing and making practical applications of all these regional studies in terms of larger composite regional studies, of their application to teaching and research, and of their relation to regional national planning. A companion volume to *Southern Regions of the United States* is Rupert B. Vance's notable new volume, *All These People: The Nation's Resources in the South*, appearing in 1945 as the most comprehensive scientific study of a regional population published up to now. Two new volumes embodying the regional synthesis and sociological theory to appear in 1945 are *The Way of the South: A Biography of the Southern United States* and *Understanding Society*.[19] The regional approach had previously been featured in their *Introduction to Social Research* by Odum and Jocher[20] and in Odum and Moore's *American Regionalism* and Odum's *American Social Problems*.[21] Other titles featuring the regional approach to study and planning included Odum's *The Case for Regional National Planning, Planning an American Region*, Odum, Becker and Others, *Regional Planning Technique*, Odum's *The Regional Approach to National Social Planning*, Vance's *Regional Reconstruction: A Way Out for the South*, Vance's *The South's Place in the Nation*, Woofter's *Southern Population and Social Planning*, Moore's *What Is Regionalism?*, Vance's *Farmers Without Land*, and Vance's *Research Memorandum on Population Redistribution Within the United States*.

For practical purposes of planning, financing, and research the program of regional social study and practice for the Institute for Research in Social Science was projected under several divisons. Naturally, there was some overlapping and considerable intertwining of the special subdivisions, the list of studies from which researches were to be chosen including more than 200 units, and the extent of future researches depending upon resources and facilities which may be made available. (The groups were: social, political, economic, and legal aspects of government; agri-

---

[18] *Recent Social Trends in The United States*, 2 vols. (New York: McGraw Hill, 1933).

[19] Both by Howard W. Odum and to be published by The Macmillan Co.

[20] Henry Holt and Co., 1929.

[21] Henry Holt and Co., 1936 and 1939.

culture and rural organization; social-industrial relations; crime and criminal justice; racial groups; special social and educational institutions; historical and cultural backgrounds and demography; cooperative and theoretical studies.) Within each of these subdivisions individual projects were selected with the following considerations in view: With the exception of the theoretical and cooperative studies, problems were selected within the State and regional field but also with a view to generic interest and value to social science anywhere. They were selected also with a view to long-time periods of research but capable of subdividing into units which are susceptible to shorter-time completion. They were selected also with a view to available materials and resources, available personnel, and practicability of successful completion. Included in the theoretical and cooperaive studies were units of regional and folk study in other parts of the United States, in Canada, Mexico, South America, as well as studies of transitional society wherever possible in other areas.

V

A great deal more might be added. Perhaps this catalogue is adequate to indicate how our theoretical assumptions and conclusions have grown "out of the day's work." That is, our theories are vitally realistic in that they emerge from study and experiment, on the one hand, and from needs and experience, on the other. It is likely that the full import of our assumptions that "sound theory is the most practical thing in the world" would not have been manifest except for another very realistic factor. This was the challenge of the region and the nation to implement social research through practical regional planning and development. This, in turn, was accentuated by the national trends toward social planning to meet the needs of depression and emergency and to carry on social theory as far as possible into reality of the American scene. The situation was more than the old proverbial "necessity is the mother of invention"; it was Thorstein Veblen's reverse application that invention is the mother of necessity in the sense that science, invention, and technology, together with world situations, having brought the nation to this point of emergency, necessity for planning and reconstruction became the chief keystone of realistic social science.

Thus, there were two principal backgrounds in which the emergence of theory and planning was reflected. One was that of social research experimentation within the frame of reference of a major region of the United States; and the other the emergency of regional planning in the nation as it evolved from the earlier concept of metropolitan planning into both a philosophy and a technique of national development. The first example was more in the nature of a laboratory and testing ground; the second was reflected in the logical attempt to meet emergencies and to comprehend in practical ways the length and breadth and power of a great nation in transition.

First, with reference to southern regional research, it seemed fair to assume that social study and social planning in order to be realistic and responsible must find their laboratory and their data within the region where the greatest reality abounds. Thus, we set up a sort of living regional laboratory where social phenomena could be studied and social planning explored. Such a laboratory, however, was not to be interpreted as provincial or local, but rather a concrete laboratory for the testing of generic premises. Problems selected for study and areas chosen for planning were to be those which would have generic value throughout all parts of the country. Thus, agricultural reconstruction, social-industrial relationships, the reintegration of agrarian culture in American life, race relations and prospects, the redistribution of opportunity and wealth, the techniques of making democracy effective in the unequal places, the organic nature of the folk life and the new realism of the people were universal problems, finding their reality, however, in the living laboratory in which they grew.

It soon became clear, however, in the next place, that so far from being provincial or limited, these regional efforts required a more thorough background and a wider knowledge for successful accomplishment than did the ordinary historical or theoretical approaches which focus merely upon principles, concepts, abstract laws, and the like. That is, it was necessary to reinforce our equipment in methods and approaches to the study of social problems; it was necessary to study more comprehensively the cultural backgrounds involved in history and anthropology; it was necessary to reinforce our knowledge with geography and other physical sciences. All this meant that it was necessary also to have a closer alignment and closer cooperation with and among all the social sciences. Not only this, but here was a frame of reference for the study of culture and economy, which, without any doubt, set the tempo for a new era in the cooperation of the social sciences with the physical sciences, in the coöperation of the so-called academic institutions and the professional schools and the great land-grant colleges and their coöperation with governmental agencies.

Thus, work in this regional laboratory for social study and planning led to two relatively new methodological approaches. One was the coördination and coöperation of the various sciences and social sciences and the other was regionalism as a methodological approach, in which not only the attack upon universal problems could be made by all the sciences and social sciences, but in which it became clear that the folk-regional society or culture constitutes the supreme unit for social study and the smallest unit in which all of the factors, including those of natural resources, human resources, and cultural conditioning, may be found.

There emerged, therefore, an important theoretical conclusion as to the rôle of regionalism in national analysis and planning. Yet the chief value after all was practical. It became clear that the understanding of one region with its backgrounds, limitations, and prospects could be attained only through a sort of science of the region, which may be likened unto a gestalt, in which all factors are sought out and interpreted in their proper perspective. That is, each part is not only related to every part, but also planning for one aspect cannot successfully be done without adequate consideration of all aspects. Seen in the light of such a premise, a region, in this case the South, reflects everything that goes into the architecture of civilization, and its problems and prospects in many ways are reflected mirror-like in such ways as to enable us to stand off and look on them objectively and work towards a better mastery.

Further than this, however, it became very clear that it was not possible to characterize one region in terms of useful measures unless and until we had characterized the rest of the nation and the other regions by similar comparisons. The regional approach, therefore, became a dynamic tool in the attempt to understand the living geography of the nation and to place each of the great regions in their proper setting to the whole.

This led still further, namely, to the conclusion that it is not only not possible for one region to develop without the coöperation of the other regions and of the Federal Government, but also that only through strong regional development may the nation as a whole be enriched. Thus, through the newer reaches of regionalism as opposed to the old sectionalism and through the almost universal trend toward centralization in government and economy, we came to a logical and scientific interpretation of the obligation of the Federal Government to coöperate with each of the regions. This obligation, of course, has been reinforced by the background of historical and political action and of cultural and economic differentials, in addition to these fundamental trends.

This still is not the end. Immediately with the movement to have regionalism transcend sectionalism and the trend toward Federal centralization over States' rights, there arise fundamental issues and many points of conflict. These issues again are of universal and generic interest to peoples everywhere to the end that centralization and totalitarian patterns may not transcend democratic form and retard progress. Thus, regionalism becomes the tool for decentralization, the buffer between Federal and State conflicts, and if there is any way to prevent totalitarianism in a great complex, urban, and industrial civilization of standardized tendency and to retain a quality civilization in a quantity world, it is through regionalism that it must be effected.

VI

In order to interpret more vividly and comprehensively this concept of American regionalism, we have often tried to approach the subject from a more or less popular viewpoint. On the above assumptions and with a view to exploring both the wide range of meanings and the "usefulness" of the concepts, we, therefore, sometimes presented the concept of regionalism under four divisions: first, as a science; second, as an American frontier; third, as a tool or technique of government; and, fourth, as a motivation or purpose.

Regionalism in the comprehensive sense in which it is now becoming dynamic and articulate in American society is a science in several meanings. First, it is a science in the sense that it represents a substantial body of scientific materials gathered by authentic research specialists using acceptable scientific methods. This body of knowledge comprehends a wide range and area, including research in geography, ecology, other biological inquiries, as well as historical, economic, and sociological research into areal situations and phenomena. Furthermore, these materials are being carefully analyzed, interpreted, and utilized in effective ways.

In the second place, regionalism may well become a science in the sense that it represents a sound inquiry into the organic character of the relation between men and resources, between areas and culture, between physical environment and cultural environment. All societies begin with the area or region and expand out into larger developments, so that culture becomes as natural as the physical, areal environment itself. Regionalism lies at the basis of the larger ecology and helps to interpret sociology as a natural science in the sense of measuring the capacity of social organisms to function within the framework of their natural environment and inherent endowment.

Regionalism may be interpreted as a science further in the sense, therefore, that it comprehends what we call the folk-regional society, which is the smallest unit through which all society can be studied. The community, for instance, does not comprehend all the factors in time area and cultural conditioning. The same may be said for the family; while the individual is too small a unit. The folk-regional society, therefore, becomes the basis for folk sociology, which must inevitably become the general science of societal development.

Regionalism may be interpreted in the scientific sense in still another way, namely, as a methodological approach to research in this regional approach. It is not only possible to utilize the general cultural sociological approach alongside the descriptive and historical inquiries, but the folk region affords the best possible laboratory for statistical and objective measurements within a frame of reference comprehensive enough to be complete but limited enough to insure thoroughness.

The regional approach also affords the best opportunity for the coöperation and coördination of all the social sciences attacking a problem and likewise for the coöperation of the physical sciences and the social sciences. This phase, however, we have discussed under our second category of

regionalism as a frontier. But more important, it will be science in the sense that we are all coming to an acceptable delineation of a relatively small number of major group-of-states regions for multiple purposes, determined by indices available for the largest number of agencies and meeting the largest number of needs, and avoiding the largest possible number of conflicts. When we study regions, therefore, we all study the same thing. We also determine the meaning of subregions for special administrative or functional purposes which we designate as districts, and there will be as many districts as may be needed in each of the major administrative areas. We also defined subregions as the great natural regions, river valley, soil, climate. And we study these and plan for these through an over-all, central, national arrangement as opposed to the States and· regions and districts of our formal regional arrangement. There is, then, of course, the final definition of the State and the zone. Regionalism will become a science when the agencies of the government approximate uniformity in the use for research, census taking, and planning the same number of regions, use the same terminology for comparative purposes, and develop a scientific public administration, in which the region becomes a balance wheel between the extreme States' rights and Federal centralization.

In the second place, regionalism is a *frontier* in several ways. We all recall, I believe, the frontier tradition of America, such that Frederick Jackson Turner was wont to say that America's culture was largely conditioned by the frontier civilization. First, there was the Seaboard, East, North, and South. Then there was the great trek across Appalachia into "Kaintuck," on to the great Northwest and great Southwest; then on into the Middle West, and the Oregon trail and the Gold Rush to the Far West, and then frontiers back again into the great plains to the Southwest.

Then you recall that "everybody" said we had no more frontiers of a physical sort, and, therefore, we must turn to the social frontiers. This, of course, was not true, although it was partially true and is still partially true. Now, the new frontiers of American regions constitute both a physical frontier of soil, resources, and the like, and a cultural frontier, both of which in their developing are analogous to the earlier frontier upon which America was built. For literally the conservation and development of the resources in relation to the people in each of these great regions is as much a needed frontier and as difficult a task as was the exploitation and conquest of the earlier frontiers. So, too, in the development of the peoples and cultures in each of the great regions we follow a universal pattern of building a great society from the many community, State, and regional units outward towards a total culture. We only need to look at new developments and defense requirements, the redistribution of population, of wealth and opportunity, to see that here is literally a new frontier important enough to call out the best of American creative effort.

The region is again a frontier in the sense that in the development of the regions of America we have for the first time the merging of the physical and the social sciences in this balance of men and resources and in the development of wealth to be used for human weal. This is also a new frontier. It is also a new frontier in the great task of the future made necessary in the modern world of supertechnology, namely, discovery of a new balance and equilibrium between supercivilization and American culture in the balance between men and machines, between men and resources. If ever there was a new frontier this is one.

Regionalism is next a tool and technique of government and development in the sense that there can be no planning American style except that it takes into consideration the fundamental principles of geographic representation. Overcentralization in planning, ignoring the rights of the States and regions, is contrary to the American principle. Exaggerated States' rights and walls built around the States in competitive process are no longer tenable in the complex inter-State American relationships.

Regionalism becomes a tool for decentralization, and through a national-regional-state-research-and planning council arrangement it becomes a sort of fourth wheel of American government, in which there is added to the judicial, the administrative, and legislative, the advisory groups, whose personnel, both in number and distinction, shall parallel those of the Supreme Court and members of the Cabinet, to which will be added representation from each of the great regions.

Regionalism then becomes the primary tool for American planning, flexible in time and geography, of, for, and by all the people, all the regions, and all the institutions. It becomes a tool for the redistribution of wealth and opportunity, because this can be done in the American way only by creating the capacity in each region to produce wealth and to consume it adequately in relation to the people and the region, and in relation to a balanced economy of man, resources, and regions in the perspective of the total national interest.

Regionalism, then, manifestly becomes a great purpose or motivation. An advanced student who had lived many years abroad and, in particular, in Russia suggested that American regionalism in the sense of this science and tool of American development is the ideal substitute for communism or the extreme utopian type of concept which so appeals to the younger people. Regionalism as a science, as a frontier, as a tool, and a purpose, is something that the young people can get hold of, in which they can participate in the development of the American life rather than merely talk about it and criticize it. In regionalism, there is the same high purpose and motivation of the earlier forefathers, recapitulating much of the great task of conserving and developing the physical resources and of developing and restating the ideals of democracy.

Manifestly, now it must be clear that there can be no concept of the region, except as it is a *component, constituent part of the total nation.* The region cannot be just an area or just a State or a separatism, or an isolated self-sufficing group of units. The very definition of the region always connotes that it is a contributing part to, of, for, and by the total nation. It is, therefore, the opposite of sectionalism, of blocs, and of ever-seeking political units. It is what we have called in America regionalism, the historical and cultural approach to national integration. Under this concept regionalism, therefore, cannot lead primarily to competition and conflict, because in the essence of regionalism will be found a strategy which matches resources and people in each region and those arrangements which compete least with those of other regions, because the total objective is enrichment of the region and the people in relation to the total national ideal. In return, this enrichment of the nation always leads to a return service on the part of the Federal Government to each region in terms of leadership, equalization fund, scientific research, expert guidance, and a fellowship and exchange of technical skills and personnel and resources.

VII

This, however, was still not the end. We return again to our earlier assumptions that sound theory is the most practical thing in the world, and by the same token it develops from the day's work in the sense that research, exploration, and survey become the bases upon which enduring conclusions are reached. Our studies of the folk and of the folk society have led us to conclude that the folk-regional society is the smallest unit through which a comprehensive study of all society may be made, and that folk sociology seeking balance and equilibrium between the folkways and the stateways, between the folk society and the state society, between voluntary action and coercion becomes the definitive sociology. In so far as the laboratory for folk sociology is the folk-regional society, sociology, as indicated in the first pages of our report, becomes a natural science in the more comprehensive and realistic sense of science and society.

Moreover, just as the study of regionalism has led us to the broader inquiry concerning the unity of all society and the study of the southern regions indicated the necessity for studying all regions in their comparative and contrasting relationships, so the study of the folk society necessitates the study of the contrasting state society. So, too, the study of the folkways as basic to culture and folk society necessitated the study of the stateways of modern technology and their impact upon culture and led to the discovery of the new phenomenon of technicways which transcend the folkways and supplant the mores in modern contemporary society. The study of technicways, therefore, becomes a major problem of inquiry, with implications to the modern world perhaps as important as any that have been presented in a long time. The technicways, therefore, become a form of measuring differences between the folkways and stateways, between the old folk culture and modern technology, and lead to the further assumption of fundamental distinction between culture and civilization. From this point it becomes necessary to explore further the possibility of balance between culture and civilization in a world where there is apparently too much civilization and too little culture.

This led us to suggest two testing grounds for university exploration into the study of this new balance between civilization and culture. The first lies within the framework of a greater Americanism approximated through the new regionalism, the theme of which I have characterized as essentially that of a great American nation, the land and the people, in whose continuity and unity of development, through a fine equilibrium of geographic, cultural, and historical factors, must be found not only the testing grounds of American democracy, but, according to many observers, the hope of western civilization. Manifestly, this is a task that requires all that all groups of scientists can do.

The second is found in the search, not for what science and technology are doing to society, but what the processes are through which such tremendous transformations are being wrought. We have voluminous reports on the effects of invention and technology on society, but little on how they come to pass. I venture to predict, therefore, an entirely new area for the combined inquiries of the physical and social sciences. This will be research into the startling new phenomena of the technicways, which, in contemporary civilization, transcend the old folkways and supplant the mores, thus, so modifying human behavior and institutions as to outmode the earlier rate of societal evolution.

Now this new frontier of the technicways does not seem to me to be merely a new series of jargon and terminology, for just as the old folkways and mores were practical ways of meeting needs in the long, cultural road of evolution, ultimately leading to the development of institutions, morals, and learning, so in this hectic world of bigness, speed, technology, super-organization, the technicways are the new ways of meeting the needs of a technological world. One only needs to look at the new technicways of war which violate all of the old folkways and agreements with reference to women, children, hospitals, institutions of learning, art; or the swift-changing episodes of our own science, economics, learning, morals, changing behavior patterns, and the demands upon our institutions which are accelerating the whole rate of our cultural evolution.

Perhaps in all of this we are appealing for a new opportunity for the social sciences, in which, working upon the great results of the physical sciences and working with them, we may attain results in some of the fields of social inventions and social technicways, which may match the flood tide of technology now sweeping down upon us. Here is a task adequate for any university and for all that the new social sciences can muster.

VIII

The implications of the technicways have in their application to modern society been indicated in many ways, and illustrations are abundant. This field, however, is a major area of research and now represents mostly certain larger premises and assumptions which are being tested both through statistical measurements and cultural analyses. From the study of the mechanical technicways, which have arisen because of modern technology, the transition to inquiry with reference to social technicways and social inventions all comprehended in the larger framework of social planning, becomes a logical necessity, and by the same token offers an even greater field of research. Another type of approach to the explanation and direction of society may be found in certain premises or social "axioms" which have arisen from the study of the folk-regional society and by contrast the development of the state society and civilization.

It seems profitable to attempt to state certain assumptions growing out of the further development of the field of folk sociology which may serve as general premises to be tested both by further inquiry and by their application to realistic situations. Among such assumptions to be tested as to accuracy of statement and validity of application are the following:

1. The folk-society, the folk-culture, is the elemental and basic culture definitive of all societies in process.

2. The folk-society, characterized by folkways and mores, may be best observed in the folk-regional society, which is the smallest comprehensive definitive unit of society. This folk-regional society is bottomed in the relative balance of man, nature, and culture.

3. Over against the folk-society has been the universal trend toward the state-society, characterized by stateways and technicways, which increases in scope and power until at its crest it approximates the megalopolitan, the technological, the intellectual, the totalitarian culture called civilization.

6. Wherever the folk-society and the state-society conflict, in the long run, the folk-society always wins both in the sense of the mastery of the one by the other and in the sense of ultimate survival. But in the process leading up to conflict the totalitarian state-society increasingly dominates and weakens the folk-society and contributes to the artificiality of civilization.

5. Whenever the folk-socity and the state-society coincide, the resulting society, within the framework of its region and resources, reflects great power for growth and development and is practically irresistible against opposing forces. And when the unity of folkways and stateways is reinforced by the technicways, society reaches its maximum achievement.

6. But when there is conflict between the folk-society and the state-society and when the demands of a supertechnology and an artificial society exceed the capacity of the folk or of their institutions to meet or adjust, there is tension, disorganization, conflict, and ultimately decay until such time as mastery is achieved through a reconstructed folk-society.

7. In the modern contemporary world, mass-trending toward that state-society which is civilization at its crest, there are new societal forces reflected in and measured by the technicways which have transcended the folkways and supplanted the mores of the earlier folk-culture, thus accelerating the tempo of modern society and giving aid to the state-society in its dominance over the folk-society.

8. Manifestly the definitive, enduring society will be found in balance and equilibrium between the folk-society and the state-society in which not only the folkways and stateways will coincide but the technicways may be directed toward the orderly processes of societal development and towards attainable margins of survival.

9. The conclusion seems justified that there is uniformity in processes and orderly development from the earlier stages of society with its natural folk-regional culture, through its gradual extension and expansion on the levels of time, geographic quality, and cultural development into the later civilization of intellectual specialization, totalitarian state, megalopolitan culture, and technological power.

10. In the technicways which are "habits of the individual, customs of the group" to meet

survival needs in this new technological world may be found ways of measuring the contemporary state-society, of indicating trends from the folk-society to the state-society, of explaining many of the phenomena of the modern world, and of laying the groundwork for conserving and reconstructing the folk-society.

11. This groundwork is comprehended in the concept and practice of social planning through which the distance between the scientific "theoretical" and the "practical" may be bridged and through which the contributions of the social sciences and the physical sciences may be utilized in societal direction.

THE WAY OF THE SOUTH

IN BOTH practical studies and theoretical implications, as we have indicated their range and nature, the total of the Southern Regional Study envisaged a better balanced regional America in which there would no longer exist the narrow sectionalisms of "America's Tragedy." The old terms "North" and "South," "East" and "West," as conflicting sections would be transcended by the logical development of well balanced regions; the Southeast and the Southwest would be no more "sectional" or isolated than would the Northeast and the Northwest or the Middle States and the Far West. Thus, one of the most important contributions of the Southern Regional Study was the clear delineation of the South into its Southeast and Southwest.

As summarized in *Southern Regions of the United States*,[1] it was pointed out that there was no longer in the United States any single entity which might be designated as "the South." More authentically, there was a Southeast and a Southwest, comparable to four other major regions designated as the Northeast, the Northwest, the Middle States, and the Far West. The old custom of massing together, for aggregate quantitative effects, a large group of "southern" States, including Missouri, Maryland, Delaware, West Virginia, Texas, and the specialized urban District of Columbia, was not only inaccurate but detrimental to genuine regional analysis and planning.

It was, therefore, neither possible nor desirable to present a single authentic picture of "the South" any more than it is of "the North" or "the East" or "the West," not only because of the magnitude and diversity of the regions but also because of the dynamics of the emerging southwestern region, comprising Texas, Oklahoma, New

[1] Howard W. Odum, *Southern Regions of the United States* (Chapel Hill: University of North Carolina Press, 1936), pp. 5–9.

Mexico, and Arizona, which would require separate analysis and interpretation no less critical and comprehensive than that for the Southeast.

One of the major contributions of the study was the working hypothesis of the relatively clear-cut differentiation between the older Southeast and the emerging Southwest, a new empire in itself. Inherent also in both content and methodology was the definitive sixfold regional division of the United States. A part of the value of this regional division was to be found in the effectiveness and comprehensiveness of these six divisions for the particular purpose of the Southern Regional Study. It was hoped, however, that this arrangement might contribute something toward a more uniform basis for regional study and planning and for experimentation with many subregional divisions for further exploration and planning.

The sixfold division basic to the study was evolved from a study of a large number of regional classifications and from many hypothetical groupings tested from various angles. It was, therefore, the most satisfactory arrangement that could be worked out. Allocation of States was made on the basis of the clustering of elemental indices, of which some seven hundred constituted the field of analysis. In addition to the *Southeast* and and the new *Southwest*, the *Northeast*, approximating Frederick Jackson Turner's "Greater New England," included Maine, New Hampshire, Vermont, Massachusetts, Rhode Island, Connecticut, New York, New Jersey, Delaware, Pennsylvania, Maryland, and West Virginia. The *Middle States*, approximating the earlier "Old Northwest" and the "Middle West," included Ohio, Indiana, Illinois, Michigan, Wisconsin, Minnesota, Iowa, Missouri. The *Northwest* included North Dakota, South Dakota, Nebraska, Kansas, Montana, Idaho, Wyoming, Colorado, Utah; and the *Far*

West added Nevada to the Pacific Coast States of Washington, Oregon, and California.

It is important to indicate here, however, something of the method by which the Southwest was differentiated from the Southeast and the Southeast redefined to exclude Maryland and Missouri. Basic to any reasonable effort to attain effective regional analysis of "the South" was the first task of delimitation and definition. What were the limits within which valid differentials could be measured and what the limits of desirable homogeneity for the purposes of analysis and planning? The first task within this assignment was to appraise the traditional "South" as a premise for such analysis. This broad grouping generally comprised seventeen or eighteen States including from the Northeast, Maryland, West Virginia, the District of Columbia, and sometimes Delaware; from the Middle States, Missouri; and in the Southwest, Oklahoma and Texas. The first task in the examination of this older and larger regional hypothesis was to seek measures of homogeneity and differentials when compared with the "border" States and adjoining regions and with the national averages.

The second task was to appraise the general historical and cultural factors which might apply to such groupings and to gauge the practicability of encompassing so large a part of the Nation in any workable techniques either of study or of planning. Tested by both of these criteria it was clear that so large and traditional a "South" was no longer a reality either in the spirit or the measure of the regions. First of all, Maryland qualified as "South" in no more than a score of a field of nearly 200 indices. And so to attempt to characterize or plan for Maryland as a region of farm tenancy or of Negro-white population or of illiteracy or of agrarian culture or of children per 1,000 women or of wealth and income or bank resources and savings or value of land and buildings or land use and industrial indices and a hundred other socio-economic factors, basic to needs and planning, was at once to invalidate the scientific validity of regional analysis. On the other hand, to add Maryland's aggregate to the Southeast in the effort to bolster up its claims and ratings would defeat the object of seeking workable differentials upon which to reach accurate diagnosis. Having rejected Maryland as a southern State, Delaware and the District of Columbia, being beyond and to the northeast, were no longer considered hypothetically within the South. Missouri, following much the same process, showed only a score or more indices of homogeneity with the South than Maryland. By the same token, it was overwhelmingly not "southern," except in certain parts of the State and in certain historical, legislative, and institutional affiliations, all of which, however, no longer appear valid as definitive characterizations.

Turning next to the western border States, Texas and Oklahoma qualify as "southern" in less than a third of the indices selected. As measured, therefore, both by a predominance of the selected indices and by general geographical, industrial, and cultural conditions, these States do not belong in the "South" of the Southeastern States. Having characterized Texas and Oklahoma as belonging to the Southwestern States, there remained the problem of classifying Louisiana and Arkansas, both west of the Mississippi, and often characterized as Southwest. Tested by the criteria, on the one hand, of the Southeast and, on the other, of Texas and Oklahoma, they qualify overwhelmingly with the Southeast and are differentiated from the emerging greater Southwest in a plurality of indices. In addition to this, they fall within the geographic bounds of practical homogeneity of culture and function. Thus the Southeastern Region of eleven States conforms to a dominance of characteristics which indicate a quite satisfactory general southern homogeneity.

This delineation of southern regions, therefore, symbolized again both the practical considerations involved in southern research and planning and the theoretical implications for the regional balance of America through the substitution of the new regionalism for the old sectionalism, and for a while it appeared as if we had succeeded. For during the 1920's and 1930's it was commonly assumed the terms "North" and "South" were no longer valid realities in the new America that was developing except as they reflected a tragic past which the Nation wanted to forget. The First World War had relegated the use of the term "The War," as referring to the Civil War, to an outmoded past that took its place alongside other epochs of "only yesterday" or that represented stepping stones of dead selves from which the Nation had already risen to higher things. And before that, perhaps during the whole of the first third of the twentieth century, there were manifest very substantial trends toward a genuinely realistic reintegration of the South in the Nation as, in the regional balance of America, the southern States assumed increasingly higher standards of achievement and a larger degree of participation and fellowship in the total American culture. The "South," as Southeast and Southwest, was taking its place dynamically in the Nation, even as the Far West, the Northwest, and all the other regions were making America strong and united by developing their own diversity of strength and seeking a new economic and cultural balance of America.

There were several reasons for these important trends, perhaps about equally balanced between the regions and the Nation as a whole. In the case of the South its leaders had inventoried her resources and her deficiencies and had begun a realistic facing of facts basic to genuine progress. In the North a new school of historians had rewritten the history of the Nation and had presented the South in fair appraisal and had also made realistic diagnosis and criticism of the northern post-Civil War administration. The South had also made extraordinary strides in nearly all phases of its culture and economy. It had built industry, developed great highways, increased its urban civilization in both the Southeast and the Southwest, faster than any other regions, had pioneered in some aspects of public welfare, public health and education, and had, with the cooperation and support of the Northeast, strengthened its colleges and universities, and especially a number of important institutions. It had begun to develop research in both the physical and social sciences and to apply the results to agriculture and industry, and it was increasingly being represented in the national councils of leadership. It had assumed a new sort of leadership in literature, and the South had become the best documented of all the regions at the same time that this was made possible by an extraordinary liberal cooperation of publishers and educational leaders and philanthropists in the Northeast. And there was pride of achievement not only in the South but in the other regions, particularly in "the wests," for what the southern regions were doing.

All this was especially marked from the period immediately following the First World War, from 1918 through to the early depression years. Then, once again, both the Southeast and the Southwest assumed increasingly larger and more positive participation in the affairs of the Nation as the democratic administration developed the New Deal. This was true in two main ways. One was the natural and logical larger ratio of southern participation in the actual Federal Government in a democratic administration. The other was in the South's participation in the measures of relief and reconstruction during the depression years when the South was sometimes "worse off" than other parts of the Nation. At any rate, the southern States put their hands to the task, and through State planning boards, through various technical ways of coöperating with New Deal agencies, through public works, work relief, agricultural adjustment, through educational coöperation, and other ways were assuming a new sort of normal and logical participation in the total national effort. Southern personnel, both in political and in appointive arrangements, was large.

Then a strange thing happened. And it happened twice, once due to the depression New Deal pressure and once due to the pressure of war, namely, a sudden revivification of the old sectional conflict and the recrudescence of the terms "North" and "South." It would have been unbelievable, if it had not actually happened, that this together with special and intensified revival of the old race conflict would bring the South to its greatest crisis and the Nation again to one of its chief domestic dilemmas since the Civil War. This dilemma, even as the promising trends of the earlier period, found its genesis about equally in the mutual relationships and action of North and South.

First, as a result of the realistic researches in the South diagnosing its resources, deficiencies, and needs, and then as a result of the New Deal administration, the Nation so rediscovered the South as to set a mark, first of backwardness and later of badness upon a region, and to undertake to remake it overnight. The revival of the term "The South," in so far as the national administration was concerned and in so far as it began to be universally used by editors and critics, came about in two ways. One was typified in the now noted slogan that the South was the Nation's Economic Problem Number One. The South was Tobacco Road. It was again missionary territory. But, whatever it was, it was "The South." In the second place, "The South" came to be synonymous with conservatism or reactionary policies due to the opposition of southern senators and congressmen and of State governors and leaders to many of the New Deal policies. "What else could you expect, he is a Southerner?" came to be a common refrain. And then "The South," with its usual sensitiveness and defense resentfulness revived with a vengeance the term "The North" which was again "trying to make the South over."

And even more than the depression New Deal, the coming of the war which was expected to bring unity to the Nation and in which the southern States led in enlistment and in all-out support, brought about the second intensification of the North-South conflict, due, of course, to the South's racial segregation, culture, and laws. The Nation realized suddenly that its ideas of the American Dream guaranteed to all its citizens equal rights and opportunities, and that, while it had gone to war for global democracy, it had in two of its own great regions a negation of such democracy. And it realized suddenly that this limitation of democracy and this segregation policy applied to the armed forces and that, being a white man's world, and the Army and Navy and Air Corps being a part of that world, the Negro in America was disgracefully discriminated against through no fault of his own. And so there was the ever-recurring question, "What can be done about the South?" And there were increasingly articulate individuals and agencies, private and public, setting themselves to the task of "making" the South change. The net result has been an unbelievable revival of the bitterness implied in the old "North" and "South" what time the South resents what it calls northern interference and what time the North tries to coerce the South again.

Then there is another factor. There may be no new South nor new North in these conflicting areas, but there is a new Negro of great force and vitality which makes compromise well-nigh impossible. The Negro himself had changed tremendously. It was not only that he had developed an important upper and middle class; it was not only that he had developed a magnificent leadership and thousands had received higher educational opportunities. It was not only that Negro youth, sensing the epochal spiritual change and racial attitudes and led by Negro leadership of the North and South, was minded to experiment with every type of equal opportunity—it was all this and more. It was as if some universal

message had come through to the great mass of Negroes, urging them to dream new dreams and to protest against the old order. It was as if there were pathos and tragedy in their misunderstanding of the main tenets of a bitter Negro leadership, and as if many of the northern Negro leaders of limited mentality had confused them with the idea that any sort of work or courtesy or cheerfulness was an index of subservience to the white man. In all of this, whether it was pathos and tragedy or admirable idealism and noble effort, the net result was a new Negro facing the old white man and joining with "The North" against "The South."

The Southern Regional Study as interpreted in *Southern Regions of the United States* had envisaged its functions primarily in terms of southern regional development but always featured as integrated into the national picture and as portraying in a scientific way the realistic culture analysis of the South. Its objectives and findings were stated in some two hundred paragraphs, among which the following need to be recalled here in order that subsequently we may characterize the cultural "Way of the South."[2]

The first objective of the Southern Regional Study was to present an adequate picture, partial but representative, of the southern regions of the United States in fair perspective to time-quality, to geographic factors, and to the cultural equipment and behavior of the people.

It was desired further to present this picture in such ways as to indicate the place of these regions in the Nation and to explain something of the dramatic struggle of a large and powerful segment of the American people for mastery over an environment capable of producing a superior civilization, yet so conditioned by complexity of culture and cumulative handicaps as to make the nature of future development problematical.

Over and above any conventional social inventory, it was important to point toward greater realization of the inherent capacities of the southern regions; and to indicate ways and means of bridging the chasm between the superabundance of physical and human resources as potentialities and the actualities of technical deficiencies in their development and waste in their use.

It was equally important to point toward a continuously more effective reintegration of the southern regions into the national picture and

[2] *Ibid.*, p. 1–3.

thereby toward a larger regional contribution to national culture and unity. To this end, it was important to make available and to reinterpret to special groups and to the public in general, within and without the regions, and in as many ways as possible, the facts basic to the understanding of the situation and to the planning of next steps.

Partly as purpose and method and partly due to the recognition of the extraordinary difficulty and importance of these tasks, it was desired to project the study upon a theoretical framework which would insure measurable reality in research and attainability in whatever programs might emerge. Such reality was, of course, manifold. It would comprehend not only measurement, but perspective and interpretation; not only the general picture of aggregates and averages, but the specific facts of distribution and such detailed analysis as would focus upon critical problems toward which continued research might be directed.

Basic to such a framework was a clear recognition of the historical and theoretical significance of the region and of the power of the folk-regional society in modern culture, as well as the very practical problem in the United States of what divisions of the Nation might meet the largest number of requirements for general regional analysis and planning and what other special regions and subregions might be effective for more specific purposes.

More specifically, such a theoretical framework aimed to give reality to the southern picture. This reality, again, was of many kinds. A part was the facing of absolute facts rather than substituting rationalizations which grew out of irrelevant comparisons or defense explanations of how things had come to be as they were. Yet another form of reality was to be found in the measurement of conditions in terms of comparison with certain selected standards and with regional and national variations. Yet, still again, a part of the reality was to be found in the clear recognition that mere comparisons with national averages or aggregates were valid only within the bounds of their particular limitations and definitions, the problem and methodology of evaluating such comparisons and differentials being a part of the task. Furthermore, the greatest measure of reality could be found in the balanced picture of basic facts rather than, and largely exclusive of, vivid extremes.

Again, such a theoretical framework aimed to be practically comprehensive enough to insure a fair picture of the major resources and forces which have determined and will determine the capacity of the southern regions. In terms of "wealth," they were natural wealth, technological wealth, artificial wealth, human wealth, and institutional wealth. In terms of a larger twofold measure, there would be, first, an inventory of natural resources together with the visible ends of technological mastery in human use aspects and in the resulting artificial wealth of the regions; and, second, an appraisal of human resources together with the visualized ends of social achievement in the development of a richer culture and social well-being.

One of the special premises of the study was reflected in the past constricting power of sectionalism in contrast to the current motivation of substituting the new regionalism for the old sectionalism in American life. Since sectional conditioning appeared more marked in the Southeast than elsewhere, the study was, therefore, projected to feature the regional-national as opposed to the local-sectional emphasis. Such a regional premise manifestly would avoid any hypotheses of a self-contained or self-sufficing South and would stimulate a greater degree of Federal interest and participation on the part of the South.

It was understood that many of the dominant forces of the regions, such as tradition, opinion, conflict, arrangements of local stateways and folkways, which constitute a part of the picture, were not measurable in terms of units that can be counted. On this assumption a part of the reality of the picture was inherent in the need and capacity for such authentic interpretation of the South's background as will give "the dignity of cultural history" to its chronological lag, its retarded frontier dominance, its agrarian culture, its youthful and immature population, its lusty vitality, its unevenness of life, and its marginal struggle for survival.

The study sought, further, to explore the southern regions as a laboratory for regional research and for experimentation in social planning. Of special importance might be the regional testing field for adjustment between industry and agriculture as the basic economic goal of government, and for the more general objective of reintegrating agrarian culture in the national picture. Again, the study was projected as a regional approach to the new demography which in both method and content might contribute largely to the revitalized study of the people and their institutions. Such a study of contemporary civilization would recognize certain values inherent in logical differentials which abound in the regions. Manifestly, such a theoretical framework must assume a less provincial and a more objective, long-time view of the South than had commonly obtained, and a more generous patience with the realities of societal evolution on the part of all those who seek reform and reconstruction.

Ten years after the publication of *Southern Regions*, in the light of continued study and observation, of planning and exploring ways and means for regional development, the hazards of a return to the older sectionalism, as indicated in the early 1930's appear even more significant. And one basis for the threatened revivification of the old sectional conflict is found in the failure of both the South and the Nation to understand and to coöperate with each other as organic, integral units of American culture. The South is not something exotic in America, set apart as a phenomenon or to be set aside or transformed by edict or wish, no matter how right the ends may be. So much is that true that the story of the South often seems to reflect the most distinctive need of the Nation as one of realistic understanding of the South in terms of a cultural and sociological analysis of what the South is, why it came to be what it is, why it behaves as it does, what the rest of the people of the Nation think of it, how they came to so think about it, and why they behave as they do.

The story of the South, therefore, is first of all an American story. In the analysis and chronology of this story the way of the South is the way of Nature. It is the way of the frontier and country life, of the heritage of the American Indian and his treatment. It is the way of the folk, the way of religion, the way of race, the way of culture. It is, therefore, the way of America always abounding in problems to settle and ways to settle them. It is the way of history and its unerring annals of what happens and of what else happens. In these ways are reflected the story of the South's earlier years and growing up; in these ways are reflected its conditioning and folkways that continue to characterize its culture even up to now. And in the way of race and caste the biography of the South pulls away somewhat from the American pattern to reflect a distinctive culture which, isolated by its earlier sectionalism and by war, now constitutes the Nation's first problem of regional balance and national integration.

We may look briefly, therefore, at certain symbols and summaries of how the "Way of the South" is characterized by each of these elements of Nature and the frontier, of race and folk, of religion and politics, of culture and history; and is thus inseparably the way of America.

First of all, the Way of the South is the way of Nature and resources set in the American framework. This was true in several ways. It was not only true in the sense in which Ulrich Phillips had explained, but in even more profound ways. Phillips began his *Life and Labor in the Old South* by discussing the weather. For that, he thought, had been the "chief agency in making the South distinctive. It fostered the plantation system, which brought the importation of Negroes, which not only gave rise to chattel slavery but created a lasting race problem. These led to controversy and regional rivalry for power, which produced apprehensive reactions and culminated in a stroke for independence. Thus we have the house that Jack built, otherwise known for some years as 'The Confederate States of America.'"

Yet the total culture of the South and its place in the Nation is not so simply explained. There was Nature in the beginning and what it did to set the incidence of a distinctive regional culture. But there was also the powerful factor of what that culture would do with Nature and her resources. In the analysis, therefore, of all the factors involved, namely Nature's first contribution in climate and situation; Nature's total endowment in resources and laws; and Nature's use in the evolving culture of the people, will be found a realistic understanding of what is called in America "The South," and what in reality is primarily distinctive southern regions of American culture.

How true this is may be seen from the consideration that one of the best approaches to the understanding of a given society is a clear picture of all resources available for development and utilization by the people of that society. There are two sides of the picture. One has to do with the nature and range, the quality and quantity of resources, and the other with their conservation, development, and use. In human society use of resources is of greater significance than range and kind. Yet in human society total resources, including human resources, will always include such factors as science, research, and planning for resource use and the social institutions through which the people work.

It is important, therefore, to emphasize the powerful rôle of Nature through natural resources, increasingly important in the modern world, but also the fact that natural resources exist, in so far as society is concerned, only as they relate to human and social resources. This is where the story of a culture comes to grips with the reality of a world in which natural and human wealth must find balance and equilibrium within the framework of each society and also in the interrelationships between different societies in conflict. For the nature and use of resources is determined in the long run by the kind of society in which they are used; just as the use to which they are put determines the nature of the society of which they are the physical basis.

In order to see how this works in a particular culture, such as the southern regions of the United States, we may classify resources into five main categories. These are natural resources, technological resources, capital resources, human resources, and institutional resources. How these are all inseparably interwoven in the fabric of human society may be seen by noting that a society which discovers and develops technological resources such as science, invention, technology, organization, management adequately to translate its natural resources into capital wealth or money resources is enabled to apply its capital wealth in the development of its institutional resources and thereby enrich its people and insure their welfare.

Another way of classifying these same types of resources is to say that there are two main categories, namely, natural resources and human resources. In order for natural resources to be developed and utilized well there is needed the technological resources of research, science, invention. In order for human resources to be developed and utilized well there is needed the technological resources of the institutions and of management and organization. In the case of natural resources the result is capital wealth or money resources and in the case of human resources the result is institutional resources to be devoted to human welfare and happiness as ends to which all resources are merely means. This is why the biography of a people begins with nature and resources as inseparable organic parts of society itself.

All this means that there is something far more significant about nature than merely physical things. Nature and resources find scarcely half of their measure in the things of nature—air, water, soil, minerals. The power and glory of nature are in her laws and in the processes of growth and development and in her capacity to produce. Nature's laws and processes are synonymous not only with science itself but are basic to human nature and human society. In reality nature is of three sorts—the material things of earth; natural laws and processes; and then the human counterparts and social relationships of man *and* nature and of man *in* nature.

And finally, we must never lose sight of the fact that the supreme climax of nature is in the personality of the individual and in the folk-character of the people. The full understanding of this implies a recapturing of the fundamental meaning of the inner personality and individual differences of people wherever they aspire to be appreciated, recognized, loved, rewarded, praised, and wherever they revolt when they are not so appraised. This means that the rediscovery and esteem of the folk personality is a supreme task in any understanding of the natural history of a culture. This reflects the profound truth that the mere redistribution of resources and technology through standardized procedures isolated from the elements of folk life brings neither satisfaction to the people nor peace and democracy in the world. This explains also why the understanding and direction of a society must be found within the framework of its regional environment and the inherent cultural endowment of the folk.

And in the South the folk were Nature-folk longer than in the rest of the Nation. The mountains and rivers, the hunting and fishing, the weather working on man to give him the Nature character—all these were elemental factors. And men partook of the hard way of Nature. Sometimes they were prophets of doom, sometimes of the rainbow's end. Sometimes they loved the bark of dog or the low of cow more than the bloom of flower or the crop of corn. Sometimes they loved the sunset and mountaintop and sometimes they brooded in isolation.

Sometimes they loved the rippling, dreamily-drifting river and sometimes they cursed its muddy-watered floods. Sometimes they loved the whispering and murmuring of pine trees, and sometimes they cut and burned them to death. Storm clouds, high winds, cold frosts, wet grounds vied with hot sun, parching winds, baked grounds and burning drought to mix the moods of the folk. There were rippling fields of oats, waving fields of wheat, tasseling tops of corn, white fleeced cotton fields, and there were horses and mules, cows and calves, hogs and chickens, hounds and cats, wild life and wild woods. And there were winter and summer, day and night, breakfast and dinner and supper. And the days went on with sickness and health and children a-borning and dying. The days were full and the folk were not so much interested in civilization as they were in culture and living in the way of Nature.

There is another way in which Nature and the American Indian were symbolic of the South that was to be and in which they had set the incidence for the southern regions of the United States. This was in the regional nature of the southern areas and cultures and the way in which sectionalism and regionalism were to fix the rôle of the South in the Nation. For whatever else the South might be, it constituted first one, and later two, of the major regions of a great Nation that was to find much of its strength in its diversity. And the total character and destiny of the Nation was to be forever conditioned by the part which the southern regions were to play in its growth and development. In the later story of the cultural and historical development of the South, this elemental regional nature of the South was to take the form of a powerful sectionalism. The story of this sectionalism is a part of the way of culture and history which we shall presently study. For the present we are interested primarily in the basic nature of that elemental regionalism in which America is so fundamentally bottomed. For it was in this that the youth-period of "The South" was nurtured.

In the oft-forgotten story of Appalachia that looks down to the sea was found the first incidence, not only of the South's physical heritage, but of the other great regions of America and the frontier influence in the culture of the New World. Here was an extraordinary and amazing new world of Nature and of men. Of Nature there were no less than seven continental divisions below a Canadian Superior Upland, each adequate for separate and distinctive empires, yet potentially seven great regions constituting one great continental unity. And of men, there could be symbolized no less than seven great culture areas, in each of which the basic modes of life and adaptation to Nature were sufficiently similar to afford

cultural homogeneity. These twin-settings of Nature and Man, on the one hand, as magnificent a picture as ever Nature provided, and, on the other, equally magnificent specimens of Nature's earth-men, constituted the New World of America, basic to the future development of the South and the Nation.

The southern members of the family of American regions grew up, like the rest of the early Nation, under the influence of their ever-changing boundaries and areas. In this influence of the frontier was to be found not only many of the forces which were to condition the culture of the South but the Nation as well. For there was a striking parallel between the early influence upon the Nation of such leaders as Washington, Jefferson, Madison, and other statesmen of the aristocratic South and the influence of such frontier leaders as Andrew Jackson, James K. Polk, and Andrew Johnson, all leaders in the new frontier approaches to American democracy. For in these leaders there was foreshadowed much of the politics of personalities and much of the tropism of the people toward political expression that was to characterize the later South in many of its major political episodes.

The products, however, were not so organic or far-reaching as the total culture effects of the frontier on the enduring character of both the Southeast and the Southwest. For just as the early plantation South had set the incidence for a regional culture of aristocracy, race, and caste, so the opening of the new Southwest, stemming out from North Carolina, thence through what was to be Tennessee, set the stage for a sturdy folk democracy that was to influence not only that part of the South but would extend northwestward through old "Kaintuck" and on to "ole man river" north and later south and beyond into Texas and Oklahoma. In both great southern levels of early Americanism the chief mode of life was the open country, the expanding frontier, and an agrarian culture that set the patterns for southern life and institutions.

This influence of the frontier was, of course, of many sorts. In general there were two fundamental conditioned results of the frontier forces, one on the character of the culture and institutions of the people and one on the character of the people themselves, particularly their psychology of the individual and the folk. These make up the culture and behavior of a people and may be used as measures of any early civilization. This is true of early American culture and its continuing traits, whether it be the folk culture of the mountain folk or of the plains dwellers or whether it apply to the product which was Walt Whitman, Nature, and Frontier Man personified; or the same would be true of the powerful folk cultures of the great open spaces of Russia, or of the product which was Tolstoy, unharassed spirit of Nature and the frontier.

The general influence of the frontier upon American culture has been appraised by Turner and others. Illustrations are numerous from the realistic study of the various frontiers of America or from the study of literature and the history of the various regions of America. When we come to apply this measure to the southern regions, it must be very clear that the task is almost synonymous with the cataloging of many of the main traits of southern culture. For here was a regional culture which featured strong individualism, great religious influences, strong sense of honor and personality, strong allegiance to the family and morals, quick tempers and emotional reactions, impatience with organization and formal law and control, love of freedom and the open spaces, and not too much emphasis upon finished standards of art, education, work. There were the frontier patterns of all earlier America as reflected in the homogeneity of native white, northern European stocks, Protestant church going, Sabbath observing, patriarchal folk, abounding in the spirit of honor fighting politics, liquor-drinking, and little love of the law.

So, too, the rural influence still constitutes a powerful factor in the individual lives and behavior of the southern people. Morning, noon, and night, spring, summer, and winter, the language of the weather becomes the language of the people. The farmer loses, wins, breaks even in his contests with rain and drouth, storm and flood, cold and heat. A sizable storm may destroy years of achievement. A year of drouth penalizes with high financial loss and personal dilemma. Blizzards and floods, weevils and worms, disease and hazard multiply their toll until the farmer's gamble becomes a part of his daily life.

For the frontier was not only powerful in its earlier character-forming influence upon the region, but conflict between frontier folkways and modern technological civilization has long been considered by those who study the psychological foundations of modern society as basic to the understanding of much that characterizes pathological behavior. Dr. Franz Alexander in his *Our Age of Unreason* thought that Frederick Jackson Turner's writings "explained the most common conflict of the American neurotic, the thwarted ambition among people trained to admire individual achievements, as their ancestors had done in the days of the Open Frontier, yet situated in a standardized industrial civilization which imposed uneventful routine and offered no real security in return." One need not agree with this conclusion to sense, however, the essential importance of the way of the frontier in the total way of the South.

As if the South up to this point did not already have enough of the total elements that go into the architecture of all cultures, there were yet to be added the powerful factors of race and caste which were to make the region different from all other regions of the Nation. Alongside, therefore, the two great streams of southern development already under way there was to be a third, the three at floodtide converging into a powerful current of mixed waters to make the symbolic muddy river of southern culture. For paralleling the plantation aristocracy was the ever-widening and swift moving stream of slavery, growing larger from the springs of population increase and the tributaries of economic and sectional conflict. And in the uttermost parts of the South was the other widening stream of migration of white groups and their varied ethnic heritage to mix and mingle with the other two.

For the source of this new stream we return, then, to our first introduction to the powerful rôle of Nature in the development of the South, namely, the influence of weather upon crops, the place of cotton among southern crops and consequently the rôle played by Negro slavery in the cotton crop and its economy and culture. For in the coming of the Negro into the picture as a slave there were introduced at once not only the factor of race but a double basis of caste, one of blood and one of sex. In the first place, before the Negro came later to be the most powerful conditioning factor in postbellum southern culture through race and sex-caste, the plantation aristocracy had already evolved into such class and caste that the distinctions between the planter aristocracy at its highest level and the white South at its lowest level had formed an almost unbridgeable chasm between the two in so far as intermarriage was concerned. That cast culture had left its inevitable weakening influence upon the upper brackets of the white South and its embittered heritage upon the rest of the white South. Then, later the organic heart of the South's bi-racial dilemma was to be found in the essential race-sex caste nature of the Negro problem, which rendered its dilemmas unsusceptible to the usual modes of adjustment. The understanding of these factors is essential to any appraisal of the way of the South as it matured into later years.

If in the story of the Negro and the South is reflected the most distinctive trait of the culture of the white South, commonly synonymous with the whole South, this trait is doubly reinforced by the universal heritage of folk culture more powerful and enduring than all the stateways of civilization. For the way of the South has been and is the way of the folk, symbolic of what the people feel, think, and do as conditioned by their cultural heritage and the land which Nature has given them. The culture of the South is the culture of the folk often in contradistinction to the civilization at its flood tide of urbanism, technology, intellectualism, and totalitarianism. This folk culture is deeply bottomed in the realities of Nature and the frontier struggle, in the heritage of multiple migrant people, in the rise and fall of an upper-folk aristocracy, and in a later powerful race and regional conflict. This is an elemental reality definitive of most of the South's culture and economy. The folk society of the South is well-nigh all-inclusive and is reflected on many levels of time and class and in the organic nature of the folk-regional society as definitive of how all societies are formed and grow up.

The elementary sources of this powerful folk society are reflected in a fourfold heritage. There was the growing up of the earlier frontier folk in their struggles with Nature and the Indian alongside the earlier folk culture which was of the vintage of Virginia and the planter aristocracy. Then for a time nearly all of the South consisted of the rural folk with their rugged individualism and their struggle with land and climate, with victory or defeat or harvest time in their blood. And there were the remnants of frontier folk symbolic of mountain culture or flatwood frustration or swamp and bayou levels of living in the out of way places throughout the Deep South. And finally there was the powerful folk society of

the Negroes themselves as both apart from and a part of the dominant white folk.

The first fruits of this heritage were easily discernible in four levels of folk culture which clearly accounted for the institutions and behavior of all the southern people in their considerable diversity, yet in such essential unity as to be characterized as the South. More accurately the southern folk society was a variegated fabric made from a fourfold pattern: the upper levels of the plantation aristocracy; the upper levels of the middle white South; the lower levels of the disadvantaged whites; and the Negro folk society itself reflecting three levels. One of these three was the folk society of the slave level distinguished in any story of universal culture and exerting a powerful influence upon the institutions and behavior of the white South. Another was the white-Negro folk society after freedom, a dual culture that always distinguished the South from the rest of the country and symbolized folk beliefs for which men were willing to die. The third was the new Negro folk society separate from and within the State society of the white South. This, again, was a magnificent example of folk culture in the making and showing remarkable vigor and power of survival, because it was of the essence of the folk.

In reality the vigorous and lusty South that was growing up in the way of Nature and the frontier, of race and the folk, could be understood only through a knowledge of the way of all culture as it develops from the earlier folk stages on through various maturing levels until it flowers in civilization. For this thing we call culture is the heart of human society and is the sum total of all the processes and products of a given people and their society at any given time and region in which they grow up and expand into wider areas and more complex relationships. Culture does not grow up overnight, neither is it changed in the twinkling of an eye. As the supreme character of human society, culture is not only what men die for, but is the product of all that for which they have lived and died, constituting also, therefore, the rich heritage of the past. Culture, moreover, is of and by all the groups, wherever found, whether dominating or not, so that the total culture of a people is interwoven into a fabric made up of variegated parts. The historian has come to recognize the fact that too often the variegated threads of folk culture have been neglected in the attempt to document and to describe society of the past.

For culture is the rich process of living and experience even more than the recorded product. The intensity and quality of culture, like a man's character and personality, dominate life and behavior and make up the very essence and drama of living society. It might very well be the Santayana "public experience . . . the stars, the seasons, the swarm of animals, the spectacle of birth and death, of cities and wars . . . the facts before every man's eyes." Many of these the documentary historian cannot see. Nor does he always get the Carl Sandburg sensing that

> The people is every man, everybody,
> Everybody is you and me and all others.
> What everybody says is what we all say.

And applied further, what everybody feels is what we all feel and what everybody does is what we all do. What we all do reflects the individual and group behavior which is culture.

All of this is of the greatest importance in the understanding of the South, its varied folk societies, its character and personality, and its institutional modes of behavior. For, within the fourfold pattern of southern folk culture there had grown up strong institutions, deeply bottomed in the culture of the old aristocratic South, the old frontier South, and the later South of the upper and lower brackets of white folk strongly conditioned by the black South of cultural tradition and of postwar change. This culture of the South was of the nature of the laws of the Medes and Persians, which changeth not in so far as it constituted the basic fabric upon which the South and the Nation were part and parcel of the same great American culture.

In the biography of a region the more intimate observations and explanation of the folk culture help us, in the words of Carl Sandburg, to sense "the feel and atmosphere, the layout and the lingo of the region, of breeds of men, of customs and slogans, in a manner and air not given in regular history." Yet to sense the stream flow of events, there is needed not only the cultural approach to history, but also and finally the historian's account of what has gone into the making of each regional culture and by the same token of the total national culture fabricated of all. Even though, in the past, much of our history may have been deficient in the first-hand knowledge of people and regions, more recent history, often

vividly and brilliantly written, with adequate documentation of the scholar, not only beckons to those who would know more but provides the authentic formal picture of the folk cultural backgrounds so essential to understanding.

The life of the South has been rich in experiences and episodes about which have centered great emotion and differences of opinion. Yet about the main facts of its birth and its growing up there can be no doubt. For here history has recorded the dates and many of the circumstances, so that, like the universal cultural evolution of the region, its history constitutes the essential reality which makes the way of the South the way of history. It might have been different under different circumstances. The South might have chosen to make it different. The Nation, were it all to do over again, even as the South, would never introduce slavery. Yet that which is written is written and the way of the South is the way of history. That which was done was done and cannot now be changed, and the understanding of what was done is essential to the understanding of the South and the Nation. There is needed, moreover, knowledge not only of whether this or that event happened, whether these or other facts were true, but also what else happened and what else was true in the total historical record. Most of the history of the South is no more nor less logical than the history of the rest of the Nation; it has simply been revivified and interpreted in such partial and partisan manner as to make it appear a thing apart.

And now finally, as we look at the "Way of the South" as it has been reflected in the backgrounds and heritage of its early formative periods, it is increasingly clear that the "Way of the South" has been, is now, and must always be the "Way of America." We have already illustrated how this was true in the historical and cultural backgrounds. It must be clear that there was tragedy and failure in the one instance where, in the attempted secession, the way of the South was not the way of America. The tragedy was of, for, and by the Nation as well as the South. It must be clear in the new southern crisis and the national dilemma that the way of the South, more than ever before, must needs be the way of America, which America, of course, the South will help remake and strengthen. This means that there can be no enduring reality of the southern regions of the United States, except as they are component parts of the better balanced and integrated Nation.

THE REGIONAL QUALITY AND BALANCE OF AMERICA

WE RETURN now to our starting point in regionalism as reflected in the first principles of Americanism. A part of the American dream of equal opportunity has always been soundly bottomed in the great range and variety of that part of the North American Continent which came to be known as the United States of America. It was in the regional quantity and quality of this Continent that the first plantings and the later fruits of American democracy set the incidence of the American way of life as distinctive from that which had gone before or that which was European. This regional nature of America was both physical and cultural and set the stage for a nation that was to be strong because of the successful integration of its great diversities in which its supreme task was to be the achieving of a realistic and adequate regional balance of America.

It follows, therefore, that the way of the South, as the way of any region, is the way of America. By the same token, the way of America is the way of its regions, explored, developed, conserved, and integrated into the unified fabric of the total Nation. Whatever America might have been under different conditions, this is the way America grew; this is the way America is; this is the way of America forward. Just as the greatest strength of America is inherent in its well developed and well balanced diversity of regions, of resources, of peoples, and of culture, so the heart of American democracy is found in the freedom of opportunity, the richness and uses of resources, the development and welfare of the people, within the framework of this diversity and an increasingly effective national government of federated States and regions.

Yet, within the framework of regional diversity may be found not only the historical pattern of national development and strength but also measures of national weakness and undeveloped potentialities alongside the tragedies of sectionalism and the wounds of civil war which have not healed in three generations. Inherent in the waste and weakness of any of the Nation's regions, in the conflict and lack of unity of its peoples, and in hazards of regional imbalance and pathology, are still lurking dangers and dilemmas capable of swelling to floodtide mass emotion, confusion and revolution in the immediate postwar modern world and after.

It must be clear, therefore, that even in normal periods of American development a key problem was always that of the regional quality and balance of America. It was so in the beginning of the great frontier expansion of uneven and unplanned development and exploitation. It was true in the earlier colonial days of pre-North and pre-South in the Nation; it was true in the post-Civil War period of the rapid multiplication of fortunes and the concentration of wealth; it was true in the heyday of the 1920's when the Nation reached its crest of achievement in the quantitative attainments of peacetime civilization. Since then the depression years of the 1930's, the early period of World War II and after have greatly accentuated the importance of planning anew for the regional balance of America. For one thing the increased tensions in matters of the Negro and race segregation and in areas of levels of living and labor organization have revivified the sectional conflict between "South" and "North" to such an extent that we have referred to this problem alone as "shadows over America." The problems of defense and war production early emphasized the importance of decentralization of industry and wealth and of reworking a master plan of transportation to insure adequate distribution. And the global situation with reference to minority peoples, races, and nationalities, has finally made clear the organic significance of this regional quality and balance of people the world over.

The way of the South, therefore, is first of all American and, second, southern. The situation is always one of double responsibility on the part of both the Nation and the South. That is, the Nation's obligation is clearly twofold. One is to so coöperate and administer the ways of American democracy and economy as to help develop the South and the other is by so doing to enrich the Nation. The Nation owes the fullest possible development of the South not only to the South, but to the other regions and the Nation at large. No problem of regional development and planning can be a simple one-way problem.

In the same way the South's task in planning for its part in the regional balance of America is twofold. One is to develop itself and the other is to get along with the rest of the country and to become increasingly a major integrated region of the Nation. There is pathos in the fact that the South's chief deficiencies and tragedies have been the result of its failure in these tasks. For its waste of resources, its failure to develop and conserve them for the enrichment of the people has resulted in vast handicaps. Yet the greater tragedy of war and continued conflict has also continued basic economic handicaps. In this search, therefore, for a better regional balance of America it is difficult to estimate which of the two tasks is primal or more fundamentally important— the development of the region or its integration into the national picture.

Clearly, however, the task is first of all a national one and a first essential is the recognition of this fact by the Nation and by the South and all the other regions. To understand the essential regional quality of America and of world problems and to translate the old sectionalism and separatism into the newer regionalism and unity clearly emerge as a *must* in the new era.

Something of the epic story of this earlier regional America may be recaptured through symbolism of America's Walt Whitman in "The Shapes Arise" or in some gigantic "Broadaxe" set to the building of a frontier nation. To sense anew the range of the incredible and swift-moving cavalcade of America "as the shapes arise" is to recapture the epic of the Nation's powerful heritage of resources set in the midst of every region and of every folk at work at every occupation in which "the main shapes" of democracy were made enduring because of the diversity of people, place, work, and wealth.

In the new regional balance of America, "as the shapes arise" there is recaptured again the powerful and colorful multiple meaning of the old "welcome" to new frontiers. "Welcome are all the earth's lands, each for its kind."

> Welcome, welcome, welcome.
> Lands of pine and oak
> Lands of lemon and fig
> Lands of gold
> Lands of wheat and maize
> Lands of sugar and rice

and all the other lands of grape, and cotton, and white potato, and sweet potato, measureless grazing lands and tablelands, lands of orchards and flax, of honey and hemp. And "welcome just as much the other more hard-faced lands," of mines, of the manly and rugged ores, of copper and coal, of lead and zinc, of iron and tin. And equally again,

> Welcome are mountains, flats, sands, forests, prairies,
> Welcome the rich borders of rivers, tablelands, openings,

Yet more, for "the shapes arise" as of the folk, too, as of those who sought, and seek again, New England and found it or Virginia and the Carolinas or the Deep South and on westward. Or those who found the waters of the Mississippi or of the Red River or deeper south on the Rio Grande; or north again by the Colorado or up beyond by the Northwest's Snake River valleys or the widening thousand-miled Columbia or by Willamette; or again back down by Death Valley and the desert lands and back again to the California Redwoods; and then eastward back again to mountain plateau and great plains and great lakes; and on to great eastern woodlands and mountaintops; and in the way places across a continent by springs and rivers and valleys and back to Appalachia that looks down to the sea. But always the folk and always "Welcome" and ever "the shapes arise." Yet of many shapes, one; of all shapes, America,

> The main shapes arise
> Shapes of democracy total, result of centuries.

First of all, it must be recalled that realistic Americanism was grounded in the physiographic measures of the Continent and in the adaptation of the people to the places where they lived. This was true not only because of the extraordinarily wide range and kinds of natural phenomena but because of the sheer size of an America in which all Western Europe, so to speak, could be lost in her mountain fastnesses or river valleys or great plains. In this happy convergence of a superabundance of natural wealth and human wealth was to be found the measures of both the Nation's extraordinary strength and power as well as her growing pains and sectional conflict.

A full understanding of this physiographic America and her people might well be begun if the observer, flying at a reasonably low altitude, should approach the Continent from the Atlantic Ocean. He would see an extraordinarily rugged Atlantic coast line from which point he would fly over the eastern seaboard with its small rivers and valleys. He would then see the great Appalachian Mountain Region extending all the way from New England down into Georgia and Alabama. Then he would continue across broad flat plains, a thousand miles of middle America, drained by great rivers, stretching from the Great Lakes to the Gulf of Mexico. From here he would fly over the great range of Rocky Mountains and high plateaus from which again he would look down on valleys and snowcapped range of mountains and then his plane might drop abruptly to land along a California coast line, now smooth and now rugged, where he would join the Pacific Ocean. In the midst of these larger parallel regions of mountains, of river valleys, of plateaus, each of which became a frontier in American expansion, he would glimpse hundreds of smaller river valley regions and no less than seventeen major river valleys symbolic of the richness of all resources and power, of flora and fauna of the great American domain. This would be the physiographic regional picture of America as the lines would run north and south. Then, flying north to south over the same regions he would encounter crosswise east to west the great climatic regions and many of those environmental factors which were to so condition people of the United States as to divide them into "North" and "South."

If, then, the observer would return for a closer regional inspection of a great nation in which he would study the combination of the physical and cultural factors he might well start in the New England Northeast. Here he would see its great coast line and fisheries, ships and shipbuilding, industries and technological equipment, centers of urban culture and commerce, an abundance of colleges, universities, art and recreation, philanthropy and wealth, and the concentration of the melting pot population. As he flew south beyond Washington he would see a different sort of American culture, yet strangely uniform in the fabric of its highways and communication. Although there are growing cities, the main character of the culture would appear rural and agricultural where, however, the traditions of the Old South were being transcended by a new balance of agriculture and industry. Here would be lands of cotton and tobacco and millions of black folk growing up and apart. Passing still further southward he would see a great Gulf Coast line with resorts and new reaches in agriculture, balanced with live stock and truck crops and also prospective of new developments in South American commerce and perhaps in the discovery of oil and chemical industries to give new incidence to southern and northern balance of America.

On across the Mississippi to Texas and Oklahoma, he would be amazed at the great plains and their cotton farming, cattle raising, turkey ranches, tropical vegetables, and empire of oil contesting with each other as the rapid increase of cities and industries transform a frontier culture again into a youthful civilization of growing pains and immaturity of years. On then across the continuing fringe of Southwest through New Mexico and Arizona, and moving into San Diego and up the Pacific Coast he would find the most exotic "American" and "Un-American" culture in which the East and West of America and the East and West of the World meet. On up into Oregon and Washington and into the first reaches of Canada he would find a culture and economy of the Pacific Far West, extending from Southern California, reputed to have the highest standard of living of any region in the world. Thence again there would be the completion of the exploration starting east again over the great mountains and plains. Here would be seen the most remarkable examples of power and irrigation dams in existence, as well as the Nation's most notable federal parks and forests, mines of copper and of gold, great expanses of winter wheat lands, and grazing lands again with sparsely settled population. Back again eastward, the observer would slip into the great industrial urban Middle States vying with the East in the concentration of wealth and manufacturing and people but also holding steadfast to the agricultural and rural tradition of America. And in the upper reaches of this river valley with its cities and industries, its tributaries would blend with the east of the western Pennsylvania and West Virginia coal fields.

If, then, the observer wished to obtain a still more detailed view of his America, there could be another more intimate picture which might be had from a three-level travel and exploration review of all the great regions. He might begin with the great Pacific Northwest and move back eastward, retracting his route by railway and automobile as well as by plane. One level would be by plane to circle over and along the great Columbia River country from its upper Canadian borders to its Oregon and Washington developments, mirroring the almost incredibly powerful Grand Coulee Dam and other seemingly superhuman achievements of the world's greatest engineering feats in which new waters may make over lands for a million folk. Yet no air view could be adequate to note the wealth of detail. Another level, therefore, is needed, namely, to go by train and observe more closely. Yet, more still is needed and a third level of travel would be to drive by automobile with such stopovers as might be desirable. From such survey could be gained a knowledge of realistic regional potentiality by adding up the meaning of all this in the totals of what regional resources and development may mean to the strength and unity of America if adequately integrated into the national culture.

And so for the other regions. For instance, such a three-level picture of the Great Plains and of the old area of the Dust Bowl, as reflected in the planning and decentralization of a war period, would reflect an amazing picture of what can go into the regional balance of America. Or again, preview to a new Missouri River Valley development would be an intensive review of the South with its Tennessee Valley, its Appalachian and Piedmont regions of industry and cotton and tobacco, its Black Belt or its deep South along the Gulf and back up the Atlantic. In such a three way level of observation of all the American regions would inhere both the facts necessary for understanding and the assumptions for planning based upon the essential needs for better balance and equilibrium between and among all the parts of America and all the levels of life.

There are still other ways in which we can sense the regional quality of America and the need and opportunity to harness its power and integrate the component parts into a still stronger and better balanced Nation. One way is through an understanding of its rivers and river valleys. And one way to approach that is through the biography of the rivers of America. As were the rivers, so were the people as they won their way in the new America and as they formed their character and fixed their loyalties. This was true whether it be in the little river valleys of a Sweetwater, Tennessee or in the composite Tennessee River Valley with all its tributaries bringing in the waters and the folk alike to the powerfully vibrant total. It is true of the tiny little creek valleys of mountain folk where their highways and creek bottoms and their names and community spirit coincided in the patterns of folk culture and identification. It was true in the big and powerful rivers, the Missouri and the Ohio, the Columbia and the Mississippi. It was true in the twenty-four rivers selected for the "Rivers of America

Series" by Farrar and Rinehart for their notable literary contributions to the understanding and enrichment of America. As it was told by Constance Lindsay Skinner, "It is as the story of American rivers that the folk sagas will be told." And in this effort to "make a whole interpretation of a few American folk" as symbolized in river localities, there is the "greater adventure, namely a composite study of the American Folk as a Nation." There could be multiplied many times the saga of the twenty-four rivers symbolized by *Kennebec: Cradle of the Americans; Upper Mississippi: a Wilderness Saga; Sewanee River: Strange Green Land; Powder River: Let'er Buck;* "history warmed by love of spacious country."

Another way in which it is possible to understand this America through its rivers is to measure the length and breadth and power of its great river valleys as integral regions of this Nation of regions and folk. There is the picture of the Tennessee Valley with its TVA as "Democracy on the March"; or the winding Columbia, upper of Canada and Washington; lower of Washington and Oregon and the Pacific, merging with the Willamette and its lesser tributaries. There is the wide expanse and the long turning of the Missouri and its prospective MRA, to match Tennessee's TVA. In these river valley regions are measurable units of culture and economy, susceptible of scientific study and planning, contributing to the diversity and unity of the American scene. A great Ohio river valley, encompassing so much from Dayton, Ohio to Dayton, Tennessee, must surely represent the need and symbol of unity because of the very diversity of its culture and people. Yet it must somehow be symbol of the regional distinctive quality and variety of the folk themselves because of the many States whose tributary it is. Such a valley, therefore, is not only measure of economy and problem; symbol of folk and nation; but also problem for central administration of government balanced with State and regional priorities.

And so are the other major river valleys, each and every one designated by the National Resources Planning Board as basic areas for water planning and river drainage problems. There were seventeen of these American river valley regions estimated to approximate one measure of the regional quality and balance of America. These regions were designated as the major river valleys of New England, the North Atlantic, the

Middle Atlantic, the Southeast, the Tennessee, the Ohio, the lower Mississippi, the Western Gulf, the Southwest Mississippi Basin, the upper Mississippi-Red River, the Great Lakes-St. Lawrence, the Missouri Basin, the Colorado, the Great Basin, California, the upper Rio Grande, and the Pacific Northwest.

The regional diversity of America may also be understood through a knowledge of what has usually been called the metropolitan regions of America, in contrast with the rural regions of the Nation. In the urban picture may be found also prevailing trends of population and industry, measures of unevenness and imbalance, and areas of conflict, as between labor and agriculture, the consumer and agricultural producer, and evidence of the need for both economic and cultural balance. For in many ways urban centers drain the hinterlands and exploit the folk and resources of the rural regions and set the incidence for inequalities of culture and opportunity. The total urban quality of the Nation may perhaps be observed best in two ways. The one is to examine the one hundred metropolitan districts as classified by the census into areas of more than 100,000 population. The other is to analyze the two great industrial-urban regions of concentrated population and wealth in the Northeast and in the Middle States regions, in both of which the dominant power of urban and organized America finds its greatest expression.

Still another approach to the understanding of the regional quality of America may be found in the historical aspects of regionalism. For, in order to understand the premises and need for this regional balance of America, and still more especially the South's rôle in its attainment, we have to go a considerable way back into America's experiences. For our main assumptions are that the promise and prospect of the Nation in the future, and more specifically the South, are to be found in the substitution of a genuinely realistic regionalism for the older historical sectionalism, which featured separatism, isolationism, competitive States and economy, and political pressures and conflict. Yet the very need makes it all the more important to understand the nature and power of the earlier American conditioning.

First, of course, was the American frontier on the several regional levels already indicated in the way of the South as the way of the frontier and its influence upon the character of American culture.

There were two fundamental aspects of this, both partially conforming to the Frederick Jackson Turner concepts of American history, but with adequate variations to "prove the rule." The first of these was the conclusion that in the process of adapting to a new geographical environment, the economic, social, and psychological demands made upon the pioneers resulted in the creation of new culture patterns which progressively became more American than European. But, unfortunately, this frontier culture set the incidence for something that was also reminiscent of European conflict, namely, American sectionalism, the significance of which "in American history is that it is the faint image of a European nation and that we need to reexamine our history in the light of this fact. Our politics and our society have been shaped by sectional complexity and interplay not unlike what goes on between European nations. The greater sections are the result of the joint influence of the geologists' physiographic provinces and the colonizing stocks which entered them. 'We must shape our national action to the fact of a vast and varied Union of unlike sections.' " The types of American sectionalism which have grown out of these premises include: First, the conflict of the North and South, which James Truslow Adams called "America's Tragedy." Next was the conflict between New England and the West, followed by a conflict between the urban and the rural, and subsequently there has been continuous secondary conflict between different geographic areas and between States.

The essential framework through which both sectionalism was evolved and upon which the new regionalism must be built had its genesis in the ever-expanding series of frontier-regions commonly designated as "wests" in American expansion. The first wests represented the approaches to the Appalachians prior to the breaking over to the real wests. These were movements from eastern New York and Pennsylvania toward the western part of these States, and subsequently the great southwest trek to the State of Franklin and towards western North Carolina and Tennessee, followed by the next westward movement which represented the exploration of Kentucky through the Rayburn Gap and similar overflow behind the Appalachians.

A next western frontier represented movements into Ohio and preliminary approach to a next great westward movement, which might be termed the great Northwest, moving up toward the Great Lakes and to the Mississippi River. Still another series of frontiers reflected the westward movement toward Alabama, Louisiana, Mississippi, and technically then the Louisiana Purchase area, and later came the great exploration of the Mormons and others across the Mississippi and the more or less isolated continuation of the westward movement. Then came the great Oregon trail and the California gold rush, followed by a rebound from the Far West and a revival of the westward movement to the Northwest into the Northern Great Plains. Following these, then, were the great southwestern movements to the Plains, including Texas, New Mexico, and Oklahoma.

Then, too, the historical development of the concept of regionalism helps to interpret the total picture. Perhaps the first of these in the order of historical priority was what was generally called a *cultural* and *literary regionalism*, in which differing groups of people, their culture, folkways, and institutions were described as definitive indices of homogeneity. This was little more than localism and conformed to the earlier sectionalism. Such a regionalism, however, has been richly documented and has a distinguished background. Next perhaps was *metropolitan regionalism*, which was a logical outgrowth of the rise of urbanism and the subsequent extension of the cities into suburban areas, which, with the multiplication of cities and the concentration of population, gave rise to two trends, namely, decentralization of residential and industrial activities and the comprehensive planning and widening inclusion of metropolitan districts. Such a regionalism, like literary regionalism, was primarily local and was focused upon the improving of a situation within given areal concentrations.

Next perhaps was what might be called the *regionalism of convenience and organization*, in which business concerns, industrial corporations, banking organizations, chain stores, educational and religious associations all found it convenient to break the great country down into divisions for practical purposes of distance, size, decentralization, and organization. This regionalism of convenience and organization naturally was a forerunner to a main type of American regionalism, namely, that of *administrative regionalism*. As a major division and movement this was primarily in the field of governmental administration, in which the Nation has been variously divided into areas, corps, districts, regions, zones, and many other terminologies growing up until more than a hundred and thirty such areal divisions have been designated by various governmental agencies for administrative purposes. Samplings are legion, such as the earlier army area corps, the federal reserve banking system, and scores of more recent New Deal administrative subdivisions, such as FSA, WPA, etc.

Finally, a very specialized combination of physiographic, economic, cultural, and administrative regionalism is that in which the Tennessee Valley Authority explores the possibilities of regional planning within specific geographic areas for both cultural and economic development and as strategy for river valley regional planning in harmony with the States and regions and Nation.

One of the best testing grounds for understanding this regional quality of America is the exploration of what the people of the several regions know about and think about each of the other regions.

> Everyone knows this land of ours:
> Sing, "My Country, 'Tis of Thee"

or

> "God Bless America"
> Everyone knows this land of ours,
> And no one knows it.

This is peculiarly true of the younger generation whose knowledge and experience leave a wide gap between general political history and modern ideological principles and philosophy set in the midst of a busy world of specialisms. This was vividly explained in one way by Constance Lindsay Skinner in the statement that, "If the average American is less informed about his country than any other national, knows and cares less about its past and about its present in all sections but the one where he resides and does business, it is because . . . few about have displayed to him the colors and textures of the original stuff of American life; or made him comrade of the folk."[1] Out of this ignorance one region of another grow conflict and misunderstandings and failure to realize on the powerful factors of union in diversity.

Yet after all the greatest evidence of the regional quality of America is found in the cultural

[1] See concluding section in each of the volumes of the *Rivers of America* series by the general editor, Constance Lindsay Skinner.

quality to loyalties within each great region. And how the people love their own regions and criticize others! "Where I come from" is still the perennial proverb for excellence. From a multitude of Southerners: "I hope I shall never have to live outside of the South long. I have enjoyed California and the Middle West and I love New York, but I don't want to live there." And of the windy great plains of the Northwest one writes: "I loved the fabulous sunsets, lakes of gold and the dreamy purple mountains." From the multitudes who love California, some would be found as "seekers of health, sunshine, change, beauty, rest; shunners of toil, care, routine and tumult; haters of closed walls, and lovers of the open air, and others, just Americans demonstrating that East and West do meet—East and West of America, East and West of war." And from New England, soldier boys temporarily in the South: "I want to go back where one can really live. I don't see why anybody would want to live in the South." And from the South, soldier boys: "I don't see why anybody would live up here in this God-forsaken Michigan winter—I want to go home." Or "Deep in the Heart of Texas" may be a symbol of all the regional romance of America. Or one writes, "It is easy to see why Lee loved Virginia so much." Another calls attention to the fact that New England assumed her culture to be most American because they defined American culture in terms of what New England had.

In his story of the *Upper Mississippi: A Wilderness Saga* Walter Havighurst has featured the regional quality of the folk. What he says of that region applies equally to the South in different measures or to any other region. "There is," he wrote, "a stamp that a country puts upon men's faces and upon their speech, and, more mystically, upon their minds. Not by coincidence did Stefanson and Lindbergh, Garland and Turner and Veblen, come from the same great prairies above the Mississippi. Their work has an affinity which makes it a single contribution, repeated in their separate fields of adventure, in earth and air, in vision and in thought. Imagination and will were required of pioneers in that wilderness. It is no accident that the Middle Border produced men resolute and original whose minds have started rivers of new thought that are enlarging still.

"Prairie men, these all saw space in their youth and lived amid tasks bounded only by the horizon. They walked toward the sky. Later, they had no fear of space—not of blank miles of ice, not of blue oceans and blue air, not of spacious ideas that swing arcs of power over the slow thought-world of tradition. Like the homestead seekers, they feared confinement more than hazard. There is a nostalgia that America knows for tasks that come only to a first generation and are not now recoverable. But the wind still blows over the prairie where the grass bent under the wagon wheel and then sprang up again. And the prairie mind still holds the instincts of horizon-land, impatient of boundaries, questing, impelled by an old need and led by purposes forever new."

All this means simply that the way of each region is the way of its culture and that each culture is inseparably identified with its regional character. This is not only nothing new but has always been recognized as a definitive part of understanding peoples and their institutions. It has always been recognized by the common people in their loyalties and devotion to their own customs and institutions and in their criticism of others. It has always been recognized by anthropologists and sociologists in their study of cultures. Regional attitudes and mores are so definite and powerful that they constitute rights and wrongs; they determine the nature of behavior and institutions. Intolerance, therefore, of the mores of a people reflects narrowness and provincialism of outlook.

In the United States there has recently developed an increasing tendency among urban intellectuals to belittle and to characterize as bad many of the mores of rural America and nearly all of the ways of the South. This would be inevitable since the types of culture differ so radically. Manifestly, however, this is one source of conflict and imbalance in the Nation, the conflicting part being unnecessary. And there is an increasing tendency on the part of the North and the South to evaluate their own attitudes and behavior highly and for each to discount those of the other, without understanding them. This reflects a strange backwardness in an age of communication and intellectual liberalism. The depth and width of the growing chasm and the reasons for it would be unbelievable if the situation were not actually true.

This regional quality of culture, behavior and institutions is, of course, as universally applicable to all regions of world society as to the United

States. The recognition of this regional quality of world society, of its imbalance, and of the need for regional arrangements for world organization and peace, while relatively new, is rapidly becoming the basic consideration in nearly all plans for stabilizing world organization. Symbolic of the swelling tide of regionalism is the conviction of Sumner Welles "that an effective international organization can be constituted only through the creation of regional systems of nations . . . under an overall international body representative . . . of all regions." But in whatever instance the point of emphasis is that it is through coöperative arrangement and the integration of diversified cultures that strength and stability are to be found.

* * *

Now, all of this is of the utmost importance if we are to sense the urgency of this problem of the regional quality and balance of America and the rôle of the South in the future development of the Nation. For in our assumption that the South is the chief testing ground for American regionalism and American democracy we have assumed also that its problems are more difficult and varied and that it has inherited a larger number of handicaps than other regions. This explains why the South must devote itself more earnestly to its regional development than other regions, and why, by the same token, the South seeks the way of reasonable national coöperation. There is no other way. The South is as it is. It is the only South we have. The Nation is as it is. It is the only Nation we have. There must surely be some way of attaining this better balance and equilibrium.

This means, again, that the oft-recurring basis upon which we seek to understand and develop the new way of the South in the Nation must be bottomed in the *new American regionalism* in contradistinction to the *old American sectionalism*. It assumes that the balancing of men and resources in the major regions of the United States is no longer a matter of generalities or of ideology alone. It assumes a science of the region in which there is agreement upon the delineation of a reasonable number of major composite group-of-States regions, through which actual planning may be done where men live and work. This means accordingly that planning is not just a matter of words and items, but of realistic action close to reality and in priority schedules of time,

place, and relationship that have to do with each actual job to be done. *Repeat and repeat, regionalism and regional planning are set forth as tools to provide precisely the definite, specific, workable ways of attaining concretely what is generally advised in contradistinction to mere ideology and education or again in contradistinction to sectional rivalries and conflict.*

Such a science of regionalism affords uniform measures upon which all can agree, and thus it becomes a tool for attaining balance and equilibrium between people and resources, men and machines, the State and the folk. It is a tool of the democratic process in that it provides for the redistribution of the good things of life and of the opportunity to work within the framework of every people's geography and of their inherent cultural equipment. It is a tool for democratic world reconstruction in the postwar world, because it is through coöperative regionalism rather than economic nationalism that the society of tomorrow can be organized for human welfare instead of for military achievements. It is a tool for social planning, because it takes into consideration the rights, privileges, resources of people and areas, and stresses self-government and self-development as opposed to coercive centralized power. It is a tool for social planning, also because it offers specific technical workable ways of developing and conserving resources for human-use ends.

Since regionalism, as the opposite pole of sectionalism, isolation, and separatism, is as true of international as well as of national affairs, it wants no self-sufficiency in economy. It wants no isolationism and separatism. There can be no region except as it is a part of the total Nation or of world society, each region being a constituent unit in the whole, and the wealth and welfare of the total measured through the integration of the wealth and welfare of each. By the same token each region can be enriched and developed only through the principle of national coöperation and representation set in the framework of both governmental and voluntaristic effort.

* * *

Such a regionalism is insurance against any economy which allows for the "haves" and the "have nots" in areas of American democracy. This is exactly what exists in the South today and what a surprising number of "scholars" have assumed must continue. There could be no justification in a well integrated American democracy for a system or set-up of public administration and philosophy which would assume the perpetuation of weakness, deficiency, and poverty in one region alongside strength, efficiency, and abundance in another. The whole situation is especially tragic when pathology and deficiency are assumed as permanent traits of a region with great potentiality of resources. It would be unbelievable if it were not true that such a framework of American democracy should come so near the realization. Regionalism, therefore, both strengthens the economic total of the Nation and avoids conflict, on the one hand, and prevents the necessity for special relief, special differentials and privileges, on the other. And, of course, it features the American credo of self-adequacy and mastery over environment.

As it relates to the universally desired redistribution of wealth and opportunity, regionalism provides the only way for such an enduring and effective redistribution by creating in each region the capacity to produce and use wisely wealth which comes from the development and utilization of resources and men within the framework of the region and the equipment of the people. This is essentially the key to the regional balance of man everywhere in which the goal is a better equilibrium between men and full resources and between men and situation, communication and transportation. This is the way to utilize science and technology in the mastery of man's problems.

* * *

The enrichment of each region, in addition to the development and use of its resources, training of its people, and the balance of its industry, contributes powerfully to the wealth of the Nation, which wealth, in turn, from Federal sources may be used in coöperative and equalizing funds for leadership, research, training, and planning essential to the democratic processes of State and regional representation. The way to train youth, for instance, and to guarantee security and reality for the American army of the new generation, to raise standards of living, to insure equal opportunity and security is to develop regional capacities and programs and to work out interregional optima rather than draining some regions for others or concentrating abnormal situations subversive to the development of a great unified Nation.

So, too, the way of defense and the way of a strong Nation in time of war is essentially in the multiple strength of all regions, each providing its part in the Nation's total and in particular to guarantee the national reserves essential for permanent defense and permanent prosperity. Such a power of regional decentralization, yet of national order, was brilliantly illustrated in the way in which Russia's strength was deployed against Germany. The way to effect a wholesome decentralization of wealth, of power, of people is explored through the regional balance of men and resources, but always with the national integration and unity of a strong people as the first concern.

On the other hand, if there is any way to prevent totalitarian overcentralization of power, it is to provide safeguards and guarantees in a sound regionalism bottomed in the American principle of geographic representation and the balance of power of the people. Furthermore, if there is any way to safeguard the American ideals of democracy of the folk and to prevent the rule of persons rather than of the rule of laws and constitution, it is through this continuing equilibration which comes from the regional balance of wealth, of control, of population, all in turn balanced with land and resources developed within the framework again of balanced communications, transportation, and exchange which makes possible the best adjustment between the people and their total heritage and environment. Here is the essential consistency of the ideals and strategy of a strong centralized government and planning to the end that there may be power and resources adequate to guarantee a strong and effective decentralization.

James Truslow Adams in his latest interpretation of the United States in *The American*, in which he seeks to define America in realistic terms, "strikes the first snag—unity in vast diversity." Yet so far from being merely an obstacle, this is in reality the explanation for the genuine liberalism which is America on all its levels of historical time, geographical regions, and cultural development. But especially the historian emphasizes the fact that "to learn what a man is you have to know a lot about his background and life." To this end he insists that "we shall have to go a long way back and follow the American through his experience and consider the influences which have been operating to make him what he is." This is especially true in the case of American regionalism, in which it is necessary perhaps to go even further back to understand how all societies grow out of the folk-regional culture. All this is doubly important because of the prevailing ignorance of history on the part of the American people and because of the failure to understand the backgrounds of American regionalism. And it is of critical importance in the new tendency toward the revivification of the old seeds of sectionalism in America and of the crisis that grows more ominous under the strain of world conflict and dilemma.

The rediscovery of the regional power and glory of America, however, through literary and historical portraiture is not all of the problem of attaining the desired regional balance. Although an understanding of the historical and cultural backgrounds and meaning of regionalism is fundamental, the problem is essentially a contemporary one of study and analysis on the one hand and of planning for the future, on the other. This involves measures of imbalance and a continuous redefinition of balance to meet the flexible needs of a rapidly changing economy and culture. Implied in the definition of balance are many factors besides the technical one of a balanced economy, such as we have already described. The heart of the problem is found in search for equal opportunity for all the people through the conservation, development, and use of their resources in the places where they live, adequately adjusted to the interregional culture and economy of the other regions of the Nation. The goal is, therefore, clearly one of balanced culture as well as economy, in which equality of opportunity in education, in public health and welfare, in the range of occupational outlook, and in the elimination of handicapping differentials between and among different groups of people and levels of culture may be achieved. In so far as the South is concerned, one way of sensing the full meaning of imbalance is in terms of the measures of inequality.

*　*　*

Yet this problem of balance and equilibrium is not all a matter of balanced economy and culture within the region. It is also a matter of adjustment and interregional balance with other regions in so far as it lies within the South's capacity to seek that balance. But also a large part of the imbalance has been due to deficiencies of national strategy in keeping the South as a colonial section whose participation in the Nation has been and is still often considered a privilege. Thus, the South has the double handicap of its own self-adapted sectionalism and the almost universal picture of cultural separatism which the rest of the country assumes to be the realistic South.

Furthermore, in so far as the lack of balance in the Nation is one of culture as well as economics, it reflects not only vast inequalities of education and welfare but lack of balance between urban and rural America, between majority and minority groups, and conflict between the East and the West, as well as North and South, between white and Negro, between capital and labor, between opposing groups of organized labor, between different classes in cities and in industries themselves. The lack of cultural balance includes overconcentration of population and pathology in the cities as well as in isolated population areas. It extends to the multiple national agencies in urban centers and is reflected in their conflicting ideologies and failure to agree upon elemental factors.

These measures of imbalance are all abundantly found in the South and have been described already in the catalogue of deficiencies which we have presented. In general the southern States rank in the lowest quartile in the statistical measurement of the most commonly used indices of adequacy so that the measure of need for balancing the region would be that of moving up into the second or first quartile or the equivalent of a hundred percent improvement in many aspects of regional economy and culture.

More vivid illustrations may be cited as basic to next steps in planning and development. For instance, there is no American university in the South either in its equal ranking with leading institutions in endowment, libraries, research or in the capacity to include in its curriculum, the attitudes and ideologies of the university education unhampered by race or creed or traditions or in the ability to secure and hold on its faculties the top scholars of the Nation. They are all southern universities. Furthermore, there is no one in the South well acquainted with the situation and realistically facing the facts who claims for any southern university full national character and no one who sees any prospect for such a university in the near future. More than this, it is generally assumed among all the university folk in the rest of the Nation, not only that the South has no first ranking university, but that it can't have such universities. Southern university professors start, therefore, with this double handicap because of which they are expected to contribute to the South only and not to the Nation or the total of knowledge and learning. If it be said that the South does not want such universities and that the rest of the Nation does not want the South to have them, this itself constitutes eloquent evidence of the regional imbalance in this field.

If then it be said that this appears as a severe arraignment of the South which has made greater strides in education than any other region, and of the North which has contributed millions of dollars in philanthropic and coöperative efforts, as well as provided many of the educational leaders for the South, this again constitutes eloquent testimony to the complex nature of the southern regional culture in the national picture. For all of these are true in the total picture. Or again, if it be added that the South has a certain quality in its institutions which attracts thousands of students from other regions who continue to like the South, that again emphasizes all the more the lack and need of equal universities in the Nation and indicates what might be done in a well balanced plan for the interregional exchange of faculties and fellowships.

Again the South has no technological institutions of the first rank to train for research and leadership in agriculture, engineering, or industry. The South has none of the great research centers in industrial research or engineering research or in business or university research and it has a very small ratio of research workers in any field, although its needs are greater than other regions The concentration of research in a few regions. and the consequent neglect of its application to regional research and to the training and employment of youth reflects one of the most marked phases of imbalance. And this goes hand in hand with the poor uses of resources and the waste of many natural resources and the lack of opportunity for nearly half of southern youth in the culture and economy of the South as it has been and as it is now trending with the hazards of diminishing cotton returns.

It follows, therefore, that the greatest measure of imbalance is found in the development and utilization of human resources. Over against the need for more industry of the sort to employ millions more of workers better trained, there are too many agricultural workers inadequately equipped by training and farm economy and their income is out of balance with the rest of the Nation or with what is needed. This imbalance, however, has two sides to it. One is in the simple lack of balanced economy between agriculture and industry, and the other has to do with lack of a balanced agriculture itself. Or to put it differently, there might be too much good industry with too much poor agriculture over against a greatly increased, diversified agriculture balanced with increased industry but with the guarantee of parity for agricultural products.

How national planning might not contribute effectively to the regional balance of America and especially how it might militate against the South may be illustrated in two sample cases. There was, for instance, in the depression 1930's an earlier publication at the time when America's consumer purchasing power was scarcely more than sixty billion dollars prepared by a national planning agency looking toward full employment. In the program, recommended under the title "Resource Utilization," it was pointed out that when the total purchasing power of the Nation reached seventy or eighty billion dollars the Nation could give full employment to all of its employables. Yet it was stated that even if the total consumers' purchasing power should rise to ninety or ninety-five or even one hundred billion dollars there would be need for scarcely any increase in agricultural workers. As applied to the South with its great mode of farmer folk, it would thus come to pass that, when the rest of the Nation was reaching its peak of prosperity on the basis of industrial America, the South would be again, as in the 1920's, in depression straits with too little employment and having the necessity of paying high prices for commodities made on the basis of high prosperity. The original program not only failed to plan for the region and its farm populations, but on the contrary assumed that the logical thing would be for the rural folk to migrate to industrial centers, where already people were congested mainly in one or two regions.

This brings us to the second type of planning which accentuates regional imbalance and works to the detriment of the South. That is, the procedure which takes the youth from one region to another, trains them, and concentrates them in the same urban industrial centers that already exist, results inevitably in the impoverishment of the region from which they are drained and is not a sound policy for the Nation or the region. Such programs fail to provide training and work opportunity for the youth of that region, and this inevitably results in deficiency areas. It assumes an uneven regional distribution in terms of "the have" and "the have-not" regions with the corollary that such regions can best be provided for through federal aid and should be expected only to come as near self-support as possible.

In the lack of balanced agriculture with its resultant inequality of opportunity for millions of southern youth, including the children of tenant farmers and the millions of youth employed in low-paying, unskilled factory work, the South is using its great reserves of workers at no more than half of their potentialities. Yet more specifically, the South is utilizing nearly a third of its labor resources, namely the Negro, at perhaps not more than a third of their full capacity both because of the lack of a balanced economy and because of the South's policy and tradition in the employment of Negroes. This means automatically, therefore, under the present premises that the South cannot expect a well balanced culture or an abundance economy comparable to what it is capable of attaining as compared with the national standard. The most distinctive measure of imbalance, therefore, is that between the white population and the Negro in which traditional unnecessary differentials infer discrimination, and lack of an adequate program of education and training have become insuperable handicaps to the attainment of a total southern economy and culture of which the South is capable.

Further measures of imbalance, as reflected primarily in the South itself, are found in the continuing sectional conflict and the emotional energies negatively expended by the southern people in the place of the devotion to positive programs and a better balanced work program. If it is said that the North's criticisms are often based upon lack of information and are often unfair and that there is growing up an increasing enmity toward the South, this again is added evidence of the complexity of the situation and of the nature of national imbalance.

If, then, it is said that all the other regions discriminate against the Negro and segregate him in all of the main avenues of life, that still has nothing to do with the handicapping effect of these practices in the South. If it be said with scientific accuracy that the people of any other region than the South would in all probability have acted exactly as have the Southerners had they been conditioned by the same environmental influences of climate, geography, economy, and culture, this still has nothing to do with the rightness and wrongness of the southern behavior. The same behavior would be the same right and wrong and would require the same correction and amelioration whenever it occurred. The fact that the total Nation is responsible and that there are obligations outside the South subtracts nothing from the reality of the South's opportunity and obligation. On the contrary it adds up again and again to a supreme challenge and offers a double prospect for success.

Within this total framework of the regional quality and balance of America in which it is not possible to separate the South from the Nation or the Nation from the South we must, therefore, proceed directly and concretely to the specific tasks which face the South and also the rôle of the rest of the Nation in regional development and integration. These tasks are essentially of two sorts: one comprehends the whole range of action programs, of doing things that need to be done, the necessity of which appears self-evident from a clear understanding of the South and its place in the Nation. The other comprehends the whole range of attitudes and beliefs and the reexamination of traditional premises upon which these beliefs are based. From our insistence that one of the first essentials of the Nation is a better understanding of all the facts involved, it is clear that the twofold nature of the tasks applies alike to the South and the rest of the Nation. Yet since it is the way of the South that we portray and the development of the South that we plan, our emphasis must necessarily be primarily upon the South and what its reasonable program will include. We begin with the action programs; with things to be done.

Again, within the framework of action programs needed there are two levels of approach. One is the general over-all planning program which comprehends the best in coöperative effort between governmental institutions and voluntaristic agencies; and the other is on the level of specific things to be done within the larger framework of planning. Manifestly, the first need is for the over-all planning program that combines as many desirable features as possible. There must be specific but broad principles and practices of federal, State, and regional planning which will meet the needs for developing the Nation's great resources and for such adequate and equitable regional distribution of the essential good things of life as will insure a greater balance and equilibrium in the Nation for all of its people. The fact that we are primarily concerned here with the South means that there is need for even higher motivation and more harmonious agreement on next steps. These include an uncompromising allegiance to the framework of American culture, a more realistic understanding of regional factors and problems, a new and practical approach to the reintegration of agrarian culture into American life, a relentless search for a better balanced economy, and always back again to the conservation and development of our resources and the training and development of the people. And there is always the need for the long road of intellectual processes, hard work, technical skill, and a more realistic facing of facts than either the South or North has so far been willing or able to attain.

We have already outlined in the previous chapter an over-all regional planning program for the South. The adoption of some such program is the first essential for adequate regional development and balances such as we have shown to be necessary in the future successful life of the South. Perhaps the main reason that it is needed is the fact that this is the only way that the South can be brought to agreement among its own conflicting forces and to work with the Nation at large. Another reason for a definite federal, regional, State, and local planning arrangement under the auspices of governmental agencies is the fact that this is the only way that it is possible to work out a practical working relationship that will provide for increasingly rapid attainment of equality of opportunity for disadvantaged groups. It has been demonstrated many times that private and voluntaristic organizations, of which the South is a veritable graveyard, cannot do the job. On the other hand, programs, combining the agencies of State and city and county in coöperation with regional agencies working with federal coöperation acceptable to the people, can not only succeed but increase respect for government and enhance the whole program of democratic services. It is only through definite workable ways of doing

things through State and regional planning that it is possible to incorporate programs for all the people, and especially for the equalizing of opportunity for Negroes. Through such arrangements respect for public administration may be accentuated at the same time that there is responsible action in the place of what is too often irresponsible agitation. Such an over-all program may become a medium through which recommendations of civic agencies and educational institutions may be tested and enacted and at the same time may initiate ways and means for inquiring into and carrying out any one or all of the action programs adjudged necessary. Manifestly, such problems as the poll tax or farm tenancy or equality of accommodations for Negroes and many other specific problems now being attacked through isolated agitation will come within the range of such regional planning.

* * *

There are then many specific things to be done within the framework of the over-all planning program. High up in the catalogue is an inventory of total resources. There has been a growing unanimity of opinion among southern students, observers, and leaders in public life that the South's greatest opportunity and obligation now are found somewhere in the field of developing, conserving, and utilizing wisely and more widely her resources. If, therefore, we provide a program and procedure which will enable us to so develop and utilize our resources as to increase our wealth, enrich our institutions, and give prosperity and welfare to the people, we will be accomplishing the most and the best that can be done for the South at this time. If this is true, the greatest single need of the South, outside its Victory programs and its general leadership and development, is very clearly the application of science to industry, agriculture, and to the development and utilization of its great resources. The ends sought are that the young people may be better trained, that scientific research may be carried on, that this research may be applied to raw materials with a view to greater manufacturing use as well as to industry and agriculture itself, and that there may be forthwith programs which will render greater income to the people, increase employment, increase wealth, and give the South a well balanced economy.

Since the primary purpose of an inventory of regional resources is inherent in the assumption of their development and wise use, it follows that a great increase in research and the training of research workers becomes a third major task inseparable from the second. For, in these areas of resource development and use the South reflects one of the most unfortunate examples of imbalance in the total national picture. For in no field of research does it excel. In every field of research it lags. Its deficiency here not only deprives its people of opportunity but also of wealth, and in addition contributes to an over-centralization of research in a few centers, adds greatly to the imbalance of the Nation, and limits the wealth of the Nation and the region.

In this South of tomorrow growing into its next great period of development, there are other aspects of its resource development and use that provide the basis for next steps. It is not only that there is needed a new inventory of total resources with new reaches of skills in research and invention to be applied to the development and use of natural resources, but there are two immediate opportunities that have to do with human resources. One of these is the more effective utilization of the people as workers, including their distribution and employment and including the very special aspects relating to the Negro people. The other has to do with the effectiveness of the schools in resource education and in training in elements of life that are basic to regional culture. The problem of the wiser use of the people and of their relation to a better regional balance of the Nation requires two separate approaches. One is the problem of employment and standards of pay and work in general for all the people, including again special attention to the employment of the Negro in the South. The other has to do with a planned redistribution and migration of the Negro throughout the other regions of the Nation.

With reference to the first aspect, planning and next steps are relatively simple in terms of the programs being worked out for the better training and equipment of youth, for the increase of industries which pay higher wages and turn out the more finished products, for the elimination of regional differentials, and for the special development of a balanced agriculture and adequate opportunity for youth on the farm. From the viewpoint of developing and using wisely natural and human resources together, there can be no doubt of the urgency, as a first task, of increasing regional industry to provide a new balanced economy and to bring new standards of equipment, of pay and of living to all the workers of the South. Symbolic of what is to be done and illustrative of what can be done is the record of three great southern industries that have already attained the highest rung in the national ladder. The first of these is the textile industry, if we take into consideration both its past achievements and what is even now already being planned for the immediate future. A second is the extraordinary record of tobacco production and manufacture with its national and international excellence. The third is the furniture industry which in some ways is the largest in the country.

Yet there is needed much more than these in the form of not only more industries but specialized types, such as chemical and processing industries, which will employ a larger ratio of skilled workers and will reward with more pay and with a larger increment of wealth left in the region. We have demonstrated that the South has the necessary natural resources; that the farmers are able and are more and more willing to produce the necessary increased variety of commodities; that the South has ample labor reserves and can train them; that there is a large reserve of capital wealth in the South available when the circumstances become favorable for investment. There is then need for leadership and what Harriet L. Herring emphasizes as "enterprisers" to do the job. There is, finally, the increasing need for developing our technological resources in the form of skills, tools, management.

In the total planning for new industry and wealth as basic to a better balanced economy and culture there is one major problem of increasing importance and difficulty. This is the problem of training and utilizing wisely the great labor resources of the Negro people. For here is a region where a fourth of its worker-resources have been utilized to scarcely more than a fourth of their possibilities and with the rapidly changing status and prospect of cotton which has been the basic field of work for Negroes, the prospects for the future offer still less promise unless there is special planning with reference to the new industrial development or for migration to other regions. In addition to this special planning there is need to plan wisely for the total situation as reflected in the problems of fair practices in labor and employment and the increasing hazard of competition in which many of the older occupations of Negroes will be taken over by whites.

* * *

This brings us face to face with the other two action programs already mentioned, the redistribution of the Negro people in the Nation and the rôle of the schools in regional development. These are, however, also primarily programs that have to do with attitudes and tradition. We may, therefore, approach our second level of special tasks, namely, those having to do with regional and national attitudes, folkways and emotions, with these two problems. And, first is the problem of planned voluntaristic migration through which the Negro people may be more evenly distributed throughout all the regions of the Nation. This requires a master strategy capable of bearing the burden of a many-sided dilemma. There is not only the difficult task of balanced distribution of the people but also that of providing ways and means of educating and training the Negro in his new environment and the considerable problem of planning work for him to do before he is relocated for his training and education.

The assumptions of such planned migration are many. First, there is to be had the consent and coöperation of the rest of the Nation outside the South. Then, there is the consent and coöperation of the Negro people. But, finally, there is the consent and good will of the South. There are other assumptions on other levels of approach. One of these assumptions is that the increasing demand for the elimination of discrimination and segregation for the Negro in American life brings with it both the willingness and the capacity of the Nation to provide facilities when there is adequate wealth and will to make satisfactory arrangements, and when legal restrictions are not present. This means, in practice, the ascertaining of the answers to the questions of how many Negroes in what classifications of age, training, family equipment, can be wisely used in what regions of the Nation and in what capacities and through what procedures.

There are other complicated assumptions, perhaps four of which are fundamental to the first consideration of any such planned migration. The first of these is that it is not possible to approximate the balanced culture necessary to guarantee the Negro equal opportunity in America in any other way than through the migration from the South, to all other regions, of at least one-half the total Negro population in the South. A second assumption is that the rest of the Nation is sincere in its militant advocacy of equal opportunity and is willing to do its part in attaining the desired ends. Another assumption is that increased provisions for training Negroes and for setting up additional industrial opportunities can be made through national, regional, and State planning agencies much more economically for the Nation than the attempt at coercive military enforcement by the Nation of a non-segregation economy advocated by many agitators. And finally there is the assumption that the South, in the face of losing a large part of its Negro population and in the light of reduced numbers would provide facilities for equal opportunity for those who remain, would eliminate all unnecessary differentials between the races, and would modify its policy of segregation in many respects.

Now manifestly, so far as any immediate results may be anticipated, such a suggested program of planned migration can be little more than a way of vivid presentation of the complexity of the situation and the urgency of need, because of the lack of reality in nearly all of the assumptions stated. Yet such a program must be faced frankly and something of its equivalent must be planned if there is to be anything like balance and equilibrium in this area of Negro-white relationships in the United States and if stark tragedy is to be avoided in the wake of present trends. If, again, it be objected that the Negroes will not agree, that the various regions of the Nation will protest that they are not prepared, and that the South itself will not coöperate, this again is another way of indicating the difficulties and hazards in the way of the South in the Nation.

* * *

In the drama of this way of the South in the Nation there is no way of hiding the fact that the supreme task for region and Nation in their search for a better regional balance of America is that of a better adjustment of race relations and opportunities with all of the implied obligations of both races and all regions. There is no way of overlooking the fact that the South's attitudes and behavior on most levels are wrong, judged from any general, abstract principle of democracy or Americanism. If it be offered in defense that New England or the people of any other region would in all probability have behaved exactly the same as the South, it still remains that New England or any other region would have been equally wrong.

If it be said that there is no record of any other peoples being successful in a compound bi-racial civilization and that race prejudice is as old as civilization and that all the other regions of the United States discriminate against the Negro in high places and in low, that still has nothing to do with the obligation of the South and the Nation to work jointly toward the amelioration of conditions. If it be said that the other regions of the Nation should study and plan for the improvement of their own situations and unfair practices, the answer would be that they are doing just that, which adds to the South's obligation to do its part.

On the other hand, since the job is one for all the Nation as well as for the South, it must be apparent that the Nation's part is also a two-way task. If, as is clear, the Nation is assuming increasing responsibility in its attitude and action toward the southern part of the problem, there are two sides to this. It is not only that the Nation's conscience is troubled over the vast injustices in the South and the verdict is that the Nation must do something about it. It is also that there is the equal responsibility for the Nation to understand the total situation, to participate in its working out on the levels of American democratic government, and plan with the South in terms of attainable reality. The Nation must surely know the nature of the problem and understand how the way of the South is the way of Nature with all her powerful conditioning forces; the way of the frontier and the folk with their loyalties and patriotism for causes for which they, both white and Negro, are willing to die; the way of religion and race, more powerful than all abstract moralities; and the way of culture and of America and of history through which the way of the South has been interwoven in the total fabric of the Nation and of the Nation in the fabric of the South.

There is another way in which the Nation's part is a two-way approach. If it is said that the Nation cannot face the world of nations and their search for global democracy unless it can forthwith reshape its own undemocratic procedures, it must be said also that America cannot lead the nations of the world toward abiding peace and fellowship through organization if it cannot prevent violent revolution and civil war within its own races and regions. The fact that there are wrongs to be righted is no license to right them through fighting and war again, especially since these wrongs are of the same sort, only less complicated and often less extensive, as the wrongs

and tragedies of the rest of the world. Some of the movements, attitudes, and activities, both North and South, within these threatening shadows over America, have come close to treason in time of war; they can bring on new war when peace has come. America can adopt the procedures of planning and interregional and interracial organization and cooperation and be ready to join with the world in international organization and coöperation for peace. Or America can join the conflicting nations and races in perpetual warfare and violence and lose its place in the leadership of the world of international organization for peace. This problem is no more a one-way obligation in the United States, with its opportunity for interregional and interracial balance than are the obligations of nations and races and folk in tragedy and travail the world over.

That's how important the problem is. That's how near America comes to crisis. That's why the shadows over America grow. That's why the supreme task, for the way of the South and for the way of the Nation is found in the problem of the regional quality and balance of America. That's why there is no other way to achieve the desired and attainable standards other than through complete coöperative State, regional, and national planning under the auspices of governmental and voluntaristic programs, adopted and enacted through the consent of the people and through new reaches in the effectiveness of education. The Nation has had no greater responsibility than this. The South has had no greater opportunity.

* * *

So comes the South to a new era in the annals of America. We return to our starting point in which a new region grew up in the tutelage of Nature and of the folk seeking the promised land through the mastery of a distinctive environment. And we recapture something of the heroic story of the region with all its tragedies and hazards and its perennial problems. And we recall the sayings of the historian that to learn the life and times of an individual we have to know a lot about his background and experiences and to learn the life and times of a region we have to know a lot about that region's experiences and backgrounds. Now, we have learned a lot about this South of the United States but we have also learned a lot about the way of Nature and culture in a magnificent reality that knows no turning back and gives no special privilege to any culture and no special priorities to any region or race. "The shapes arise" anew challenging a new youth and maturity of the South and Nation to be strong, as America is strong to meet all tasks.

> She receives them as the laws of Nature, receiving them, she is strong,
> She, too, is a law of Nature—there is no law stronger than she is.

In the knowledge about the way of America and the way of emergency and crisis, there is warning as well as promise:

> And whether I come to my own today or in ten thousand or ten million years,
> I can cheerfully take it now, or with equal cheerfulness I can wait.

We return to another starting point in our story of the South, namely the four traits of the American way: the American dream of equal opportunity; the American endowment of Nature; the American strategy of conquest and mastery; and the American heritage of exploitation and waste. The biography of the South, rich in all these, is still the biography of Americans.

> With firm and regular step they wind,
> They never stop,
> Succession of men, Americans, a hundred million,
> One generation playing its part and passing on,
> Another generation playing its part and passing on in its turn.

And never America in general shall diminish one whit the specific part which the South shall play in the total epic; or the concrete task of the Nation in the southern epoch. And always Southerner same as Northerner; Easterner same as Westerner; Negro same as white; and always again, "Take my leaves, take them South and take them North, make welcome for them everywhere. . . . In the name of these States surround them East, and West. . . ."

THE REGIONAL LABORATORY FOR SOCIAL RESEARCH AND PLANNING

IMPLIED in the assumptions of a regional University center of social research and planning is the availability of the regional laboratory. This term must for the most part at present symbolize the need and the general concept of scientific work in the social sciences, rather than an actual specific working laboratory comparable to those of the natural sciences. Yet the regional laboratory as utilized by the Institute for Research in Social Science has actually consisted of three major levels. One is the South itself as the area from which materials are gathered and in which research is conducted. A second is the sub-regional laboratory of thirteen counties proposed as the central focus for as many concrete projects as practicable. The third is the physical laboratory and workshop and its correlated activities in Alumni Hall at the University of North Carolina. We may look briefly at each of these.

THE SOUTH AS A GENERAL LABORATORY

In using the South as a term for the general living laboratory for regional research and development, there is ample precedent and urge.

For instance, when Columbia University set up its Department of Sociology the recommendations submitted emphasized the importance of the City of New York as a great laboratory for the study of human society. The City of Chicago has often been designated as the laboratory for the pioneering work in human ecology of the Department of Sociology in the University of Chicago. In North Carolina, President Edward Kidder Graham not only popularized the University but made its work increasingly dynamic by referring to the State as the University's campus and laboratory.

In its efforts to make its research realistic the Institute for Research in Social Science at the University of North Carolina added the principle of providing that most of its study and research be done in the southern regional area which it chose as its over-all laboratory. Its policy provided for *planned cooperative research* in this laboratory rather than merely individual research in the history and theory of cultures or in areas of foreign relations, no matter how important. One of the first contributions of the Southern Regional Study was to delineate scientifically the Southeast and the Southwest as clearly defined areal laboratories of the South which were to be no more sectional than any other of the regions, Northeast, Southeast, Northwest, Southwest, Middle States, and Far West. Such a regional division not only provided comparable laboratories but tended to relegate to the past the narrow constraining terms "North," "South," with their implications of conflict and sectional isolation.

There is yet another observation of great importance here. It is that the practical community or regional study, which must be tested in the white light of application and double checking in the laboratory in which it was made, must stand a harder test and therefore be more scientific than the mere historical and theoretical research into scholarly archives and original sources. The researchers must know more anthropology, more geography, more sociology, more economics, more political science, and more statistics, *not less*. The regional study, therefore, becomes the broader, organic inquiry, capable of contributing to genuine theory more than the mere documentation and analysis of historical theory.

THE SUBREGIONAL LABORATORY FOR SOCIAL RESEARCH AND PLANNING

As exploring the whole area of methods and programs of social research and planning, the Subregional Laboratory for Social Research and Planning has been projected and delineated with a view to meeting the need for a relatively concrete *permanent working laboratory* for the Institute for Research in Social Science at the University of North Carolina.

The area of the special laboratory includes thirteen contiguous counties, approximating a miniature Piedmont South, with ten counties in North Carolina and three in Virginia. The counties are: Alamance, Caswell, Chatham, Durham, Granville, Guilford, Orange, Person, Rockingham, Wake, in North Carolina; Halifax, Henry, Pittsylvania, in Virginia.

Such a laboratory is universally recognized as an essential next stage in social research and planning and especially in programs of regional effort. It is generally agreed that adequate results can no longer be attained without such a laboratory.

The Subregion is not an area to be studied or surveyed or planned. Nothing *has* to be done *to* it or *about* it.

It is rather a laboratory area in which research and planning *may* be done in accordance with occasion, facilities, and resources, commensurate with the needs and opportunities for new and more realistic studies and for implementing theories and findings that have evolved from previous studies and the desires and participation of the people.

In so far as research and planning may be projected and completed the area provides a suitable laboratory for concrete and intensive studies in whatever units may be undertaken and in the long run the aggregate result may well comprehend the most complete and comprehensive and experimental planning possible.

The laboratory is continuous. It may be used or it may not be. It may be utilized at some times and not at others. Parts of it may be used and parts not. What is done in one county may not necessarily be done in all. What is done for one field of interest may not be done for others. There is no compulsion either in the work to be done or in time limits in which it must be done.

As in any laboratory the range and nature of research and planning will be determined by the need, the facilities, the opportunities, the personnel, the methods available. These in turn will be conditioned by the programs, needs, techniques, and trends of the social science and social work groups, on the one hand, and by the needs, opportunities and availability of the counties on the other.

As is the case in other laboratories, the Subregion will provide not only for research and planning but for training leaders and specialists.

It is available for exploration and experiment in coöperative research and coördinated planning. It is equally available as testing grounds for research and programs for local, State, regional, or national implementation.

The laboratory is especially adapted to the coöperation of the social sciences and the physical sciences, in such studies as ecology, agriculture, soils, diet, climate, farm chemurgy, land-use planning.

The laboratory is especially available for the coöperation of the several colleges and universities whenever desirable. Within the Subregion are the three units of the University of North Carolina; in neighboring Durham, Duke University; other colleges include Elon, Greensboro, Guilford, High Point, Meredith, Wake Forest, Bennett, Negro Agricultural and Technical College, North Carolina College for Negroes, Shaw University, St. Augustine's College. The Subregion also includes the State capital with its many resources and departmental agencies.

The three counties in Virginia provide opportunity not only for comparative studies of contiguous counties in different States but also afford a laboratory for coöperative effort between institutions and research agencies in North Carolina and Virginia, such as the University of Virginia with its Institute for Research in the Social Sciences and the Virginia Polytechnic Institute, whenever such coöperation may be desirable, or practicable.

In 1939, when Alumni Building was completely renovated and remodeled according to specifications which planned and equipped the building for use by the Division of Public Welfare and Social Work, the Department of Sociology, the editorial offices of SOCIAL FORCES, and the Institute for Research in Social Science, plans provided for a Laboratory Workshop on the Fourth Floor, which should feature and implement the Subregional Laboratory for Social Research and Planning. Accordingly such a Laboratory Workshop was developed around a large room for exhibits, study, and assemblies, with smaller workshops including rooms for map making, drafting, conferences, and statistical laboratory.

THE LABORATORY WORKSHOP

The Laboratory Workshop proper is a room about 75' by 45' covering approximately 3375 square feet of floor space. In order to give as much wall space as possible for exhibits and to facilitate the use of visual aids, the lighting is from overhead and the ventilation is indirect. The walls are covered with Burlap Wall surfacing mounted on Masonite which makes them suitable for convenient and rapid mounting of maps, charts, pictures, etc. Portions of the north and south walls are lined with built-in bookshelves, 42" in height, with slanting top about 20" wide with a one inch rail at the lower edge. The shelves are spaced to accommodate large books such as atlases and folders containing maps, as well as for ordinary books, journals, pamphlets, etc. In addition there are some half dozen large tables which are available for study as well as for special exhibits. For assemblies, there are provided about one hundred comfortable, attractive chairs.

Wall materials may be said to be of three kinds: (1) illustrative material for special sessions and discussions; (2) materials and methods for more leisurely study; (3) testing materials for teaching

and publication. For example, the exhibit prepared for A University Conference on Population Research, Regional Research, The Measurement of Regional Development, held in the Spring of 1940, included both permanent and temporary maps and charts and featured world regions along with the southern regions. The plan adopted then has since been generally followed with new and up-to-date materials continually supplanting the old and with changing emphases for special institutes and conferences. Following this arrangement, the west wall is devoted to maps of world regions, featuring certain geographic and specialized regions within the limits of space and function. This is in the form of an exhibit for permanent study by those interested in areal distributions and regional problems from whatever viewpoint.

The north wall is devoted to the southern regions, utilizing the same general classification of resources as *Southern Regions of the United States*, namely, natural wealth, technological wealth, capital wealth, human wealth, and institutional wealth. Panel one is devoted to natural resources, their measurement, conservation, development, and use. Panel two features technological resources, including education, training, skill, science, organization as they relate to the development of natural resources. Panel three is devoted to capital wealth and income. Panel four carries exhibits in population and human wealth. Panel five is devoted to special institutional efforts. Panel six presents certain trends and developments in all of these from 1930 to 1944 and lays the basis for the projection of trends.

The south wall is divided into two major parts. The first is devoted to regional and subregional classifications of the United States, and gives samplings and illustrations from the many regional divisions now in use or proposed, featuring especially the significance and technique of subregional analysis of particular areas. The second panel is given over entirely to the North Carolina Subregional Laboratory for Social Research and Planning, the major portion of which presents photographic portraiture as exploration in the field of research through photography.

The east wall is devoted primarily to regional planning, to raising certain questions, and pointing to next steps and new programs of research and planning.

While all exhibits have been installed by the Institute for Research in Social Science, a number of agencies, institutions, and individuals have at all times coöperated, including especially the regional activities of the Federal Government. An extension of this service has been suggested in the request of a number of institutions for reproduction of the maps and charts in quantity for teaching purposes.

The shelves carry printed and mimeographed materials supplementing the wall exhibits. These include the resources and deficiencies of the southern regions as outlined in Howard W. Odum's *Southern Regions of the United States*, and as enumerated above, namely, natural wealth, human wealth, capital wealth, technological wealth, institutional wealth. There is another important section featuring TVA materials, while the shelf running along the south wall is given over entirely to social planning—national regional, state. On the tables are collections on community planning, veteran rehabilitation, the Negro, international relations, social studies texts, with special featuring of such series as the University of North Carolina Social Studies Series, the publications of the Institute for Research in Social Science, contributions from regions other than the Southeast. Of interest and value, too, are the pamphlet series such as Public Affairs Pamphlets, National Planning Association series, Headline Books, etc.

The Laboratory Workshop is also equipped for showing moving pictures and slides. A 16 mm. motion picture projector and a portable screen, preferably one with a beaded surface, should be considered essential permanent equipment, together with a tri-purpose strip film projector for showing "stills" and a lantern projector which will take book pages either directly from the book or mounted on light cardboard. Minimum requirements, in addition to the overhead lighting and indirect ventilation, are proper electric wiring and facilities for darkening the room. Storage space for films and facilities for inspecting, repairing, and shipping audio-visual aids should be provided within easy access.

The half dozen or more tables—each 8 feet by 3 feet—are placed at convenient intervals in the rear of the room. Six persons can work at each of these tables without crowding. The student works here much as in a reserve reading room of a University library. It is highly advantageous to have the wall maps, charts, and other exhibits that may be under current discussion in the lectures and general discussions conveniently accessible when the pertinent reading is being done. Greatest effectiveness is attained if this room is used for study under the supervision of a person competently acquainted with the subject matter of the study program as it is being developed as well as completely familiar with all materials and exhibits, in order to be able to give the student adequate information and assistance.

THE SMALLER WORKSHOP UNITS

Map Room. This room, designed for the making of maps and practice in the study of mapping, is of moderate size, accommodating about 10 persons at one time. Satisfactory lighting arrangements are essential. Built-in cabinets furnish storage space for equipment and supplies. One or more four drawer vertical steel files, either letter or legal size, are indispensable for filing maps, photographs, etc., properly catalogued according to subject, subregion, county, etc. This not only preserves materials but makes them easily accessible. A master card file gives additional value since other groupings and classifications can be designated in this way.

A particularly valuable feature is a cabinet for classifying and storing maps too large for the regular files. This should be at least 6½ ft. long, 4 ft. wide, and about 40 inches high. Placed at one end of the room, but with free space on all four sides and with a well-finished top surface, such a cabinet provides not only storage space but an excellent work table. Since maps and exhibits in this cabinet will be of varied sizes and on different weights of paper and kinds of material, a horizontal shelf arrangement is probably more practical, even though there is less conservation of space and materials are not quite as accessible as they would be if filed vertically.

The student should have an opportunity here to familiarize himself with basic standard equipment and supplies needed in the reproduction and mounting of maps and graphic materials for publication or exhibit. Minimum equipment for this room, therefore, should include: a large globe; several well-constructed drawing tables, which should be "light tables," i.e., tables fitted with an insert of frosted glass in the top and with a light bulb beneath so arranged as to focus light through the glass from beneath the table, for use in making tracings of maps; one or more Pantographs (Dietzgen) for enlarging maps; one or more lettering sets, such as Leroy Lettering Set (manufactured by Keufel and Esser Co., New York) or Wrico Lettering Guides and Pens (Wood-Reagan Instrument Co.); simple drawing instruments; cutting boards.

Basic supplies should include various types and grades of drawing paper; graph paper; outline maps, such as regional maps of the United States, developed by the Institute from Goode's Series of Base Maps, by permission of the University of Chicago Press; India ink, thumb tacks, pencils, art gum, ink erasers, etc.; Scotch tape; crayons or water colors; mounting boards (photo mount boards); kodak dry mounting tissue; liquid rubber cement; waxed pine strips to be used in mounting exhibits; stapler and staples.

Special mention should be made here of the use of Zip-A-Tone, a product of Paratone, Inc., which, because of its usefulness for graphic design, shading and coloring maps, etc., should be among the basic supplies in any map or drafting room. It is a labor saving device, which takes the place of much of the arduous work of the draftsman. Moreover, the uninitiated student can learn to use Zip-A-Tone easily and quickly, whereas drafting is a highly skilled technique, perfected only after much study and practice. Zip-A-Tone consists of transparent screens, each 8 x 12 inches, with a highly glazed surface and a waxed base, printed in black and red (which also photographs black) in more than two hundred line and dot patterns. The screens are cut to the proper size and shape with a cutting needle and smoothed flat with a bone burnisher. Zip-A-Tone leaves no wax on the drawing and, therefore, can be removed readily in case of inaccuracy or needed change. Leading engravers use and recommend it. A uniformity, such as can be produced only by the most skilful draftsman, is assured. From the many patterns offered, various series can be worked out. The Paratone Company will also manufacture special screens, when these are needed and ordered in sufficient quantity, especially when the design is one that will add value to their ever-growing array of patterns.

Although especially good for reproducing materials for printing, mimeographing, etc., Zip-A-Tone does not have permanent exhibit value. It can be used for short-time exhibits but where materials are to be left on the walls for some time, the Zip-A-Tone loosens from the paper, curls, and finally drops off. For exhibits of a more or less permanent nature, the skill of the draftsman is still a requisite.

Drafting Room. This might well be considered an adjunct to the Map Room. If space is limited, the making and altering of statistical charts, graphic designs, and maps, mounting materials for wall display, etc., could be done in one section of the map room. However, it is advantageous to have a small separate room for this purpose, even though there may be some duplication of equipment and supplies, so that the person or persons especially employed for this rather exacting work, can proceed without undue interruptions from students, even when the draftsman serves also as a part-time instructor in cartography or graphic presentation.

General Workshops. Of added value are small conference rooms or workshops in which from five to fifteen persons can work together at desks or around tables. Here again adequate lighting and ventilation are a requisite. Rooms should be comfortably but not elaborately furnished. One of these rooms might well be large enough to accommodate desks for two or three research assistants working on special assignments over a period of weeks or months, or visiting fellows or scholars who might need such accommodations for shorter periods.

Statistical Laboratory. A statistical laboratory with minimum equipment of one or more automatic calculators, adding machines, typewriters, together with drafting and mounting equipment and supplies, as listed above or convenient access to rooms in which these are available, is an essential unit in any Laboratory Workshop. With equipment of this kind it is particularly important to standardize on certain makes, such as Monroe calculators, Burroughs or Monroe Adding machines, Royal typewriters, especially in the interest of adequate servicing.

There should be sufficient electric floor outlets, placed at convenient intervals, to accommodate all the machines. Instead of having each machine on a separate desk or table, it has been found practicable to have specially built long tables at which several students can be working at the same time. If the room is large enough, these can be from 12 to 15 feet in length, about 28 inches wide, and in height from 26 to 29½ inches. It is well to have two tables of different heights to accommodate persons of different stature and preference. In addition, there should be one large table of standard size and height, a portable drawing stand, and one or two small typewriter tables. Straight backed, armless, but comfortable chairs should be furnished. In addition to cabinets for storage space and open shelves for source materials, lockers, which can be assigned individually, should be provided for work in progress, especially in cases where the statistical laboratory is being used by students who do not have other special desk or office space.

There should be available on the shelves all United States census publications, including, besides a complete set of the latest decennial census, a set of Statistical Abstracts, preliminary census releases, Census of Manufacturing, etc. Other government reports such as those of the Social Security Board, Office of Education, Bureau of Agricultural Economics, Monthly Labor Review, together with State reports—as many as possible should be accessible for immediate use. Several good texts on statistics, a file of the *Journal of the American Statistical Association*, logarithmic tables, slide rule, and other statistical aids are all part of the essential equipment of a statistical laboratory.

Objectives of the Laboratory Workshop. The objectives of such a Laboratory Workshop as described above are threefold: (1) the stimulation of interest by means of the project method involving purposeful and pertinent group and manual activity; (2) the injection into the study program of an element of realism, by means of placing the student in contact with particular data and confronting him with specific problems to be worked out on the basis of these data; (3) the attainment of the student of some technical proficiency in statistical methods and in the graphic presentation of statistical facts on charts and maps.

To this end the facilities of the Laboratory Workshop of the Institute have already been made available not only to students, both graduate and undergraduate, and classes in the University, but to numerous conferences including A University Conference on Population Research, Regional Research, the Measurement of Regional Development, 1940; Conferences on Marriage and Family Relations; Tomorrow's Children; North Carolina Chapter of the American Association of Social Workers; Public Welfare Institutes; Interracial Student Conferences sponsored jointly by Duke University, the North Carolina College for Negroes, the University of North Carolina, and the Division of Coöperation in Education and Race Relations; an ASTP unit from August 1943 to March 1944;[1] two special

summer workshop groups: A Laboratory Study of Southeastern Regional Problems, Potentialities, and Planning in 1942, and a Social Studies Institute in 1944; Institute for Law Enforcement Officers. In addition, it is in constant use for special lectures and seminars.

The Laboratory Workshop of the Institute for Research in Social Science at the University of North Carolina includes, in addition to the rooms already mentioned, a lounge or small conference room, and a kitchenette. This is not an absolute requisite but is a valuable adjunct in giving a touch of informality, as well as cordiality, to special groups and meetings. Small gatherings, particularly committee meetings, can be held directly in the lounge, while larger meetings can take place in the Laboratory Workshop proper, with an informal get-together and the continuation of discussion in the lounge afterward.

Direction of the Laboratory Workshop. It should be emphasized that although not absolutely essential to the Laboratory, the full and successful operation of a complete Laboratory Workshop unit depends to a considerable degree upon having it under the full-time direction of a competent person. This director should have no or only light formal teaching duties in the program, but should keep constantly in touch with the course of all instruction that involves workshop activity. To that end a thoroughly competent person is needed, one who fully understands the comprehensive purposes of the program. While it is not likely that any one person would have a professional knowledge of all the fields involved, it is desirable that the director of the workshop activities should be something more than a technician or a study-hall assistant. While an important and substantial part of his job should be to supervise the periods of workshop activity, his paramount function should be that of co-ordinating and integrating these activities with each other and with the other phases of the instructional and research program. Some of the hours of actual physical supervision of workshop activities naturally have to be delegated to others who participate in the program.

---

[1] As an illustration of how the Laboratory Workshop may be adapted to the needs of a particular group, in this instance ASTP, see, C. B. Robson, Notes on Equipping an Adequate Workshop for Area Study in Schools for Officer Candidates in Military Government. Submitted by the University of North Carolina, March 1943 (Mimeographed). Some of the material from this memorandum is reprinted here.

TWO DECADES OF SOCIAL FORCES

THE JOURNAL OF SOCIAL FORCES, founded in 1922, and becoming SOCIAL FORCES in 1925, might very well be said to have been the product of the Departments of Sociology at the University of North Carolina and Columbia University. For it was founded in November 1922 by Howard W. Odum, head of the Department of Sociology and director of the School of Public Welfare at the University of North Carolina, strongly seconded by Franklin Henry Giddings, professor of sociology at Columbia University and dean of living American sociologists at that time. For it was Professor Giddings' enthusiasm for the JOURNAL to be set up as a national medium of sociology and his preparation of a series of leading articles on the scientific study of human society that were the deciding factors in the establishment of the new sociological journal. For two years Professor Giddings contributed leading articles which were subsequently published by the University of North Carolina Press under the title, *The Scientific Study of Human Society*, and which in some ways was Professor Giddings' favorite book. Professor Giddings also made provision to donate his personal library to the University of North Carolina where his books have been catalogued as the Franklin H. Giddings' Collection of Sociological Literature.

Although SOCIAL FORCES has published more than twice as many articles by authors outside the southern regions as in the South, it early adopted the policy of featuring regional research and planning as one medium of its social study and interpretation. Since that time its major emphasis has been, in addition to its broad field of sociological research and theory, primarily that which featured the regional quality and balance of America. This emphasis, in turn, stemmed from the need and contributions of southern regional research and sociology. Something of the range and nature of this work is described in other divisions of the present special issue of SOCIAL FORCES.

As indicative of the regional-national character of SOCIAL FORCES may be cited its official relation to the national and Southern Sociological Societies and the number and range of its contributions. For the years just preceding the establishment of the *American Sociological Review* as the official organ of the American Sociological Society, SOCIAL FORCES was one of the official journals of the Society. It has been also the official journal of the

Southern Sociological Society since the Society's organization in 1936.

SOCIAL FORCES has published in its first twenty-two volumes, through Volume 22, 1943–1944, more than 1750 articles and 4450 book reviews and notes, representing some 1300 authors from all the States and regions of the United States, as well as a few from Canada, the South American republics, and foreign authors from Europe and the Orient.

Analysis of the articles and authors shows a wide distribution, including the leading American sociologists, many scholars from the other social sciences, many distinguished publicists and educators. Among the presidents of the American Sociological Society were Franklin H. Giddings and R. M. MacIver of Columbia University; W. F. Ogburn, Ellsworth Faris, Ernest W. Burgess, and Robert E. Park of the University of Chicago; Howard W. Odum and Rupert B. Vance of the University of North Carolina; Edward Alsworth Ross and John Lewis Gillin of the University of Wisconsin. Others, one each from other universities, were L. L. Bernard, Washington University; Emory S. Bogardus, University of Southern California; F. Stuart Chapin, University of Minnesota; Charles A. Ellwood, Duke University; Henry Pratt Fairchild, New York University; John M. Gillette, University of North Dakota; Edward Carey Hayes, University of Illinois; George A. Lundberg, Bennington College; E. H. Sutherland, University of Indiana; Dwight Sanderson, Cornell University; Kimball Young, Queens College.

Among the authors from the other social sciences were Charles A. Beard, Wesley C. Mitchell, John Dewey, Charles H. Judd, Frank Lorimer, Walton Hale Hamilton, Clark Wissler, Robert Redfield, Leonard White, William E. Dodd, Roscoe Pound, Avery Craven, Thomas Nixon Carver, Shelby Harrison, Grace Abbott, Sophonisba Breckinridge, Floyd Allport, E. A. Hooten, Ellsworth Huntington, W. Carson Ryan, Frank H. Knight William H. Kilpatrick.

Among the distinguished editors, publicists, and educators at large were Woodrow Wilson, Edwin A. Alderman, Charles A. Beard, Walter Lippmann, Edwin R. Embree, Jackson Davis, Gerald W. Johnson, Henry Noble MacCracken, Harry Woodburn Chase, A. E. Morgan, Rexford Tugwell, William Allen White.

In addition to the Department of Sociology, the School of Public Welfare, and the University of

North Carolina Press, which gave momentum to SOCIAL FORCES in its earlier years, the Institute for Research in Social Science, founded soon after SOCIAL FORCES began publication, has contributed largely to the regional contributions. The total contributions of the Institute and the nature of its work are described elsewhere. Although SOCIAL FORCES has published several hundred contributions for the Institute, it has followed its own divisions in the classification of its contributions. In addition to the Library and Workshop, it has featured the following divisions with the number of contributions listed under each. A classification of approximately 1755 articles which have appeared in Volumes 1 through 22, according to the present departmental set-up, shows the following distribution: Contributed Articles, 563; Teaching and Research in the Social Sciences, 258; Public Welfare and Social Work (exclusive of announcements of conferences of social work), 217; Community and Neighborhood, 208; Marriage and the Family (begun in 1930), 103; Race, Cultural Groups, Social Differentiation, 169; Government, Politics, Citizenship, 153; Social Industrial Relationships, 84. Library and Workshop has carried reviews of some 3281 books, briefer comments on another 1178, making an approximate total of 4459 books. In addition, almost 800 "Guides to Periodical Literature" have appeared in the pages of SOCIAL FORCES.

To illustrate the range and distinction of contributions, samplings with their authors might well include:

General Articles. "The Measurement of Social Forces" by Franklin H. Giddings; "Robert E. Lee: An Interpretation" by Woodrow Wilson; "Law and Morals" by Roscoe Pound; "Culture and Sociology" by William F. Ogburn; "Henry Hughes, First American Sociologist" by L. L. Bernard; "Social Security and American Traditions" by Jesse F. Steiner; "Sociology and Human Welfare" by Ellsworth Faris; "Scientific Method in Sociology" by Charles A. Ellwood; "Are Human Movements Independent of Wars?" by William Allen White; "Crisis and Reform of the Western World" by Herbert von Beckerath; "A New Definition of Social Institutions" by F. Stuart Chapin; "Roads to Social Peace" by Edward Alsworth Ross; "Charles Horton Cooley" by Walton Hale Hamilton; "The South and the New Society" by Walter Lippmann; "Mobility, Ecological and Social" by Radhakamal Mukerjee; "Sociologists in the Present Crisis" by Stuart

A. Queen; "Education and the Good South" by Edwin R. Embree; "Some Sociological Aspects of the Fascist Movements" by Talcott Parsons; "Security and Adjustment—The Return to the Larger Community" by Rupert B. Vance.

Teaching and Research in the Social Sciences. "Methods of Teaching: Impressions and a Verdict" by Robert E. Park; "Exploration and Survey" by Franklin H. Giddings; "Sampling Theory in Sociological Research" by Thomas C. McCormick; "The Need and Opportunity for Experiment in Social Psychology" by J. F. Dashiell; "Of What Use Is Dimensional Sociology?" by Stuart Carter Dodd; "Research in Progress and Available Data for Research in State Departments of Public Welfare in the Southeastern Region, 1936–1938" by Wiley B. Sanders; "Exploring for the Causes of Crime" by Emory S. Bogardus; "Experimental Sociology in the United States" by H. C. Brearley; "A Reclassification of Urban-Rural Population" by T. J. Woofter, Jr. and Edith Webb; "The Social Responsibilities of the State University" by Harry Woodburn Chase.

Public Welfare and Social Work. "Recent Advances in the Administration of Poor Relief" by Robert W. Kelso; "Family Case Work Faces the Future" by Paul L. Benjamin; "The In-Service Training of Public Welfare Workers" by Wilma Van Dusseldorp; "The Interdependence of Sociology and Social Work" by Ernest W. Burgess; "Education for Public Welfare and Social Work: from the Point of View of the State University" by Roy M. Brown; "The Migrant Family and Social Agencies in Washington" by Marion Hathway; "Economic Factors in the Making of a Criminal" by John L. Gillin; "Case Work Aspects of Administration" by Arthur E. Fink.

The Community and Neighborhood. "Some Aspects of Village Demography" by T. Lynn Smith; "Community Organization for War and Peace" by Dwight Sanderson; "Theories of Community Organization" by Jesse F. Steiner; "Is Community Organization Social Work?" by Walter Pettit; "The Changing Culture of the City" by Walter J. Matherly; "The College in Relation to Community Analysis and Development" by Gordon W. Blackwell; "A Preview of Community Recreation" by Harold D. Meyer; "Spatial Distance and Community Organization Pattern" by R. D. McKenzie.

Marriage and the Family. "Education for Family Life and National Defense" by Ernest R. Groves; "The Child: Welfare Objective and

Scientific Concept" by James H. S. Bossard; "Some Domestic Relations Laws that Counsellors in Marital Difficulties Need to Know" by John S. Bradway; "The Adjustment Behavior of Bereaved Families: A New Field for Research" by Thomas D. Eliot; "The Program of Marriage Instruction at the University of North Carolina" by Donald S. Klaiss; "The Variance Between Legal and Natural Causes for Divorce" by Ernest W. Mowrer; "The Bearing of Nervous and Mental Disorders on the Conservation of Marriage and the Family" by Raymond S. Crispell, M.D.

Race, Cultural Groups, Social Differentiation. "Race and Culture in the Modern World" by Alexander Goldenweiser; "Race in Politics" by T. J. Woofter, Jr.; "The Place and Importance of Population Studies in Relation to the Negro Population of the South" by Charles S. Johnson; "The New Mobility and the Coastal Island" by Lee M. Brooks; "Problems of Adjustment of Race and Class in the South" by Monroe N. Work; "Some Methods of Studying Race and Culture" by Floyd N. House; "Does the South Owe the Negro a New Deal?" by Guy B. Johnson.

Government, Politics, Citizenship. "The Typical Life Cycle of Dictatorships" by J. O. Hertzler; "Bureaucratic Structure and Personality" by Robert K. Merton; "Social Science and Social Action in Agriculture" by Carl C. Taylor; "The Melting Pot in the United States" by Harry Best; "The Psychology of the Bi-Party System" by Walter James Shepard; "The Changing Backgrounds of Southern Politics" by Clarence H. Nixon; "The Rural Tax Problem" by Clarence Heer; "The Democratic Processes and the Formulation of Agricultural Policy" by M. L. Wilson.

Social Industrial Relationships. "The Seasonal Worker and Unemployment Compensation Benefits" by R. Clyde White; "The Social Problem of Labor Organization Casualties" by Harriet L. Herring; "The Supposed Necessity for an Industrial Reserve Army" by Thomas Nixon Carver; "Decentralization of Industry in the New Deal" by M. L. Wilson; "American and Foreign Labor Legislation: A Comparison" by Alice Hamilton; "Industry's Responsibility for Unemployment" by G. T. Schwenning.

Library and Workshop. Feature reviews of: Pitirim Sorokin's *Social and Cultural Dynamics* (4 vols.), by A. E. Tibbs; Quincy Wright's *A Study of War* (2 vols.), by Howard W. Odum; Sir William Beveridge's *Social Insurance and Allied Services*, by Eric Fischer; Pareto's *Mind and So-*

ciety (4 vols.), by Harry Estill and Bernice Milburn Moore; Dodd's *Dimensions of Society* and Lundberg's *Foundations of Sociology*, by Donald W. Calhoun; Kulischer's *The Displacement of Population in Europe*, by Louis O. Kattsoff and Werner J. Cahnman.

In Volumes 20, 21, 22, and 23 special emphasis has been placed upon regionalism including the trends toward regional analysis and planning for international organization. Indicative of the nature and range of these articles were the issues in which regionalism constituted the special feature of contributed articles. These included "A Sociological Approach to the Study and Practice of American Regionalism," by Howard W. Odum; "Regionalism and Plans for Postwar Reconstruction: The First Three Years," by James T. Watkins; "World Reconstruction and European Regionalism," by Nicholas Doman; "Regionalism in China's Postwar Reconstruction" by Cheng Ch'eng-K'un; "Regionalism as Illustrated by the Western Hemisphere: Solidarity of the Americas," by Charles E. Martin; "Regionalism, Science, and the Peace Settlement," by George A. Lundberg; "Theoretical Aspects of Regionalism," by Svend Riemer; "Regionalism: Some Critical Observations," by Rudolf Heberle; "Some Sociological Aspects of American Regionalism" by J. O. Hertzler; "Statistical Methods for Delineation of Regions Applied to Data on Agriculture and Population," by Margaret Jarman Hagood. This present anniversary issue continues that feature.

Among the associate editors who contributed especially to the earlier issues and to the success of the Journal was Jesse F. Steiner, then professor of Social Technology at the University of North Carolina and now professor and head of the Department of Sociology at the University of Washington. He has continued as associate editor and friend throughout the whole period. Other associate editors have been: E. R. Groves, since 1928; L. L. Bernard, since 1929; Rupert B. Vance, since 1931; E. C. Branson, D. D. Carroll, H. D. Meyer, L. R. Wilson, 1922–23; Gerald W. Johnson, 1923–28; Katharine Jocher, 1928–31.

The number and nature of articles published by SOCIAL FORCES dealing with southern problems is presented in the special bibliography of southern regional titles in a separate part of this issue. The number and identification of authors is shown in the alphabetical list which follows.

CONTRIBUTORS TO SOCIAL FORCES

Volume *1* to Volume *22*

1922 to 1944

A

Abbott, Grace
Abel, Theodore
Achiss, Thelma D.
Ackerson, Luton
Adams, Florence S.
Adams, Matthew P.
Albig, William
Alderman, Edwin A.
Alexander, Frank D.
Alexander, Franz
Alexander, Will W.
Alfred, Helen
Allard, Winston
Allen, Chester
Allen, Francis R.
Allison, Thomas W.
Allport, Floyd H.
Alpert, Harry
Anderson, Floyd J.
Anderson, H. Dewey
Anderson, Nels
Anderson, V. V.
Anderson, W. A.
Andrews, Columbus
Angell, Robert C.
Anthony, Donald
Armstrong, James W.
Arndt, Karl J.
Asay, Ivan
Ashton, Elma H.
Atkins, Willard E.
Atkinson, Mary Irene
Atkinson, R. K.
Atwood, Wallace W.
Axel, Robert

B

Babcock, James O.
Baber, Ray Erwin
Bagby, English
Bailey, W. F.
Bain, Joe
Bain, Read
Baker, Edith M.
Baker, Sibyl
Ballinger, W. J.
Bane, Frank
Barash, Meyer
Barker, Robert H.
Barker, Ruth E.
Barkley, Key L.

Barnes, Harry Elmer
Barnett, H. G.
Barnhart, E. Kenneth
Barnhart, Nat G.
Bassett, John Spencer
Bates, Alan
Bates, Sanford
Bauder, Russell
Beach, Walter G.
Beard, Charles A.
Beard, Mary R.
Becker, Donald
Becker, Howard
Beckwith, Burnham P.
Beecher, John
Beecroft, Eric
Beer, Ethel S.
Beers, Howard W.
Beery, A. Frances
Bell, Earl H.
Bellamy, Raymond
Benedict, Ruth
Benjamin, Paul L.
Bennett, John W.
Berman, Nathan
Bernard, Frances Fenton
Bernard, Jessie
Bernard, L. L.
Bernheimer, Charles S.
Berry, Brewton
Best, Harry
Beuick, Marshall
Bidgood, Lee
Biesanz, John
Biesanz, Mavis
Bingham, Walter V.
Binkley, Robert C.
Bittner, W. S.
Bixler, J. S.
Blackburn, Burr
Blackwell, Gordon W.
Blaha, Arnost
Blanchard, Albert C.
Blanchard, Phyllis
Bloodworth, Jessie A.
Bloom, Leonard
Boardman, George R.
Boettiger, L. A.
Bogardus, Emory S.
Bonapart, Joseph
Bond, N. B.
Bonney, Merl E.
Bookman, C. M.

Boots, Ralph S.
Borders, Karl
Bornemann, Alfred
Bossard, James H. S.
Bowden, A. O.
Bowden, Witt
Bowen, Ezra
Bowen, Howard
Bowman, Claude C.
Bowman, LeRoy E.
Bowne, Henrietta
Brackett, Jeffrey R.
Bradley, Clifton J.
Bradley, Evelyn
Bradley, Frances Sage
Bradley, Phillips
Bradshaw, F. F.
Bradway, John S.
Bragstad, A. S.
Brandeis, Alice G.
Branson, E. C.
Brearley, H. C.
Breckinridge, S. P.
Brevis, Harry Jacob
Brinton, Hugh P.
Bristol, L. M.
Britt, Steuart Henderson
Broda, R.
Brody, Alexander
Bronner, Charlotte
Brooke, Myrtle
Brooks, E. C.
Brooks, Evelyn C.
Brooks, Lee M.
Brown, George K.
Brown, Ina Corinne
Brown, J. F.
Brown, John A.
Brown, Marian Kaufman
Brown, Roy M.
Brown, W. O.
Brunner, Edmund De S.
Bruno, Frank J.
Bryson, Gladys
Buchanan, D. H.
Buck, A. E.
Buckman, Rilma
Buell, Bradley
Buell, J. B.
Burchard, Edward L.
Burgess, Ernest W.
Burgess, J. Stewart
Burgess, Robert W.

Burleson, F. E.
Bush, Mrs. L. B.
Bushnell, C. J.
Bushong, Eugene M.
Butler, Amos W.
Butterfield, Kenyon L.
Byers, Joseph P.

C

Cahnman, Werner J.
Caldwell, Morris G.
Caldwell, Sheila M.
Caldwell, Wallace E.
Calhoun, Arthur W.
Calhoun, Donald W.
Calverton, V. F.
Cameron, Anna M.
Cameron, Merton K.
Cantril, Hadley
Cape, Thomas Wilson
Capers, Ellison
Carlton, Frank T.
Carman, Harry J.
Carner, Lucy P.
Carpenter, Niles
Carr, Lowell Julliard
Carroll, Mollie Ray
Carroll, Monroe S.
Carstens, C. C.
Carter, Hugh
Carter, Isabelle K.
Carver, Thomas Nixon
Cason, Clarence E.
Cassatt, Anna A.
Cassidy, Harry M.
Cavan, Ruth Shonle
Cavers, David F.
Chaddock, Robert E.
Chaffee, Grace E.
Chandrasekhar, S.
Chapin, F. Stuart
Chapman, L. F.
Chase, Harry Woodburn
Chase, Lucetta C.
Chenault, Lawrence R.
Cheng, Ch'eng-K'un
Cheyney, Alice S.
Chivers, Walter R.
Church, George F.
Clapp, Raymond F.
Clark, Carroll D.
Clark, William A.
Clarke, Edwin L.
Clarke, Helen I.
Cline, Denzel C.
Clow, F. R.
Cobb, John Candler
Coe, George Allen

Coggin, George W.
Colcord, Joanna C.
Cole, William E.
Coleman, Laurence Vail
Coleman, Lee
Comer, Harry F.
Conant, Richard K.
Conard, Laetitia M.
Cone, Grace
Connor, R. D. W.
Cook, Lloyd A.
Cooley, Edwin J.
Cooper, John Irwin
Cooper, Peter
Cope, Persis M.
Copeland, Lewis C.
Copeland, William A.
Cornell, William A.
Corson, John Jay, 3rd
Cottam, Howard R.
Cottrell, Louise
Coulter, Charles W.
Coulter, Isabella Kellock
Coutu, Walter
Cowdrick, Edward S.
Cowper, Mary O.
Cox, Cordelia
Cox, Oliver C.
Coyle, Grace L.
Crafts, L. W.
Craig, Elizabeth
Craighead, T. J., Jr.
Crane, Harry W.
Craven, Avery
Crawford, W. Rex
Cressey, Paul Frederick
Cressman, Charles P.
Cressman, Luther S.
Crispell, Raymond S.
Criswell, W. S.
Crook, Margaret B.
Crook, W. H.
Cross, William T.
Crosser, Paul K.
Cuber, John F.
Cummins, E. C.
Curtis, H. S.
Cutler, J. E.

D

Daggett, Harriet S.
Dahlberg, Arthur O.
Dankert, C. E.
Dashiell, J. F.
Davidson, Donald
Davidson, Percy E.
Davis, Alice
Davis, Arthur K.

Davis, Horace B.
Davis, I. G.
Davis, Jackson
Davis, Jerome
Davis, Kingsley
Davis, Ralph N.
Dawson, Carl A.
Dawson, Edgar
Dawson, John B.
Dawson, Joseph Martin
Day, George M.
Daykin, Walter L.
Dealey, James Quayle
Deardorff, Neva R.
Deering, Tam
De Forest, Charles M.
DeGraff, Harmon O.
Delson, Harry
Demaree, Ralph G.
Demerath, N. J.
Demmon, E. L.
Dent, Carl E.
Detweiler, Frederick G.
Devine, Edward T.
Dewey, John
Dewsbury, Ethel M.
Dexter, Elisabeth A.
Dexter, Robert C.
Dickins, Dorothy
Dietrich, Ethel B.
Diggs, Mary Huff
Dinsmore, Charles Allen
Dodd, Stuart Carter
Dodd, William E.
Dodson, Linden S.
Dollard, John
Doman, Nicholas
Dorn, Harold F.
Douglas, Dorothy Wolff
Douglas, Marjory Stoneman
Douglas, Paul H.
Douty, H. M.
Dow, G. S.
Downs, Robert B.
Draper, E. S.
Dreher, William C.
Droba, D. D.
Dublin, Louis I.
Du Bois, Florence
Du Bois, W. E. B.
Ducoff, Louis J.
Duerbeck, Edwin M.
Duncan, H. G.
Duncan, Otis Durant
Duncan, Winnie Leach
Dunford, Francis Marion
Dunham, H. Warren
Dunning, Dorothy

Dunning, John C.
Dunseath, S. Glover
Dutcher, Elizabeth

E

Earle, Mrs. Genevieve B.
Eaton, Mary Alice
Eaves, Lucile
Ebaugh, Cameron Duncan
Ebaugh, Laura Smith
Eberling, Ernest J.
Edens, Boyce M.
Edmunds, Allen T.
Edwards, Allen D.
Edwards, Vinson A.
Eggan, Fred
Eggen, J. B.
Egger, Rowland
Eiseley, Loren C.
Eldridge, Anita
Eldridge, Hope Tisdale
Eldridge, Seba
Eldridge, T. B.
Eleazer, R. B.
Eliot, Thomas D.
Ellingwood, Albert Russell
Ellwood, Charles A.
Elmer, Manuel C.
Embree, Edwin R.
Engel-Frisch, Gladys
Engelman, Uriah Z.
Engle, Earl T.
Ensminger, Douglas
Entman, Sidney
Epstein, W.
Estabrook, Arthur H.
Estabrooks, G. H.
Estey, J. A.
Eubank, Earle Edward
Eutsler, Roland B.
Evans, James Gilbert
Evans, Kenneth
Everett, Ray H.
Ewing, Russell H.

F

Fairchild, Henry Pratt
Faison, Georgia H.
Falk, Myron
Faris, Ellsworth
Faust, S. W.
Feder, Leah H.
Fenlason, Anne F.
Fesler, James W.
Fields, Harold
Fink, Arthur E.
Finney, Ross L.
Firey, Walter

Fischer, Eric
Fisher, Clyde Olin
Fisher, Isaac
Fisher, Mary S.
Flanders, Dwight P.
Fleming, James E.
Fleming, Robert
Fletcher, Mildred
Fletcher, Ralph
Flippin, Percy Scott
Folks, Homer
Folse, C. L.
Folsom, Joseph K.
Forbes, Allyn B.
Forbush, William Byron
Ford, James
Ford, Robert N.
Foreman, Paul B.
Forster, G. W.
Foster, Robert G.
Francis, Robert C.
Frank, Lawrence K.
Frankel, Emil
Frazer, Keener C.
Frazier, E. Franklin
Frissell, Sydney D.
Fryer, Douglas
Fuller, Richard C.

G

Galitzi, Christine
Galloway, George B.
Galpin, C. J.
Garey, L. F.
Garnett, W. E.
Garrett, Constance
Garrison, K. C.
Gaylord, Gladys
Gee, Wilson
Gehlke, C. E.
Geisert, Harold Loran
Gettys, Warner E.
Gibson, John M.
Giddings, Franklin H.
Gilbert, Jeanne G.
Gillette, John M.
Gillin, John
Gillin, John Lewis
Gillman, Joseph M.
Gilmore, Harlan W.
Gist, Noel P.
Gittler, J. B.
Givler, Robert C.
Glenn, Mary Wilcox
Glueck, Eleanor Touroff
Godfrey, James L.
Goldenweiser, Alexander
Goldthorpe, Harold

Gomillion, Charles G.
Goodenough, Florence L.
Goodsell, Willystine
Goodwin, Cardinal L.
Gosnell, Cullen B.
Gosnell, Harold F.
Gould, Kenneth M.
Grafton, Thomas H.
Graham, Gladys Murphy
Graper, Elmer D.
Grattan, C. Hartley
Graves, W. Brooke
Gray, Greta
Green, Fletcher M.
Greene, J. E.
Greene, Lee S.
Gregory, E. W., Jr.
Grier, N. M.
Grove, Elsa Butler
Groves, Ernest R.
Groves, Gladys Hoagland
Gruenberg, Frederick P.
Guessaz, Louis A., Jr.
Guild, June Purcell
Guthrie, Elton F.
Gwin, J. Blaine

H

Haas, Hans
Haenzel, William M.
Hagood, Margaret Jarman
Haines, George (IV)
Hale, Oron James
Hall, Arnold Bennett
Hamburger, Kaete
Hamilton, Alice
Hamilton, C. Horace
Hamilton, J. G. de Roulhac
Hamilton, Walton H.
Hamrick, W. P.
Hancock, Gordon B.
Hankins, Dorothy
Hankins, Frank H.
Hansen, Marcus L.
Harap, Henry
Harding, T. Swann
Hargan, James
Harlan, Howard H.
Harland, J. P.
Harms, Ernst
Harper, Ernest Bouldin
Harper, Roland M.
Harper, William A.
Harris, Abram L.
Harris, Frederick
Harris, Julia Collier
Harris, Thomas L.
Harrison, Shelby M.

Hart, Helen
Hart, Hornell
Hart, Joseph K.
Hartman, Edward T.
Hartsough, Mildred
Harvey, O. L.
Harvey, Ray F.
Hathway, Marion
Hauser, Philip M.
Hausheer, Herman
Hawkins, Gaynell
Hawley, Amos H.
Hayes, C. Walker
Hayes, Edward Cary
Hayes, Wayland J.
Hayner, Norman S.
Haynes, Fred E.
Hazen, H. H.
Head, Elizabeth
Healey, James C.
Heath, Milton S.
Heberle, Rudolf
Heer, Clarence
Heinberg, John Gilbert
Heiss, M. W.
Henderson, Donald E. V.
Henderson, Elmer W.
Herman, Thelma
Herrick, C. Judson
Herrick, Francis H.
Herring, E. Pendleton
Herring, Harriet L.
Herskovits, Melville J.
Hertz, Frederick
Hertzler, J. O.
Herzog, George
Hewes, Amy
Hexner, Ervin
Higby, Chester P.
Hightower, Raymond L.
Hill, Howard C.
Hill, Mozell C.
Hiller, E. T.
Hilmer, Hermann
Himes, Norman E.
Hirsch, Walter
Hirsh, Joseph
Hirst, Dallas
Hitt, Homer L.
Hixenbaugh, Elinor Ryan
Hobbs, S. H., Jr.
Hodges, Robert M.
Hoffer, Charles R.
Hoffer, Frank W.
Hoffsommer, Harold
Hogue, Richard Wallace
Hoijer, Harry
Holben, Ralph P.

Holden, Alice M.
Hollander, Edward
Hollis, Ernest V.
Holsey, Albin L.
Holt, John B.
Homan, Paul T.
Hood, Robin
Hooker, Elizabeth R.
Hooten, E. A.
Hoover, Calvin B.
Hoover, Glenn E.
Houdini
House, Floyd N.
House, Robert B.
Howard, T. Levron
Howerth, I. W.
Howes, Raymond F.
Howett, Harry H.
Hoyt, Elizabeth E.
Hoyt, Homer
Hubbard, E. H.
Hudnut, Ruth Allison
Hudson, R. F.
Hudson, W. M.
Hughes, Everett Cherrington
Hulett, J. E., Jr.
Humphrey, Norman D.
Hunt, Edward Eyre
Huntington, Ellsworth
Hypes, J. L.

I

Israel, Henry
Ivey, John E., Jr.

J

Jackson, George Pullen
Jackson, Leroy F.
Jackson, Thorstina
Jackson, W. C.
Jacobs, Theo
Jaffary, Stuart K.
James, Arthur W.
James, Harlean
James, Virginia
Jameson, Samuel Haig
Janow, Seymour
Jarrett, Mary C.
Jenks, Leland H.
Jensen, Ellen C.
Jensen, Howard E.
Jocher, Katharine
Johnson, Charles D.
Johnson, Charles S.
Johnson, Earl S.
Johnson, Fred R.
Johnson, Gerald W.
Johnson, Glenn R.

Johnson, Guion Griffis
Johnson, Guy B.
Johnson, J. Herman
Johnson, Kate Burr
Johnson, Rex M.
Johnston, Josephine
Jones, Caroline W.
Jones, Cheney C.
Jones, Lester M.
Jones, M. Ashby
Jones, Marshall E.
Jones, William B., Jr.
Jordan, A. M.
Jordan, Orvis F.
Josephs, William
Josey, Charles C.
Judd, Charles H.

K

Kahn, Dorothy C.
Karpf, Fay B.
Karpf, Maurice J.
Karpinos, Bernard D.
Kattsoff, Louis O.
Katz, Daniel
Keeler, Miriam
Keenleyside, Hugh L.
Keezer, Dexter M.
Keister, Albert S.
Keith, Alice B.
Keith, John A. H.
Keller, A. G.
Kelso, Robert W.
Kendall, Glenn
Kendrick, B. B., Jr.
Kendrick, Benjamin B.
Kennedy, Albert J.
Kennedy, Renwick C.
Kerner, Robert J.
Key, V. O., Jr.
Kibler, T. L.
Kilpatrick, William H.
Kimball, Reginald Stevens
Kimble, G. Eleanor
King, A. K.
King, Charles E.
King, Joe J.
Kinneman, John A.
Kirby, James P.
Kirk, John H.
Kirkpatrick, Clifford
Kirkpatrick, E. L.
Kiser, Clyde V.
Klaiss, Donald S.
Klein, Earl E.
Kluckhohn, Clyde
Knight, B. W.
Knight, Edgar W.

Knight, Frank H.
Knight, Howard R.
Knight, Melvin M.
Knowles, Morris
Knox, John B.
Koenig, Samuel
Kolb, J. H.
Kolb, William L.
Kolehmainen, John I.
Kollmorgen, Walter
Krout, Maurice H.
Krueger, E. T.
Kuhlman, A. F.
Kulp, Daniel H., II
Kutak, Robert I.

L

Ladu, Lena B.
LaFuze, G. Leighton
Laing, James T.
Lam, Margaret M.
Lambin, Maria Ward
Lamson, Herbert D.
Lancaster, Lane W.
Landecker, Werner S.
Landheer, Barth.
Landis, Benson Y.
Landis, Judson T.
Landis, Paul H.
Lane, Harold E.
Langer, William L.
LaPiere, Richard T.
Larson, Olaf F.
La Sater, Marion Newcomb
Lasker, Bruno
Lasswell, Harold D.
Lastrucci, Carlo L.
Lawes, Lewis E.
Lawrence, George H.
Leap, W. L.
Lebrun, Harvey
Lee, Alfred McClung
Leeper, Mary E.
Lehman, Harvey C.
Lenroot, Katharine F.
Leonard, R. F.
Leonard, S. E.
Levenbach, Marius G.
Lewis, Alfred G. Baker
Lewis, Burdette G.
Lewis, Edward E.
Lewis, Myron F.
Lewis, Nell Battle
Leybourne, Grace G.
Leyburn, James G.
Lind, Andrew W.
Lindeman, E. C.
Lindenberg, Sidney J.

Lindesmith, A. R.
Lindstrom, D. E.
Link, Eugene P.
Liphshitz, I. N.
Lippmann, Walter
Lively, C. E.
Loeber, Maude
Logan, George B.
Logan, Joseph C.
Loomis, Alice
Loomis, Charles P.
Lorimer, Frank
Loukas, Christ
Love, Cornelia
Lovejoy, Gordon W.
Lovejoy, Owen R.
Lowie, Robert H.
Lowrie, S. Gale
Lucasse, Walter W.
Lumley, Frederick E.
Lumpkin, Katharine DuPre
Lundberg, George A.
Lundborg, Herman
Lurie, Harry L.
Lynch, Ruth G.
Lyon, Leverett S.

M

MacCracken, Henry Noble
MacCurdy, George Grant
MacFadyen, Dugald
MacIver, Robert M.
Maclachlan, John
MacLeod, William Christie
MacRory, Boyd E.
Madison, Charles I.
Maller, Julius B.
Malzberg, Benjamin
Mandelbaum, David G.
Mangold, George B.
Mangus, A. R.
Manning, Seaton Wesley
Mark, Mary Louise
Marquette, Bleecker
Marsh, A. W.
Marshall, Robert
Martin, Charles E.
Martin, E. S.
Martin, James W.
Martin, Robert R.
Maslow, A. H.
Masters, Ervilla Alice
Masuoka, Jitsuichi
Matherly, Walter J.
Mathews, Shailer
Matthews, Harold J.
Mauldin, W. Parker
Maxey, Chester C.

May, Geoffrey
Mayer, Joseph
Mayo, Selz C.
McAlister, A. W.
McCain, John Walker, Jr.
McClenahan, Bessie Averne
McCloy, Shelby T.
McClusky, Howard Y.
McCobb, Helen Irene
McCombs, Carl E.
McCord, Fletcher
McCormick, Thomas C.
McCutchen, Duval T.
McDougle, Ivan E.
McGoldrick, Joseph
McGuinn, Henry J.
McHale, Kathryn
McKay, Henry D.
McKelvey, Blake
McKenzie, R. D.
McLauchlin, Muriel
McLean, Angus Wilton
McLennan, William E.
McVoy, Edgar C.
Meacham, William Shands
Meadows, Paul
Meier, Norman C.
Meigs, Emily B.
Mell, Mildred Rutherford
Melvin, Bruce L.
Menefee, Selden C.
Meroney, W. P.
Merriam, Charles E.
Merton, Robert K.
Messenger, Ruth
Meyer, Harold D.
Meyer, Max F.
Michels, Robert
Michelson, Truman
Miles, Arthur P.
Miles, Catharine Cox
Miles, R. W.
Miller, Herbert Adolphus
Mims, Edwin
Mitchell, Donald
Mitchell, George S.
Mitchell, Samuel Chiles
Mock, Clark
Montgomery, J. H.
Moody, E. F.
Moody, V. Alton
Moore, Bernice Milburn
Moore, Bruce V.
Moore, Elon H.
Moore, Harry Estill
Moore, Harry H.
Morgan, Arthur E.
Morgan, E. L.

Morgan, Ruth Dodd
Morgan, William H.
Moron, Alonzo G.
Morris, Albert
Morris, F. Grave
Morse, H. N.
Morse, Josiah
Mosca, Gaetano
Moseley, Jessie O.
Moss, Cora B.
Motvani, K. L.
Mowrer, Ernest R.
Mowrer, Harriet R.
Mudge, G. O.
Mudgett, Mildred D.
Mueller, John H.
Mukerjee, Radhakamal
Mukherjee, B. B.
Muntz, Earl E.
Murchison, John P.
Murdock, George P.
Murphy, Gardner
Murray, James J.
Myers, Earl D.
Myers, Howard B.
Myers, Robert C.
Myrick, Helen L.

N

Nathan, N. Ben
Neer, Imogene
Nelson, Arthur J.
Nelson, Lowry
Neptune, Donna Wicks
Nesbitt, Florence
Newbold, N. C.
Newcomb, Rexford
Newell, Bertha Payne
Newell, Jane I.
Newsom, Vida
Nichols, Jeannette Paddock
Nickle, Clarence E.
Niederfrank, E. J.
Nimkoff, Meyer F.
Nixon, H. Clarence
Normano, J. F.
North, Cecil C.
Notestein, Frank W.
Novak, Emil

O

Oatman, Miriam E.
O'Brien, John
O'Brien, John Francis
O'Brien, Robert W.
Odum, Eugene P.
Odum, Howard W.
Ogburn, William F.

Olds, Edward B.
O'Leary, Ellen J.
O'Leary, John B.
Opie, Thomas F.
Orton, William
Orton, William A.
Osborn, Frederick
O'Shea, M. V.
Outland, George E.
Overholser, Winfred
Oyler, Merton

P

Paget, Edwin H.
Palmer, Gladys L.
Palmer, Mary B.
Pam, Hugo
Pangburn, Weaver
Panunzio, Constantine
Pape, Leslie M.
Parenton, Vernon J.
Parham, Bettie Esther
Parish, John C.
Park, Robert E.
Parker, Frederick B.
Parker, Ida R.
Parshley, Howard M.
Parsons, Herbert A.
Parsons, Philip Archibald
Parsons, Talcott
Passin, Herbert
Pate, James E.
Patten, Walter
Patterson, Caleb Perry
Patterson, Ernest Minor
Peacock, Helen M.
Peck, Harvey W.
Peele, Catherine Groves
Pegg, Carl Hamilton
Pendleton, Helen B.
Penick, Edwin A.
Pennington, Edgar Legare
Perrigo, Lynn I.
Perry, Clarence Arthur
Peters, Iva L.
Pettit, Walter W.
Phelps, Harold A.
Piersel, W. G.
Pihlblad, C. Terence
Pinney, Harvey
Polk, William
Popenoe, Paul
Porter, Dorothy B.
Porterfield, Austin L.
Poteat, William Louis
Potter, Ellen
Pound, Roscoe
Powell, Fred Wilbur

Pratt, Anna B.
Pratt, George K.
Pratt, Joseph Hyde
Pressley, Luella Cole
Price, Daniel O.
Price, Frances E.
Price, Guy V.
Price, Harry B.
Price, Maurice T.
Pritchett, C. Herman
Pritchett, Henry Lucien
Provus, Severn
Pruette, Lorine
Puckett, Newbell Niles
Punke, Harold H.
Puschner, Emma C.

Q

Queen, Stuart A.
Quinn, James A.

R

Rainey, Glenn W.
Ralston, Andrew
Ralya, Lillian L.
Ralya, Lynn L.
Ramos, Arthur
Ramsdell, Leroy A.
Raper, Arthur F.
Rapport, Victor A.
Ratchford, Benjamin Ulysses
Ratcliffe, S. C.
Ratner, Julius
Reckless, Walter C.
Redfield, Robert
Reed, Ellery F.
Reeder, R. R.
Reeves, F. W.
Reid, Ira De A.
Reinecke, John E.
Reinhardt, James M.
Remer, Alice Winter
Renaud, Etienne B.
Renner, George T.
Resnik, Reuben B.
Reuss, Carl F.
Reuter, E. B.
Rhyne, Jennings J.
Ricci, John E.
Rice, Stuart A.
Richardson, Frank Howard
Richardson, William P.
Ricks, James Hoge
Ridgway, Florence Holmes
Riemer, Svend
Riley, John Winchell
Riley, Thomas J.
Ritchie, Albert G.

Roberson, Nellie
Robert, Percy A.
Robinson, Duane
Robinson, Edward S.
Robinson, Virginia P.
Rodnick, David
Rogers, Agnes
Rogers, Ethel
Rogler, Charles C.
Rosenbaum, Betty B.
Rosenberg, S. L. Millard
Rosenquist, Carl M.
Ross, Arthur M.
Ross, Earle D.
Ross, Edward Alsworth
Ross, F. A.
Ross, Harold
Ross, Miriam I.
Roucek, Joseph S.
Rozzelle, C. E.
Rubinow, I. M.
Ruff, Robert H.
Ruggles, Arthur H.
Rumyaneck, J.
Russell, Clyde
Russell, John C.
Russell, Josiah Cox
Ryan, Bryce
Ryan, W. Carson

S

Sahler, Helen
Saibel, Bernard
Sandelius, Walter E.
Sanders, Irwin T.
Sanders, Wiley B.
Sanderson, Dwight
Sanford, Gilbert A.
Sapasnekaw, Jacob
Sarkar, Benoy Kumar
Sarvis, Guy Walter
Satterfield, M. Harry
Schettler, Clarence
Schmadel, Marion
Schmid, Calvin F.
Schmid, Robert C.
Schmidt, Louis Bernard
Schmiedeler, Edgar
Schneider, Herbert W.
Schneider, Joseph
Schuler, Edgar A.
Schwenning, G. T.
Scott, Elmer
Sedman, Virginia Rankin
Seligmann, Herbert J.
Sen Gupta, N. N.
Sewell, William H.
Shane, Aileen

Shanks, Henry T.
Shankweiler, Paul W.
Shaw, Clifford R.
Shea, Alice Leahy
Sheffield, Ada E.
Shenton, Herbert N.
Shepard, Walter James
Sherman, John H.
Sherwell, Guillermo A.
Shinn, John C.
Shipman, Gordon D.
Shivers, Lyda Gordon
Shotwell, Mary G.
Shulman, Harry M.
Sibley, Elbridge
Sibley, James L.
Siegel, Morris
Simpson, George
Sims, Newell L.
Sitterson, J. Carlyle
Skaug, Arne
Skidmore, Rex A.
Slotkin, J. S.
Smedes, H. R.
Smertenko, Johan J.
Smith, Anna Greene
Smith, Carrie Weaver
Smith, Charles M.
Smith, Christopher
Smith, Dorothy Wysor
Smith, Elna N.
Smith, Helen Alden
Smith, John F.
Smith, Mapheus
Smith, Margaret G.
Smith, Marion B.
Smith, Mary Phlegar
Smith, Maurice Greer
Smith, Russell Gordon
Smith, T. Lynn
Smith, T. V.
Smith, William C.
Snedden, David
Snelling, Paula
Snyderman, George S.
Sorokin, Pitirim A.
Spencer, Sarah H.
Spengler, Joseph J.
Sprague, Theodore W.
Spruill, Julia Cherry
Spykman, Nicholas John
Standing, T. G.
Stanford, W. R.
Staples, Ruth
Starr, Harris E.
Stearns, A. W.
Steelman, J. R.
Steely, Fred Lynn

Steiner, Jesse F.
Stephan, A. Stephan
Stephan, Frederick F.
Stern, Bernhard J.
Stevens, Raymond B.
Steward, Gustavus Adolphus
Stewart, Ethelbert
Stewart, Margaret Winfield
Stillman, Charles C.
Stocking, Collis
Stone, Olive M.
Stouffer, Samuel A.
Stout, D. B.
Stout, D. G.
Stowe, A. Monroe
Street, Elwood
Strong, George W.
Strong, Samuel M.
Strow, Carl W.
Sturdivant, Joanna Farrell
Stutz, John G.
Sullenger, T. Earl
Sullivant, Willes
Sutherland, E. H.
Swift, Linton B.
Swift, Wiley H.
Sytz, Florence

T

Taeuber, Conrad
Taeuber, Irene B.
Taft, Donald R.
Talbot, Nell Snow
Tannous, Afif I.
Taylor, Alva W.
Taylor, Carl C.
Taylor, Carter
Taylor, Charles T.
Taylor, Maurice
Teggart, Frederick J.
Tenenbaum, Samuel
Terry, Edward A.
Tetreau, E. D.
Thomas, Dorothy Swaine
Thomas, Franklin
Thomas, Margaret A.
Thompson, Edgar T.
Thompson, Holland
Thompson, Warren S.
Thomsen, Arnold
Thorne, Alison Comish
Thorner, Isidor
Thorp, Willard L.
Thurnwald, Richard C.
Thurow, Mildred B.
Tibbitts, Clark
Tibbs, A. E.
Tigert, John J.

Tillett, W. F.
Tillinghast, Anne Williams
Timmons, B. F.
Tippy, Worth
Titus, Charles H.
Todd, Arthur J.
Todd, T. Wingate
Townsend, H. G.
Trabue, Marion Rex
Treudley, Mary Bosworth
Troncoso, Moises Poblete
Trump, Elizabeth V.
Tufts, James H.
Tugwell, Rexford G.
Turner, W. S.
Tuttle, Emeth
Tuttle, F. W.
Tuttle, Harold Saxe
Tyler, Dorothy
Tylor, W. Russell

V

Vaile, Gertrude
Vance, Rupert B.
Van Dusen, Albert P.
Van Dusseldorp, Wilma
Van Kleeck, Mary
Van Royen, William
Veblen, Florence
Verry, Ethel E.
Vincent, John Martin
Vincent, Melvin J.
Visher, Stephen S.
Vogt, Paul
Von Beckerath, Herbert

W

Wade, John
Wager, Paul W.
Wagner, M. E.
Wakeley, Ray E.
Walker, Curtis H.
Wallace, Richard W.
Wallis, Wilson D.
Waples, Douglas

Ward, Paul W.
Ware, Caroline F.
Warner, Kenneth O.
Waterman, Willoughby C.
Watkins, James T., IV
Watson, Frank D.
Watson, James
Watters, Mary
Wead, Margaret
Weatherford, W. D.
Weaver, Leon
Weaver, Robert C.
Webb, Edith
Weeks, H. Ashley
Weil, Gertrude
Weinfeld, William
Weintraub, Philipp
Weld, W. E.
Weldon, W. C.
Wentworth, Mildred
Wesley, Oscar
Westefeld, Albert
Whelden, C. H., Jr.
Whelpton, P. K.
White, Carl M.
White, Edna Noble
White, Leonard D.
White, Leslie A.
White, R. Clyde
White, William Allen
Whitney, Vincent H.
Whittley, R. L.
Wilder, Francis S.
Willard, D. W.
Willey, Malcolm M.
Williams, Aubrey W.
Williams, B. O.
Williams, Carl A.
Williams, Eric
Williams, L. A.
Williams, Melvin J.
Wilson, Logan
Wilson, Louis R.
Wilson, M. L.
Wilson, Warren H.

Wilson, Woodrow
Winston, Robert W.
Winston, Sanford R.
Wirth, Louis
Wise, Harry
Wish, Harvey
Wissler, Clark
Witherspoon, Pauline
Witmer, Helen Leland
Witty, Paul A.
Wolf, H. D.
Wood, Arthur Evans
Wood, Arthur Lewis
Wood, Margaret Mary
Woodard, James W.
Woodbury, Robert M.
Woodhouse, Chase Going
Woodhouse, Edward James
Woodruff, Clinton Rogers
Woods, Erville B.
Woodward, C. Vann
Woodward, Julian L.
Woofter, T. J., Jr.
Woolston, Howard B.
Work, Monroe N.
Wright, Mary Hamilton
Wyckoff, G. P.
Wyckoff, Viola

Y

Yeatman, Trez P.
Yeaxlee, Basil A.
Young, C. L.
Young, Erle Fiske
Young, Ina V.
Young, Kimball
Young, Pauline V.

Z

Zander, Alvin
Zimmerman, Carle C.
Zimmermann, Erich W.
Zittel, Ruth Ellen
Zumbrunnen, A. C.
Zutermann, Erna

TOWARD REGIONAL DOCUMENTATION

IT HAS often been said that the South has been the most completely documented region of any in the Nation and that it has also had a larger body of both romantic and realistic literature than any other region. Whether this be true or not, the nature and range of regional documentation and literature available offer abundant evidence of both opportunity and obligation to interpret the South adequately as an integral part of American culture, rather than as an exotic section of the Nation.

It has sometimes been said that the public often tires of so much writing about the South and that contrariwise it never tires of the endless stream that flows on and on. Perhaps both of these impressions are true, yet the second is perhaps more nearly demonstrable since it can be measured in terms of best sellers, Pulitzer awards, the quantity of books produced, and the never-ceasing demand. Yet it is doubtful if any real inventory of southern studies and literature has ever been attempted since there is no authentic and comprehensive southern bibliography available. One of the units of the Sesquicentennial Celebration of the University of North Carolina, therefore, is planned in the form of such a bibliography, classified in such definitive categories as to indicate the total picture of southern regional development and documentation. The bibliography is being prepared by Anna Greene Smith under the auspices of the Institute for Research in Social Science. The general categories for cataloguing and analysis include: The Status of Southern Bibliography; Special Features of Southern Documentation; Popularity of Southern Literature, including Pulitzer Awards and Best Sellers; Southern Fiction Written by Southern Writers and Southern Fiction by Other Authors; Dramatic Writings and Production; Biography; Comprehensive Treatises on the South, including Social-Economic Studies and Reviews by Publicists; Special Cultural and Economic Studies; Historical Studies; Nature and the Folk; Nature and Resources; The Negro; Needed Further Documentation.

The purpose of this present brief paper may be simply stated. It is to illustrate further the nature and range of regional study and interpretation undertaken and presented during the last twenty years by the Institute for Research in Social Science and by SOCIAL FORCES. In another paper in this special issue of SOCIAL FORCES the number and nature of authors and the number of contributions are described. It remains only to present a representative list of special articles dealing with southern regional subjects published by SOCIAL FORCES together with a catalogue of books, articles, and manuscripts sponsored by the Institute for Research in Social Science.

It must be emphasized here that this sampling of regional titles is limited entirely to SOCIAL FORCES and the Institute for Research in Social Science at the University of North Carolina for the reason that the story of these is required for this particular occasion. There were notable examples of other special regional studies from other southern centers, such as Virginia, Louisiana State, Duke, Oklahoma, Vanderbilt and Peabody, Fisk and Atlanta, as well as a host of special studies from the land-grant colleges and other southern institutions and agencies, and especially the Commission on Interracial Coöperation, since 1944 the Southern Regional Council, at Atlanta. Of the southern periodical media, in addition to SOCIAL FORCES, there were *The Virginia Quarterly Review*, *The Sewanee Review*, *The South Atlantic Quarterly*, *The Southwest Review*, and *The Southern Review*, and still later the *Southern Economic Journal* and *The Southern Historical Review*, in addition to the State historical publications and the State educational and school journals. These, of course, are all reported in the Regional Bibliography to which reference has been made.

First we review briefly, in chronological order, the main contributions of SOCIAL FORCES in the field of regional study and interpretation. It may be noted that in these articles, as in the regional studies and programs, the evolution is from local studies and analysis to wider inquiries into total regional problems, implemented, then, into theoretical discussions and conclusions. One need only glance at the last page of these samplings in comparison with the first page to note the marked contrasts. Here again the procedure is one from community studies to regionalism, with an increasing emphasis placed upon responsible theory. In this developing order, too, may be observed something of the wider regional-national range of SOCIAL FORCES articles and the decreasing ratio of contributions devoted to southern themes written by southern authors and the increasing number of national themes and authors.

SOCIAL FORCES

CONTRIBUTIONS DEALING WITH SOUTHERN REGIONAL SUBJECTS

VOLUME 1. "State Programs of Public Welfare in the South," Burr Blackburn, November, 1922; "The North Carolina Study of Prison Conditions," Wiley B. Sanders, November, 1922; "Certification of Superintendents of Public Welfare," S. E. Leonard, November, 1922; "Institutes for Public Welfare," Mrs. Clarence A. Johnson, November, 1922; "The Church-By-The-Side-Of-The-Road," A. W. McAlister, November, 1922; "The Tennessee State Conference," R. F. Hudson, November, 1922; "The Approach to the South's Race Question," M. Ashby Jones, November, 1922; "A Usable Piece of Community Machinery," Will W. Alexander, November, 1922; "The Southern Summer Schools for Rural Pastors," Robert H. Ruff, November, 1922; "A Rural State's Unlettered White Women," E. C. Branson, November, 1922; "A University Plan," Howard W. Odum, November, 1922; "The Organized Work of Women in One State, Part I, Nellie Roberson, November, 1922; "Race Relations," Howard W. Odum, November, 1922; "The Use of Books and Libraries in North Carolina," Louis R. Wilson, January, 1923; "The South as a Field for Sociological Research," L. A. Williams, January, 1923; "Courses in Rural Social Science," John F. Smith, January, 1923; "Parole in North Carolina," A. W. McAlister, January, 1923; "Parole in Kentucky," Joseph P. Byers, January, 1923; "The North Carolina Prison Conference," Wiley B. Sanders, January, 1923; "The South Carolina Conference," Ellison Capers, January, 1923; "Summer Schools for Pastors of the Methodist Episcopal Church, South," A. C. Zumbrunnen, January, 1923; "Conference for Negro Education in Raleigh," N. C. Newbold, January, 1923; "The Negro Offender," W. C. Jackson, January, 1923; "Multiplying Dollars for Negro Education," Isaac Fisher, January, 1923; "The Virginia Inter-Racial Committee," R. W. Miles, January, 1923; "The North Carolina Inter-Racial Committee," R. W. Miles, January, 1923; "The South Carolina Inter-Racial Committee," R. W. Miles, January, 1923; "Social Occasions and Contacts in a Rural County," E. C. Branson, January, 1923; "The Organized Work of Women in One State, Part II," Nellie Roberson, January, 1923; "A Regional Library Association," Mary B. Palmer, January, 1923; "Farm Tenancy in the Cotton Belt: How Farm Tenants Live," E. C. Branson, March, 1923; "Mr. Babbitt Arrives at Erzerum," Gerald W. Johnson, March, 1923; "Personnel Studies in Southern Industries," Harriet L. Herring, March, 1923; "Applying Democracy to Some Unequal Places in Georgia," Boyce M. Edens, March, 1923; "Child Labor in North Carolina, 1912–1922," Wiley H. Swift, March, 1923; "A Cripple Census Week in North Carolina," Emeth Tuttle, March, 1923; "A Forward Move in Georgia," Burr Blackburn, March, 1923; "Texas Council of Statewide Agencies," Elmer Scott, March, 1923; "The North Carolina Conference for Social Service," Nell Battle Lewis, March, 1923; "The Social Service Program of the Protestant Episcopal Church," Edwin A. Penick, March, 1923; "Fundamental Principles Underlying Inter-Racial Co-Operation," Howard W. Odum, March, 1923; "The Tuskegee Conference," Albin L. Holsey, March, 1923; "The Second Generation of Race Relations," W. F. Tillett, March, 1923; "Books for Country Readers in Kentucky," Florence Holmes Ridgway, March, 1923; "A Survey of Conditions Affecting Children of Bradley County Arkansas," Frances Sage Bradley, March, 1923; "The North Carolina Municipal Association," T. B. Eldridge, March, 1923; "Social Work of Women's Organizations in the Churches. I. Methodist Episcopal Church South," Bertha Payne Newell, March, 1923; "Reading, Writing, and Leadership," Howard W. Odum, March, 1923; "A Decade of Social Progress in North Carolina," Kate Burr Johnson and Nell Battle Lewis, May, 1923; "Mileposts of Progress in Georgia," Burr Blackburn, May, 1923; "The Virginia Plan," Frank Bane, May, 1923; "Louisiana Notes," G. P. Wyckoff, May, 1923; "Mississippi Beginnings," N. B. Bond, May, 1923; "A Sociological Interpretation of the New Ku Klux Movement," Guy B. Johnson, May, 1923; "Training Colored Social Workers in the South," Edward Franklin Frazier, May, 1923; "Farm Tenancy in the South. Part II. The Social Estate of White Farm Tenants," E. C. Branson, May, 1923; "Southern Women and Lynching," May 1923; "The Social Responsibility of the State University," Harry Woodburn Chase, September, 1923; "Hands Across the States," Pauline Witherspoon, September, 1923; "Alabama State

Conference Plans," James L. Sibley, September, 1923; "Studies of Negro Education," Howard W. Odum, September, 1923; "The Social Program of the Stanley McCormick School," Leroy F. Jackson, September, 1923; "An Educational Opportunity for Industrial Girls," Lucy P. Carner, September, 1923; "The Organized Work of Women in One State. Part III." Nellie Roberson, September, 1923; "The Transfer of Leadership," Howard W. Odum, September, 1923.

VOLUME 2. "Issachar Is a Strong Ass," Gerald W. Johnson, November, 1923; "Rural Standards of Living in the South," Roland M. Harper, November, 1923; "The Rise of the Rural Problem," Carl Taylor, November, 1923; "Training for Rural Leadership: II. The North Carolina Plan," Wiley B. Sanders, November, 1923; "Harnessing College Power to Promote Public Welfare in the South," Jeannette Paddock Nichols, November, 1923; "Developing a State Through Student Club Work," S. H. Hobbs, Jr., November, 1923; "Georgia Legislation," Burr Blackburn, November, 1923; "A Council of the Church Schools of the South," Howard W. Odum, November, 1923; "The Negro on a Strike," T. J. Woofter, Jr., November, 1923; "Money an Indisputable Argument," N. C. Newbold, November, 1923; "The Long Lane: A Study in Rural Conservatism," N. B. Bond, November, 1923; "Southern Pioneers in Social Interpretation: I. Madeline McDowell Breckinridge," S. P. Breckinridge, November, 1923; "The Influence of War Travel on One Rural State. From the Letters of Quincy Sharpe Mills to Laconic Illiteracy," R. B. House, 1923; "Walter Hines Page: A Southern Nationalist," R. D. W. Connor, January, 1924; "The Orphanage Population of One Southern State," Mary G. Shotwell, January, 1924; "The Dallas Institute for Social Education," Gaynell Hawkins, January, 1924; "Social Legislation in South Carolina," Pauline Witherspoon, January, 1924; "A Tennessee Reorganization Program," Howard W. Odum, January, 1924; "Louisiana," Willes Sullivant, January, 1924; "Progress in Alabama," James L. Sibley, January, 1924; "The Race Problem in Cross Section. The Negro in 1923," Monroe N. Work, January, 1924; "Rural Standards of Living in the South. II. Interrelations of Certain Demographic Factors," Roland M. Harper, January, 1924; "Robert E. Lee: An Interpretation," Woodrow Wilson, March, 1924; "The Southern Mill Village Complex," Howard W. Odum, March,

1924; "I. The Southern Cotton Mill Village: A Viewpoint," M. W. Heiss, March, 1924; "II. Does the Mill Village Foster Any Social Types?", Jeannette Paddock Nichols, March, 1924; "Field Work Training in Community Organization," Jesse F. Steiner, March, 1924; "The State Conferences for Social Work," Howard W. Odum, March, 1924; "The Negro Migration and Its Consequences," Guy B. Johnson, March, 1924; "Sectionalism and Its Avoidance," Edward Alsworth Ross, May, 1924; "Southern Pioneers in Social Interpretation. IV. Charles Brantley Aycock," Edwin A. Alderman, May, 1924; "A Decade of Progress in Alabama," Mrs. L. B. Bush, May, 1924; "Extremes and Means in Racial Interpretation," Melville J. Herskovits, May, 1924; "Critical Attitudes North and South," Gerald Johnson, May, 1924; "Cotton and Some Aspects of Southern Civilization," R. Clyde White, September, 1924; "The Land of 'I Reckon' and the Land of 'Hadn't Ought'," Edgar Legare Pennington, September, 1924; "Scientific State Building," W. E. Garnett, September, 1924; "What Racial Equality Means to the Negro," Andrew Ralston, September, 1924; "The Rural South," Wilson Gee, September, 1924; "A More Articulate South," Howard W. Odum, September, 1924.

VOLUME 3. "The South Carolina Conference," Aileen Shane, November, 1924; "Southern Regional Child Welfare Conference," C. C. Carstens, November, 1924; "Southeastern Library Conference," Cornelia Love, November, 1924; "Rural Economic Co-operation and Community Organization," Benson Y. Landis, November, 1924; "Development of the Textile Industry in South Carolina," W. P. Hamrick, November, 1924; "The Search After Values," Howard W. Odum, November, 1924; "Southern Pioneers in Social Interpretation. VI. Woodrow Wilson: A Challenge to the Fighting South," Gerald W. Johnson, January, 1925; "Judge Longstreet of Georgia," John Wade, January, 1925; "Booker T. Washington, Pioneer," Monroe N. Work, January 1925; "North Carolina—Publisher and Reader?," L. R. Wilson, January, 1925; "The Search After Values," Howard W. Odum, January, 1925; "Know Your Home State. Discussion III," S. H. Hobbs, Jr., March, 1925; "Psychological Factors in Negro Health," E. Franklin Frazier, March, 1925; "Morituri Te Salutamus," Harriet Herring, March, 1925; "The Southern Textile Social Service Association," M. W. Heiss, March, 1925; "University Research and Training in Social Science," Howard W. Odum, March, 1925; "Artists and Chroniclers," Gerald Johnson, March, 1925; "Conflicting Forces in Negro Progress," Francis Marion Dunford, May, 1925; "Newspaper Advertisements and Negro Culture," Guy B. Johnson, May, 1925; "The Labor Union Problem in the Southern Textile Industry," George S. Mitchell, May, 1925; "A Southern Promise," Howard W. Odum, May, 1925.

VOLUME 4. "The Teaching of Sociology in the South," T. J. Woofter, Jr., September, 1925; "Community Relationships," J. B. Gwin, September, 1925; "A New Field for the Negro Social Worker in the South," Helen B. Pendleton, September, 1925; "The Collapse of the Farmer-Labor Bloc," Fred E. Haynes, September, 1925; "Cotton-Cloth: A Type Study of the Social Process. I," Mary O. Cowper, September, 1925; "The Intellectual Status of Children in Cotton Mill Villages," L. A. Williams, September, 1925; "The South's Challenge to University Men," Marion Rex Trabue, December, 1925; "The Physician and Mental Ills in Mississippi," N. B. Bond, December, 1925; "A White and Black World in American Labor and Politics," Abram L. Harris, December, 1925; "Seven Southern State Capitals," Harlean James, December, 1925; "The Discovery of the People," Howard W. Odum, December, 1925; "The Social Philosophy of Ellen Glasgow," Edwin Mims, March, 1926; "Distribution of Five Years of Ph.D. Research in the Social Sciences," F. W. Hoffer, March, 1926; "Making the Visible Arts Visible in North Carolina," William Polk, March, 1926; "The Negro Church in the United States," Newbell N. Puckett, March, 1926; "Employee Representation Plan of the Durham Hosiery Mills," Joanna Farrell Sturdivant, March, 1926; "A Social Interpretation: South Carolina," Josiah Morse, June, 1926.

VOLUME 5. "A Social Interpretation: Tennessee," Ernest J. Eberling, September, 1926; "An Alabama Institute," Myrtle Brooke, December, 1926; "Negro Art: African and American," Melville J. Herskovits, December, 1926; "A New Technique in Folk Lore," Read Bain, December, 1926; "Negro Folk Beliefs," Clyde Russell, December, 1926; "The Beginnings of Industrial Social Work," Harriet L. Herring, December, 1926; "Crime in the Superior Courts of North Carolina," Francis S. Wilder, March, 1927; "Has the Negro Arrived?" W. S. Turner, March, 1927;

"The Beginnings of Industrial Social Work," Harriet L. Herring, March, 1927; "An Experiment in Rural Social Organization," Jesse Frederick Steiner, June, 1927.

VOLUME 6. "The South and the New Society," Walter Lippmann, September, 1927; "Health Education and Welfare Agencies in Georgia Counties," Burr Blackburn, September, 1927; "An Approach to State Planning," Edward Eyre Hunt, September, 1927; "The Community Chest in Virginia Cities," Gladys L. Palmer, December, 1927; "The Penitentes: A Folk-Observance," Mary Watters, December, 1927; "An Adventure in County Public Care of Children," Frank W. Hoffer, March, 1928; "A Stock-Taking Conference on the Negro," Guy B. Johnson, March, 1928; "A Survey of Virginia State and County Governments," A. E. Buck, March, 1928; "Tracing the Development of Welfare Work in the North Carolina Textile Industry," Harriet L. Herring, June, 1928; "Leaders in Village Communities," Elizabeth R. Hooker, June, 1928; "The Negro and the Farm Crisis," T. J. Woofter, Jr., June, 1928; "Defining Public Welfare as a Function of Government in Virginia," Arthur W. James, June, 1928; "Industrial Development and Population Growth," P. K. Whelpton, June, 1928.

VOLUME 7. "The Pauper Idiot in Kentucky," Arthur H. Estabrook, September, 1928; "The Negro and the Changing South," W. S. Turner, September, 1928; "The Social Sciences in Southern Colleges and Universities," Curtis H. Walker, December, 1928; "An Institute on Community Planning," June P. Guild, December, 1928; "Evolution of Population and Dwelling in the Indian Southwest," Etienne B. Renaud, December, 1928; "The Negro Community, A Cultural Phenomenon," E. Franklin Frazier, March, 1929.

VOLUME 8. "Twenty Years' Pioneering in Race Relations," Herbert J. Seligmann, September, 1929; "The Concept of the Region," Rupert B. Vance, December, 1929; "Homicide in South Carolina: A Regional Study," H. C. Brearley, December, 1929; "Toward Preliminary Social Analysis; I. The Southern Mill System Faces a New Issue," Harriet L. Herring, March, 1930; "Toward Preliminary Social Analysis: II. Economic Aspects of the Gastonia Situation," Benjamin Ulysses Ratchford, March, 1930; "Social Mobility Among Farm Owner Operators," W. A. Anderson, March, 1930; "Do Disasters Help,"

J. Blaine Gwin, March, 1930; "Agricultural Credit and the Negro Farmer: I," Roland B. Eutsler, March, 1930; "Agricultural Credit and the Negro Farmer: II," Roland B. Eustler, June, 1930.

VOLUME 9. "The New Mobility and the Coastal Island," Lee M. Brooks, October, 1930; "A Well Governed County," Edward A. Terry, October, 1930; "A Karl Marx for Hill Billies. Portrait of a Southern Leader," Rupert B. Vance, December, 1930; "The Negro and Homicide," H. C. Brearley, December, 1930; "The Social Problem of Labor Organization Casualties," Harriet L. Herring, December, 1930; "Research by Southern Social Science Teachers," Benjamin B. Kendrick, March, 1931.

VOLUME 10. "Notes on the Study of Regional and Folk Society," Howard W. Odum, December, 1931; "Keeping up with Culture in Texas and the Southwest," Joseph Martin Dawson, December, 1931; "A Study of Emotional Instability and Intelligence of Women in the Penal Institutions of North Carolina," Lena B. Ladu and K. C. Garrison, December, 1931; "Social Development in the Mill Village: A Challenge to the Mill Welfare Worker," Harriet L. Herring, December, 1931; "We Vote Solid! A Note on Southern Political Folkways," John Maclachlan, March, 1932; "The Effects of the Present Credit System on Southern Agriculture," Garnet W. Forster, March, 1932.

VOLUME 11. "The Changing Background of Southern Politics," H. Clarence Nixon, October, 1932; "Negroes Who Run Afoul the Law," Hugh Penn Brinton, October, 1932; "County-State Relations in Virginia," Rowland Egger, October, 1932; "Nashville Makes a Venture," Marion Newcomb LaSater, December, 1932; "The Standard of Living of Negro Farm Families in Albemarle County, Virginia," W. L. Leap, December, 1932; "Comparative Costs of County Government in the South," Clarence Heer, December, 1932; "Civilization of Southeastern Kentucky," Roland M. Harper, March, 1933; "The Effect of Unemployment and Short-Time During 1931 in the Families of 200 Alabama Child Workers," Katharine Du Pre Lumpkin and Dorothy Wolff Douglas, May, 1933; "The Gerrymander System in Georgia," Cullen B. Gosnell, May, 1933; "Labor Unrest in North Carolina, 1932," H. M. Douty, May, 1933.

VOLUME 12. "Social Isolation of the French Speaking People of Rural Louisiana," H. W. Gilmore, October, 1933; "The Negro and the Depression in North Carolina," Guy B. Johnson, October, 1933; "Industrial Relations in the South and the NIRA," Harriet L. Herring, October, 1933; "What of Submarginal Areas in Regional Planning," Rupert B. Vance, March, 1934; "The Tennessee Valley Regional Plan," T. J. Woofter, Jr., March, 1934; "Regionalism Vs. Sectionalism in the South's Place in the National Economy," Howard W. Odum, March, 1934; "Some Small-Town Folk Beliefs of the Carolina Piedmont," John Walker McCain, Jr., March, 1934; "Twenty-three Years of Teaching in a Negro Medical School," H. H. Hazen, May, 1934; "Contrasts Between Northern and Southern and Urban and Rural Negroes in the United States," Roland M. Harper, May, 1934.

VOLUME 13.[1] "The Case for Regional-National Social Planning," Howard W. Odum, October, 1934; "Where Regionalism and Sectionalism Meet," Donald Davidson, October, 1934; "The Prospect for Optimum Regional Production in the Southern Regions," Milton S. Heath, October, 1934; "The Subregions of the Southeast," T. J. Woofter, Jr., October, 1934; "Rural-Urban Migration in the Tennessee Valley Between 1920 and 1930," C. Horace Hamilton, October, 1934; "The Displaced Tenant Farm Family in North Carolina," Gordon W. Blackwell, October, 1934; "Some Aspects of Mortality in Florida, 1921–1930," Albert C. Blanchard, October, 1934; "Black Belt Aristocrats. The Old South Lives on in Alabama's Black Belt," Renwick C. Kennedy, October, 1934; "Some Costs of Economy in Schools," Harriet L. Herring, October, 1934; "A City in Depression—Greensboro, North Carolina," Albert S. Keister, October, 1934; "Does the South Owe the Negro a New Deal?" Guy B. Johnson, October, 1934; "A Comparison of Race Relations in South Africa and the Southern States," John H. Kirk, October, 1934; "The Share Croppers' Union in Alabama," John Beecher, October, 1934; "A Half Century of Southern Penal Exploitation," Blake McKelvey, October, 1934; "A Bibliography on Southern Labor," Robin Hood, October, 1934; "Recent Farm-Ownership Changes in the Cotton Belt and Their Significance for Migration," Edward E. Lewis, December, 1934; "Race Discrimination and Negro Personality," Walter R. Chivers, December, 1934; "Balancing State Budgets in Southern Commonwealths Dur-

[1] Number 1 in this volume was a special issue featuring The South in the Depression.

ing the Economic Crisis," James E. Pate, December, 1934; "Was the American Conflict a War Between States," Robert W. Winston, March, 1935; "The AAA and the Cropper," Harold Hoffsommer, May, 1935; "Personality and Cultural Research in the Tennessee Valley," William E. Cole, May, 1935.

VOLUME 14. "Socio-Economic Aspects of Territorial Planning with Special Reference to the Mississippi Valley Plan," W. Russell Tylor, December, 1935; "Southern Population and Social Planning," T. J. Woofter, Jr., October, 1935; "Does It Cost Less to Live in the South?" William F. Ogburn, December, 1935; "Voting in Tennessee 1900–1932," Charles H. Titus and Joe Bain, December, 1935; "How the Conservative Negro Intellectual of the South Feels about Racial Segregation," Bettie Esther Parham, December, 1935; "The Emergence of the Metropolitan Community in the South," Walter J. Matherly, March, 1936; "Negro Education in Northern Alabama," Paul W. Shankweiler, March, 1936.

VOLUME 15. "Family-Capitalism in a Community of Rural Louisiana," Harlan W. Gilmore, October, 1936; "The Initial Experience with Census Tracts in a Southern City," Walter C. Reckless, October, 1936; "The Social Scientist in the Tennessee Valley Authority Program," T. Levron Howard, October, 1936; "The Southern Crisis and Social Control," Wayland J. Hayes, October, 1936; "Regions," William F. Ogburn, October, 1936; "The Newspaper and Race Relations," William Shands Meacham, December, 1936; "Family Life Cycle Analysis," Charles P. Loomis, and C. Horace Hamilton, December, 1936; "Teaching Sociology in Colleges and High Schools," Part III. The Correlation of the Teaching of Sociology in High Schools and Colleges, Harold D. Meyer, December, 1936; "Racial Factors and Economic Forces in Land Tenure in the South," Monroe N. Work, December, 1936; "Recent Changes in the Farm Population of the Southern States," T. Lynn Smith, March, 1937; "The 'Drag' of Talent Out of the South," Wilson Gee, March, 1937.

VOLUME 16. "The Historic Pattern of Sociology in the South," L. L. Bernard, October, 1937; "A Population Policy for the South," B. O. Williams, October, 1937; "Teaching Marriage at the University of North Carolina," Ernest R. Groves, October, 1937; "Problems of Adjustment of Race and Class in the South," Monroe N. Work, October, 1937; "The Tennessee Valley Authority as a Government Corporation," C. Herman Pritchett, October, 1937; "A Study of Land Tenure in the South," Harry Wise, December, 1937; "Gullies and What They Mean," Arthur Raper, December, 1937; "Urban Adjustments of Migrants from the Southern Appalachian Plateaus," Grace G. Leybourne, December, 1937; "The Removal of Families from Tennessee Valley Authority Reservoir Areas," M. Harry Satterfield, December, 1937; "Some Findings of a Standard of Living Study Made of White Farm Families on Sand Mountain, Alabama," Ervilla Alice Masters, March, 1938; "Present Status and Future Trends in the Southern White Family," Bernice Milburn Moore, March, 1938.

VOLUME 17. "The State of Sociology in the United States and Its Prospect in the South," Howard W. Odum, October, 1938; "Research in Progress and Available Data for Research in State Departments of Public Welfare in the Southeastern Region, 1936–1938," Wiley B. Sanders, October, 1938; "The Sociology of Crises: The Louisville Flood of 1937," Robert I. Kutak, October, 1938; "Notes on the Social Organization of a French Village in South Louisiana," Vernon J. Parenton, October, 1938; "Some Occupational Trends in the South," Kenneth Evans, December, 1938; "Poor Whites of the South," Mildred Rutherford Mell, December, 1938; "Analyses of Racial Differences within Seven Clinical Categories of White and Negro Mental Patients in the Georgia State Hospital, 1923–32," J. E. Greene, December, 1938; "The Profession of Social Work in the South," Stuart K. Jaffary, December, 1938; "White Relief in North Carolina, 1865–1867," Alice B. Keith, March, 1939; "The Demographic Basis of Old Age Assistance in the South," T. Lynn Smith, March, 1939; "A Study of Virginia's Rural Marginal Population," Allen D. Edwards, March, 1939.

VOLUME 18. "The Trend of the Interregional Migration of Talent: The Southeast, 1899–1936," Harold Loran Geisert, October, 1939; "Economic Factors in Negro Migration—Past and Future," Robert C. Weaver, October, 1939; "The Outside Employer in the Southern Industrial Pattern," Harriet L. Herring, October, 1939; "Distinctive Cultures in the Southeast: Their Possibilities for Regional Research," John MacLachlan, December, 1939; "The Treatment of Juvenile Offenders in Tennessee: A Study in Integration," William B. Jones, Jr., December, 1939; "Modern Trends in Penology," L. F. Chapman, December, 1939;

"Some Contrasts in Levels of Living in Industrial, Farm, and Part-time Farm Families in Rural Mississippi," Dorothy Dickins, December, 1939; "A Sample Study of Migration to Knoxville, Tennessee," W. Parker Mauldin, March, 1940; "Parole in Alabama," J. Herman Johnson, March, 1940; "Family Life in a Rural Community," Frank D. Alexander, March, 1940; "The Program of Marriage Instruction at the University of North Carolina," Donald S. Klaiss, May, 1940.

VOLUME 19. "Education and the Good South," Edwin R. Embree, October, 1940; "Urban Development in the Southeast: What of the Future?" E. S. Draper, October, 1940; "Experience in Developing a Community Program of Education," Glenn Kendall, October, 1940; "Public Housing from a Community Point of View," Alonzo G. Moron, October, 1940; "Bulgarians and Southern Rural Whites in Contrast," Irwin T. Sanders, October, 1940; "The Economics of Migration and Southern Poverty," James Gilbert Evans, October, 1940; "Methodological Notes for Studying the Southern City," Ira De A. Reid, December, 1940; "The Planter in the Pattern of Race Relations in the South," Edgar T. Thompson, December, 1940; "Rôle of the Poor Whites in Race Contacts of the South," W. O. Brown, December, 1940; "Rôle of the Indian in the Race Relations Complex of the South," Leonard Bloom, December, 1940; "The Growing South," T. J. Woofter, Jr., March, 1941; "Sociological Analysis Through Field Course Procedure," Gordon W. Blackwell, March, 1941; "Federal Action Programs and Community Action in the South," W. E. B. Du Bois, March, 1941; "Status of Chinese in the Mississippi Delta," Robert W. O'Brien, March, 1941; "A Regional Study of the Negro," W. G. Piersel, March, 1941; "Some Contrasts in Women Employed in Two Types of Industries in Mississippi," Dorothy Dickins, May, 1941.

VOLUME 20. "The Place and Importance of Population Studies in Relation to the Negro Population of the South," Charles S. Johnson, October, 1941; "Some Problems of Social Work Education from the Point of View of the State University," Arthur E. Fink, October, 1941; "The College in Relation to Community Analysis and Development," Gordon W. Blackwell, October, 1941; "The Social Structure of New-Ground Settlements in the Mississippi Delta," Rudolf Heberle, December, 1941; "The Influence of the

Negro on the Culture of the South," Charles G. Gomillion, March, 1942; "Population Redistribution in Louisiana," Homer L. Hitt and T. Lynn Smith, March, 1942.

VOLUME 21. "Negro Leadership in Rural Georgia Communities: Occupational and Social Aspects," Vinson A. Edwards, October, 1942; "Community Adjustments in Reservoir-Affected Communities," R. F. Leonard, December, 1942; "Recreation Planning in the Tennessee-Cumberland Rivers Watersheds," Allen T. Edmunds, December, 1942; "Southern Regional Folkways Regarding Money," William Fielding Ogburn, March, 1943; "The South's Forest Frontier and the War," E. L. Demmon, May, 1943; "The Rôle of the Commission on Interracial Coöperation in War and Peace," William E. Cole, May, 1943; "The Rôle of the Library in the Southeast in Peace and War," Louis R. Wilson, May, 1943.

VOLUME 22. "Some Regional Indices of Agricultural Equipment Basic to Southern Regional Planning," Harriet L. Herring, October, 1943; "The Implications of Regionalism to Folk Sociology with Illustrations from the Southern Regions," Hope Tisdale Eldridge, October, 1943; "Food Preparation of Owner and Cropper Farm Families in the Shortleaf Pine Area of Mississippi," Dorothy Dickens, October, 1943; "Development of the Public Health Movement in the Southeast," Francis R. Allen, October, 1943; "The Impacts of the War on the Rural Community," Douglas Ensminger, October, 1943; "Two Factors in Urban Population Growth," Selz C. Mayo, October, 1943; "A Research Note on Desired Family Size," Gilbert A. Sanford, October, 1943; "Social Classes: A Frame of Reference for the Study of Negro Society," Mozell C. Hill and Thelma D. Ackiss, October, 1943; "The Employment of Negro Women as Domestic Servants in New Orleans," Harlan Gilmore and Logan Wilson, March, 1944; "Consumer Problems and the Coöperative Movement in the Curricula of Southern Negro Colleges," Lee M. Brooks and Ruth G. Lynch, May, 1944; "Observations on Regional Differentials in Coöperative Organization," Charles M. Smith, May, 1944; "Social Status and Physical Appearance among Negro Adolescents," Mozell C. Hill, May, 1944.[2]

[2] This listing closes with Volume 22, Number 4, May 1944. October and December 1944–Numbers 1 and 2 in Volume 23 are not included.

INSTITUTE FOR RESEARCH IN SOCIAL SCIENCE

PUBLICATIONS AND MANUSCRIPTS (Arranged Chronologically)

I. BOOKS AND MONOGRAPHS

Southern Pioneers in Social Interpretation. By Howard W. Odum (ed.). Chapel Hill: University of North Carolina Press, 1925. Pp. 221.

The Negro and His Songs. By Howard W. Odum and Guy B. Johnson. Chapel Hill: University of North Carolina Press, 1925. Pp. 306.

Systems of Public Welfare. By Howard W. Odum and D. W. Willard. Chapel Hill: University of North Carolina Press, 1925. Pp. 302.

An Approach to Public Welfare and Social Work. By Howard W. Odum. Chapel Hill: University of North Carolina Press, 1926. Pp. 178.

Negro Workaday Songs. By Howard W. Odum and Guy B. Johnson. Chapel Hill: University of North Carolina Press, 1926. Pp. 278.

American Marriage and Family Relationships. By Ernest R. Groves (with William F. Ogburn). New York: Henry Holt and Company, 1928. Pp. 479.

Rainbow Round My Shoulder. The Blue Trail of Black Ulysses. By Howard W. Odum. Indianapolis: Bobbs Merrill Company, 1928. Pp. 323.

The History of Taxation in North Carolina During the Colonial Period, 1663–1776. By Coralie Parker. New York: Columbia University Press, 1928. Pp. 178.

County Government in North Carolina. By Paul W. Wager. Chapel Hill: University of North Carolina Press, 1928. Pp. 447.

Social Work and the Training of Social Workers. By Sydnor H. Walker. Chapel Hill: University of North Carolina Press, 1928. Pp. 241.

Transportation in North Carolina. A Study of Rate Structure and Rate Adjustment. By Roland B. Eutsler. Philadelphia: University of Pennsylvania doctoral dissertation, 1929. Pp. 65.

Welfare Work in Mill Villages: The Story of Extra-Mill Activities in North Carolina. By Harriet L. Herring. Chapel Hill: University of North Carolina Press, 1929. Pp. 406.

John Henry: Tracking Down a Negro Legend. By Guy B. Johnson. Chapel Hill: University of North Carolina Press, 1929. Pp. 155.

Financing Extra Curricular Activities. By Harold D. Meyer and Samuel McKee Eddleman. New York: A. S. Barnes and Company, 1929. Pp. 132.

Wings on My Feet. Black Ulysses at the Wars. By Howard W. Odum. Indianapolis: Bobbs-Merrill Company, 1929. Pp. 309.

An Introduction to Social Research. By Howard W. Odum and Katharine Jocher. New York: Henry Holt and Company, 1929. Pp. 488.

Capital Punishment in North Carolina. By Lawrence A. Oxley and others. Raleigh, North Carolina: North Carolina State Board of Charities and Public Welfare, 1929. Special Bulletin No. 10. Pp. 173. Illustrated.

Folkbeliefs of the Southern Negro. By Newbell Niles Puckett. Chapel Hill: University of North Carolina Press, 1926. Pp. 644. Illustrated.

The North Carolina Chain Gang. By Jesse F. Steiner and Roy M. Brown. Chapel Hill: University of North Carolina Press, 1927. Pp. 194. Illustrated.

A State Movement in Railroad Development. The Story of North Carolina's First Effort to Establish an East and West Trunk Line Railroad. By Cecil K. Brown. Chapel Hill: University of North Carolina Press, 1928. Pp. 300.

Public Poor Relief in North Carolina. By Roy M. Brown. Chapel Hill: University of North Carolina Press, 1928. Pp. 184.

Phonophotography in Folk Music. American Negro Songs in New Notation. By Milton Metfessel with an introduction by Carl E. Seashore. Chapel Hill: University of North Carolina Press, 1928. Pp. 181. Illustrated.

William Gregg: Factory Master of the Old South. By Broadus Mitchell. Chapel Hill: University of North Carolina Press, 1928. Pp. 331.

Human Factors in Cotton Culture. By Rupert B. Vance. Chapel Hill: University of North Carolina Press, 1929. Pp. 346.

Constitutional Development in the South Atlantic States, 1776–1860. By Fletcher M. Green. Chapel Hill: University of North Carolina Press, 1930. Pp. 328.

The Negro Sings a New Heaven. By Mary A. Grissom. Chapel Hill: University of North Carolina Press, 1930. Pp. 101.

Income and Wages in the South. By Clarence Heer. Chapel Hill: University of North Carolina Press, 1930. Pp. 68.

A Social History of the Sea Islands. By Guion Griffis Johnson. Chapel Hill: University of

North Carolina Press, 1930. Pp. 227. Illustrated.

Folk Culture on St. Helena Island. By Guy B. Johnson. Chapel Hill: University of North Carolina Press, 1930. Pp. 183.

King Cotton Is Sick. By Claudius T. Murchison. Chapel Hill: University of North Carolina Press, 1930. Pp. 129.

An American Epoch. Southern Portraiture in the National Picture. By Howard W. Odum. New York: Henry Holt and Company, 1930. Pp. 379.

Some Southern Cotton Mill Workers and Their Villages. By Jennings J. Rhyne. Chapel Hill: University of North Carolina Press, 1930. Pp. 214.

Black Yeomanry. A Study of Negro Culture on St. Helena Island, South Carolina. By T. J. Woofter, Jr. New York: Henry Holt and Company, 1930. Pp. 290. Illustrated.

The State Highway System of North Carolina. By Cecil K. Brown. Chapel Hill: University of North Carolina Press, 1931. Pp. 260.

Textile Unionism and the South. By George S. Mitchell. Chapel Hill: University of North Carolina Press, 1931. Pp. 92.

Cold Blue Moon. Black Ulysses Afar Off. By Howard W. Odum. Indianapolis: Bobbs-Merrill Company, 1931. Pp. 278.

The Plight of Cigarette Tobacco. By T. J. Woofter Jr. Chapel Hill: University of North Carolina Press, 1931. Pp. 99.

Homicide in the United States. By H. C. Brearley. Chapel Hill: University of North Carolina Press, 1932. Pp. 249.

Report of the Tax Commission of North Carolina, 1932 to Governor O. Max Gardner. Part II by Clarence Heer, with the assistance of Hugh P. Brinton and Robin Hood.

Human Geography of the South. A Study in Regional Resources and Human Adequacy. By Rupert B. Vance. Chapel Hill: University of North Carolina Press, 1932. Pp. 596. Revised edition, 1935.

Administrative County Government in South Carolina. By Columbus Andrews. Addendum by Marion A. Wright. Chapel Hill: University of North Carolina Press, 1933. Pp. 245. (In cooperation with the Committee on Government.)

Lynching and the Law. By James Harmon Chadbourn. Chapel Hill: University of North Carolina Press, 1933. Pp. 221. (A cooperative study with the Southern Commission in the Study of Lynching and The Commission on Interracial Cooperation.)

Marriage. A Text for College Men and Women. By Ernest R. Groves. New York: Henry Holt and Company, 1933. Pp. 563.

The Elimination of Tax Conflicts. By Clarence Heer. Memorandum submitted to the Interstate Commission on Conflicting Taxation of the Interstate Assembly, 1933 (mimeographed).

Negro Child Welfare in North Carolina. By Wiley B. Sanders. Chapel Hill: University of North Carolina Press, 1933. Pp. 326.

Races and Ethnic Groups in American Life. By T. J. Woofter, Jr. New York: McGraw-Hill Book Company, 1933. Pp. 247.

Swing Your Mountain Gal. Sketches of Life in the Southern Highlands. By Rebecca Cushman. Boston: Houghton Mifflin Company. 1934. Pp. 150. Illustrated.

The American Family. By Ernest R. Groves. Philadelphia: J. B. Lippincott Company, 1934. Pp. 500.

Pro-Slavery Thought in the Old South. By William S. Jenkins. Chapel Hill: University of North Carolina Press, 1935. Pp. 381.

The South Looks at Its Past (A unit in the Southern Regional Study). By B. B. Kendrick and A. M. Arnett. Chapel Hill: University of North Carolina Press, 1935. Pp. 196.

The Regional Approach to National Social Planning. With Special Reference to a More Abundant South and Its Continuing Reintegration in the National Economy. By Howard W. Odum. Chapel Hill: University of North Carolina Press, and New York: The Foreign Policy Association, 1935. Pp. 31.

Regional Reconstruction: A Way Out for the South. By Rupert B. Vance. New York: Foreign Policy Association. and Chapel Hill: University of North Carolina Press, 1935. Pp. 31.

Southern Regions of the United States (Findings of the Southern Regional Study). By Howard W. Odum. Chapel Hill: University of North Carolina Press, 1936. Pp. 664. Maps, charts, tables. 2d printing, 1937; 3d printing, 1943.

Preface to Peasantry. A Tale of Two Black Belt Counties. By Arthur F. Raper. Chapel Hill: University of North Carolina Press, 1936. Pp. 423. Illustrated (A cooperative study with The Commission on Interracial Cooperation).

How the Other Half Is Housed. A Pictorial Record of Sub-Minimum Farm Housing in the South. By Rupert B. Vance. Chapel Hill: University of North Carolina Press, 1936. Pp. 16. (Southern Policy Papers No. 4.)

The South's Place in the Nation. By Rupert B. Vance. New York: Public Affairs Committee, 1936. Pp. 32. (Public Affairs Pamphlets No. 6.)

Southern Population and Social Planning. By T. J. Woofter, Jr. Chapel Hill: University of North Carolina Press, 1936. Pp. 10. (Southern Policy Papers No. 1.)

Part-Time Farming in the Southeast. By Harriet L. Herring and others. Works Progress Administration, Research Monograph IX. Washington: U. S. Government Printing Office, 1937. Pp. 317.

Manual for Southern Regions of the United States. By Lee M. Brooks and others. Chapel Hill: University of North Carolina Press, 1937. Pp. 194. Maps. (A Southern Regional Study publication.)

The American Woman. The Feminine Side of a Masculine Civilization. By Ernest R. Groves. New York: Greenberg, 1937. Pp. 438.

The Wasted Land. By Gerald W. Johnson. Chapel Hill: University of North Carolina Press, 1937. Pp. 110. (A Southern Regional Study Publication.)

Ante-Bellum North Carolina. A Social History. By Guion Griffis Johnson. Chapel Hill: University of North Carolina Press, 1937. Pp. 935.

What Is Regionalism? By Harry Estill Moore. Chapel Hill: University of North Carolina Press, 1937. (Southern Policy Papers No. 10.)

Juvenile Court Cases in North Carolina, 1929-1934. By Wiley B. Sanders and W. Curtis Ezell. Raleigh, North Carolina: State Board of Charities and Public Welfare, 1937. Pp. 53. 27 tables. (A cooperative study with the State Board of Charities and Public Welfare.)

Farmers Without Land. By Rupert B. Vance. New York: Public Affairs Committee, 1937. Pp. 32. (Public Affairs Pamphlets No. 12.)

American Regionalism. A Cultural-Historical Approach to National Integration. By Howard W. Odum and Harry Estill Moore. New York: Henry Holt and Company, 1938. Pp. 693. Maps, charts, tables.

Women's Life and Work in the Southern Colonies. By Julia Cherry Spruill. Chapel Hill: University of North Carolina Press, 1938. Pp. 426. Illustrated.

Research Memorandum on Population Redistribution Within the United States. By Rupert B. Vance. New York: Social Science Research Council, 1938. Pp. 134.

Mothers of the South. Portraiture of the White Farm Tenant Woman (a unit in the analysis of the Subregional Laboratory). By Margaret Jarman Hagood. Chapel Hill: University of North Carolina Press, 1939. Pp. 252.

Business Education in the Changing South (A unit in the Southern Regional Study). By Walter J. Matherly. Chapel Hill: University of North Carolina Press, 1939. Pp. 342.

Rural Relief and Recovery. By Rupert B. Vance. Washington: U. S. Government Printing Office, 1939. Pp. 32. (In cooperation with the Works Progress Administration—Social Problems No. 3.)

The Family and Its Social Functions. By Ernest R. Groves. Philadelphia: J. B. Lippincott Company, 1940. Pp. 631.

An Introduction to Sociology. Third edition, revised. By Ernest R. Groves and Harry Estill Moore. New York: Longmans, Green and Company, 1940. Pp. 737.

Southern Industry and Regional Development. By Harriet L. Herring. Chapel Hill: University of North Carolina Press, 1940. Pp. 103.

Paths to Maturity. Findings of the North Carolina Youth Survey, 1938-1940. By Gordon W. Lovejoy (Coordinator), 1940. Pp. 258. (Mimeographed.)

The Legal Status of the Negro. By Charles S. Mangum, Jr. Chapel Hill: University of North Carolina Press, 1940. Pp. 436.

American Democracy Anew. An Approach to the Understanding of Our Social Problems. By Howard W. Odum and others. New York: Henry Holt and Company, 1940. Pp. 614.

Statistics for Sociologists. By Margaret Jarman Hagood. New York: Reynal and Hitchcock, Inc., 1941. Pp. 934.

Alabama Past and Future. By Howard W. Odum and others. Chicago: Science Research Associates, 1941. Pp. 401. (The States at Work Series.)

Sharecroppers All. By Arthur F. Raper and Ira De A. Reid. Chapel Hill: University of North Carolina Press, 1941. Pp. 381.

Christianity and the Family. By Ernest R. Groves. New York: Macmillan Company, 1942. Pp. 229.

Sex Fulfillment in Marriage. By Ernest R. Groves and others. New York: Emerson Books, Inc., 1942. Pp. 319.

Race and Rumors of Race. Challenge to American Crisis. By Howard W. Odum. Chapel Hill: University of North Carolina Press, 1943. Pp. 245.

Conserving Marriage and the Family. A Realistic Discussion of the Divorce Problem. By Ernest R. Groves. New York: Macmillan Company, 1944. Pp. 138.

All These People. The Nation's Human Resources in the South. By Rupert B. Vance. With the statistical collaboration of Nadia Danilevsky. Chapel Hill: University of North Carolina Press, 1945. Pp. 488.

Understanding Society. An Introduction to the Study and Direction of American Society. By Howard W. Odum. New York: Macmillan Company. (MS in press.)

The Way of the South. A Biography of the Southern United States. By Howard W. Odum. New York: Macmillan Company. (MS in press.)

II. ARTICLES AND CHAPTERS

"Recent Literature on the Negro." By Guy B. Johnson. *Social Forces*, III (1925), 315–19.

"Newspaper Advertising and Negro Culture." By Guy B. Johnson. *Social Forces*, III (1925), 706–9.

"The County Unit as a Basis of Social Work and Public Welfare in North Carolina." By Howard W. Odum. *Proceedings of the National Conference in Social Work, 1926*, pp. 461–67.

"Swing Low, Sweet Chariot." By Howard W. Odum. *Country Gentleman*, XCI (March 1926), No. 3, pp. 18–19, 49–50.

"Workmen's Compensation in North and South Carolina." By William H. Wicker and Robert A. McPheeters. *North Carolina Law Review*, IV (1926), 47–84.

"Down That Lonesome Road." By Howard W. Odum. *Country Gentleman*, XCI (May 1926), No. 5, pp. 18–19, 79.

"Recent Contributions to the Study of American Negro Songs." By Guy B. Johnson. *Social Forces*, IV (1926), 788–92.

"Black and White at the Negro Fair." By Guy B. Johnson. *Opportunity*, IV (1926), 223–25.

"The Beginnings of Industrial Social Work." By Harriet L. Herring. *Social Forces*, V (1926–27), 317–24; 502–7.

"Governmental Responsibility for Social Work." By Howard W. Odum. *Ohio Welfare Bulletin* (December 1926).

"The Monroe Doctrine and the Panama Congress." By Guion Griffis Johnson. *Studies in Hispanic-American History.* Edited by William Whatley Pierson, Jr. *The James Sprunt Historical Studies*, XIX (1927), 53–73.

"Crime in the Superior Courts of North Carolina." By Francis S. Wilder. *Social Forces*, V (1927), 423–27.

"John Henry." By Guy B. Johnson. *Southern Workman*, LVI (1927), 158–60.

"Double Meaning in the Popular Negro Blues." By Guy B. Johnson. *Journal of Abnormal and Social Psychology*, XXII (1927), 12–20.

"Research and Study in Public Welfare." By Howard W. Odum. *University of Virginia Public Welfare and Citizenship*, September, 1927.

"Labor Day at Henderson." By Harriet L. Herring. *Baltimore Evening Sun*, September 5, 1927.

"The Musical Talent of the Negro." By Guy B. Johnson. *Southern Workman*, LVI (1927), 439–44.

"12 Cents, the Troops, and the Union." By Harriet L. Herring. *Midmonthly Survey*, LIX (1927), 199–202.

"John Henry, A Negro Legend." By Guy B. Johnson. *Ebony and Topaz*, edited by Charles S. Johnson (New York: Opportunity Press, December, 1927), pp. 47–51.

"John Henry." By Guy B. Johnson. *Southern Workman*, LVI (1927), 158–60.

"Double Meaning in the Popular Negro Blues." By Guy B. Johnson. *Journal of Abnormal and Social Psychology*, XXII (1927), 12–20.

"John Henry." By Guy B. Johnson. A feature story written for the Southern Commission on Interracial Cooperation for distribution in southern white papers in the spring of 1928. Also sent to representative Negro papers in the spring of 1928.

"Wagram: Blood Relationship and Tradition as Organizing Forces." By Harriet L. Herring. Chapter III in *The American Community in Action.* By Jesse F. Steiner. New York: Henry Holt and Company, 1928.

"Eno Mills: An Economically Saturated Community." By Guy B. Johnson. Chapter II in *The American Community in Action.* By Jesse F. Steiner. New York: Henry Holt and Company, 1928.

"Human Factors in Social Research and Social Work." By Howard W. Odum. *Proceedings, New Jersey Conference of Social Work,* 1928.

"Long Creed: Neighborhood Rivalry and School Consolidation." By Arthur F. Raper. Chapter XII in *The American Community in Action.* By Jesse F. Steiner. New York: Henry Holt and Company, 1928.

"Ferrum: Factions and Social Complexes in a Cotton Mill Town." By J. J. Rhyne. Chapter VI in *The American Community in Action.* By Jesse F. Steiner. New York: Henry Holt and Company, 1928.

"The Blues, Negro Sorrow Songs." By Guy B. Johnson. *Carolina Magazine,* LVIII (February, 1928) pp. 3–13.

'A Stock-Taking Conference on the Negro." By Guy B. Johnson. *Social Forces,* VI (1928), 445–47.

"Methods of Research in Studying the Family." By Katharine Jocher. *Family,* IX (1928), 80–85.

"Decisions and Rulings—North Carolina." By Clarence Heer. *Bulletin of the National Tax Association* (June, December, 1928; November, 1929).

"Tracing the Development of Welfare Work in the North Carolina Textile Industry." By Harriet L. Herring. *Social Forces,* VI (1928), 591–98.

"The Negro and the Farm Crisis." By T. J. Woofter, Jr. *Social Forces,* VI (1928), 615–20.

"How New Is the South in Social Work?" By Howard W. Odum. *Survey,* LX (1928), 329–30.

"The Family in 1927." By Ernest R. Groves. *American Journal of Sociology,* XXXIV (1928), 150–56.

"The Ante-Bellum Town in North Carolina." By Guion Griffis Johnson. *North Carolina Historical Review,* V (1928), 372–89.

"The Negro and Musical Talent." By Guy B. Johnson. *Music Supervisors Journal,* XV (1928), 81, 83, 96.

"Working Mothers and Their Children." By Harriet L. Herring. *Family,* IX (1928), 234–36.

"The Case Method in Social Research." By Katharine Jocher. *Social Forces,* VII (1928), 203–11.

"Is the Negro in America Accommodated or Assimilated?" By Guy B. Johnson. *Living Stone,* XXIV (Livingstone College, December, 1928), No. 11, pp. 5–6.

"The Taxation of Public Service Corporations." By Clarence Heer. *Report of the Tax Commission, 1928* Raleigh, North Carolina, 1929, p. 223.

"Recreational and Cultural Activities in the Ante-Bellum Town of North Carolina." By Guion Griffis Johnson. *North Carolina Historical Review,* VI (1929), 17–37.

"Race in Politics: An Opportunity for Original Research." By T. J. Woofter, Jr. *Social Forces,* VII (1929), 435–38.

"Cycles of Cotton Mill Criticism." By Harriet L. Herring. *South Atlantic Quarterly,* XXVIII (1929), 113–25.

"Social Characteristics of Ante-Bellum North Carolina." By Guion Griffis Johnson. *North Carolina Historical Review,* VI (1929), 140–57.

"History of the Family for 1928." By Ernest R. Groves. *American Journal of Sociology,* XXXIV (1929), 1099–1107.

"Legal and Administrative Restrictions Affecting the Rights of Married Women to Work." By Mary Phlegar Smith. *Annals of the American Academy of Political and Social Science,* CXLIII (1929), 255–64.

"Cotton Culture and Social Life and Institutions of the South." By Rupert B. Vance. *Publications of the American Sociological Society,* XXIII (1929), 51–59.

"Regional Portraiture." By Howard W. Odum. *Saturday Review of Literature,* VI (July 27, 1929), 1–2.

"Black Ulysses Goes to War." By Howard W. Odum. *American Mercury,* XVII (1929), 385–400.

"The Rural Tax Problem." By Clarence Heer. *Social Forces,* VIII (1929), 109–18.

"Black Ulysses in Camp." By Howard W. Odum. *American Mercury,* XVIII (1929), 47–59.

"The Public Dollar." By Clarence Heer. *Bulletin of the National Tax Association,* October, 1929.

"The Metamorphosis of the Docile Worker." By Harriet L. Herring. *Greensboro Daily News, et al.,* October 27, 1929.

"Peace or War in Southern Textiles." By Harriet L. Herring *Greensboro Daily News, et. al.,* November 3, 1929.

"Homicide in South Carolina: A Regional Study." By H. C. Brearley. *Social Forces,* VIII (1929), 218–21.

"The Concept of the Region." By Rupert B. Vance. *Social Forces,* VIII (1929), 208–18.

"Taxation of Public Service Corporations." By Clarence Heer. *Report of the Tax Commission to Governor O. Max Gardner,* State of North Carolina, 1930, pp. 171–204.

"The Southern Industrial Problem, as the Social Worker Sees It." By Harriet L. Herring. *Proceedings of The National Conference of Social Work, 1930,* pp. 309–14.

"Cotton and Contrabands." By Guion Griffis Johnson. Chapter II in *Black Yeomanry.* By T. J. Woofter, Jr. New York: Henry Holt and Company, 1930.

"Folk Values in Recent Literature on the Negro." By Guy B. Johnson. *Folk-Say,* II (1930), 359–72.

"St Helena Songs and Stories." By Guy B. Johnson. Chapter III in *Black Yeomanry.* By T. J. Woofter, Jr. New York: Henry Holt and Company, 1930.

"The Speech of the Negro." By Guy B. Johnson. *Folk-Say,* II (1930), 346–58.

"Changing Regions of the American South." By Rupert B. Vance. *Proceedings,* Southern Educational Conference, 1930.

"John Henry, Man or Myth?" By Guy B. Johnson. Feature story for the National Everyweek Syndicate, published in various Sunday papers in January and February, 1930.

"King Cotton Is Sick." By Claudius T. Murchison. *Virginia Quarterly Review,* VI (1930), 48–64.

"Agricultural Credit and the Negro Farmer." By Roland B. Eutsler. *Social Forces,* VIII (1930), 416–25, 565–73.

"Toward Preliminary Social Analysis: I. The Southern Mill System Faces a New Issue." By Harriet L. Herring. *Social Forces,* VIII (1930), 350–59.

"St. Helena Gullah Tales." By Guy B. Johnson. *The Inlander,* X (1930), No. 3, pp. 6–9.

"Borough Representation in North Carolina." By Mary Phlegar Smith. *North Carolina Historical Review,* VII (1930), 177–89.

"The Family." By Ernest R. Groves. *American Journal of Sociology,* XXXV (1930), 1017–26.

"The New Mobility and the Coastal Island." By Lee M. Brooks. *Social Forces,* IX (1930), 99–103.

"The Southern Labor Supply." By Rupert B. Vance. *University of North Carolina Extension Bulletin,* X (1930), No. 2, pp. 16–21.

"The Negro and Homicide." By H. C. Brearley. *Social Forces,* IX (1930), 247–53.

"The Social Problem of Labor Organization Casualties." By Harriet L. Herring. *Social Forces,* IX (1930), 267–73.

"A Karl Marx for Hill Billies: Portrait of a Southern Leader." By Rupert B. Vance. *Social Forces,* XI (1930), 180–90.

"Trends in Family Life in the United States." By Ernest R. Groves. *Stockholm Journal,* XXXII (1931), 993–1002.

"The Sociological Viewpoint in Education for Racial Adjustment." By Howard W. Odum. *Education and Racial Adjustment.* Report of Peabody Conference on Dual Education in the South (November, 1931), pp. 56–59.

"The Frontier: Cultural and Geographical Aspects." By Rupert B. Vance. *Encyclopaedia of the Social Sciences,* VI (1931), 503–5.

"Human Aspects of the Geography of the American South." By Rupert B. Vance. *University of North Carolina Extension Bulletin,* X (1931), 12–24.

"Early Industrial Development in the South." By Harriet L. Herring. *Annals of the American Academy of Political and Social Science,* CLIII (1931), 1–10.

"The North Carolina State and Local Tax System as of January 1, 1931." By Clarence Heer. *Federal and State Tax Systems.* Second edition, January 1, 1931. The Tax Research Foundation.

"A Summary of Negro Scores on the Seashore Music Talent Tests." By Guy B. Johnson. *Journal of Comparative Psychology,* XI (1931), 383–93.

"The Negro Spiritual: A Problem in Anthropology." By Guy B. Johnson. *American Anthropologist,* XXXIII (1931), 157–71.

"History of the Family for 1930." By Ernest R. Groves. *American Journal of Sociology,* XXXVI (1931), 993–1001.

"Problems of Industrial Adjustment." By Harriet L. Herring. Proceedings of the Third

Southern Conference on Education. *University of North Carolina Extension Bulletin*, X, No. 9 (May, 1931).

"Changing Problems of Race Adjustment." By Guy B. Johnson. Proceedings of the Third Southern Conference on Education. *University of North Carolina Extension Bulletin*, X, No. 9 (May, 1931).

"Folk and Regional Conflict as a Field of Sociological Study." By Howard W. Odum. *Publications of the American Sociological Society*, XXV (1931), 1–17.

"Courtship and Marriage Customs in Ante-Bellum North Carolina." By Guion Griffis Johnson. *North Carolina Historical Review*, VIII (1931), 384–402.

"Social Development in the Mill Village: A Challenge to the Mill Welfare Worker." By Harriet L. Herring. *Social Forces*, X (1931), 264–71.

"The Epic of Brown America." By Howard W. Odum. *Yale Review*, XXI (1931), 419–21.

"Notes on the Study of Regional and Folk Society." By Howard W. Odum. *Social Forces*, X (1931), 164–75.

"What Is the Negro Rate of Increase?" By T. J. Woofter, Jr. *Journal of the American Statistical Association*, XXVI (1931), 461–62.

"Lynchings, Fears, and Folkways." By Howard W. Odum. *Nation*, CXXXIII (1931), 719.

"Trends in Public Welfare." By Howard W. Odum. *Proceedings of the National Conference of Social Work, 1931*, pp. 441–50.

"Parent Education." By Ernest R. Groves. *Annals of the American Academy of Political and Social Science*, CLX (1932), 216–22.

"History of the Family for 1931." By Ernest R. Groves. *America Journal of Sociology*, XXXVII (1932), 942–48.

"Interpolation for Populations Whose Rate of Increase Is Declining." By T. J. Woofter, Jr. *Journal of the American Statistical Association*, XXVII (1932), 180–82.

"Comparative Costs of County Government in the South. By Clarence Heer. Social Forces, XI, (1932), 263–68.

"A Challenge to the Social Sciences." By Katharine Jocher. *Social Forces*, XI (1932), 303–5.

"Taxation and Public Finance." By Clarence Heer. Chapter XXVI in Volume II of *Recent Social Trends in the United States*. Report of the President's Research Committee on Social Trends. 2 vols. New York: McGraw-Hill Book Company, 1933.

"Negro-White Relationships." By Guy B. Johnson. Pp. 192–203, of Chapter X in "Race Prejudice and Discrimination," *Races and Ethnic Groups*. By T. J. Woofter, Jr. New York: McGraw-Hill Book Company, 1933.

"Public Welfare Activities." By Howard W. Odum. Chapter XXIV in Volume II of *Recent Social Trends in the United States*. Report of the President's Research Committee on Social Trends. 2 vols. New York: McGraw-Hill Book Company, 1933.

"The Status of Racial and Ethnic Groups." By T. J. Woofter, Jr. Chapter XI in Volume I of *Recent Social Trends in the United States*. Report of the President's Research Committee on Social Trends. 2 vols. New York: McGraw-Hill Book Company, 1933.

"Revival Movements in Ante-Bellum North Carolina." By Guion Griffis Johnson. *North Carolina Historical Review*, X (1933), 21–43.

"Aycock of North Carolina." By Rupert B. Vance. *Southwest Review*, XVIII (1933), 288–306.

"New Frontiers of Leadership in Public Affairs." By Howard W. Odum. *Public Opinion and the Press*. Atlanta: Emory University Press, 1933, pp. 52–71.

"Regionalism vs. Sectionalism in the South's Place in the National Economy." By Howard W. Odum. *Social Forces*, XII (1933) 338–54.

"What of Submarginal Areas in Regional Planning?" By Rupert B. Vance. *Social Forces*, XII (1933), 315–29.

"A Reclassification of Urban-Rural Population." By T. J. Woofter, Jr. and Edith Webb. *Social Forces*, XI (1933), 348–51.

"The Tennessee Valley Regional Plan." By T. J. Woofter, Jr. *Social Forces*, XII (1933), 329–38.

"The Camp Meeting in Ante-Bellum North Carolina." By Guion Griffis Johnson. *North Carolina Historical Review*, X (1933), 95–110.

"History of the Family for 1932." By Ernest R. Groves. *American Journal of Sociology*, XXXVIII (1933), 873–79.

"Notes on Recent Trends in the Application of the Social Sciences." By Howard W. Odum. *Social Forces*, XI (1933), 477–88.

"Common Errors in Sampling." By T. J. Woofter, Jr. *Social Forces*, XI (1933), 521–25.

"The Interstate Commission on Conflicting Taxation." By Clarence Heer. *Tax Magazine*, XI (1933), 218–20.

"Industrial Relations in the South and the NIRA." By Harriet L. Herring. *Social Forces*, XII (1933), 124–31.

"The Negro and the Depression in North Carolina." By Guy B. Johnson. *Social Forces*, XII (1933), 103–15.

"Is There Too Much Food?" By Emily White Stevens. *New Republic*, LXXVI (1933), 297.

"Tax Injunctions and Suits to Recover Taxes Paid Under Protest in North Carolina." By Edwin M. Perkins. *North Carolina Law Review*, XII (1933), 20–42.

"Changes in American Life." By Ernest R. Groves. *New Era*, XV, (London, 1934), 95–98.

"Domestic Adjustment and Character." By Ernest R. Groves. *Character*, I (1934), 1.

"The Industrial Worker." By Harriet L. Herring. Chapter XVII in *Culture in the South*. A Symposium edited by W. T. Couch. Chapel Hill: University of North Carolina Press, 1934.

"John Henry." By Guy B. Johnson. Pp. 363–65 in *Negro Anthology*, made by Nancy Cunard, 1931–1933. London: Nancy Cunard at Wishart and Company, 1934.

"Negro Folk Songs." By Guy B. Johnson. Chapter XXV in *Culture in the South*. A Symposium edited by W. T. Couch. Chapel Hill: University of North Carolina Press, 1934.

"The Profile of Southern Culture." By Rupert B. Vance. Chapter II in *Culture in the South*. A Symposium edited by W. T. Couch. Chapel Hill: University of North Carolina Press, 1934.

"Folk Rationalizations in the 'Unwritten Law'." By Rupert B. Vance and Waller Wynne, Jr. *American Journal of Sociology*, XXXIX (1934), 483–92.

"Squatters, New Style." By Harriet L. Herring. *Baltimore Evening Sun*, January 23, 1934.

"The Sales Tax and Transactions in Interstate Commerce." By Edwin M. Perkins. *North Carolina Law Review*, XII (1934), 99–119.

"Severance Taxes in Alabama." By Herschal L. Macon. *Tax Magazine*, March and April, 1934.

"An Approach to Race Adjustment." By Howard W. Odum. *Woman's Press*, (April, 1934), 96–97.

"Braxton Bragg Comer: Alabama's Most Audacious." By Rupert B. Vance. *Southwest Review*, XIX (1934), 244–64.

"Sociology in 1934." By Ernest R. Groves. *Education*, LIV (1934), 569.

"Social Planning and the New Deal." By Howard W. Odum. *News and Observer* (Raleigh, North Carolina), May 20, 1934.

"The Power of Congress to Levy Taxes for Distribution to the States." By Edwin M. Perkins. *North Carolina Law Review*, XII (1934), 326–49.

"Human Factors in the South's Agricultural Readjustment." By Rupert B. Vance. *Law and Contemporary Problems*, I (1934), 259–74.

"Marriage and Modern Life." By Ernest R. Groves. *Bulletin of the State University of Iowa, Child Welfare Pamphlets,* No. XXXVI (1934), 1–9.

"The Share Croppers' Union in Alabama." By John Beecher. *Social Forces*, XIII (1934), 124–32.

"The Displaced Tenant Farm Family in North Carolina." Gordon W. Blackwell. *Social Forces*, XIII (1934), 65–73.

"Some Costs of Economy in Schools." By Harriet L. Herring. *Social Forces*, XIII (1934), 85–91.

"A Bibliography on Southern Labor." By Robin Hood. *Social Forces*, XIII (1934), 133–37.

"Does the South Owe the Negro a New Deal?" By Guy B. Johnson. *Social Forces*, XIII (1934), 100–03.

"The Case for Regional-National Planning." By Howard W. Odum. *Social Forces*, XIII (1934), 6–23.

"Some Factors in the Development of Negro Social Institutions in the United States." By Guy B. Johnson. *American Journal of Sociology*, XL (1934), 329–37.

"Regional Planning and Social Trends in the South." By Rupert B. Vance. *Proceedings*, Southeastern Library Association, Memphis, Tennessee, 1935.

"Planning the Southern Economy." By Rupert B. Vance. *Southwest Review*, XX (1935), 111–23.

"Sex Adjustment of College Men and Women." By Ernest R. Groves. *Journal of Educational Sociology*, VIII (1935), 353–60.

"Taxation and the Schools. An Analysis of the Effects of Recent Changes in the Methods of Financing Public Schools in North Carolina, together with a Survey of Various Sources of State Revenue." By Clarence Heer. University of North Carolina *News Letter*, February 6, 1935.

"Isolation or Integration?" By Guy B. Johnson. *Opportunity*, XIII (1935), 89–90.

"A Sociological Approach to National Social Planning. A Syllabus." By Howard W. Odum. *Sociology and Social Research*, XIX (1935), 303–13.

"Education, Segregation, and Race Relations." By Guy B. Johnson. *Quarterly Review of Higher Education Among Negroes*, III (1935), 89–94.

"State Action Under the Federal Estate Tax Credit Clause." By Edwin M. Perkins. *North Carolina Law Review*, XIII (1935), 271–90.

"Adaptations of Family Life." By Ernest R. Groves. *American Journal of Sociology*, XL (1935), 772–79.

"Migratory Divorces." By Ernest R. Groves. *Law and Contemporary Problems*, II (1935), 293–301.

"Critical Appraisal of Tax Statutes, in a Survey of Statutory Changes in North Carolina in 1935." By Edwin M. Perkins. *North Carolina Law Review*, XIII (1935), 355–499, tax statutes at 405–435.

"Orderly Transitional Democracy." By Howard W. Odum. *Annals of the American Academy of Political and Social Science*, CLXXX (1935), 31–39.

"Is Agrarianism for Farmers?" By Rupert B. Vance. *Southern Review*, I (1935), 42–57.

"Implications of the Concepts 'Region' and 'Regional Planning'." By Rupert B. Vance. *Publications of the American Sociological Society*, XXIX (1935), 85–93.

"Some Methods of Reducing Race Prejudice in the South." By Guy B. Johnson. *Southern Workman*, LXIV (1935), 272–78.

"The Natural Increase of the Rural Non-Farm Population." By T. J. Woofter, Jr. *Milbank Memorial Fund Quarterly*, XIII (1935), 311–19.

"Southern Population and Social Planning." By T. J. Woofter, Jr. *Social Forces*, XIV (1935), 16–22.

"Folk Implications in Pareto's Sociology." By Harry Estill Moore and Bernice Milburn Moore. *Social Forces*, XIV (1935), 293–300.

"The Influence of State Competition in the Adoption of Regressive Taxes: The North Carolina Sales Tax." By Edwin M. Perkins. *North Carolina Law Review*, XIV (1935), 53–73.

"Promise and Prospect of the South: A Test of American Regionalism." By Howard W. Odum. *Proceedings*, Eighth Annual Session of the Southern Political Science Association, December 26, 1935.

"Alabama's Place in the South." By Howard W. Odum. *Proceedings*, Institute of Public Affairs, University of Alabama, 1936.

"Cotton and Diversification." By Howard W. Odum. *Problems of the Cotton Economy*. *Proceedings*, Southern Social Science Research Conference Held in New Orleans, March 8, 1935. Section III, pp. 50–71. Dallas, Texas: Arnold Foundation, 1936.

"The Cotton Belt on the Move." By Rupert B. Vance. *The South Today*, Southern Newspaper Syndicate Release to the Press, 1936.

"Cotton and Tenancy." By Rupert B. Vance. *Problems of the Cotton Economy*. *Proceedings*, Southern Social Science Research Conference Held in New Orleans, March 8, 1935. Section II, pp. 18–39. Dallas, Texas: Arnold Foundation, 1936.

"The Old Cotton Belt." By Rupert B. Vance. Chapter III, pp. 124–63, *Migration and Economic Opportunity*. Edited by Carter Goodrich. Philadelphia: University of Pennsylvania Press, 1936.

"The TVA and the Southern Utilities." By Rupert B. Vance. *The South Today*, Southern Newspaper Syndicate Release to the Press, January 12, 1936.

"Testing Grounds for Social Planning. The Promise of the South, a Test of American Regionalism." By Howard W. Odum. *Plan Age*, II (1936), No. 2, pp. 1–26.

"Realistic Premises for Regional Planning Objectives." By Howard W. Odum. *Plan Age*, II (1936), No. 3, pp. 7–21.

"Changing Economy of the Southeast." By Rupert B. Vance. *Occupations*, XIV (1936), 309–14.

"The Economic Future in the Old Cotton Belt." By Rupert B. Vance. *Southern Workman*, LXV (1936), 85–92.

"Social Security and Public Welfare in the 30's." By Howard W. Odum. *Minutes and Materials*, Second Annual Institute, North Carolina State Employment Service and National Reemployment Service, pp. 61–64. Chapel Hill: University of North Carolina, June 15–20, 1936. (Mimeographed).

"Regional Planning with Reference to the Southeast." By Rupert B. Vance. *Southern Economic Journal*, III (1936), 55–65.

"Despite Potentialities the South Is an Area of Scarcity Instead of a Land of Abundance." By Howard W. Odum. In the series, *The South Today*. Published in twelve southern newspapers through the Southern Newspaper Syndicate, August, 1936.

"Planning for the State's Public Welfare." By Howard W. Odum. *Public Welfare News Letter* (Raleigh, North Carolina), October, 1936.

"Six Americas in Search of a Faith." By Howard W. Odum. *Independent Woman*, XV (1936), 309, 334–36.

"Little Man, What Now?" By Rupert B. Vance. *Southern Review*, I (1936), 560–67.

"The Advisory Commission of Cuba." By David A. Lockmiller. *Hispanic American Historical Review*, XVII (1937), 1–29.

"Hazards of Modern Marriage." By Ernest R. Groves. *Duke Bar Association Journal*, V (1937), No. 2, pp. 66–74.

"Problems of Reintegration in Agrarian Life." By Harry E. Moore and Bernice M. Moore. *Social Forces*, XV (1937), 384–90.

"Some Contributions of Psychology to Social Case Work." By Margaret Jarman Hagood. *Social Forces*, XV (1937), 512–19.

"These Southern Regions." By Howard W. Odum. *Alabama School Journal*, LIV (1937), No. 9.

"Notes on the Technicways in Contemporary Society." By Howard W. Odum. *American Sociological Review*, II (1937), 336–46.

"From Sections to Regions." By Howard W. Odum. *Saturday Review of Literature*, XVI (June 12, 1937), No. 7, p. 5.

"Negro Racial Movements and Leadership in the United States." By Guy B. Johnson. *American Journal of Sociology*, XLIII (1937), 57–71.

"A New Realism of the People." By Howard W. Odum. *Education and Human Relations*. Report of the Second Southern Area Institute of Human Relations, Chapel Hill, North Carolina, July, 1937.

"Industrial Relations and the Social and Economic Life of the South." By Howard W. Odum. *New Factors in Industrial Relations*

(A summary of the Eighteenth Annual Industrial Conference, Blue Ridge, North Carolina, July 15–17, 1937), pp. 67–74.

"The South—Population Seedbed of the Nation." By Rupert B. Vance. *The South Today*. Southern Newspaper Syndicate Release to the Press, August 15, 1937.

"The Family: Old Functions and New." By Bernice Milburn Moore. *Texas Parent-Teacher Magazine*, September, 1937.

"The Human Aspects of Chemurgy." By Howard W. Odum. *Farm Chemurgic Journal*, I (1937), 60–71.

"Teaching Marriage at the University of North Carolina." By Ernest R. Groves. *Social Forces*, XVI (1937), 87–96.

"Divorce." By Ernest R. Groves. *1938 Britannica Book of the Year*, p. 213.

"History of the Family." By Ernest R. Groves. *Dictionary of American History, 1938*, pp. 241–43.

"The Promise of Graduate and Research Work in the South." By Howard W. Odum. *Inauguration and Symposium at Vanderbilt University*, Nashville, Tennessee, 1938, pp. 99–108.

"What About the Federal Equalization Fund for Education?" By Howard W. Odum. *Southern Newspaper Syndicate*, 1938.

"Cultural Diversity on American Life." By Rupert B. Vance (as member of the Technical Committee on Population Problems of the National Resources Committee). *Problems of a Changing Population*. Washington: National Resources Committee, 1938.

"The Regional Distribution of Economic Opportunity." By Rupert B. Vance (as member of the Technical Committee on Population Problems of the National Resources Committee). *Problems of a Changing Population*. Washington: National Resources Committee, 1938.

"Rural Distress and Relief in the Southeast." Testimony before a Special Committee of the United States Senate, March 7, 1938. By Rupert B. Vance. *Hearings Before a Special Committee to Investigate Unemployment and Relief*. United States Senate, 75th Congress, Vol. II, pp. 1011–1016, 1556–1560. Washington: Government Printing Office, 1938.

"The Psychic Side of Marital Maladjustment." By Ernest R. Groves. *Social Forces*, XVI (1938), 396-400.

"Present Status and Future Trends in the Southern White Family." By Bernice Milburn Moore. *Social Forces*, XVI (1938), 406–10.

"American Regionalism. The Implications and Meanings of Regionalism." By Howard W. Odum. *Progressive Education*, XV (1938), 229–39.

"The Clement Attachment: An Episode of Reconstruction Industrial History." By Harriet L. Herring. *Journal of Southern History*, IV (1938), 185–98.

"Rebels and Agrarians All: Studies in One-Party Politics." By Rupert B. Vance. *Southern Review*, IV (1938), 26–44.

"New Sources of Vitality for the People." By Howard W. Odum. *Journal of The American Dietetic Association*, XIV (1938), 417–23.

"Rural Relief in the South." By Rupert B. Vance. *The South Today*, Southern Newspaper Syndicate Release to the Press, June 5, 1938.

"New Standards for Family Living." By Ernest R. Groves. *National Parent-Teacher Magazine*, XXXIII (1938), 13–15.

"The State of Sociology in the United States and Its Prospect in the South." By Howard W. Odum. *Social Forces*, XVII (1938), 8–14.

"Some Occupational Trends in the South." By Kenneth Evans. *Social Forces*, XVII (1938), 184–90.

"Implications of Topological and Field Theoretical Psychology for Sociology." By Margaret Jarman Hagood. *Social Forces*, XVII (1938), 267–71.

"Poor Whites of the South." By Mildred Rutherford Mell. *Social Forces*, XVII (1938), 153–67.

"Marriage and Divorce in 1939." By Ernest R. Groves. *1939 Britannica Book of the Year*, pp. 414–15.

"Patterns of Race Conflict." By Guy B. Johnson. Chapter V in *Race Relations and the Race Problem*. Edited by Edgar T. Thompson. Durham: Duke University Press, 1939.

"Racial Competition for the Land." By Rupert B. Vance. Chapter IV in *Race Relations and the Race Problem*. Edited by Edgar T. Thompson. Durham: Duke University Press, 1939.

"What Is the Answer?" By Howard W. Odum. *Carolina Magazine*, LXVIII (1939), No. 5, pp. 5–8.

"The South as Testing Ground for the Regional Approach to Public Health." By Howard W. Odum. *Journal of the American Medical Asso-ciation*, Spring, 1939. Also *Proceedings*, Annual Congress on Medical Education and Licensure, Chicago, February 13 and 14, 1939, pp. 14–17.

"An Examination of Regional Differentials in Fertility by Analysis of Variance and Covariance. By Margaret Jarman Hagood and Mary Alice Eaton. *Social Forces*, XVII (1939), 495–502.

"A State Experiment in Contraception as a Public Health Service." By Margaret Jarman Hagood. *Journal of Contraception*, IV (1939), 103–06, 118.

"The Position of the Negro in the American Social Order in 1950." By Howard W. Odum. *Journal of Negro Education*, VIII (1939), 587–94.

"Of a Closer Cooperation Between the Physical and the Social Sciences." By Howard W. Odum. *Harvard Alumni Bulletin*, XLI (1939), 1124–28.

"Personality in a White-Indian-Negro Community." By Guy B. Johnson. *American Sociological Review*, IV (1939), 516–23.

Discussion of B. O. Williams, "The Impact of Mechanization of Agriculture on the Farm Population of the South." By Margaret Jarman Hagood. *Rural Sociology*, IV (1939), 313–14.

"Of New Social Frontiers in Contemporary Society." By Howard W. Odum. *Frontiers of Democracy*, VI (1939), No. 47, pp. 15–17.

"The Trend of the Interregional Migration of Talent: The Southeast, 1899–1936. By Harold Loran Geisert. *Social Forces*, XVIII (1939), 41–47.

"The Outside Employer in the Southern Industrial Pattern." By Harriet L. Herring. *Social Forces*, XVIII (1939), 115–26.

"Biology in Sociology." By Hope Tisdale. *Social Forces*, XVIII (1939), 29–40.

"Can Human Nature Be Changed"; "Individualism, Democracy and Social Control." By Rupert B. Vance. Pp. 12–18, 28–32 in *Standards of Value for Program Planning and Building*. Proceedings of school for Washington Staff of the Bureau of Agricultural Economics, October, 1939. Washington: United States Department of Agriculture, October, 1939. (Mimeographed.)

"The Next Generation Marries." By Donald S. Klaiss. Pp. 49–64 in *Tomorrow's Children*. Proceedings of the Southern Conference on Tomorrow's Children. November, 1939. New

York: Birth Control Federation of America, 1939.

"Regional Development and Governmental Policy." By Howard W. Odum. *Annals of the American Academy of Political and Social Science*, CCVI (1939), 133–41.

"A Desirable Policy for the Conservation and Development of the South's Human Resources." By Rupert B. Vance. Pp. 35–48 in *Tomorrow's Children*. Proceedings of the Southern Conference on Tomorrow's Children. November, 1939. New York: Birth Control Federation of America, 1939.

"Negro Leadership and Strategy." By Guy B. Johnson. *Virginia State College Gazette*, XLV (1939), No. 3, pp. 10–16.

"The Geography of Distinction: The Nation and Its Regions, 1790–1927." By Rupert B. Vance. *Social Forces*, XVIII (1939), 168–79.

"Human and Material Resources of the South." By Rupert B. Vance. *Journal of the Florida Educational Association*, XVII (1939), 7–8, 28–29.

"Marriage and Divorce in 1940." By Ernest R. Groves. *1940 Britannica Book of the Year*, pp. 430–31.

"Probable Trend of Migration from the Southeast." By Rupert B. Vance. Statement and Testimony at the Montgomery, Alabama, *Hearings Before the Select Committee to Investigate the Interstate Migration of Destitute Citizens*. House of Representatives, 76th Congress, Third Session, Part 2, pp. 406–422. Washington: Government Printing Office, 1940.

"An Index Number for Measuring Rural Farm Welfare." By Mary Alice Eaton. *Alpha Kappa Delta Quarterly*, IX (1940), No. 2, 14–17.

"Interregional Relations." By Elwyn Mauck. *Annals of the American Academy of Political and Social Science*, CCVII (1940), 124–30.

"On the Southern Frontier" (editorial). By Howard W. Odum. *Southern Frontier*, I (1940), 1, 4.

"Population and the Pattern of Unemployment, 1930–1937." By Rupert B. Vance and Nadia Danilevsky. *Milbank Memorial Fund Quarterly*, XVIII (1940), 27–43.

"How Can the South's Population Find Gainful Employment?" By Rupert B. Vance. *Journal of Farm Economics*, XXII (1940), 198–206.

"Technicways in American Civilization." By Alice Davis. *Social Forces*, XVIII (1940), 317–30.

"The Disposition of Income in Relation to Levels of Living in the South." By Rupert B. Vance. *Proceedings of the Sixth Annual Southern Social Science Research Conference, March 7–9, 1940.* (Mimeographed.)

"Is the South the Nation's Number One Problem?" By Howard W. Odum. *Scholastic*, XXXVI (1940), No. 8, pp. 8–9, 16.

"How Did the United States Come About." By Ernest R. Groves. *Living*, II (1940), 46–48.

"The Program of Marriage Instruction at the University of North Carolina." By Donald S. Klaiss. *Social Forces*, XVIII (1940), 536–39.

"Selling Mill Houses to Employees." By Harriet L. Herring. *Textile World*, XC (1940), No. 5, 78–79; No. 6, 54–55, 114–15.

"Tennessee's War of the Roses." By Rupert B. Vance. *Virginia Quarterly Review*, XVI (1940), 413–24.

"How Did the United States Come About?" By Ernest R. Groves. *National Parent-Teacher*, XXXV (1940), 12–15.

"Education in the Secondary Schools of the South." By Howard W. Odum. *Southern Association Quarterly*, IV (1940), 523–29.

"Prevenception, the Health Department and the Practicing Physician." By Donald S. Klaiss and William Richardson, M.D. *North Carolina Medical Journal*, I (1940), 468–71.

"Three-fold Task Awaits South's Development" (editorial). By Howard W. Odum. *Southern Frontier*, I (1940), No. 10, pp. 1, 4.

"Population and the Pattern of Unemployment in the Southeast, 1930–1937." By Rupert B. Vance and Nadia Danilevsky. *Southern Economic Journal*, VII (1940), 187–203.

"A Decade of Marriage Counseling." By Ernest R. Groves. *Annals of the American Academy of Political and Social Science*, CCXII (1940), 72–80.

"Time and the Technicways. An Experiment in Definition." By Alice Davis. *Social Forces*, XIX (1940), 175–89.

"Bibliography: Books and Pamphlets of Interest to Teachers and Specialists in the Field of Marriage and the Family." By Ernest R. Groves. *Social Forces*, XIX (1940), 236–43.

"The First Credit Course in Preparation for Family Living." By Ernest R. Groves. *Social Forces*, XIX (1940). 236–43.

"Areas of Educational Effectiveness." By Ernest R. Groves. *Education for Family Life*, 19th

Yearbook, American Association of School Administrators, Chapters V–VI, pp. 74–107 (1941).

"Interrelations of Population Trends and Land Tenure in the Southeast." By Rupert B. Vance. Chapter II in *The People, the Land and the Church —in the Rural South*, pp. 85–96, Farm Foundation, Chicago, Illinois, 1941.

"The South's Human Resources in Total Defense." By Rupert B. Vance. Chapter II in *Essays on Southern Life and Culture, a Symposium in Commemoration of the Semicentennial of Henderson State Teachers College*, Arkadelphia, Arkansas, 1941, pp. 41–54.

"The Family in Peace and War." By Ernest R. Groves. *Highways to Peace*, Fifth Parent Education Yearbook of the National Congress of Parents and Teachers, January, 1941.

"Sale of New England Mill Houses." By Harriet L. Herring. *Textile World*, XCI (1941), 64–66.

"North Carolina Goes to Town." By Myron F. Lewis. *North Carolina Education*, VII (1941), No. 5, pp. 167–68, 182.

"Towards the South at Its Best." By Howard W. Odum. *Mississippian* (Spring, 1941).

"The Interaction of School and Community in a Democratic Society." By Gordon W. Blackwell. *Journal of Educational Sociology*, XIV (1941), 427–31.

"Sociological Analysis Through Field Course Procedure." By Gordon W. Blackwell. *Social Forces*, XIX (1941), 356–65.

"Education for Family Life and National Defense." By Ernest R. Groves. *Social Forces*, XIX (1941), 519–22.

"The Problem of the Mixed Marriage." By Ernest R. Groves. *Ladies' Home Journal*, LVIII (May, 1941), 92–94.

"The Role of Regionalism and the Regional Council in National Planning." By Howard W. Odum. *National Conference on Planning*, 1941. Proceedings of the Conference held at Philadelphia, Pennsylvania, May 12–14, 1941. Chicago: American Society of Planning Officials (1941), pp. 316–26.

"The First Credit Course in Preparation for Family Living." By Ernest R. Groves. *Marriage and Family Living*, III (1941), 67–9. *Social Forces*, XX (1941), 140.

"Educational Principles and Processes." By Ernest R. Groves. *Ladies' Home Journal*, LVIII (June, 1941), 92–3.

"School Life Expectation and Marriage Expectation: An Attempt to Apply the Technique of Life Table Construction to Other Fields of Sociology." By Rupert B. Vance and Nadia Danilevsky. *Proceedings of the Conference on Analysis and Interpretation of Social and Economic Data*. North Carolina State College, Raleigh, North Carolina, 1941, pp. 72–78. (Mimeographed.)

"The Negro and Crime." By Guy B. Johnson. *Annals of the American Academy of Political and Social Science*, CCXVII (1941), 93–104.

"The College in Relation to Community Analysis and Development." By Gordon W. Blackwell. *Social Forces*, XXI (1941), 70–76.

"Regional Approach to the Study of High Fertility." By Rupert B. Vance and Nadia Danilevsky. *Milbank Memorial Fund Quarterly*, XIX (1941), 356–74.

"Four Years of Contraception as a Public Health Service in North Carolina." By George M. Cooper and others. *Public Health*, XXXI (1941), No. 12.

"Regionalism and Social Planning: A Footnote to the Organic Role of Regionalism in National Planning." By George Simpson and John E. Ivey, Jr. *Social Forces*, XX (1941), 185–95.

"Regionalism—A Technique for Large-Scale Social Planning and Democratic Checks." By Howard W. Odum. *New Leader* (February 28, 1942), pp. 3 and 6.

"Bibliography No. 2: Books and Pamphlets of Interest to Teachers and Specialists in the Field of Marriage and the Family." By Ernest R. Groves. *Social Forces*, XX (1942), 371–77.

"The Process of Urbanization." By Hope Tisdale. *Social Forces*, XX (1942), 311–16.

"Studying the South First Hand." By Gordon W. Blackwell. *Educational Record*, XXIII (1942), 271–82.

"The American Family in Our Present Crisis." By Ernest R. Groves. *Christian Home*, I (1942), 3–6.

"A Sociological Approach to the Study and Practice of American Regionalism." By Howard W. Odum. *Social Forces*, XX (1942), 425–36.

"Threefold Task Awaits South's Development." By Howard W. Odum. *The Need to Eat Is Not Racial*. Atlanta, Georgia: Commission on Interracial Cooperation (May, 1942), pp. 10–11.

"The Way of the South. A Regional Approach to the Promise of American Life." By Howard W. Odum. *Christendom*, VII (1942), 377–89.

"Correlates of Stage of Family Development Among Farm Families on Relief." By Gordon

W. Blackwell. *Rural Sociology*, VII (1942), 162–74.

"Patterns of Regionalism in the Deep South." By Howard W. Odum. *Saturday Review of Literature*, XXV (Sept. 19, 1942), No. 38, pp. 5–7.

"War on the Home Front." By Gordon W. Blackwell. *Progressive Education*, XIX (1942), 319–22.

"The South at Its Best." By Howard W. Odum. *Baptist Student*, XXII (1942), No. 1, pp. 3–5.

"The University, Scholarship and the People." By Howard W. Odum. *College of Education Record* (University of Washington), IX (1942), 1–9.

"What Kind of a Family Do We Wish to Develop in America." By Ernest R. Groves. *Marriage and Family Living*, IV (1942), 5–6.

"When Blueprints Won't Work." By Ernest R. Groves. *Christian Home*, January, 1943.

"The Glory That Was. And the Southern Grandeur That Was Not." By Howard W. Odum. *Saturday Review of Literature*, XXVI (January 23, 1943), No. 4, pp. 9–10, 35–36.

"Statistical Methods for Delineation of Regions Applied to Data on Agriculture and Population." By Margaret Jarman Hagood. *Social Forces*, XXI (1943), 287–97.

"Marital Frustration." By Ernest R. Groves. *Hygeia*, XXI (1943), 271, 296, 297.

"Marriage Department: Husbands and Wives." By Ernest R. Groves. *American Family*, I (1943), 3–5.

"Effects of the War on the Agricultural Working Force and on the Rural-Farm Population." By Louis J. Ducoff and others. *Social Forces*, XXI (1943), 406–12.

"Sociology in the Contemporary World of Today and Tomorrow." By Howard W. Odum. *Social Forces*, XXI (1943), 390–96.

"Development of a 1940 Rural-Farm Level of Living Index for Counties." By Margaret Jarman Hagood. *Rural Sociology*, VIII (1943), 171–80.

"Development of the Public Health Movement in the Southeast." By Francis R. Allen. *Social Forces*, XXII (1943), 67–75.

"The Implications of Regionalism to Folk Sociology with Illustrations from the Southern Regions." By Hope Tisdale Eldridge. *Social Forces*, XXII (1943), 41–43.

"Criteria for Administrative Regions." By James W. Fesler. *Social Forces*, XXII (1943), 26–32.

"Bibliography No. 3: Books and Pamphlets of Interest to Teachers and Specialists in the Field of Marriage and the Family." By Ernest R. Groves. *Social Forces*, XXII (1943), 82–86.

"War and the Adolescent." By Ernest R. Groves. *Christian Home*, II (October, 1943), 22–24.

"Some Regional Indices of Agricultural Equipment Basic to Southern Regional Planning." By Harriet L. Herring. *Social Forces*, XXII (1943), 33–40.

"Human Resources and Public Policy: An Essay Toward Regional-National Planning." By Rupert B. Vance. *Social Forces*, XXII (1943), 20–25.

"Towards a More Dynamic Regional National Planning." By Howard W. Odum. *Proceedings* of the American Society of Planning Officials, 1943.

"The American Heritage." By Howard W. Odum. *Proceedings* of the Twentieth Annual Educational Conference and the Ninth Annual Meeting of the Kentucky Association of Colleges and Secondary Schools, University of Kentucky. Bulletin of the Bureau of School Service, XVI (December, 1943), No. 2, pp. 51–59.

"Crisis in the Making." By Howard W. Odum. *Crisis*, L (1943), 360–62, 377–78.

"Social Control and the Technicways." By Frederick B. Parker. *Social Forces*, XXII (1943), 163–68.

Articles on Folk, Folk-Regional Society, Folk Society, The Region, Regional Planning, Regionalism, Technicways. By Howard W. Odum *Dictionary of Sociology*, edited by Henry Pratt Fairchild. New York: Philosophical Library, 1944.

"The Hospital Patient." By Ernest R. Groves. *Hygeia*, XXII (1944), 12, 54, 55.

"A New Era in Race Relations." By Howard W. Odum. *Pulse*, I (1944), No. 12, pp. 6–8.

"The Legend of the Eleanor Clubs." By Howard W. Odum. Condensed from the book, *Race and Rumors of Race*. *Negro Digest*. II (1944), No. 4, pp. 17–22.

"Patrick Geddes' Heritage to 'The Making of the Future.'" By Howard W. Odum. *Social Forces*, XXII (1944), 275–81.

"Consumer Problems and the Cooperative Movement in the Curricula of Southern Negro Colleges." By Lee M. Brooks and Ruth G. Lynch. *Social Forces*, XXII (1944), 429–36.

"Contemporary American Domestic Problems and Their Meaning for Religious Education." By Ernest R. Groves. *Religious Education*, XXXIX (1944), 135–40.

"Social Security and Adjustment: The Return to the Larger Community." By Rupert B. Vance. *Social Forces*, XXII (1944), 363–70.

"Living After the War." By Gordon W. Blackwell. *Southern Association Quarterly*, VIII (1944), 342–50.

"Postwar Planning in North Carolina. A Program for Industrial Development." By Harriet L. Herring. *Popular Government*, X (1944), No. 6, pp. 8–12.

"The Social Background of Wartime Adolescents." By Ernest R. Groves and Gladys Hoagland Groves. *Annals of the American Academy of Political and Social Science*, CCXXXVI (1944), 26–32.

"Americans All." By Howard W. Odum. *Negro Digest*, III (1944), No. 1, p. 44.

III. MANUSCRIPTS

Studies in County Government and County Affairs. By Paul W. Wager, Brandon Trussell, Myron Green, Charles T. Edwards, Edward A. Terry, Columbus Andrews, Clifton J. Bradley, under the direction of E. C. Branson. 1924–1930. Pp. 50 to 200.

Leisure Time Activities of Adolescents in North Carolina. By Mabel Boysworth. 1925. Pp. 64.

Town Government in North Carolina. By Roy Eugene Brown. 1925. Pp. 138.

Cotton Cloth: A Type Study of the Community Process. By Mary O. Cowper. 1925. Pp. 126.

Notes on Vocational Guidance. By Cordelia Cox. 1925. Pp. 83.

Rural Occupations for Women. By Cordelia Cox. 1925. Pp. 74.

A Study of the Need of Rural Elementary Educational and Vocational Guidance. By Cordelia Cox. 1925. Pp. 79.

Adolescent Leisure Time Activities in Mississippi. By Kate Fulton. 1925. Pp. 81.

Social Aspects of County Organization: A Study of Rural Leadership in Orange County, North Carolina. By Coyle Ellis Moore. 1925. Pp. 84.

Case Studies of Mill Village Population in Gaston County. By Jennings J. Rhyne. 1925. Pp. 231.

Public Welfare Problems of Chapel Hill. By Elizabeth G. Smith. 1925. Pp. 79.

Reading Habits of North Carolinians. By Orlando Stone. 1925. Pp. 74.

A History of Social Work in Durham County. By Margaret Battle Bridgers. 1926. Pp. 169.

The Administrative Cost of Crime with Special Reference to Durham County. By Lee M. Brooks. 1926. Pp. 60.

Rural Electrification. By Addison T. Cutler. 1926. Pp. 94.

A Statistical Analysis of Crime in North Carolina. By Aileen Gramling MacGill. 1926. Pp. 85.

Folk Interpretations of Social Values as Found in Folk Songs and Ballads. By Clyde Russell. 1926. Pp. 162.

The Rural Working Girl in Durham, North Carolina. By Clyde Russell. 1926. Pp. 50.

Types of Crime in North Carolina. By Francis S. Wilder. 1926. Pp. 93.

Case Studies of Delinquent Girls in North Carolina. By Margaret C. Brietz. 1927. Pp. 256.

A Comparative Study of Growth in Mental and Physical Abilities of Mill and Non-Mill Children. By Graham B. Dimmick. 1927. Pp. 212.

Negro Agricultural Credit Conditions in North Carolina. By Roland B. Eutsler. 1927. Pp. 130.

Extent and Types of Juvenile Delinquency and Dependency in Durham, North Carolina. By Charles Horace Hamilton. 1927. Pp. 35.

A Statistical Summary of Arrests and Disposition in Durham, North Carolina. By Charles Horace Hamilton. 1927. Pp. 7.

A Study of the Musical Talent of the American Negro. By Guy B. Johnson. 1927. Pp. 89.

Backgrounds of Delinquent Boys in North Carolina. By Clyde V. Kiser. 1927. Pp. 36.

Liquor Law Violations in Durham and Person Counties, North Carolina. By Clyde V. Kiser. 1927. Pp. 12.

Life Histories of Rural Negro Teachers in the South. By George E. Pankey. 1927. pp. 137.

Physical Education in North Carolina. By Mary Phlegar Smith. 1927. Pp. 101.

The Peanut Industry and the Peanut Cooperative Marketing Association. By Boone D. Tillett. 1927. Pp. 169.

A Study of Homicides in South Carolina, 1920–1926. By H. C. Brearley. 1928. Pp. 62.

100 Country Dwelling Negroes and Their Crimes in Durham, North Carolina. By Hugh Penn Brinton. 1928. Pp. 24.

Mental and Physical Growth of Children in Different Occupational Groups. By A. M. Jordan. 1928. Pp. 128.

The Organization and Administration of Public Welfare in Orange County, North Carolina. By George H. Lawrence. 1928. Pp. 77.

Social Factors and School Progress. By Gustave E. Metz. 1928. Pp. 147.

Some Inequalities of Educational Opportunities in North Carolina Elementary Schools. By Roy W. Morrison. 1928. Pp. 148.

Mob Action in the South. By John Roy Steelman. 1928. Pp. 437.

Reading as a Southern Problem. By Louis Round Wilson. 1928. Pp. 57.

The Tri-State Tobacco Growers Cooperative Association. By Clifton J. Bradley. 1929. Pp. 100.

A Study of Primary Group Isolation. By Lee M. Brooks. 1929. Pp. 289.

The Vocational Ambitions of North Carolina High School Students. By Gustave E. Metz. 1929. Pp. 42.

A Survey of Rural Illegitimacy in Orange County, North Carolina, 1923–1927. By Janet Quinlan. 1929. Pp. 82.

The Negro in Durham. By Hugh Penn Brinton. 1930. Pp. 465.

Social-Economic Characteristics of the Mississippi Delta. By Virginia L. Denton. 1930. Pp. 448.

A Follow-Up Study of Juvenile Court Cases in Orange County, North Carolina, 1919–1929. By Mary Katharine Fleming. 1930. Pp. 118.

Folk Beliefs and Practices in Central North Carolina. By Elizabeth Lay Green and Paul Green. 1930. Pp. 414.

A Gaston County Cotton Mill and Its Community. By Bertha Carl Hipp. 1930. Pp. 101.

A Survey of the North Carolina Prison System (made for the Governor's Prison Commission). By Howard W. Odum and others. 1930. Pp. 164.

Social-Economic Characteristics of the Black Prairie and Red Hill Regions of Mississippi and Alabama. By Elton C. McNeil. 1930. Pp. 55.

Municipal Development in North Carolina, 1665–1930. By Mary Phlegar Smith. 1930. Pp. 432.

The Kentucky Mountaineer. A Study of Four Counties of Southeastern Kentucky. By Harriette Wood. 1930. Pp. 112.

Administrative County Government in Mississippi. By Columbus Andrews. 1931. Pp. 150.

Tillman and Blease as "Popular" Leaders in South Carolina. By William C. Ezell. 1931. Pp. 103.

The After-Prison Life of Released Prisoners. By J. Paul McConnell. 1931. Pp. 120.

Crime in North Carolina. By Lena Mae Williams. 1931. Pp. 301.

Problems of the Small Town in North Carolina. By Ina V. Young. 1931. Pp. 165.

A Case Study of the Tarboro Lynching. By N. Clifford Young. 1931. Pp. 65.

A Survey of Warren County, North Carolina. By Columbus Andrews. 1932. Pp. 176.

The Diet Pattern of the South: A Study in Regional Sociology. By Emily Stevens Maclachlan. 1932. Pp. 140.

A Fiscal History of North Carolina, 1776–1860. By Hershal L. Macon. 1932. Pp. 452.

Farm Life of the Upper Middle Class in Piedmont North Carolina After the Civil War. By Edith Webb. 1932. Pp. 137.

Public Welfare Administration in the United States. By Howard W. Odum, Roy M. Brown, Clarence Heer, Katharine Jocher, Mary Phlegar Smith, D. W. Willard, and others. 1930–1932.

Preliminary manuscripts, bibliographies, and source materials prepared, 1930–1932, as basic materials for "Public Welfare Activities," by Howard W. Odum, Chap. XIV, in *Recent Social Trends in the United States* (New York: McGraw-Hill Book Company, 1933). These materials include the following: Trends in Public Welfare, by Howard W. Odum, pp. 89; Trends in County Organization and Units, by Roy M. Brown, pp. 39; Trends in Public Welfare Costs, by Clarence Heer, pp. 145; Trends in the National Conference of Social Work, by Katharine Jocher, pp. 110; Trends in Municipal Administration of Public Welfare, by Mary Phlegar Smith, pp. 143; Trends in State Systems of Public Welfare, by D. W. Willard, pp. 470; Trends in the Administrative Control of Prisons from the Point of View of Public Welfare, by Roy M. Brown, pp. 39; The Growth of Public Welfare, by Howard W. Odum, pp. 102; Bibliographical Materials from *Proceedings* of the National Conference of Social Work, *Journal of Abnormal and Social*

Psychology, Atlantic Monthly, Journal of Criminal Law and Criminology, The Family, Harper's, Journal of Social Hygiene, Mental Hygiene, Social Forces, Social Service Review, Survey, etc.; also bulletins, articles, monographs, etc.; pages not numbered.

The Development and Application of the Social Sciences and Social Research. By Howard W. Odum and others. 1932. Pp. 200.

West Southern Pines: An Episode in Negro Self-Government. By Joseph Herman Johnson. 1933. Pp. 103.

A Social Study of High Point, North Carolina. By Sarah Margaret Smith. 1933. Pp. 175.

State Public Welfare in the Southeast: An Approach to Regional Planning in the Field of State Public Welfare. By Gordon W. Blackwell. 1934. Pp. 210.

A Study of Some Reformatory Systems for Women Offenders in the United States with Particular Reference to the Industrial Farm Colony at Kinston, North Carolina. By June Rainsford Butler. 1934. Pp. 138.

Wage Differentials Between Negro and White Workers in Southern Industry. By Charlotte Califf. 1934. Pp. 102.

A State in Depression. Directed by Howard W. Odum, T. J. Woofter, Jr., and Harriet L. Herring. 1933–1934. A series of studies made in cooperation with the CWA, the TVA, and the FERA in North Carolina, showing the effects of the depression on the life and people in North Carolina, including: Public Administration in the Fifteen North Carolina Counties of the Tennessee Valley Area, by Columbus Andrews, pp. 69; State Centralization of the Public Schools in North Carolina, by Mabel Bacon and W. H. E. Johnson, pp. 377; Blank Farm: An Example of Tenancy Under a Corporation (under the auspices of the NCERA), by Gordon W. Blackwell, pp. 7; Rural Relief Families in North Carolina (under the auspices of the NCERA), by Gordon W. Blackwell, pp. 85; also Greene County, pp. 53; Mountain Families, pp. 113; Bertie County, pp. 40; Columbus County, pp. 69; Onslow County, pp. 77; Piedmont Counties, pp. 104; Stokes County, pp. 57; Tyrell County, pp. 40; Washington County, pp. 40; The Problem of the Displaced Tenant Farm Family in North Carolina (in cooperation with the NCERA), by Gordon W. Blackwell, Roy M. Brown, and Harriet L. Herring, Greene County, pp. 57; Nash County, pp. 75; Wilson County,

pp. 120; Summary of Greene, Nash, and Wilson Counties, pp. 25; Survey of Idle Land and Vacant Houses Available for Displaced Tenant Farm Families in Wilson County, pp. 35; A Study of Living Costs of North Carolina Teachers, by Harriet L. Herring, pp. 105; A City in Depression—Greensboro, North Carolina, by A. S. Keister, pp. 71; Effects of the Depression on Education in the South, by Edgar W. Knight, pp. 52; A Study of Three North Carolina Cities in Depression—Asheville, Greensboro, Rocky Mount, by Chester P. Lewis, pp. 101; Asheville, pp. 89; Survey of Those Who Entered the University of North Carolina in 1926–27, 1927–28, 1928–29, and 1929–30 with Reference to Their Percentile Rank and Length of Stay in School, compiled under the direction of Herman Schnell, pp. 25; North Carolina: Which Way Is Forward, by Irene Strieby, pp. 184.

New Leisure: How Is It Spent? By Frances Hampton. 1935. Pp. 113.

A Sociological Study of the Tri-Racial Community, Robeson County, North Carolina. By Earnest D. Hancock. 1935. Pp. 128.

The Second United States Intervention in Cuba. By David A. Lockmiller. 1935. Pp. 343.

The Social Welfare Movement in the South: A Study in Regional Culture and Social Organization. By Lyda Gordon Shivers. 1935. Pp. 408.

Financial Aspects of City Planning: An Objective Study of Planning Commissions in Cities of Greensboro, High Point, and Durham, North Carolina. By Hilliard B. Wilson. 1935. Pp. 74.

Population as an Area of Study in Social Planning: An Introduction to the Southeastern Region of the United States. By Robert Newton Woodworth. 1935. Pp. 176.

A Survey of the Catawba Valley. 2 vols. (A Cooperative Study with the Tennessee Valley Authority.) By T. J. Woofter, Jr., Rupert B. Vance, Harriet L. Herring. 1935. Pp. 408.

Southern Regional Study: Work Memoranda. 1932–1936.

The Chief Economic Opportunities in the South. By S. H. Hobbs, Jr., with the assistance of W. P. Young. Pp. 56.

Commercial Fertilizer in the Economy of the Southeastern Region. By John M. Maclachlan. Pp. 37.

Agricultural Readjustment with Special Reference to the Dairy Industry in the Southeast. By

Howard W. Odum and John M. Maclachlan. Pp. 51.

Higher Standards of Food Consumption in the Southern Regions. By Emily Stevens Maclachlan. Pp. 85.

Farm Tenancy in the South. By John M. Maclachlan and E. C. Branson. Pp. 39.

Mississippi: A Picture of Potentiality. By John M. Maclachlan. Pp. 350.

Business Education in the South. 2 vols. By Walter J. Matherly. Pp. 769.

Commercial and Business Schools and Courses. By Walter J. Matherly. Pp. 200.

Regional Folk Culture. By Helen Irene McCobb, Edith Webb, Emily Stevens Maclachlan, and others. Pp. 60.

Southern Regions and National Economy. By Howard W. Odum. Pp. 36.

Southern Regions: An Introduction to Regional Analysis and Democracy. By Howard W. Odum. Pp. 91.

Southern Regional Study. Part I. By Howard W. Odum. Pp. 199.

The Social Population of the Southwest. By Jennings J. Rhyne. Pp. 463.

Library Planning in the South. By Irene Strieby, Icelle Wright, Alberta Bush, and John McNeil. Pp. 47.

Wholesaling and Retailing in the Chattanooga Marketing Area. By Malcolm D. Taylor. Pp. 35.

Wholesaling and Retailing in the Knoxville Marketing Area. By Malcolm D. Taylor. Pp. 44.

Theses Relating to the Social and Economic Problems of the Tennessee Valley. Pp. 65.

The Southwest Economic Region. By Raymond D. Thomas. Pp. 84.

Rate Levels in Relation to the Economic Development of the Southeast. By George Lynch Tillery. Pp. 21.

Submarginal Areas and Populations in Regional Planning. By Rupert B. Vance. Pp. 49.

Forest Resources of the South. By Paul W. Wager. Pp. 126.

Report on Tennessee Valley Study. By T. J. Woofter, Jr. With an Introduction and summary by Howard W. Odum. Pp. 52.

Submarginal Counties of the Southeast. 3 vols. I. Agriculture; II. Minor Civil Divisions; III. Population, Occupation, and Educational Data. Compiled under the direction of T. J. Woofter, Jr., with CWA personnel (an extension of the Report on Tennessee Valley Study). Pp. 303.

Southern Regional Study: Bibliography. More than 5000 pp. Not numbered.

Southern Regional Study: Indices and Source Tables. Not numbered.

The North Carolina Industrial Worker, 1880–1930. By Harry M. Douty. 1936. Pp. 396.

Occupations in the United States and the South, 1910–1930. By Ruth Yeomans Schiffman. 1936. Pp. 261.

Commercial Recreation in the Southeast: A Study of Commercial Recreation of a Region. By Oliver Bruce Thomason. 1936. Pp. 282.

Fifty Years of Electrical Development in North Carolina. Edited by Charles E. Waddell. 1936. Pp. 105.

Seventeen Hundred Economically Handicapped Families: A Study of Families in Orange County, North Carolina, Aided by Federal Emergency Relief. By Katherine Lewis Barrier. 1937. Pp. 93.

A Sociological Study of Police in North Carolina with Special Reference to Personnel Selection. By James Payne Beckwith. 1937. Pp. 73.

A State and Its Children, 1900–1936: As Measured by the Children's Charter. By Effie Estelle Doan. 1937. Pp. 143.

Mothers of the South: A Population Study of Native White Women of Childbearing Age of the Southeast. By Margaret Jarman Hagood. 1937. Pp. 302.

Mississippi: A Regional Social-Economic Analysis. By John Miller Maclachlan. 1937. Pp. 556.

An Analysis of Public Welfare Services to 422 Cases in Orange County, North Carolina, January 1 to December 31, 1936. By Jean McCaig. 1937. Pp. 55.

State Differences in the Southeast As Indicated in a Decade of State Bibliographies. By Myrtle Powell Mizell. 1937. Pp. 350.

Age and Sex Distribution of the People as Conditioning Factors in Cultural Participation: A Study in the Regional Demography in the United States. By Bernice Milburn Moore. 1937. Pp. 387.

The Theories of Regionalism. By Harry Estill Moore. 1937. Pp. 346.

Social Resources of the Southeast: A Definition and Classification of Agencies and Institutions, Public and Private. By Vincent Heath Whitney. 1937. Pp. 352.

Florida, 1920–1935: A Case of Interstate Migration. By Richard H. Ashby. 1938. Pp. 103.

A Follow-Up Study in Juvenile Delinquency: The Careers of Eighty-Eight Delinquent White Boys Committed to Jackson Training School by the Durham, North Carolina, Juvenile Court (1922–1935) and Their Post-Adustment. By Robert King Bailey 1938. Pp. 108.

Americanisms as Characterized by Representative Writers. By Lee Amos Coleman. 1938. Pp. 105.

Changing Occupational Distribution in the South with Special Emphasis on the Rise of Professional Services. By Kenneth Evans. 1938. Pp. 217.

Curriculum Training for Recreational Leadership in Institutions of Higher Learning in the Southeastern Region. By Fred Fletcher. 1938. Pp. 85.

The Balance of Inter-State Migration in the Southeast, 1870–1930, with Special Reference to the Migration of Eminent Persons. By Harold L. Geisert. 1938. Pp. 393.

Preliminary Prospectus of the North Carolina Subregional Laboratory for Social Research and Planning. By Howard W. Odum and Margaret Jarman Hagood with the assistance of Nadia Danilevsky and others. 1938. Pp. 92.

The North Carolina Conference for Social Service: The Record of Twenty-Five Years, 1912–1937. Compiled by Harriet L. Herring with the assistance of Margaret Clark Neal and WPA workers. 1938. Pp. 271.

The Jews in North Carolina: A Study in Occupational Distribution. By William H. Levitt. 1938. Pp. 90.

A Social-Economic Analysis of a Mississippi Delta Plantation. By Raymond McClinton. 1938. Pp. 109.

A Definitive Study of the Poor Whites of the South. By Mildred Rutherford Mell. 1938. Pp. 313.

A State and Its University: North Carolina, 1900–1930. By Howard W. Odum and Harriet L. Herring. 1938. Pp. 64.

The Negro Churches of Chapel Hill. By Agnes Brown. 1939. Pp. 122.

Agrarian Conflicts in Alabama: Sections, Races, and Classes in a Rural State, 1800–1938. By Olive M. Stone. 1939. Pp. 604.

The Negro in Mississippi, 1865–1890. By Vernon Lane Wharton. 1939. Pp. 543.

Some Regional Variations in Standards of Living. By Francis Sidney Wilder. 1939. Pp. 314.

Care of the Aged in the Piedmont Subregion. By Alline Campbell. 1940. Pp. 67.

Illustrations of How the Technicways in the Modern Community Modify the Folkways. By Phyllis Brumm Cannon. 1940. Pp. 129.

What is American? A Lexicographic Analysis of Alleged American Characteristics, Ideals, and Principles. By Amoss Lee Coleman. 1940. Pp. 516.

The Administration of the National Labor Relations Act in North Carolina. By Ruth Crowell. 1940. Pp. 123.

An Introductory Study of Interrelationships Among Federal, State, and Local Public Relief Administrations and of the Economy and Social Welfare of the Community. 2 vols. By Virginia Lyn Denton (in collaboration with Margaret Jarman Hagood, Fred Bunting, and Robert Hodges. Preface by Roy M. Brown). 1940. Pp. 460.

The Negro in Greenville, South Carolina. By Joseph Turpin Drake. 1940. Pp. 274.

The Climate of the Southeast: A Preliminary Investigation of the Theoretical and Factual Problems of Southern Climate. By Mary Alice Eaton. 1940. Pp. 490.

Statistical Notes Based on the Cases Disposed of in the Superior Courts of North Carolina from 1900–1938, by Race, and for the Counties of the Subregion. By Harold Garfinkel. 1940. Pp. 64.

A Study of the Durham Recreation Department. By C. Manly Loomis. 1940. Pp. 105.

The North Carolina Youth Survey, 1938–1940. By Gordon W. Lovejoy. 1940. Pp. 352.

A Preliminary Study of the Planter Aristocracy as a Folk Level of Life in the Old South. By Melville Fort Corbett. 1941. Pp. 204.

A Study of Differential Fertility in North Carolina. By Jerry Daniel. 1941. Pp. 74.

An Inquiry into the Number, Range, and Functions of Agencies Rendering Public Services in the Subregional'Laboratory for Social Research and Planning at the University of North Carolina. By Virginia Lyn Denton. 1941. Pp. 73.

A Study of Bisexual Folkways and Their Modification into Technicways on the College Campuses in the United States. By Bernard N. Desenberg. 1941. Pp. 18.

The North Carolina Conference for Social Service: A Study of Its Development and Methods. By Virginia Wooten Gulledge. 1941. Pp. 114.

Folk Medicine. By Nell Hines. 1941. Pp. 20.

Chronology of the Present South, 1913–1940. By Arthur S. Link. 1941. Pp. 205.

Rural Poverty and Relief in the Southeast, 1933–1935. By Selz Cabot Mayo. 1941. Pp. 295.

Recent Changes in Negro Farm Tenure. By Robert J. Milliken. 1941. Pp. 50.

Psychological Implications of the Growth of Technicways. By Frederick B. Parker. 1941. Pp. 19.

Analysis of Occupational Characteristics and Their Social and Econonic Correlates for the 93 Metropolitan Centers, 1930. By Daniel O'Haver Price. 1941. Pp. 70.

The Negro Tobacco Worker and His Union in Durham, North Carolina. By John Donald Rice. 1941. Pp. 120.

The Case of the South in Milk Production. By Philip Schinhan. 1941. Pp. 95.

Southern Folkways of Work. A Study of Folkways as a Cause of Regional Poverty. By Willis Weatherford. 1941. Pp. 56.

A Population Study of Youth in the Southeast Region. By Trezevant Player Yeatman. 1941. Pp. 158.

The Sociological Approach to a Clothing Study. By Alice Bowie. 1942. Pp. 78.

Government Participation in Recreation. By Frances Tull Cooke. 1942. Pp. 117.

The Growth of the Technicways: A Study in Societal Change. By Alice Davis. 1942. Pp. 410.

The Organization, Administration, and Program of the Recreation Commission of Greensboro, North Carolina. By Hughes Davis. 1942. Pp. 187.

Culture of the Centerville-Mosel Germans in Manitowc and Sheboygan Counties, Wisconsin. By Oscar Frederick Hoffman. 1942. Pp. 292.

The Measurement of Social Adjustment by Comparison of Self-Ratings and Group-Ratings of the Same Individuals. By Edmund Kenneth Karcher, Jr. 1942. Pp. 68.

Inter-Racial and Intra-Racial Homicide in Ten Counties in North Carolina, 1930–1940. By Harold Garfinkel. 1942. Pp. 398.

The Wilson Movement in the South: A Study in Political Liberalism. By Arthur Stanley Link. 1942. Pp. 218.

Rural Social Subregions of North Carolina: Application of Factor Analysis to the Problem of Sub-regional Delineation. By Robert J. Milliken. 1942. Pp. 57.

Urbanization: A Study of the Process of Population Concentration in the United States and Its Relation to Social Change. By Dorothy Hope Tisdale. 1942. Pp. 226.

WPA—A Study of Some of the Measurable Characteristics of Work Relief Recipients in Eight North Carolina Counties. By Martha Hebbert Wilson. 1942. Pp. 90.

A Compilation and Analysis of Statistics Relating to American Marriage in 1930. By Mary Isabelle Wolf. 1942. Pp. 79.

Agricultural Reform in the Georgia Piedmont, 1820–1860. By James Calvin Bonner. 1943. Pp. 382.

A Survey of Certain Defense Publications with Special Reference to Their Utilization in Community Institutions. By Margaret MacDowell Douglas. 1943. Pp. 75.

The Social Participation of Part-Time Farmers in North Carolina. By Abbott Lamoyne Ferriss. 1943. Pp. 136.

Underregistration of Births, United States, 1939; State, Regional, Race and Rural-Urban Differences. By Ellen Hull Neff. 1943. Pp. 89.

A Comparative Study of Three Experiments in Rural "Community" Reconstruction in the Southeast. By Donald M. Royer. 1943. Pp. 70.

The South's Participation in the National Conference of Social Work: As One Index of the Leaders of Social Work in the South, 1918–1942. By Caroline Blue. 1944. Pp. 53.

Growth and Plan for a Community: A Study of Negro Life in Chapel Hill and Carrboro, North Carolina. By Charles Maddry Freeman. 1944. Pp. 218.

Inquiry into the Pattern of College and University Leadership in the South Since 1900. By Leslie Woodzelle Syron. 1944. Pp. 123.

A Statistical Study of the Social Work Personnel in the North Carolina County Departments of Public Welfare, November, 1941. By Anne Williams Tillinghast. 1944. Pp. 188.

The Patterns of Village Life: A Study of Southern Piedmont Villages in Terms of Population, Structure and Role. By Vincent Heath Whitney. 1944. Pp. 350.

Part II

ON REGIONAL ANALYSIS
AND INTERPRETATION

THE PLACE OF PLANNING IN SOCIAL DYNAMICS

RUPERT B. VANCE

THE student of social change can do no better, it would seem to me, than continually to remind himself that society exists both as product and as process. If the energies of men are merged and channeled in a hundred different processes to result in a hundred different social products, we can assert that the process is essentially one of change, but the product is essentially one of social order. Continuous changes are thus essential to the maintenance of an adjusting and readjusting social organization.

In the ongoing trend of society the process is social change, but the end-product is the development of social order. In such an analysis it is customary to point out an economic process which produces the economic equilibrium, a cultural process which hands down the cultural heritage, and a political process which serves to focus the energies of men on the decisions that must be made as new issues arise. Certainly in the Aristotelian sense politics is the policy-making process.

It is within the framework of social dynamics that the concept of social planning finds its place.[1] If society were static, as it obviously is not, social planning would have the task of changing the social order from one state of inertia to another. Just as there is no final stage of order at which we presume social dynamics will halt, there is no final plan with which the process of planning will cease. Planning is both product and process and from the dynamic point of view, the process is of greater importance than any particular product.

While planning represents an important reaction against the static view of society, it has met varied responses from both the students and the proponents of social change. In a foreword to a valuable book on social planning we read these words of dissent by Herbert Read:

Planning has become the catchword of our age: not merely one suspects because it is a necessity inherent in our historical situation, but also because it offers for many people a welcome escape from the ambiguities of political action. It is the "scientific" attitude in social relations and to be scientific is better than to be moral. It happens that I personally belong to that minority which still believes that morality and therefore science, is always subordinate to the idea of sublimity; I believe that nothing would ever have been achieved in the sphere of social reform without a fiery and irrational concept of revolution, a concept at the opposite pole to any notion of scientific planning. "It is the idea of revolution which has carried the proletariat from its degradation," [wrote Kautsky], and I cannot believe that the immense problems of the future are to be solved on altogether "reasonable" lines.[2]

Mr. Read's reliance on what he is pleased to call irrationality will shake no responsive chord among those devoted to the values of science. Admitted that in a relatively few periods in history the ultimate range of social dynamics has been found in that drastic form of reorganization known as revolution, the determination of social policy is not limited to emotional and irrational procedures of group conflict. There is still the basic assumption that the energies of men can be directed by the intelligence of men.

SOCIAL RESEARCH AND POLICY FORMULATION

In a democracy the determination of policy is regarded as a rational process involving the adjustment of various group interests to the general welfare in terms of national goals to be sought. Basic to the process are (1) the social values held by members of a given society, (2) the indication of new goals to be sought, and (3) the readjustment of policy and procedures toward the new goals. The first indication that new goals should be sought is often given by research which demonstrates the conditions of maladjustment which have developed under previous social policies.

If the conditions disclosed by research prevent the realization of values held by the society or if

---

[1] This discussion may be regarded as an extension of the point of view developed in "Toward Social Dynamics," *American Sociological Reviews*, X:2 (April, 1945). For permission to anticipate the discussion in my forthcoming, *All These People*, I am grateful to the University of North Carolina Press.

[2] Herbert Read in Foreword to E. A. Gutkind, *Creative Demobilization: Principles of National Planning*, (New York: Oxford University Press, 1944), I, xiii.

they impinge on policies already adopted, they threaten national and group interests sufficiently to lead to the consideration of new policies. On this basis we can say that social research itself is affected with a public interest and bears a function in policy making.

When the issues are stated in this fashion it is doubtful whether any large group in our society would care to challenge the importance of social science in the formulation of public policy. There are, however, many considerations which operate to make the relation more complicated than the above statement suggests. Many of those who are devoted to the values of research doubt the competence of social scientists to write what we may call the prescriptions for public policy. This attitude, which is held by many sociologists and economists, does not involve doubt of the scientific value of social facts as facts. It is related, among other things, to the danger of bias involved in the selection of social facts. Since there exists in every society the danger of confusing individual class, and group interests with the national interests, there is the tendency on the part of the public to confuse the function of the impartial scientist with that of the biased advocate. It is this confusion which some careful researchers seek to avoid by confining their work to a bare statement of facts without pointing out implications and interpretation. A second element closely related to bias is the fact that no specialist can hope to know or fully appreciate the bearing of other specialisms on his conclusions. Thus, for example, it would be possible for a majority of the experts in social work to advocate a policy which the majority of economists would oppose. A third reason for caution is the gap that exists between public policy and public administration. Thus many desirable goals are likely to go unrealized in public policy because of difficulties in administration.

Accordingly whatever competence the social sciences may attain, it is generally agreed that the determination of public policy does not fall within their scope. There are many reasons for this conclusion beside the fact that the world has never been ruled by the philosopher-kings that Plato visualized in his *Republic*. These reasons can be summarized by saying that the social studies aspire to be sciences while the determination of public policy must remain an art. As an art it involves the compromise of conflicting claims of rival parties and groups in the interest of the total welfare. Basic to the scientific viewpoint is the feeling that facts are objective entities and this cannot be ruled out of existence by political compromises. By participation in the conflict over policy making, economists and sociologists have feared to lose the objectivity and freedom from bias essential to science.

Unlike a work of art which may be regarded as an entity—a good in itself—the literature of information raises the question: to what end? This is especially true of social and economic research whose findings are related to a national and cultural context. Such research may have two possible implications: (1) It may be designed to arrive at general natural laws or hypotheses similar to those prevailing in the natural sciences. In this respect neither sociology nor economics has yet been able to complete a rounded picture of the universe in which it operates. (2) On the other hand, research may serve as the basis for the development of public policy in a given field. This is not the whole purpose of social research as conducted in our colleges and universities, but its importance may be suggested by the statement that if public policy is not based on information it will obviously be based on misinformation or none at all.

It is of course logical to contend, as some do, that national policy is normally based on prejudice and emotion and that facts count only as they serve to reenforce tradition. The mistake involved in this reasoning may be clarified by saying that while social values, including the national interest and legal and constitutional commitments, undoubtedly operate to determine the policies that will be based upon a given set of facts, social facts themselves serve to determine not only what is feasible but often what is desirable. Social policy accordingly may be regarded as the conclusion of a logical syllogism whose major premise is the social values held by the group and whose minor premise is the social facts in so far as they can be developed by research.

Obviously, the social values of any society exert a determining force. The same set of facts, if they existed in Russia and the United States, could lead to opposite policies simply because of the different sets of values on which the two governments are predicated. What remains to be pointed out, however, is that over long periods of time the complex of social values themselves are subject to rational redirection on the basis of new conditions, new facts, or even of old facts newly discovered.

Thus there exists a certain validity behind the demand that an analysis of maladjustments in society be accompanied by a discussion of the issues involved in the reformulation of policy. It is the seriousness of the situation that gives to research its initial relevance; and it is only by the nature and profundity of the changes recommended that the reader can judge the seriousness of the condition discussed. Then there is the question of relative competence. Admitting that the politician is competent to estimate the force of public opinion behind the demands of various groups, he may make use of this knowledge only to solve the question of how best to win the next election. Knowledge of the facts must go over into the determination of public policy and here the results of research are the nearest to competence.

Thus in spite of his modesty the social scientist who uncovers and analyzes social facts will be asked: What do you recommend? As an honest man who values his own integrity, as a citizen who admits a public duty, and as an expert in whose training society has made an investment, the social scientist after admitting his reservations of ignorance and bias must indicate his choices of policy for whatever they may be worth. Nor should he be overwhelmed by this assumption of high responsibility, for he may rest assured that even his facts will be discounted by practical men of affairs as impossible theory while his cautious recommendations will be regarded as partisan statements by every faction whose interests they oppose. But if his facts are facts and still disregarded, he may take what consolation he can to himself in the knowledge that they also will count in the long run to come.

PUBLIC POLICY AND SOCIAL PLANNING

The implementation of social policy is found in the process we have come to call social planning. What is the nature of planning in a democracy characterized as is our society by a liberal capitalistic economy? In the first place, as John Dewey once pointed out, the ideal to be sought, is not a *planned society* but a continuously *planning society*. There is as far as we know no permanent solution to economic and social problems. Society exists as a continual process of adjustment and readjustment of its multiple groups and individuals. Unless society is continually adjusting and readjusting its elements fall so far out of balance that integration and equilibrium are not achieved. Lags and injustices arise and disequilibrium and disorganization ensue.

Throughout history the methods of meeting these maladjustments have been sporadic reforms, revolutions, civil wars, and international war. William Graham Sumner once defined revolution as a liquidation of the accumulated maladjustments in the mores. Revolutions sometimes destroy the mould of society and then break down at the point where they attempt to carry over to the new economic and political order. To some extent social planning can be regarded as a new movement that has arisen in modern society as a result of the failure of older attempts at social change. It is not Utopian, it is not revolutionary; in some respects it is not even reformist. Its aim is to prevent the need for these violent changes before they occur. Its goal is not a definitely planned society, fixed once and for all, but a continually planning and replanning society. The process itself is dynamic, for the goal is not static organization but one continually adjusting and changing as new goals are set and old ones achieved.

Democracies like other societies must face the danger of crises and wars but in the more normal course of events it can be said that social planning had its beginnings in the need of governments to plan their budgets ahead. Social and economic planning as is often said depends on prediction and control. These measures are involved in the process of balancing appropriations and expenditures. In addition, the budget itself comes to be regarded not as an accountant's statement but as incorporating long-run plans and measures of control. In adopting these measures government is simply following the best procedures of business where corporations have found it necessary to plan policy in advance of current operations.

Scientific knowledge is needed to determine the direction in which society is likely to move and control measures are required to effect needed adjustments. Adjustment and security may be regarded as the keynotes of society's planning just as they are the goals of free individual initiative and self-development. Social security as governmental policy may fail if it attempts to provide social insurance for inefficient economic alignments. Adjustment is more dynamic, for it represents not only the efforts that individuals and groups make to remedy their own undesirable situations but includes the additional incentives and pressures that society may use to hasten these desirable changes. The processes of seeking more education and migrating to areas of greater economic opportunity represent individual adjustments that also operate in the interests of greater economic security of the total society. By aiding in such adjustments liberal governments can develop the control measures adequate to social planning in a democracy.

Once assured that processes of continued adjustment are facilitated, government may then make the attempt to underwrite certain minimum guarantees against those dangers of unemployment and old age for which the individual in our society is unable to prove adequate adjustment. No social security program, however, can hope to succeed in a dynamic world if it cancels out the push toward adjustment. The assurance of continuing adjustment and readjustment among the various sections of a national economy is prerequisite to the success of any system of social security. No government, however rich, can afford to underwrite the social insurance for a system held rigid by economic barriers and monopolies.

IDEOLOGIES OF THE SOUTH IN TRANSITION

WILLIAM FIELDING OGBURN

REGIONS differ not only in climate, resources, production, and vital statistics, but also in customs and social attitudes, but being less accurately measurable these are often omitted from scientific studies of regions and left to the novelist and traveler for description. Nevertheless they are important and are among the most interesting of the characteristics which differentiate one region from another. Thus the inhabitant of the South is, in popular opinion, different because of a variety of attitudes, such as his chivalry toward women, his race prejudice, his hospitality, his leisureliness, his preference for the military life, his manners, and his acceptance of social classes. These attitudes contrast greatly with those in other parts of the United States where there is a strong belief in women's rights, where Negro children go to school with whites, where speech is frank, and where one social class is held to be as good as another.

IDEOLOGIES AND MORES

Social attitudes are very dear to the people who hold them. Indeed they become matters of belief and thus exert a strong influence like religious sanctions, and are binding like morals. Thus to behave like a gentlemen is one of the highest attainments in the social values of a southerner. Honor is a shining virtue. To act ungentlemenly and dishonorably is condemned more than most sins. Similarly in northern cities, no one would dare to admit that he was undemocratic, that he belonged to a superior class. The brotherhood of man is his belief, without distinction of color or creed. Also high in his scale of values is efficiency, the measure and reward of which is success. Not to be efficient is to be dubbed a failure, no matter how kind or good one may be. What could be worse than to be called a failure?

So our social attitudes become rights and wrongs. They are cherished like the beatitudes or are condemned like the practice of the Philistines. We can hardly discuss them calmly. They tend to become eternal truths for all people at all times. Thus, it is good for everyone to follow the codes of conduct set for a gentleman. Everyone should in every age believe in the brotherhood of man and that all men are created equal.

Sociologists have sought to signalize this emotional binding force of our cherished social attitudes by calling them mores. Thus it is said mores make right and wrong. For instance, democracy is right and slavery is wrong. It follows that a person living under a particular set of mores cannot speak against them, any more than in the present war one could speak out in the United States in praise of Hitler. One cannot speak in favor of slavery, for our mores are against slavery, though slavery was held to be good among the Greeks and at various other times and places in the world. The mores tend to restrict our vision, to make us contemporary-minded. They narrow our view like a fog. Thus we cannot see how slavery could have been proper in ancient Greece. We cannot understand how polygamy could have been suited to any people.

The mores of the South and of the North are different on many subjects. One is the Negro. Since each region believes in its own mores, and since the mores are antagonistic, each is heartily condemned by the other. Segregation and social inequality of the Negro are held desirable in the South, while in the North such an attitude is considered most unjust. Which is right?

Furthermore these attitudes are changing. The South is becoming more liberal toward the Negro while in the Northern cities property owners in urban residence sections are active in trying to keep the Negro from living in the neighborhood. There is thus some confusion in regard to social attitudes. The South is not only in conflict with the North but also with itself. For new social attitudes are developing in the South which are antagonistic to the social attitudes of the Old South. Thus the sheltered daughter of the old days is today going to a coeducational college and sometimes her free and easy behavior is a consternation to the older generation. There is confusion over the proper place and conduct of women in society. The older generation and the new are in conflict. Which is right?

SOCIO-ECONOMIC SYSTEMS AND MORES

The purpose of this essay is to try to bring some clarity and order in this confusion. The first point is that there is a correlation between a socio-economic system and its social attitudes, and that the mores which are right for any one socio-economic system are not necessarily right for different systems. Thus in the Old South the system was agricultural; in the northern industrial cities the social order is based on the factory system. Each system has its own attitudes, for instance, on child labor.

In the Old South child labor was good. The old-time southerner was really astounded to hear that in the North they were not letting children work, and making laws to prevent it. For among self-sufficing farmers child labor, that is, the industriousness of children, is greatly to be desired. That is the way the young learned to become farmers and capable housewives, for there were no agricultural schools. It was necessary for the boys to learn to care for the animals, to plow, to harvest, to mend wagons and broken tools, and for girls to learn to cook, to sew, to spin, to weave, to make medicines, to preserve fruits, to manage a house. To keep a playful youngster at these tasks required considerable pressure. If a child played too much, or did not do his chores, he was likely to come to a bad end, it was held. "An idle mind is the devil's workshop." The apprentice system—child labor—whereby a youngster learned to be a wheelwright or a lawyer was admirable. These were the virtues that Benjamin Franklin praised. Loafing and play were condemned, much as frivolity is disapproved by college deans today.

This ideology regarding child labor was not, of course, peculiar only to families with children, or only to self-sufficing farmers. Like the clouds or the weather it covered the region, even the villages, towns, and the new cities, populated from rural regions. Also while this attitude toward the industriousness of children was particularly appropriate to the self-sufficing farm of pre-Civil War or pre-Revolutionary days, it hung over into the twentieth century. For the mores change slowly.

In the industrial North the situation was quite different. There were factories where children went to work before daylight, worked all day in rooms where the air was bad and where there was little sunshine. In winter they came home after dark. Their wages were low. The tasks were routine and did not call for the varied talents that were so useful around the farm. They were tired at night. Their chief opportunity for play was on Sunday, but on the Sabbath recreation was tabooed. Therefore child labor was bad. Here the ideology was play and more play for children and no child labor for the young. The economic conditions were those of the factory system, and a new ideology on child labor arose, appropriate to this system.

Hence it is easy to see how the peoples of the urban States of the North, who were passing child labor laws which were good and moral, in their missionary zeal would want to impose them upon the agricultural southern States. When the southern States, with few factories and many farms, did not respond, they were considered by the northerners as benighted. The idea of the adaptation of the mores to the economic conditions was not appreciated by the editorial writers in the Boston newspapers. In the course of time factories came to the South and also child labor legislation.

In the case of child labor there are two ideologies, each appropriate to its own economic system. In this illustration there is observable the myopic influence of the mores. The vision is restricted to one economic system. The adherents of each system condemn the other. The southerner needed the labor of his child on his own farm and after all it was his child and not the State's. He resented implications as to his morality and he was astounded at the child labor laws of the North. The victorious North was for imposing its system on the South whether it fitted or not, and the northerner had scant understanding of the socio-economic system of the South. Each had his perspective limited. The northerner was on the winning side in this battle of the mores, for the old agricultural order was receding in the South, and factories with their new ideologies were coming to southern cities.

As the cotton factories came South, there was a lag in attitudes toward them. At first the factories were new and few, and the old mores of the need of industriousness for the young was all pervading. So the new mores of child labor, like all new social movements, had to fight their way against the opposition of the old.

THE FORCE OF TRADITION

It has been shown that each economic system has its own ideology. But this fact does not wholly explain the southern attitudes. The rural west is agricultural also and is quite different from the Old South in many of its attitudes. It is true that western agriculture is different from southern, yet this difference is not satisfactory as an explanation. For peculiarities of southern ideologies, it must not be assumed that agriculture in the southern States created them, as the factory system of the northern cities created the ideologies of the North. The South imported its attitudes from England. England of the eighteenth and earlier centuries was rural, too, with self-sufficing agriculture. The colonists came from England and brought ideologies with them. In the South with its predominantly rural life these attitudes of pre-industrial England took root and flourished better than in the non-agricultural North.

The southerner's attitude toward social classes, for instance, is much like the attitudes toward social classes held in England before the rise of cities, and also in France and other European countries. There are observers who think the southerner's views on social classes derived from his experience with the Negro. It is much more probable that they were brought over from England and persisted under the conditions of life in the South.

In discussing the ideologies of classes and democracy in the South and in the North, and indeed of other ideologies to be presented later, the purpose is not to present them scientifically and objectively. Rather they will be presented sympathetically with the idea of trying to show how the southerner feels toward his beliefs and what the social attitudes of the northerner mean to the city dwellers of that region. The reader should be able to see how each set of mores appears to be right and proper, even though they may be antagonistic. Also there is in this paper no particular interest in the extent to which the views are held in a region, such as might be collected from questionnaires. Instead a somewhat idealized statement will be presented, in order that the outlines may be seen more sharply.

SOCIAL CLASSES AND DEMOCRACY

The southerner never thought much about social classes because that is all he had ever known. He brought them over from eighteenth century England where they have persisted until the present, much as they have persisted in the South. The southerner took classes for granted, just as he takes the atmosphere around him for granted. It was not a matter for comment or debate. There were in the South three classes; the large upper class, a small class of poor whites, and the Negroes. The Negroes were slaves and were considered to be an inferior people. The poor whites were ignored. They were not good farmers. They didn't have much refinement. Many of them were illiterate. But a member of the upper classes seldom thought of his superiority. He had no occasion to strut; to have done so would have been bad form. The superiority of the upper class was obvious.

It never occurred to the southerner of the upper classes that he was socially responsible for the lower classes. That was their own problem. He believed in heredity and never thought that the upper classes were unjust to the lower classes.

In fact he had little idea of class; but he did of

family. The families with which his family associated were really his conception of class. There was much pride in family. There were, of course, various degrees of prominence among families, as there were grades in the landed gentry of England or levels in the aristocracy of France. That one's family and their friends had standards, values, and achievements no doubt gave some sense of superiority, much as there are feelings of superiority among nations today. Thus the inhabitant of the United States has no shame in feeling that his country is better than Mexico. Family pride was somewhat like the pride one has today in his church, his club, his athletic team. There was a family standard in courtesy, in skilled management, in fair dealing, in industry, in hospitality, in acquisition of the arts and learning. These the family name stood for. The family made every effort to maintain and improve its status. They brought their children up to honor the family name. If a member or relative showed signs of weakening, the other members made efforts to keep him in line and not to allow dishonor to be brought on the family name. The family was the one agency of social achievement. Families of culture, of education, of wealth were proud of their achievements or their standing and they wanted their children to associate with children of other families of culture, to intermarry with them. The families one associated with were in the social class to which one belonged. The social classes were thus collections of families.

The system was a stable one among landholders in a settled agricultural society; more so than in a city where property does not remain in a family line for many generations in an age of great change.

The southerner was very appreciative of the importance of good associates. A mother knows that she does not want her boy to associate with bad boys. This idea is the same as that stressed by sociologists who speak of the influence of groups on personality. As Professor W. I. Thomas says, "A person cannot rise much above or fall much below the level of the group with whom he associates." This leads to a "consciousness of kind" so that members of one family like to associate with families of good standing. Therefore, family and class were good, matters of pride, nothing to be ashamed of.

What was the evil of such a system? Did it not maintain high levels of achievement? Did it not keep individuals from backsliding from standards? If other families did not do so well was it not their own fault, thought these self-sufficient farmers.

The southerner found it difficult to understand how, in the cities of the North, the lower classes were glorified, how to be born in a log cabin or on the lower east side was something about which to boast, how the brotherhood of man meant that one's child should associate with any Tom, Dick or Harry, how a family with untrained-taste in art, with no musical acquaintance, with no achievement in education, with no travel abroad could be rated on a par with a family which had these advantages. He thought it inconsistent that in northern cities superiority may be claimed for a college, a business, a city, a club, but not for a family or a social class. He found the cult of the common man and the democratic dogma, strange attitudes. The tastes of the masses were of the level of the tabloid, the wild western moving picture, the comic strip, the pulp magainze. His was a family system based on landed property in a stable agriculture with considerable belief in heredity and not much experience with the "uplift" of governments and social movements.

In the northern cities, a man may start life as a common laborer and wind up the head of a steel corporation. Hence one man is as good as another. If the common laborer was born in a log cabin, then the log cabin is a symbol of his achievement and hence a matter of pride. The cities are centers of opportunity. There are schools for everyone. A boy graduating from the grammar school can go to high school, which opens many opportunities, one of which is a college education. Thus class barriers are swept away. Ability rises to the top. A city family can hardly hold its wealth for several generations as landowners can do in a stable agricultural society. The factory has broken up the family system of agricultural times. The family name doesn't mean much. It is the individual that counts, not association of families. The family ceases to be the one great social institution for achievement. It is replaced by the civic organization, by the government, by clubs. Civic pride replaces family pride. But above all democracy means that the lower classes are not to be held down to inferior positions by the powerful upper classes. The everlasting glory of democracy is that the poor need not remain poor but can rise in the economic and social scale. Democracy is supported by the sciences of sociology and biology which show no superiority of one race over another and which show the difference in ability of the classes to be much a matter of environment. The century of the common man does not mean so much a glorification of the standards and tastes of the lower classes, but rather a century of opportunity for the common man, freed from the obstacles of special privileges and unequal opportunities.

With the vote and the public schools and the purchasing power of high wages, the common man becomes very popular with the politicians, with the advertisers, with the newspapers, with the cartoonists, with the moving picture producers, and with the radio speakers and artists. There arises the ideology of the common man. Walt Whitman is his poet; Abraham Lincoln his political ideal. An ideology of the common man is built up resting upon freedom, equality, brotherhood, no privilege, no snobbishness, the virtue of honest toil, the rights of man, fair dealing, no distinctions of race and equal opportunity. The material values of the standard of living are praised more than spiritual assets. These virtues and values were supported by the powerful pressure of "Main Street." Democracy has all the compelling force of the powerful mores. None dare speak against it. To criticize democracy is no more permitted than to praise fascism.

From this point of view, the southerner with his poll tax disbarring the poor from voting, is an obstacle to progress. His treatment of the Negro is an indescribable injustice, as it denies to him the opportunities which democracy brings. The southerners are reactionaries who oppose the use of government to raise the lot of the common man. His pride of family and social class is seen as reactionary Bourbonism, as the entrenchment of special privilege, or it becomes the butt of ridicule. Southern aristocrats, along with moonlight and magnolias, plantations and Kentucky colonels were suitable material for the comic opera.

Thus, again we have two different and conflicting attitudes toward the social classes and democracy characteristic of the landed gentry and of the industrial cities.

FAMILY AND MARRIAGE

Attitudes toward the family are also different. In the Old South, the family was the main economic institution and the most powerful social one. It was the agency of attainment, of rising in the world, of care for dependency. As such, the family name was more important than the first name. It was the family rather than the individual. Marriage brought social status, property, membership in a social class, protection, associates for one's children. It also meant a business partnership, whose success rested on the ability of the husband as a provider and of the wife as a household manager. Thus in choosing a mate, romantic love was only one of many other factors. A young person should marry in the same class, into a good family. A marriage partner should be capable as well as good looking, and was appraised as a prospective father or mother of children.

The family being an economic institution, man and wife were business partners, with man as the head and woman a capable manager. There was a definite division of labor free of jurisdictional conflict. Divorce disorganized this economic institution. Virtue of women was a cornerstone of this type of family and there were just two types of women, good and bad. Women's place being in the home, they were trained not only in skills, but in graces, manners, and charm to make the relationship work smoothly. Particularly were women brought up in the social graces to please men, economic heads, property owners, protectors and fighters.

In the new northern cities, young people marry as individuals not as members of families. Family prestige means little, so great is the flux in the social scale. Family and relatives, instead of giving strength, status, and support, are troublesome and unwelcome in small city apartments where goods are all bought. Class lines are not much of an influence in marriage, for universal education and the rewards of efficiency in business mean that any individual is eligible as a marriage partner. There are not many household duties in a childless family living in a steam-heated apartment with a delicatessen store around the corner. Thus companionability and love tend to be the only factors determining the choice of mates. If a young couple love each other, they may marry, no matter what are the other conditions, and if a married couple do not love each other, to continue living together is a sin. So divorces are frequent. Women can get jobs in offices, stores, and factories. Hence they take on the attitude and practices of men. Comradeship replaces chivalry.

Women are people, not just females. The family domicile is said to be a suite of rooms over a garage, a parking placing for the night. Personality, happiness, companionship, and the giving of opportunities to children are the only goals of family life.

These antagonisms in the ideologies of marriage and the family of the landed gentry and of the city dwellers are illustrated by the abdication of the British throne by Edward Windsor to marry an untitled American divorcee. The royalty held to the status concept while the American point of view was that of romantic love, so adequately presented in the moving picture.

FRIENDSHIP AND ACQUAINTANCE

Among neighborly self-sufficing farmers there is little occasion for hypocrisy or pretense in personal relations. Friendship can be genuine, though there is an effort for such farmers to be friendly and neighborly, and perhaps some pretense is involved, but in a society with slow change the amenities are observed with good manners. There is, of course, dislike, even feuds, among rural families. Indeed, there are cliques of families; but these cliques are based upon choice. The right to choose one's friends or associates ranks high in the hierarchy of a southerner's values. This right of choice is a source of difficulty in the southerner's adaptation to democracy. Under the cult of the common man must he be friends with anyone? Has he no right of choice, of preference under the dogma of the brotherhood of man? Among the self-sufficing landed gentry you like a friend for what he is, not for what you can get out of him. To "use" a friend for selfish purposes was very much condemned in the Old South. There were certainly limits to which one could impose on a friend.

This attitude toward friendship made it difficult for the southerner with his ideas of family and class to adjust to the new tools of democracy, particularly voting. The politician very quickly practices the art of exploiting personal associations and friendliness, if not friendship, in order to get votes, as for instance kissing the baby of a prospective voter for whom he has no special friendliness. Thus it was said in the Old South that a man could not be a gentleman and be in politics. A member of the landed gentry objected to "currying favor," as it was expressed. This conception of friendship is much in evidence in Sir Walter Scott's novels of social life in rural England, which were widely read in the Old South.

The southerners also found it difficult to adjust to the tools of the trader, as did also the English gentry. To the gentry the trader "curried favor" in order to increase his customers. He was ingratiating for ulterior motives. This conflict between the folkways of the trader and the landowner in England is well known.

It is not to be implied that the Old South had only beautiful friendships. The picture is idealized and not supposed to be representative. It was rather the code, and codes are not always strictly adhered to.

In cities, friendship is somewhat different. There it is surprising how many occupations depend upon the good will and friendliness of others. Thus the doctor must have patients, the lawyer, clients. The merchant needs customers and the banker depositors, whereas the independent farmer needs only to make his land produce. Consider the case with the salesman. His job is to make you buy something whether you want to or not, whether it is good for you or not. In cities, honors, rewards, and approbations go to extraverts who are popular and have the most "friends." One collects friends because they are useful. The model is the politician. The insurance salesman is another illustration.

Friendships in cities tend to become acquaintanceships. Indeed many city dwellers do not have a conception of friendship. A friend is someone who likes you well enough to let you use him. There is a reciprocity about it. You help me to get on and I will help you. Some years ago there appeared a book of great popularity called, *How to Win Friends and Influence People*. To a southerner of the old school, the title sounds iniquitous. It is immoral to influence people, except in religion and in the case of children and relatives. To influence people is to violate the sanctity of their personality, to interfere with their freedom. As to winning friends, in the old ideology, why try to win them? You have them or you do not, according to your temperament. If you are a solitary person like Thoreau, you do not need to have many friends. People who win friends are like the politician and the insurance salesman. This from the ideology of the old South.

From the ideology of the urban North, why not influence people? To sell them insurance is a good thing. If more people can be persuaded to buy automobiles, the world will be better for it. If people use you and your friendship for good purposes, then you can use them for the same reason. Thus progress is advanced. Cooperative and voluntary collective effort depends upon such "friends" in urban regions. Among independent farmers there is less need for such a pattern of friendships.

MANNERS AND MORALS

The differences in the mores of the North and the South are not always to be explained by the socio-economic system and by the heritage of tradition. Another factor is the rapidity of change. Thus in the Old South where cotton and tobacco were planted generation after generation and change was very slow, codes of behavior could be followed by each succeeding generation. Manners are codes of behavior laid out in detail to curb the selfishness and egotism in the little acts of life. Morals and law deal with more important curbs. Both morals and manners need to be learned in detail to fit any situation. Both are much easier to learn and enforce in a stationary society than in a rapidly changing one. Where there is rapid change, new sets of rules must be made to fit each succeeding change. These may be no sooner learned than they must be changed for another set.

Hence in the Old South, manners were much in evidence. Great care was taken to teach them to children. Less emphasis is placed upon manners in the cities of the North, necessarily, for there the rapidity of change following the new inventions and the waves of migrants makes it difficult to have good manners. Also the manners tend to be somewhat different. For instance, a southerner considers it bad form in making a business call to launch immediately into setting forth his proposition. First, one asks about the health of the other, the condition of his family (if he be known well), the state of general business, or even about the weather. Only after these preliminaries may one proceed to the business at hand. In the North, all the gestures are considered unnecessary, a waste of time, and inefficient. In the South, it is not good taste to appear too aggressive; for aggression is selfishness which is kept under cover by manners. In the North, aggressiveness is one of the most desired of all traits, for it spells efficiency, hustle, and success. People, not schooled in

manners, are often confused by their niceties of speech, and have fears of making a *faux pas*. Hence manners are derided as excess baggage in favor of simplicity and directness. But the essential difference between the North and the South in manners is due to the different rates of change in the two regions.

SUCCESS AND VALUES

An outstanding difference in ideologies between these two regions, the South and the North is in their attitudes toward success, and how much sacrifice in values one is permitted to make to attain success.

In the North success is worshipped like a god. This attitude flows from the abundance of rich rewards and the widely spread opportunities in the industrial North. These rewards come from the mass production of machinery run by mechanical power. In the twentieth century industrial regions are rich and agricultural poor, that is relatively so. The economic prizes of the factory system are much greater than those of fertile valleys. In 1820, before the era of factories, Charleston, South Carolina and New York City had about the same amount of wealth. Now the industrial States are where the wealth is. Universal education opens these opportunities to all. The race is on. Success is immeasurably desired. The plaudits are for the successful. As in the days of the Klondike gold rush the rewards are for the ruthless aggressor. The cult in the cities is efficiency, to be a "go-getter," a "live wire". The ideal for youth is to be a hustler, aggressive, "up-to-date." To be a failure is to be scorned or to be ignored, to be passed by. Accomplishment, speed, production, efficiency, "stream lining," executive ability, aggressiveness, hustle are the particulars of these social values. Ruthlessness may be excused if it gets results. With the struggle to be first, moderation and balance cease to be valued in favor of the extreme, that is the best, first place. Boasting is not only permitted, but considered all right, even admired in the successful. Efficiency is beautiful; and the results are good, very good.

It is not surprising then that, in order to attain success, many values and virtues may be sacrificed. Thus one "uses" friends, or sacrifices friendship, recreation is neglected, health abused. Competition is of the cutthroat variety with a wreckage of neuroses following. Legislators may be bribed, and shady deals pulled off. The word "honor" disappears from usage. "Currying favor" of those who can help is common practice. The temptation is very great to forget the Ten Commandments and the Sermon on the Mount. It is as though in the ranking values success is at the top. But the ends justify the means. Think of the opportunities for doing good which come to the successful. Colleges may be endowed, cancer institutes supported, and art galleries set up. Then, too, most success is in doing something eminently worth while, as Henry Ford did in supplying tractors to farmers. So success becomes part of the new mores.

In the Old South of agricultural landowners, there were other values more important than success. Among the values a youngster learned at his mother's knee, the word "success" was seldom mentioned. A lad was urged to be good, noble, a man of honor, to keep his word, and to be a gentleman. To be a "Christian gentleman" was the ideal. Of course, everyone wants to be a success, that is they do not want to be a failure. But, in an agricultural society of landowners, great and spectacular successes were rare. Property was fairly stable from one generation to another, and a prominent family might remain so for several generations. So success was desired but not extravagantly. If a person was trustworthy, reliable, truthful, considerate, lived up to his promises, respected women, did not boast, fought for the right, he was a success. So success was not a particularly important word in the lexicon. Above all one must not stoop to succeed.

Even leisure, a good time, horse racing, shooting quail, and the social amenities were not to be sacrificed in order to get rich. A leisurely social life with its pleasures and associations were values not to be put aside in a mad pursuit of wealth.

Then, too, it was not good, definitely not good, to love money too much. There was a contempt or ostracism of those who chased the "almighty dollar," too eagerly. To say of a man, "He will do anything for money" was an insult. To be stingy with money was the sign of littleness, of narrowness. On the other hand, generosity was praised. One said with pride, "This is something money cannot buy." To offer money for anything other than very standard materials, such as real estate, drygoods, etc., or for other than standard services, such as a shopkeeper supplies, was very likely to give offense. It was quite definitely

necessary to warn the young against too much love of the "filthy lucre." Indeed, it was all right for a gentleman to have a contempt for money. A family without much money, if they had a good name, possessed the social requisites, and exercised the virtues, would be much more esteemed socially, than a very wealthy, newly-rich family without the proper tastes and manners.

The insistence on standards of goodness, character, and honor are found wherever a stable society exists, even among the primitive peoples. The lack of appreciation of success is correlated with a status and a stationary society, especially one where family standing and landed property are inherited. The attitude of hostility toward money is that of a self-sufficient farming society where money is little known and used only for a limited number of purchases. Money symbolized a strange, new economy in which riches were deified, and it was felt as a hostile intrusion into the scheme of values of the landed gentry.

These southerners who followed other values than success were viewed by the efficiency devotees of the North as lazy, pleasure loving, unprogressive, and inefficient. How could a southerner sit on his front porch contentedly drinking his mint julip negligent of the rich rewards of progress? His balanced life of moderation was measured against the single-minded pursuit of the extreme, success, and was judged wanting. Thus in the scale of values in the social systems of the South and of the North, success was differently emphasized and the price to be paid for it was differently estimated.

CONCLUSION

A selected list of ideologies of the Old South and the urban North have been described and found to be different. Neither region appreciates the social values of the others. In general those of the South came from rural England of earlier centuries, and were products of an agricultural society not changing very rapidly. Though agricultural they spread over the towns and villages and somewhat to the cities. On the other hand the ideologies of the North arose from industrial cities, changing rapidly, with great wealth, and a shifting population.

In the stream of social change cities are spreading, factories are coming to the South, and with them the ideologies of the North. At the same time the ideologies of the landed gentry are receding. Thus in the South the mores are in transition. There is conflict and confusion. The future will be clarified somewhat by recognizing the economic origins of these ideologies and why they have come about.

But the correlation of the mores and the socio-economic system is not perfect. The economic system is an important factor in determining some mores, but it is not the sole determinant. Otherwise the ideologies of English, German, and American industrial cities would be the same; and those of the landed gentry in France, England, and the United States would be all alike. But they are not. The existing tradition in any region forces some adjustment of the ideologies of the machine when it is imported. This adaptation comes about through choice, which rests on the attitudes of the people.

This is illustrated by a question I once asked a fencing instructor, an elderly man from France. Realizing that occupations often determine attitudes, I said to him, "I suppose you regret the passing of the duel?" "Well," he said "isn't it rather disgusting to have your intimate affairs mulled over by the courts and their hanger-on lawyers, and to have your personal affairs spread before the populace in the pages of the yellow journals? Wouldn't it be better to settle them other ways?" Each group of mores has its own values, if we can only see them. It does not behoove a person of broad mind and education to fail to understand that the mores of other peoples and of other times have their good points. Intolerance toward the mores of other peoples shows a narrowness of outlook. The northern cities are centers of dispersal for the new conquering mores that are spreading over the land. But their missionaries show a narrowness of understanding and an intolerance of the ideologies of other regions. And in the South some of the sectional patriots are equally narrow and lacking in understanding of these new social attitudes and values that are being rapidly adopted.

The new ideologies of the democratic industrial cities will be modified somewhat as they spread to the South, adapted to the southern tradition. Here is where the choice of the southern people comes in. In the countries that had the duel among the gentry—England, France, and Germany—the daily newspapers publish very little of the intimate affairs of the people and scandals, much less than the press in the United States, where the duel never flourished, though dueling in its absence may not be the sole explanation. The ideologies of the South are in transition, the problem of the southerners is to preserve the best of the old values and to select from the virtues of the new. But there is not complete freedom of will, for the socioeconomic systems are powerful forces in affecting ideologies. It is the old problem of free will and determinism.

SOCIAL CHANGES AND THEIR EFFECTS ON
RACE RELATIONS IN THE SOUTH

CHARLES S. JOHNSON

THERE has been a disposition, on the part of some observers, to regard the increasing evidences of racial tension in the South and in the country at large as prima facie evidence of the deterioration of race relations. In an earlier article[1] it was speculated that the racial incidents in themselves were not conclusive, rather that they were symptoms of basic social changes which, in the long run, might well prove wholesome. Recent developments seem to support these speculations. For not only have these developments appeared to be shaping themselves into a new pattern, but many southern leaders are beginning to recognize that the new conditions require new attitudes and techniques and are ready to take action which, a short while ago, seemed remote and unlikely.

The usual assumptions back of the popular estimates about the state of race relations have been that where there is quiescence and an undisturbed status quo there are most satisfactory and wholesome race relations. But just such quiescence may be an indication of immobility and social stagnation. The racial as well as various other social tensions that have followed in the wake of the war are a symptom of social changes; and these changes in themselves may be interpreted as the incidental effects of profound forces moving toward a new equilibrium.

As might be expected in a time of rapid change, many of these developments are imperfectly understood and regarded as a threat to traditions and customs of central importance. Racial incidents continue to occur, and there is considerable surface display of hostility. Where there is preoccupation with race and relative racial positions in the social system of the region, it is inevitable that many developments which are essentially non-racial in character will be invested with dangerous racial implications.

Total war is a cataclysmic national event that shakes and loosens many traditions from their deep moorings, whether these traditions are economic, religious, racial or romantic. The impersonal and direct imperatives of sudden war cannot trace a careful path around the embedded orthodoxies of race any more than can a flood or earthquake. When these racial traditions have been disturbed, when the comfortable patterns of living have been broken or warped, a sense of insecurity is inevitable. New guides to behavior must be worked out, new situations must be met and solved by reference to new or at least altered values. The race problem in such situations becomes more personal, and in becoming more personal it becomes more emotional.

The changes that the war brought to the South reached into the lives of its people and brought about several major crises. Although the South is primarily agricultural, it shared richly in the appropriations for cantonments, shipyards, and munitions plants. Industrial production in general was enormously accelerated. A result was the uprooting and migration of hundreds of thousands of workers from relatively isolated and rural areas to the cities and production centers. They carried their personal backgrounds with them into these new situations, and tried, as was natural, to find a basis of adjustment which would enable them to keep the old values so necessary to their sense of personal security. This alone was a personal and an industrial revolution of great significance crowded into a brief period. The major training camps for the ten million or more troops are in the South, and this has brought into new and disturbing contact northern Negroes and northern whites with southern Negroes and southern whites. The demands for manpower have pressed against the customary racial occupational categories; high wages, together with national minimum wage legislation have disturbed another traditional racial differential. The familiar and seemingly indispensable Negro domestic, unprotected by employment legislation and long underpaid by national standards, has disappeared into the new war industries, leaving a trail of dismay and bitter resentment among housewives.

Changes have also been taking place in southern agriculture. The country has given up millions of its workers to the city, yet it has been able to

[1] See SOCIAL FORCES, 23 (October 1944), pp. 27–32.

101

increase its production with fewer hands, thereby closing the door to the return of many of the emigrés. And the shadow of the automatic cotton picker looms over the remaining workers of both races.

Another outgrowth of the war has been the increasing disposition of the Federal government and the Nation at large to feel a sense of responsibility for the reaffirmation and implementation of democratic principles in all parts of the Nation. This emphasis on putting the American creed of democracy into practice has been made necessary by the nature of the war and the character of our enemies. It has had unique effects in some areas of the southern region where the principle has encountered patterns and customs with reference to the Negro population tending in the opposite direction. This has caused uneasiness among some of the white population and increasing awareness and hopefulness, if not complete faith, among many of the Negroes. The specific steps which have been interpreted as threatening to the traditional racial patterns have included: (a) extensions of various types of New Deal legislation in the South, with some effort to insist upon equitable distribution of funds or benefits involved; (b) national campaigns for the abolition of the poll tax; (c) campaigns for the broadening of the social security laws (which would affect most directly the southern region in the agricultural and domestic service fields, and marginal workers, both white and Negro); (d) Federal court decisions virtually compelling the equalization of educational expenditures for whites and Negroes, taking away the legal basis of the white primary, and denying the right of a union which has legal power to bargain for all employees, to discriminate on the basis of race, creed or color; (e) legislative efforts to outlaw discrimination, including the campaign for a Permanent Fair Employment Practice Committee.

These measures have appeared to many white southerners to be forcing racial adjustments on a new level ahead of public readiness for such changes, and a result has been resistance to this pressure from the outside, impatience with outside interference, reassertion of the regional policy of racial segregation, and a determination to handle the regional racial problem under conditions imposed by the region itself. However, there has recently been a growing recognition that change of some kind, whether imposed from the outside or directed from within, is bound to come, and a

willingness in some quarters to move independently to meet the new conditions. An example is the action of the Georgia legislature, under the leadership of Governor Arnall, in repealing the poll tax with almost startling suddenness, and another example, more directly bearing on race relations, is the importance given at a recent meeting of southern Governors to the urgent necessity of equalizing educational facilities.

A careful count over a period of ten months in 1943 showed 111 racial incidents in the South of sufficient importance to be given attention in the national press. During 1944 and the early months of 1945 similar incidents have been occurring, arising from similar causes, but there are indications of a slight decrease in the number of incidents and a possible rearrangement of the causes, in order of numerical importance. The 1943 order was as follows: (1) incidents growing out of new racial contacts in industrial employment; (2) incidents associated with congestion and racial etiquette in various modes of transportation; (3) incidents associated with crimes committed or suspected, and the police handling of these situations; (4) incidents involving conflicts between Negro service men and civilian or military police, or other civilians; (5) incidents involving Negro status, with respect to civil rights, the racial etiquette, etc.; (6) other incidents, including attempts of Negroes to vote, migrate, move into a non-Negro area, challenge of white status, and lynching.[2]

A rapid survey of racial incidents in the South in the last month of 1944 and the first month of 1945 shows a total of six incidents reported nationally, none of which involved more than a few individuals. Almost all were associated either with transportation or police methods in relation to Negroes. One incident arose out of picketing by Negro women workers. Although police handling and court disposition of Negro cases continues to follow the old patterns in many places, there is an increasing number of reports of newer trends. In one instance in Alabama a Negro father preferred charges of rape against two white men, and the men were convicted and fined, although the charge was changed to assault and

[2] It is interesting to note that in the North and West where there have also been numerous instances of racial tension, the two most important causes have been incidents associated with employment or upgrading of Negroes and incidents involving efforts of Negroes to find a place to live.

battery. A Georgia court reversed the conviction of two Negro girls on charges of disorderly conduct, and openly flayed the original conviction as evidence of race prejudice. Lynchings in 1944 dropped to two, a new low.

The most serious of the employment incidents since the beginning of the war was, of course, the Mobile affair, in which an attempt to introduce essential Negro workers on new shipbuilding jobs met resistance from white workers. Attitudes regarding labor and labor organization are less tolerant in the southern region than in some other sections of the country, and the issues of race and labor react upon each other and cannot always be separated. The highest temperatures have been registered in the areas of greatest labor demand. The demands of production schedules, under the stress of the war emergency, have tended to overcome popular resistance to the altering of caste lines in general occupational fields, and there has recently been increased racial accommodation in the war plants. Yet there are still many plants in the South producing essential war materials and calling upon Federal agencies for assistance in securing workers from outside the South, which continue to bar locally available and competent Negroes altogether. Where Negroes are employed, the principle of segregation, actual or token, has been preserved in most instances, both with respect to physical contact on the jobs and higher and lower grades of work.

The point of most frequent physical contact between whites and Negroes is in transportation, and more minor clashes have occurred in these relationships than in any other. The new conditions of population congestion, shortage of carriers, the use of raw personnel replacements for the more experienced drivers and conductors, and the flexible and frequently indeterminable limits of racial segregation on public carriers tend to reduce the *customary* patterns of segregation to highly volatile issues of *personal* status in racial situations. Where travel of members of the Armed Forces is involved a new element is introduced of the symbol of the United States uniform, and what it represents in different minds. So complex has this situation become that Mr. Virginius Dabney, Editor of the Richmond, Virginia *Times-Dispatch*, advocated for Virginia the abolition of laws for separation on carriers in the State, since they restricted and irritated without preserving their original intent to keep the races apart. The Maryland legislature, in similar vein, recently voted to do away with the segregation laws on public carriers actually to facilitate the handling of essential transportation.

Where there is at the same time inadequacy of carrier space and a racial etiquette that demands first service to white passengers, it is inevitable that there should be numerous and various challenges by Negroes of the etiquette, if they are to travel at all. Moreover, the minor patterns of the etiquette vary widely among cities, and mistakes are easy to make and may be interpreted as deliberate flaunting of the principle of segregation and of the dictum of proper racial respect. This has frequently been the issue in racial conflict situations involving Negro soldiers from the North who have been sent to the South for military training. The arming or deputizing of bus drivers in these situations seems to have proved an inadequate solution of the difficulty.

Crimes and the police handling of such situations as appear to have racial significance have very often reflected fears on the part of the police that unruly Negroes would get out of the racial as well as legal controls. This is not a new problem, but an old one greatly accentuated by war conditions. Ordinary crimes of Negroes against Negroes, normally high, have not held any important or new implications for race relations. It has been observed, however, in a growing number of southern cities—twenty-one, according to our records—that the use of Negro police has salutary effects.

The presence of northern Negro service men in the small southern towns near their camps has been fairly generally resented by the white population, and there have been numerous unsuccessful efforts to influence the Army to train these Negroes in the North. It is understandable how problems would arise with the sudden pressure of Negro soldiers on leave against the narrow recreational limits of the Negro quarter of a small southern town. The community fears of violence on the part of Negroes, in resentment of unfamiliar practices, have been justified in several cases, and the Negro violence has been all too often anticipated by a demonstration of white violence. A study of thirty-odd reported cases of violence involving Negroes in the armed forces in 1941, and 1942, and 1943 showed that there is a typical pattern, and that such incidents can occur in the North as well as in the South, and even in overseas areas where two opposite conceptions clash, namely, the conception of Negro soldiers that they are American citizens entitled to impartial, nondiscriminative treatment regardless of color, and the conception of white soldiers or civilians that they are inherently superior by virtue of their race and entitled to manifest evidence of their superiority in the discriminative treatment of Negroes.

Other examples of recent racial clashes in the South have followed fairly familiar patterns. Of importance to underlying racial sentiment and tensions, although not usually responsible for overt conflict, is the widespread experience of white middle-class households with their Negro domestic servants. The inconvenience of being without the familiar Negro domestics has proved to be one of the most intimate effects of the war in many households. Some of these domestics have gone temporarily to better paying war jobs, some have been able, as a result of family allowances from soldiers, to stay at home and care for their own households, and some have just quit work. Although this is a contingency to be expected in war time, it has become one of the most serious barriers to interracial tolerance and good will. This basically economic movement has been invested with the deepest private and political fears and disaffections of the southern white-middle-class, and has been the occasion of a vast array of unwholesome rumors. However, the very absurdity of these rumors, and their failure to materialize in the manner expected seems to have weakened their intensity in recent months, perhaps indicating a wider understanding of what has actually been happening.

The disaffections, fears, resentments, and gloomy forebodings of the racial fundamentalists have found articulate expression in the halls of the national Congress, where they have associated their reactions to the New Deal government and to the President and his family with their concern for preserving the racial *status quo*; and in the gratuitous but emphatic resolutions of the South Carolina legislature regarding the manifest destiny of the white race. In spite of the vociferousness of these elements, however, election results in November indicated that even poll tax constituencies no longer consider exploitation of the race issue as the best possible political platform. Several of the most vocal champions of "white supremacy" as a shibboleth were defeated, and their places were taken by exponents of the more liberal and constructive southern viewpoint. If other states follow Georgia in eliminating the poll tax, increased popular participation in elections should continue

this trend, even though other ways may be devised to restrict Negro voting.

While the Negro in the South has made many types of adjustment to the southern cultural pattern, there seems to be general agreement and a great deal of objective evidence that his attitude is increasingly one of protest. A southern sociologist recently published an article on "The Negro's New Belligerency," which noted that "in recent months the Negro's usual protests have become a mighty chorus of discord."[3] A recent poll by the Denver Opinion Research Center, as well as the Negro press itself, bears this out to some extent, although Negroes in the North are more unanimous and outspoken in their resentment than those in the South. There can be little doubt that the development of this protest reaction has been stimulated by the war, with its emphasis on the defense of democracy, and by situations arising out of the war; but even without the war, education, increasing means of communication such as the press and the radio, and social and economic changes would probably have produced similar results in the long run.

Much has been made of the fact that the southern cultural pattern is actually a caste system; and with respect to mental attitudes in the region on matters of race and the historical adjustment of the majority of Negroes, it has been substantially that. A true caste system, however, is based on the acceptance by each individual of his place in the system, which is rigid and not subject to change. This pattern is ruled out in the American South by the basic democratic philosophy of the American creed, to which the South as well as the North adheres in principle. This creed has power enough in the South to make it impossible to exclude the Negro altogether from opportunities for education and self-advancement. The inevitable result has been that Negroes have become, on the one hand, increasingly aware of unfair and discriminatory treatment, and on the other, less well adapted to fit into the traditional "place." The new factors introduced by war conditions have created a situation favorable to and, indeed, requiring change, and a climate of public opinion in which the expression of protest is on the whole less dangerous.

This protest, of course, is expressed in a variety of ways, depending upon the educational back-

[3] H. C. Brearley, "The Negro's New Belligerency," *Phylon*, V (fourth Quarter, 1944), 339–45.

ground, economic position, and character of the Individual. Negro leaders in the South have sometimes accepted segregation while calling for equality of opportunity and an end to discrimination. There is some evidence, however, that this point of view is fundamentally a matter of expediency rather than conviction. The signers of the Durham declaration of October 20, 1942, who are regarded as conservative by many segments of Negro opinion, stated, "We are fundamentally opposed to the principle and practice of compulsory segregation in our American society," although they indicated a common-sense willingness to work in the southern bi-racial system to help achieve an ultimate democratic society. The fact is that Negroes cannot for reasons of self-respect accept segregation and all of its implications as an ultimate solution of race relations in a true democracy because to do so would be to accept for all time a definition of themselves as something less than their fellow men. In the South, however, they have shown on the whole a disposition not to push the issue embarrassingly even in such matters as graduate and professional education, but to seek areas of cooperation where progress could be made without directly threatening the dogma of separation.

The mass of southern Negroes naturally do not express their protest in any such conscious terms, although race consciousness is increasing. Protest behavior may range from withdrawal and self-segregation to inefficiency on the job, or aggressive manners. In the more isolated areas where education and social and economic change have had least effect there may be very little feeling of protest on the part of the Negro, and this gives a semblance of justification to the conviction that the old patterns were harmonious and thus more acceptable. This situation, however, is probably a function of mental and physical isolation which cannot long be maintained in a dynamic society. It should be noted that migration itself, which often occurs from just such areas as these, is a form of protest.

It has been suggested in this paper that the racial climate is at present bad, but that the over-all trend is wholesome and promising. There are numerous indications of forces other than disruption at work in the total situation:

(a) In spite of the tensions, threats, abuses and limitations of the racial system, large-scale racial violence has seldom occurred and gives no indication of occurring, although the frictions and antagonisms threaten to continue indefinitely. Lynchings have almost disappeared, in large part through the efforts of the South itself, and particularly the southern women.

(b) The pressure of population over the long run is being relaxed by the migration of both whites and Negroes to the North and West.

(c) Constant improvements in education are changing the character of race relations by gradually removing one of the sources of personal insecurity.

(d) The increased industrialization and unionization of the region has been increasing the number and character of natural contacts between whites and Negroes in the most numerous population class. The necessities for labor and class solidarity have shown themselves vital enough to overcome many racial customs and traditions.

(e) Many white southerners, while struggling with a dilemma for which there appears to be no solution that is both acceptable and consistent, have shown themselves ready to work with Negro southerners for the removal of particular discriminations, or for the establishment of better facilities, and these instances of cooperation have brought better understanding in certain areas.

(f) The new regional approach developed by southern social scientists and the new social viewpoint in some southern political leaders have made for an increasing awareness of certain problems faced by the South which are not racial but economic, geographic, and social. This has stimulated in turn a willingness to work for the general improvement of conditions in the area which includes whites and Negroes alike.

(g) Southern colleges and universities have been increasingly contributing to a more objective approach to problems of race relations by establishing courses, programs, and study projects bearing on this field; and as a result of this and related factors more southern young people are showing a disposition to question old traditions and to try out new approaches.

The trend toward substitution of worker solidarity for racial solidarity may prove in the long run to be the most significant of the forces mentioned above. There are at least 500,000 Negroes in unions in the South, and many of these unions are considering for the first time the value of effective co-relations as a basis for workers' security in the region and in the Nation. The mine and smelter workers in Birmingham, Alabama, to take one of the many examples, have not only formed unions in which whites and Negroes participate on an equal basis, but have pressed for upgrading of Negroes on the same basis as whites, in the face of the protests of local traditionalists. An interesting if not so significant inversion of this trend was the recent effort of a Memphis employer to fight the holding of a union election on the ground that the union discriminated against Negroes. If postwar developments do not cause unions to revert generally to exclusiveness and if the Federal Government through the FEPC and the Supreme Court continues to insist upon equal opportunities in labor groups as well as in employment, the trend toward industrialization of the South should bring with it changes in the old racial mores that can be beneficial to the entire area and population. For even though it might appear to be an advantage to the racial scene to maintain fixed inequalities, the full economic development of the South can only be handicapped by this policy.

Academic instruction and research and the livelier intellectual atmosphere of some of the southern colleges are also exerting an influence which will widen and deepen as those who are influenced by it take their places in southern society. A survey in 1941 found 187 southern colleges for white students doing work in the field of the Negro and race relations. Of these, 53 offered at least one full course in the field, 20 were doing independent research, 80 supplemented course instruction with programs dealing with the subject, and 58 carried on some type of interracial activities in most of which students participated. The Negro colleges, as might be expected, take an even greater interest in the subject and make a real effort to give their students an understanding of the background of present problems and an opportunity for interracial experience.

Perhaps even more significant than direct study of race relations is the influence of southern universities in developing a new approach to southern problems. The kind of regional program first suggested by such agencies as the Institute for Research in Social Science at the University of North Carolina is now being activated by organizations of southerners such as the Southern Regional Council, the Southern Conference for Human Wel-

fare, and the Southern Electoral Reform League. The Southern Regional Council organized in 1944 with a broad base of southern leadership in many fields was recently able to adopt unanimously recommendations including employment of all persons on the basis of ability, abolition of the white primary, and equalization of educational opportunities, health facilities, and transportation facilities.

Churches over the South are giving new and increasing study to the problem of race relations and are joining with other groups in efforts to modify the more pressing injustices. Here as in the colleges, southern youth seem more disposed to view racial situations in the light of Christian and democratic principles rather than in the twilight of tradition.

At the present moment the whole question of race relations, not only in the South but in the country as a whole, is being held in a kind of suspension awaiting the end of the war and the unpredictable developments which will follow. This is not to say that there is nothing going on now in this field, for the fact is there is an unprecedented amount of attention being given to the question, a continuance of racial tensions in all parts of the Nation, and much activity by organized groups. There is, however, a general feeling that the deciding influence will be the character of social, political, and economic developments in the United States and in the world when the war ends. We can chart the constructive and the disruptive forces, but we cannot know which will prevail without knowing whether postwar America will be able to provide jobs and a standard of living to a degree which will at least make the possibility of progress seem real. Predictions as to the effect on race relations of the return of white and southern servicemen have varied from gloomy mutterings that "blood will flow" to the statement by a retiring Governor of North Carolina that "men who come back from the war, white and colored, are going to have an even better desire to work these things out." There is at least a recognition on the part of southern leaders that demobilization, reconversion, and their attendant problems require careful planning and constructive action. The extent to which such action is taken and is effective, both in the South and in the Nation at large, will be decisive not alone for race relations but for the health of the Nation.

RESEARCH AND REGIONAL DEVELOPMENT
AN INQUIRY INTO THE RANGE AND ROLE OF RESEARCH IN THE SOUTH

EDITH WEBB WILLIAMS

THE social scientist can rarely escape the pressure of a double obligation in all his work. The need for valid generalization is so great in his field that emphasis upon fundamental topics and scientific methodology can never be forgotten or slighted, but at the same time the material which he studies tends to exert upon him pressure to select subjects of investigation relevant to the immediate needs and the recognized aspirations of men. An inquiry into the role played by research in southern States satisfies both obligations. The importance of research activities and institutions in modern society justifies their selection for study, and it would be difficult to find a topic more directly related to the regional development of the southeastern United States.

Research has come to be one of our magic words, a word with which to conjure. Research has given us our prized machines, it has produced health-preserving drugs, it will win the war, and it will provide jobs and prosperity after the war. The scientist in a laboratory filled with complicated apparatus shakes a test tube, and, presto, something wonderful and new emerges. The processes and the people involved are remote from most of us, and are expected to be more mysterious than not. The ordinary man does not try to understand, except perhaps to the extent of being convinced that "research pays." The fundamental research which precedes the application, the rigorous training of the scientific worker, and, most important of all, the applicability of the logic and objectivity of science to all phases of life—these provide only a dim background for the magical drama in which all attention is focussed on the end result, the thing produced.

In this role of a new and superior magic, research in the natural sciences can no doubt continue to provide successively more impressive results. There will be no end of weapons and labor savers and entertaining gadgets. To the thoughtful person these results alone do not fulfill the promise of a science which is essentially a method of achieving understanding and power derived from understanding, a method not re-

stricted to physics and chemistry, a promise not fulfilled by accumulations of intricate and varied objects. To such persons it seems important to inquire into the role played by research in our society, not merely as a phase of the technique of production, but also as a social phenomenon whose influence reaches throughout the fabric of our culture. We need to know to what extent the promise of scientific research is failing to be realized, and in what areas. For this we need to know how much research we have and what kinds, who works at it, who supports it, who controls it, who benefits from its accomplishments. We also need to know where we do not have it and why. If our reiterated belief in the efficacy of research has a factual foundation, we should concern ourselves about our research resources and how they are being used. These are matters intimately related to the welfare of all of us. The valuable series of studies which the National Resources Planning Board made of the research resources of the nation[1] has not received the attention it deserves, nor provoked the further inquiry into the subject which should have followed it.

The social scientist particularly needs to give close attention to this institutional complex, made up of a professional group clearly set off by training and the nature of its work and perhaps by characteristic attitudes, of attitudes of others toward this group, its work and its place in society, of the interaction between this complex and other parts of the social whole, of the effects of the findings of science and the spirit of science upon the ways and attitudes and ideals of society.

The two factors thus suggested make this proposal of research upon research timely and necessary. One is the high value placed on scientific

[1] National Resources Committee, *Research—A National Resource, I. Relation of the Federal Government to Research*, December, 1938; National Resources Planning Board, *Research—A National Resource, II. Industrial Research*, December, 1940; National Resources Planning Board, *Research—A National Resource, III. Business Research*, June, 1941 (Washington: Government Printing Office).

endeavors and the faith that they will solve our problems and bring our hearts' desires. The other is the significant place of research activities in our social and economic orders. This is already sufficient to merit study as a part of our attempt to understand the working of those orders, and it will increase if the strong faith in science continues to characterize our times.

The war has dramatized the value of research so that more people are aware of it, at least in certain fields, but this worth has for some years been recognized by many who have seen it in terms of financial gain and by others who have understood the significance of continuous and varied research to the general welfare of all the people. A concrete demonstration of this recognition can be given in terms of money expended for research before the war affected the situation. A careful estimate put the national expenditure for industrial research at around $300,000,000 in 1940.[2] The Federal Government spent approximately 2 percent of its total budget on research before the war, the amount in 1936–1937 being $120,000-000.[3] Universities spent around $50,000,000 annually on research, some allotting 25 percent of their incomes for this purpose.[4] These figures are indicative only. They are estimates, not complete tabulations, and they take no account of the investigations carried on by departments of State governments and legislative committees, of the business and economic studies conducted by individual concerns and trade associations, of private agricultural experimentation.

The extent of research, as indicated by these figures, represents tremendous expansion in a relatively short period of time, chiefly between the two great wars of the twentieth century. The growth has not been even, but has been concentrated in certain fields of endeavor and in certain geographical areas. Most of the expansion of industrial research has been in a limited number of industries and by a limited number of companies. In some industries research is almost nonexistent. Governmental efforts account for most of the expansion in the field of agriculture. Some sciences have been used more than others. All types of research in all fields of interest have developed in

certain parts of the country, with other parts lagging far behind.

The causes and the results of all this variation are not simple, but there are many points which suggest a need for investigation. In the industrial field it seems to be the case that the companies which have large research organizations have tended to prosper. It also seems that only the prospering industry or company finds the money to finance research. Furthermore, extensive research activities tend to be found only with highly concentrated wealth and control. The authoritarian organization of industry seems to make possible a more effective use of science than has been achieved in other phases of our society. In agriculture, by way of contrast, most research is publicly supported and it has to be supplemented with a system for "extending" its results to the farmers. The expense of modern research and the advantages of cooperative effort on a problem have apparently pushed the individual and the small economic unit out of the research world. On the other hand, we know little about the effect of centralized control and direction of research efforts on initiative and inventiveness. It seems quite clear that the concentration of economic power which comes with control over the development of new products and processes is a problem to which a democratic society must find some solution.

Outside the industrial field there are equally important questions which need investigation. The distinction between fundamental and applied research is found primarily in the immediate ends of the inquiries, but the two tend to be different also in organization, in sources of financial support, and in the social roles they play. A few industrial companies carry on basic research, but for the most part, this is left to endowed institutes, to universities and colleges, and to governmental agencies. This is true in both social and natural sciences. These agencies are all, in a broad sense, supported by the people as a whole; they are seeking knowledge on the assumption that an increase in knowledge will help all the people; and their findings are generally available. The relationship between these agencies and those individuals or groups which need and use the results of their research is one of social importance.

Within this company, the colleges and universities occupy a peculiar position because they also train the research workers who will carry on in both fundamental and applied fields, in both the

[2] National Resources Planning Board, *Research: A National Resource, II. Industrial Research*, p. 1.

[3] National Resources Committee, *Research: A National Resource, I. Relation of the Federal Government to Research*, p. 3.

[4] *Ibid.*, p. 177.

natural and the social sciences. The amount of training given outside the academic world has been increasing, but the bulk of it still remains there, and the basic training will undoubtedly continue to take place there. Since the contributions of research in the future depend on the quantity and quality of trained personnel which will be available, inquiry into these research and training centers is of great importance. Added significance is given to such inquiry by the fact that almost all research in the social sciences takes place in these institutions. Since we have failed signally in achieving mastery in the social world, either in the accumulation of useful knowledge or in the application of it, basic questions need to be asked and answered with regard to research in the social sciences.

It is not surprising that the more wealthy regions of the country should have more research facilities of all kinds, nor that the tendency is to expand facilities where they already exist. It seems desirable, however, to inquire into the wisdom of permitting this trend to continue, with its influence upon the perpetuation of present regional imbalances in development and the consequent weakening of the national whole. In addition to the general gains from research findings wherever made, there are apparently more specific and greater gains made by the region in which the investigations take place. Our country differs so much in its different parts that study of resources and conditions in one may throw no light on the problems of another, even if the results are released freely. It would seem that regional and local research is needed on regional and local problems, both problems having to do with production and the use of natural resources and problems in the social life of the people. This is not only to insure study of specific local materials, but also to build up the appreciation and use of research findings. The final social goal is acceptance and use of knowledge, and this is aided by the presence within an area of research institutions and personnel. Appreciation of scientific methods and findings and willingness tò use them and to support them come through first hand contacts with the processes and results of research. It is only in this way that the great potentialities of science in its broadest sense can be realized through a penetration of its proved successful techniques and approaches into the daily practices of all men.

This outstanding fact about our research re-

sources, their centralization, suggests two dangers. One is that too much power is thereby concentrated in too few hands for a healthy democratic society. The other is that too many people are thereby denied the advantages and benefits which accrue from research. If these are real dangers, it would be well to discover it now. If modern research can not be carried on efficiently except in large units, we may have to develop safeguards in the form of some kind of social control. If greater gains to the country as a whole will come with decentralization of at least some kinds of research, the fact should be established. There are some subjects of inquiry where duplication of effort seems obviously wasteful, but there are other less basic ones which seem to call for varied and numerous approaches.

As a first step in examining the research complex and its role in modern society, this paper proposes to explore the research resources of the Southeastern States, a part of the country which admittedly constitutes a national problem because of its failure to develop its resources, both natural and human, to the extent which would seem possible if a whole-hearted application of science to materials were made. The South is one of the regions of the United States where research does not exist on a scale commensurate with that in other parts of the country or with the opportunities for development presented by its natural resources. In no field has the South taken a leading place in research. This is evidenced by all available measures.

Typical is the picture of expenditures for research in agriculture, the traditional economic backbone of the region. In 1942–1943 there were 4,680 research workers (full- and part-time) in agricultural experiment stations in all the States. The eleven Southeastern States had 18 percent of these.[5] In 1940 the Southeast had 33.5 percent of the total rural population.[6] To put it another way, the Southeast had fewer research workers in agricultural experiment stations per million rural population than any other region. This farming region had 44 of these agricultural research workers per million rural population, while the country as

[5] United States Department of Agriculture, *Report on the Agricultural Experiment Stations* (Washington: Government Printing Office, 1943), Table I, pp. 98–99.

[6] *Sixteenth Census of the United States, 1940. Population*, I, Table 7, p. 19.

a whole had 81, the industrial Northeast 100, the Middle States 93, the Far West 159. Research in the agricultural experiment stations is partly financed by federal grants, and although some of these grants are allotted on the basis of rural population, the older ones provide equal amounts to all States. In total federal grants, therefore, the South with its large rural population does not fare as well, on any reasonable basis of comparison, as other parts of the country. Nor do State appropriations to the stations make up the difference. Southern States make smaller appropriations for agricultural research in proportion to their rural populations than do the States of other regions.

The number of articles published in scientific journals during the year by the staff members of the various stations is reported to the Office of Experiment Stations in the United States Department of Agriculture.[7] This may be used as a partial index of the quality of the personnel and the research accomplished. In all stations there were 45 articles per 100 research workers in 1942–1943. In the Southeast there were about 28, the lowest figure for any region. The industrial Northeast led all regions with 69 articles per 100 research workers. Even considering the many factors that may affect publication, the difference seems of some significance and is evidence for the claim, often made, that all kinds of investigations flourish when conducted in an area where others are being made. These figures are for experiment station activities alone. There is some private agricultural research, particularly in plant breeding, and there is a vast amount of agricultural research conducted directly by the United States Department of Agriculture in the South as well as elsewhere.

Industrial research in the Southeast has lagged so far behind the development elsewhere that it was almost nonexistent until recent years. In the National Research Council's survey of industrial research laboratories in 1938 the 11 Southeastern States reported 5 percent of the laboratories and 3 percent of the research personnel.[8] They had

21 percent of the population.[9] In the number of industrial research workers per 10,000 wage earners in manufacturing, the Southeast is behind all other regions. There is no outstanding industrial research institute in the whole Southeast. Recently, however, there has been a definite trend toward the expansion of industrial research in the region. The rate of growth in both laboratories and personnel reported between 1927 and 1938 was more rapid in the Southeast than in any other region. This was largely because the numbers in 1927 were so small, but the trend continued at least until 1940, when the last National Research Council *Directory* was published. Between 1938 and 1940 the number of laboratories reported from the Southeast increased from 113 to 191, 69 percent. It is not possible to find out what effect the war has had on the total picture. By depleting personnel it has sharply reduced the research programs of some industries, but in other instances war related research has been expanded. War conditions and interest in planning for postwar industry have resulted in increased interest in research on the part of southern industrial groups. Several cooperatively financed industrial research institutes have been organized and will be ready for full operation when personnel and equipment become available.

Available material does not permit similar regional analysis of business and economic research but indirect evidence points to a like condition. Only business and industrial concerns with large resources can afford to maintain research departments. The South has relatively few such concerns. It is getting more branch producing units all the time, but the home office, the control, and usually the research remain centered at the point of origin. For companies without the resources for individual research, economic studies, as well as fundamental research, can be financed cooperatively through trade associations. Southern business and industry participate in these associations, both regional and national ones, although the exact extent of the participation is difficult to estimate. If the factor of location of headquarters is important in determining the trend of activities, the South remains on the fringes of the interests of national associations, and these are the ones with the most extensive research programs. The United States Department of Commerce directory,

---

[7] United States Department of Agriculture, *loc. cit.*

[8] George Perazich and Philip M. Field, *Industrial Research and Changing Technology*, Works Projects Administration, National Research Project, Report No. M-4 (Philadelphia, January 1940), Appendix A, Table A-11, p. 72 and Table A-10, pp. 69–71.

[9] *Statistical Abstract, 1941*, Table 12, p. 10.

Trade and Professional Associations of the United States, for 1942 shows 60 percent of the 2,800 listed associations located in three cities—New York, Chicago, and Washington. There are 16 cities with 20 or more associations each. Two of these are in the South, New Orleans with 21 associations and Atlanta with 20. These 41 associations may be compared with the 1,497 in the Northeast. [10] No one of the outstanding private institutes for research in economics and business is located in the South.

All available indexes of university research facilities show the South to be deficient to a serious degree. It is in the graduate school that real research training is given, and the Ph.D. degree is generally accepted today as a requirement for the highest level of research personnel in all fields. A compilation of the Ph.D. degrees given in the United States for a three-year period preceding the full impact of the war on education (1939–1942) shows the condition of southern university graduate training clearly. Out of 1,718 chemistry degrees, 76 were granted in the Southeast; out of 199 engineering degrees, not one was granted in the Southeast; out of 467 physics degrees, 16 were granted in the Southeast; out of 190 agriculture degrees, 2; out of 494 economics degrees, 34; out of 217 sociology degrees, 17; out of 205 political science degrees, 7. With 67 institutions granting degrees in chemistry the Southeast had 6; with 27 granting engineering degrees, the Southeast had none; with 53 granting physics degrees, the Southeast had 4; with 26 granting agriculture degrees, the Southeast had 2; with 45 granting economics degrees, the Southeast had 5; with 38 granting political science degrees, the Southeast had 5; with 40 granting sociology degrees, the Southeast had 5. [11]

[10] D. J. Judkins, *Trade and Professional Associations of the United States,* Washington: Bureau of Foreign and Domestic Commerce, United States Department of Commerce, Industrial Series No. 3, 1942, p. 177.

[11] E. A. Henry, (Ed.), *Doctoral Dissertations Accepted by American Universities, 1939–1940.* Number 7 (New York: The H. W. Wilson Company, 1940), Table III.

E. A. Henry (Ed.), *Doctoral Dissertations Accepted by American Universities, 1940–1941.* Number 8 (New York: The H. W. Wilson Company 1941), Table III.

E. A. Henry, (Ed.), *Doctoral Dissertations Accepted by American Universities, 1941–1942.* Number 9

An indication that place of training is related to the location of research activities is found in data on a highly selected group of younger scientists (those first starred in *American Men of Science* in 1927, 1933, or 1938). A study has been made showing where they were born, where they received their training, and where they were located in 1938. [12] The tendency for training at the higher levels to be concentrated in a few centers is clear; and it is equally clear that large numbers of the trained individuals remain in these same areas. A relatively small proportion of the total number of this selected group was born in the Southeast, but the proportions trained and located in the region are still smaller.

Somewhat comparable material for a selected group of social scientists presents the same general picture. This comes from an analysis of biographical data for the Postdoctoral Research Training Fellows of the Social Science Research Council from 1925 through 1939. [13] These fellowships "are usually awarded to persons who have already demonstrated their capacities for doing effective research under the usual conditions of employment in academic or public life..." [14] Approximately 6 percent of the number born in this country were born in southeastern States. The Southeast provided undergraduate training to about 3 percent of the total number for whom information on this point is available; it provided graduate training to less than 1 percent; and about 5 percent of the number who were located in collegiate work in 1939 were in the Southeast.

The significance of analyses of these two groups comes chiefly from the fact that each is a selected group representing the highest level of research talent, one in the natural sciences and one in the social sciences. In both cases it is evident that the Southeast does not contribute what it should in the way of talent or training, and that it does not share in the benefits that come from the presence of superior scientists at work on the problems of the region.

(New York: The H. W. Wilson Company, 1942), Table III.

[12] S. S. Visher, "Distribution of the Younger Starred Scientists," *American Journal of Science,* 237 (January 1939), 48–65.

[13] Social Science Research Council, *Fellows of the Social Science Research Council, 1925–1939* (New York: Social Science Research Council, 1939).

[14] *Ibid.,* Introduction, p. viii.

Graduate training in research requires superior teachers. Of the total number of starred scientists in the 1938 edition of *American Men of Science* who were then located in colleges and universities, the Southeast had 3 percent.[15] This amounts to less than 3 per thousand faculty members.[16] In the Nation at large there were 13 per thousand faculty members; in the Northeast, 20. When this 3 percent is put with the 5 percent of the group of social scientists, selected for research talent, it suggests one reason why so few of the best research people come out of the southern universities. These figures do not constitute a complete measure of the adequacy of southern university faculties to give training in research, but it indicates a situation which calls for attention. Perhaps it means that the most able scientists are drawn to areas where there is more money. Perhaps it means that scientists in southern schools cannot realize their potentialities because they are overburdened with teaching loads and underprovided with equipment and libraries and research assistants. Southern university faculties are clearly aware of the need for increased research. The number of bureaus and institutes of research and engineering experiment stations which exist in the region are proof of efforts to improve research conditions. Some of these have done excellent work, but many have never been given more than nominal financial support.

Good research scientists require good equipment and good libraries and time to carry on investigations. All these cost money. Careful estimates of amounts spent annually for research by colleges and universities have been made by the National Resources Committee. No southern school spends more than $1,000,000 on research, but there are 14 outside the region which do. There are, in addition, 15 which spend between $500,000 and $1,000,000. Of these the Southeast has one, Duke University.[17]

There are 40 members of the Association of Research Libraries in the country, of which 5 are in the Southeast, located in the universities which grant most of the graduate degrees given in the

region. The 5 libraries cannot meet the standards set by the great research libraries of the Nation, but the record of expenditures in recent years indicates an awareness on the part of the institutions concerned of the importance of library materials. In 1938–1939 the 5 institutions spent a larger percentage of their total budgets on their libraries than the percentage for all 40 institutions.[18] The difficulty is that the total budgets of these institutions are relatively so small that, in spite of strenuous efforts, the regional differential in research library facilities increases.

The South is also lacking in special research collections on specific subjects, especially in scientific fields. R. B. Downs reports that there is no extensive textile collection in the region despite the importance of cotton.[19] L. R. Wilson has pointed out to the author in conversation that there is no first-rate collection of materials on soils in this agricultural region. The possibilities of cooperation in this field are being shown in a number of university programs for joint library service. Such plans eliminate duplications and make possible the maximum benefits from the money expended by all cooperating groups. Recent moves toward the establishment of industrial research institutes, such as the Southern Research Institute at Birmingham and the Institute of Textile Technology at Charlottesville, include plans for technical libraries.

The poor standing of southern universities in various attempts to rate graduate schools and departments on their general excellence has been pointed out too many times to need reiteration. A criterion of particular relevance to the research facilities of the schools is the number of research fellowships and scholarships made available through national foundations and private industry. National Research Council fellowships in the natural sciences have been given since 1919 in order "to strengthen the foundations of science in the United States." The statement of the Council regarding cooperation of educational institutions is as follows:

National Research Fellows are appointed to conduct their investigations at institutions which cooperate in

---

[15] National Resources Committee, *op. cit.*, Table II, p. 174.

[16] The number of faculty members is taken from the report (unpublished) of a survey conducted by the National Roster of Scientific and Specialized Personnel of the War Manpower Commission in December, 1942.

[17] National Resources Committee, *op, cit.*, p. 190.

[18] From a compilation made by the Princeton University Library. Manuscript available from Princeton University Librarian.

[19] *Resources of Southern Libraries* (Chicago: American Library Association, 1938), p. 304.

meeting their needs, which differ widely from those of students seeking instruction only. Experienced investigators, actively engaged in productive research, are needed to inspire and guide the work of the Fellows; research laboratories, adequately manned with technicians, and amply supplied with materials, instruments, tools, and other facilities, are indispensable; and funds to provide supplies and to satisfy the continuing requirements of research must be available. Above all, there must exist the stimulating atmosphere found in institutions in which scientific investigation flourishes.[20]

Between 1919 and 1944 there have been 1,315 appointments for study in the natural sciences (excluding medical sciences) at universities and colleges in this country or at research and technical institutions or for study abroad.[21] Of these, only 8 have been given for work at institutions in the Southeast.[22]

The conditions governing the location of fellowships given by private industry are more varied. Nevertheless, the assumption that the companies want their expenditures to bring maximum returns in training and research findings seems justified. The most recent industrial grants summary[23] shows a total of 956 research fellowships and grants supported by private industry. Of these, 53 are in southeastern universities or agricultural experiment stations.

Examinations of the institutions where Social Science Research Council Fellows have carried on their advanced study indicates a similar situation in the social sciences. Of 232 Postdoctoral Research Training Fellowships from 1925 through 1939,[24] only 2 were used for study in southeastern universities. Of 111 Fellowships in Agricultural Economics and Rural Sociology granted between 1928 and 1933,[25] not one was used for study in a southeastern university. The places of study of the special Southern Fellows supported by the Council between 1929 and 1933 do not constitute a measure of the relative merits of southern schools, but it is interesting to note the figures. There were 59 fellows,[26] with 2 studying at two different schools. Of these fellows 21 studied in the Northeast, 20 in the Southeast, 2 in the Southwest, 16 in the Middle States, and 2 in the Far West.

Further multiplication of evidence is not necessary to show that this southeastern region has little part in the research life of the Nation. Both fundamental and applied research activities are at a minimum within its area. If scientific research is to provide the solutions to the economic and social problems of our times, this region must rely in large part upon other parts of the country to provide these solutions, unless the present situation is changed. The fact that applied, as well as basic, investigations are lacking, suggests that one goes along with the other, and that it is not practical to expect extensive developments in the applied field based entirely upon fundamental investigations carried on elsewhere.

The capacity of southern people and institutions to conduct successful research and the benefits which the region can derive from research programs have been demonstrated by the special regional grants based on needs which have been made by the General Education Board, the Rockefeller Foundation, the Julius Rosenwald Fund, and the Guggenheim Foundation. Over the years several hundred such fellowships and grants have been made and the resulting trained personnel has been noteworthy. The foundations have been richly rewarded in the concrete results, but the South has not yet met its full obligations. The region has not demonstrated either capacity or willingness to support its own research. The paucity of training facilities for research personnel and the lack of opportunity for satisfactory research careers in the region are undoubtedly related, but it may well be that both are more fundamentally related to basic folk attitudes toward change based upon objective analysis and the folk valuation of scientific knowledge. There is great need for inquiry by the social scientist into the influence of folkways and folk beliefs upon the processes of mate-

[20] National Research Council, *National Research Fellowships in the Natural Sciences for 1944–1945*, p. 5.

[21] One person may have an appointment for two or more institutions; these are counted as separate appointments.

[22] National Research Council, *National Research Fellowships, 1919–1938*, p. 81, and announcements of fellowships for 1939–1940, 1940–1941, 1941–1942, 1942–1943, 1943–1944, and 1944–1945.

[23] Callie Hull and Mildred Mico, "Research Supported by Industry Through Scholarships, Fellowships, and Grants," *Journal of Chemical Education*, 21:4 (April 1944), 180–191.

[24] Social Science Research Council, *op. cit.*, Introduction, pp. viii–xiii.

[25] *Ibid.*, pp. xxi–xxii.

[26] *Ibid.*, p. xxiv.

rial change and improvement, and, on the other hand, an opportunity to observe the effects upon the folk of the slowly increasing adoption of scientific research by industrialists and farmers who are interested in the money benefits they expect from it. Attitudes toward the purposes of educational institutions and toward freedom of thought and inquiry are involved here, and the natural scientist is affected by these almost as much as the social scientist. This approach to a study of society through inquiry into one of the most important institutional complexes of modern society offers a rich field both for the student of social life and for the person who is interested in the improvement of the conditions of life, particularly when the area involved is one where need for improvement is great and failure to appreciate and use research seems to be related to the need.

SOCIOLOGY AND SOCIOLOGICAL RESEARCH IN THE SOUTH*

EDGAR T. THOMPSON

A TIME FOR APPRAISAL

WE USED to think of the South as a culturally passive area where people assumed that what had always been would always be. Unlike the urban North, where change initiated from within seems almost to have been the very life principle of the society itself, change in the feudal and agrarian South has appeared as something forced from without in the form of market fluctuations and northern carpetbaggers.[1] The South has seemed to live inside its people like an instinct. The Middle West, on the other hand, has appeared in the inhabitants of that area more like a habit. Time and new surroundings can break a habit, but an instinct is unbreakable and unchangeable.

The past and the future of sociology and of sociological research in the South is an appropriate theme for discussion at a time when the southern instinct is being discarded along with all the other alleged instincts. For this region, like other parts of the world, is seething with active and contra-dictory movement, and sociologists have long regarded social change as one of the cardinal problems of their science. Today the ordinary citizen and reader of newspapers can hardly escape reflection upon the meaning of the changes going on so rapidly around him, while sociologists are required by the very nature of their occupation to probe deeply for these meanings. Our study of the nature and meaning of social change will include, naturally, a consideration of the changes that have taken and are taking place in the science in which we have a professional interest. It is obvious that changes in society and changes in sociology are not unrelated. Sociological study in the South, like sociological study everywhere else, has never proceeded in a vacuum. On the contrary, it has gone forward in close relationship to the movements of change in the community where sociologists live and carry on their work. We ourselves are part of the object of our study. It is true, of course, that the sociological fraternity extends far beyond the boundaries of region and State. Science has a world-wide character, and research in it is carried on through the infections of enthusiasm and discussion over which no one group, race, or nation has a monopoly. Nevertheless, there are certain situational imperatives in every society which have much to do with the generation, the transmission, and the increase of knowledge, and it is therefore well for us to try to understand southern sociology in its regional and institutional setting.

It seems obvious that if we could secure such an understanding we would be in a better position

---

* Read before the Eighth Annual Meeting of the Southern Sociological Society, Atlanta, Georgia, April 1, 1944.

[1] During the course of his tour of the South in the 1850's Frederick Olmsted said of southerners: "They say this uneasiness—this passion for change—is a peculiarity of our diseased Northern nature. The Southern man finds Providence in all that is: Satan in all that might be" *A Journey in the Seaboard Slave States in the Years 1853–1854* (New York: G. P. Putnam's Sons, 1904), I, 2.

to aid in the reorientation of southern sociology for the tasks ahead. Just now when our whole outlook on the future seems to be undergoing change is a good time to face the east a little more exactly and to seek again the proper bearings and relations of sociology. A time when we seem to have reached a dividing point in the history of our civilization is a good time to do a little stock-taking and a good time to do a little soul-searching. It is a good time to ask ourselves some of the more elementary questions we ask our beginning students such as, What is knowledge? What kind of knowledge is scientific knowledge? What is sociological knowledge? What is research? What is the place of valuation in science and in scientific research? We would do well to clear our minds of some of our pet conceptions over which we now stand guard as though they were property rights and approach these questions and others like them with a certain primitive innocence.

But sociology has been determined and probably will continue to be determined, not so much by rules of logical necessity, as historically and on the basis of interest. Sociology has been determined by what has been done and what is being done by men who call themselves sociologists. If sociology is what sociologists think about, talk about, and write about, then we have a good many sociologies, perhaps about as many sociologies as we have sociologists. Nevertheless, there is little doubt but that region and *Zeitgeist* have impressed themselves upon the sociological movement and have helped define its problems. Certainly this has been true of the South. "It is certainly no accident," Myrdal remarks, "that a 'regional approach' in social science has been stressed in the South."[2] Neither is it an accident that in the old Southern Sociological Congress the South possessed what probably was the first of the regional sociological societies. Like Catholic sociology and rural sociology, southern sociology has been deeply concerned to defend rather than to analyze a body of mores. For this reason Catholic sociology has remained entirely outside the American Sociological Society, rural sociology has been in and out, and southern sociology has been in but until now, perhaps, not entirely at home in it.

[2] Gunnar Myrdal, *An American Dilemma*, (New York: Harper, 1944), I, 70 footnote.

An effort to outline the historical relations of the South to sociology might with some profit and insight be organized around the three prepositions, *for*, *of*, and *in*, most often used to indicate the relation of objects to actions. I shall speak of sociology *for* the South as that sociology which, as a body of doctrine, has been used or is being used either to resist impending change or to promote social change. Sociology *of* the South is a sociology which has achieved and is achieving the meritorious result of advancing somewhat our understanding of the object studied but which is not itself thereby advanced. Sociology *in* the South is a sociology which, viewing the South as a kind of social laboratory, undertakes to exploit the rich experiences of southern life to advance our knowledge of human nature and the processes of social change generally.

SOCIOLOGY FOR THE SOUTH

When in 1854 George Fitzhugh published his *Sociology for the South* he had in mind, as did certain contemporaries of his, a sociology battling in behalf of a regional interest and a sectional sentiment. To understand what the argument was all about let us note how the South arose first as a *region*, or a part of a region, and then later as a *section*.

The South was originally differentiated as part of an economic region in an expanding world of commerce and production for commerce after the sixteenth century. Advances in communication and cheap water transportation turned the Atlantic into an inland sea and gave the warmer lands in and surrounding the Caribbean and Gulf of Mexico divisions of labor in the larger community of western civilization as producers of agricultural staples for the markets of Europe. The South, with outlets along the Atlantic coast and the Gulf of Mexico, became the northern part of the Gulf-Caribbean region. The agricultural resources of this tropical or semi-tropical region were found to supplement those of northern Europe, and the profitable market invited large-scale development. Throughout the region the labor requirements of large-scale agriculture led to the displacement of native populations by new populations imported from Europe but more especially from Africa. In the absence of a self-distributing labor market, and in a situation where there was more land than there was labor to till it, agricultural entrepreneurs could secure and hold labor only by means of slavery, and the slavery was fastened upon the imported Negroes. The institution of the plantation arose in this region as a factory for producing the staples and at the same time as a means of accommodating peoples of diverse race and culture to each other. The region became a natural habitat for the plantation, and the plantation in turn defined and characterized the region. Many plantation societies have since developed in other parts of the world, notably in southeast Asia and in the Pacific.

The northern part of the Gulf-Caribbean region, the part we call "the South," became a part of a political entity to which the other parts of the same region did not belong. The fact that, as a part of the United States, the South had its North —had, in other words, political ties with a people who seemed to stand about engaging in constant and irritating criticism of the southern way of life—led the people of the South to that degree of conscious reflection and justification of their customs which lifted them to the level of mores.[3] Thus the South became differentiated as a section through conflict with other sections of the United States. Sectionalism was induced in the South, Craven tells us, "by a drive launched first against her labor system and then broadened into an attack against the character of her people and their entire way of life."[4] North and South came to form different conceptions of themselves but they were, nevertheless, differentiated as counterparts of each other out of the same dialectical process. Struggling within the limits of the same *Lebensraum* the contest for ascendency in the Union was for the way of life of each section a struggle for existence.[5] It was George Fitzhugh

who first made the remark, later to be repeated by Lincoln, that the Nation could not continue to exist half slave and half free.

Strong sectional feeling is without much doubt mainly responsible for the fact that the leading form of social scholarship in the South has long been in the field of history. In sectionalism as in nationalism it is the historian along with the orator and the poet who functions to define and express the hopes, the fears, and the cause of a people. The historians of the South have functioned, as historians everywhere have functioned, to create and preserve the values of their society. They have done this through the method of contrast, a method which has served to emphasize the differences between the South and other parts of the United States. It is not too much to say that, not only have they worked under the influence of sectional feeling, but they also have been prime movers in its creation.

Now if southern history has functioned to traditionalize the life of the South, sociology made its appearance in this area before the Civil War in an effort to naturalize and to rationalize that life. Only recently have we begun to realize the importance of the slavery controversy upon the beginnings of sociology in the United States. In 1849 George Frederick Holmes, a naturalized southerner originally from the plantation society of British Guiana, began to discuss the necessity for a "sociology" to oppose the liberalism of his day. Holmes was familiar with the writings of Auguste Comte, with whom he corresponded, and by 1852 was the foremost interpreter and critic of Comte in America. He was the doctrinal predecessor of Henry Hughes of Mississippi, called by Bernard the "first American sociologist," and of George Fitzhugh of Virginia.[6] There were important differ-

---

[3] The old plantation society of Brazil, unlike the American plantation society, apparently did not experience criticism from other sections of Brazil nor to any considerable extent from the mother country of Portugal. This is one very important factor, among others, in the very different history of plantation Brazil.

[4] A. O. Craven, *The Repressible Conflict, 1830–1861*, (Baton Rouge: Louisiana State University Press, 1939), p. 27.

[5] What the spokesmen of the Old South contended for was, as W. G. Brown put it, "not slavery alone, not cotton and rice and sugar-cane, not agriculture alone, but the whole social organism, the whole civilization .... The representatives of the planting interest must do more than stand on the defensive ... they must rule." *The Lower South in American History* (New York: The Macmillan Co., 1902), pp. 57–58.

[6] Hughes published his *A Treatise on Sociology* in 1854, the same year Fitzhugh brought out his *Sociology for the South*. See L. L. Bernard, "Henry Hughes, First American Sociologist," *Social Forces*, XV (December 1936), 154–174; L. L. Bernard, "The Historic Pattern of Sociology in the South," *Social Forces*, XVI (October 1937), 1–12; H. G. and Winnie Leach Duncan, "The Development of Sociology in the Old South," *American Journal of Sociology*, XXXIX (March 1934), 649–656; Harvey Wish, "George Frederick Holmes and the Genesis of American Sociology," *American Journal of Sociology*, XLVI (March 1941), 698–707; Harvey Wish, *George Fitzhugh, Propagandist of the Old South* (Baton Rouge: Louisiana State University, 1943); L. L. and Jessie Bernard, *Origins of American Soci-*

ences between these men, of course, but they all were united in a common effort to establish intellectual sanctions for slavery. In view of our present tendency to associate sociology with liberal doctrines it may come as a surprise to find the subject beginning its career in America as a vigorous and often extravagant defender of the vested interests. As a matter of fact, however, these early southern sociologists were thinking well within the Comtean solution of the problem of freedom versus order. They differed from Comte in segments of their thought, and Comte probably would not have approved the slavery which they were concerned to justify, but they shared in the essential conservatism of his views.[7]

It has been suggested that "the sense of belonging to a definitely ordered society may have been one reason why southerners were the first Americans to make much use of the word 'sociology'."[8] All these sociologists wrote in a spirit inspired by "the sense of belonging to a definitely ordered society," but it was Fitzhugh, the best known and the most influential of them, who felt most sensitively the threat of gathering forces opposed to the

southern order. It was Fitzhugh who best stated the issues involved and who so addressed himself to them as to carry the controversy aggressively into the camp of the opposition. In doing so he defined sociology in such a way as to make of it not merely a doctrine supporting the southern position, but also a "science" directly at war with an enemy of its own, namely, political economy. "Political economy," Fitzhugh explained, "is the science of free society," *i.e.*, the science supporting laissez faire, free competition, and democracy. Fitzhugh opposed the teaching of political economy in southern universities and once spoke of the necessity of giving that "science" the *coup de grace*. Apparently the science being groomed to do this was sociology.[9]

Fitzhugh did not base his defense of slavery and of the southern order upon grounds of racial and biological superiority except incidentally, and in this respect he departed from other rationalizers of the slave order. Fitzhugh elevated the proslavery argument to the level of a "slavery principle," which in turn was raised to the level of a "conservative principle," which in its turn is finally the principle of control and subordination which he found running through all forms of human association—marriage, the family, the state. This more abstract principle *is* sociology.

It is not necessary to elaborate the particular use Fitzhugh made of his doctrine nor the particular form taken by the doctrine itself. Let it suffice for us to recognize that sociology in the hands of the sociologists of the Old South *was* a doctrine and as such was a part of the ideology of southern sectionalism. Doctrines are formulations and rationalizations of a faith evolved during the course of controversy and oriented toward political action. Once formulated there is a

---

ology (New York: Thomas Y. Crowell Co., 1943), Ch. XVI, "The Critical and Systematic Work of George Frederick Holmes in Social Science." An interesting attempt to put the social thought of the Old South in systematic order may be found in Julian S. Bach Jr., "The Social Thought of the Old South," *American Journal of Sociology*, XLVI (September 1940), 179–190. Another early American sociologist was Stephen Pearl Andrews. Andrews, born in Massachusetts, became a wealthy slaveholder and lawyer in Mississippi, then returned to the North to become an abolitionist. See Harvey Wish, "Stephen Pearl Andrews, American Pioneer Sociologist," *Social Forces*, XIX (May 1941), 477–482.

[7] In a recent article Robert A. Nisbet has shown us how sociology arose in France as a reaction against the excesses of the French Revolution and of the Revolution's attack upon the traditional French order of family and community. "The origins of sociology in France," Professor Nisbet says, "were characterized by a reversion, in certain respects, to ideas which had flourished during the medieval period. Comte's admiration for the Middle Ages was profound, and to no small degree this civilization served as an inspiration to this thinking." Nisbet, "The French Revolution and the Rise of Sociology in France," *American Journal of Sociology*, LXIX (September 1943), 156–164.

[8] Charles S. Sydnor, "The Southerner and the Laws," *The Journal of Southern History*, VI (February 1940), 19.

[9] Fitzhugh does not exactly say this but it seems to be assumed throughout his book and this is the interpretation placed upon his "sociology" by those who reviewed the book in contemporary periodicals. In the Preface to *Sociology for the South* he apologized for using "the newly-coined word Sociology" but there seemed to be no other term adequate to describe the remedy for the ailments of Free Society. The word sociology was "not in use in slave countries," he said, because "Slave Society, ancient and modern, has ever been in so happy a condition, so exempt from ailments, that no doctors have arisen to treat it of its complaints, or to propose remedies for their cure." In other words, slave society, already having sociology, had no conscious need to formulate it.

tendency to regard them as objective "principles" and appeal to them as men appeal to a just God. It is satisfying to feel that we fight on the side of eternal principles and not merely that the principles are fighting for us. Doctrines are therefore very important in collective action and they deserve a high place in the study of society, but they never constitute a scientific explanation of society. We lose our competence to understand and to deal with them when we ourselves become doctrinaires.

Just how and when sociology in the South changed from a conservative to a liberal doctrine we do not know, but the change was under way shortly after the Civil War. In April, 1867, Miss Anna Gardner, a young northern woman who conducted a school for Negroes in Virginia, wrote a local white printer to ask him to make a donation of printed diplomas to the school. She had heard that Mr. Southall, the printer, was a "true friend" of the cause of Negro education. Mr. Southall replied that, while he was as deeply interested in the welfare of the Negro race as anyone, he was not willing to furnish the diplomas because he opposed the teaching of "sociology" to Negroes and he shared in the opinion of white citizens of the community that Miss Gardner was guilty of teaching social equality. Miss Gardner defended the teaching of "sociology" with the quotation, "Whatsoever ye would that men should do to you, do ye even so unto them."[10] Other and similar uses of the word indicate that sociology was being understood by southerners as a doctrine of a radically different sort scarcely fifteen years after Fitzhugh and others had employed it as a doctrine in defense of the slave order.

The tendency to interpret sociology as a liberal doctrine has continued down to the present time and the disposition to do so is perhaps stronger in the South than in any other part of the Nation. Or at least a glance through the topics listed in the annual census of research in progress issued by the Southern Sociological Society indicates that such an interpretation predominates. Whether speaking for the South, or to it, it appears that many of our sociologists are and have been more interested in their own preaching than in people. Now we have seen what doctrinal obsessions have done to corrupt the scientific spirit in such totali-

[10] Walter Fleming, *Documentary History of Reconstruction* (Cleveland: The A. H. Clark Co., 1906–07), II, 183–184.

tarian countries as Germany, where the theory of relativity was held to be a Jewish attack on "Nordic physics," and in Russia where such statements as "we stand for the party in mathematics" and "we stand for Marxist-Leninist theory in surgery" appear in scientific journals. While spurning such "science" we need to become aware of the possibility of ethnocentrism in scientific circles in our own society, especially in the social sciences. Nordic physics is no more invalid as science than the Christian sociology sometimes offered in American college courses. Our decided preference as citizens for the values of democratic society should not blind us as scientists to the fact that science is not advanced by conversion from one set of doctrines to another. The climate of democracy is undoubtedly more favorable to a free system of science than totalitarian climates, but the pressure of democratic dogmas may in some respects be as inimical to science as the pressure of totalitarian dogmas. Our chronic debate over the question of values in sociology, a question which ought long ago to have been settled, is perhaps one expression of the influence of the pathos of democracy in social science. Another is our suspicion of theory as such and our insistence upon immediate and practical results from research.

Democratic doctrines have set up goals and assumptions which have been accepted as "facts" and "principles" in much the same way that other societies have accepted other goals and assumptions as "facts" or "principles." It may be suggested that much of what we are calling sociological research in the South consists of a documentation of "facts" for or against some system of values in connection with social problems. Such "research" exhibits the ideology of the liberal or reformer and results, consequently, in a low level of abstraction. The very word research is often used so loosely that it has come to mean almost anything.

Every science seems to have its sworn enemy. Astronomy has its astrology, chemistry its alchemy, and sociology—well, the enemy of sociology is cleverer; it calls itself sociology, too.

SOCIOLOGY OF THE SOUTH

The sociology of the South is the sociology of one who, whether southerner or nonsoutherner, native or outsider, endeavors to maintain something of the detachment of the stranger as he looks at the South and examines it. For him the South together with its contents is a social object to be studied as he studies other social objects like a family or a city area. The genesis of the conception of the South as an object of sociological investigation perhaps dates back to observations made by travellers in this section from Europe and from the North.

In 1880 Horace E. Scudder noted that "the South is still a foreign land to the North."[11] It had long been such and to some extent continues to be. To the urban North the Far or Lower South became in time the Deep South inhabited by natives whose customs and superstitions must have seemed almost as strange as those of the natives of Deep Africa. It was a land remote, dark, deep, and mysterious. The reports of travellers who went into this region and lived to return made interesting reading for the cosmopolites of the North. Frederick Law Olmsted, among others, reported and analyzed the workings of southern society before the Civil War, and such men as Whitelaw Reid, Carl Schurz, Ray Stannard Baker, and others continued to visit and report on the state of the South after the War. Many of these men, if not most of them, were newspaper men and journalists and of course were not regarded, and did not regard themselves, as social scientists. But they did introduce something of the objectivity of the stranger into their observations which even for us today possess considerable insight and value. The transition from the use of the South as an object of muckraking by northern journalists to its use for anthropological field work by northern investigators has been made in recent years by John Dollard, Hortense Powdermaker, W. Lloyd Warner, and others. Their contributions to an understanding of the society of this section have been most important and are most welcome. Incidentally let it be noted here that the observations about the South of both northern journalists and social scientists have almost invariably focussed upon the issue of race and race relations.

Sociology in the Old South had its origins outside educational institutions but its development in the post-bellum South has occurred through college and university channels.[12] Thus in the South, as elsewhere, the transmission and increase of sociological knowledge have fallen largely within the ambit of the academician. Now in the pursuit of knowledge much depends upon who is doing the pursuing, whether priest, teacher, or man of leisure. We are not well prepared to say just how sociology has been shaped by the kind of institution which has monopolized it but it is reasonably certain that the influence has been great. The nature and degree of that influence upon southern sociology might better be understood if we investigated it in connection with the special history and role of southern higher education, and such an investigation might prove very revealing. We might, for one thing, better appreciate the significant differences in the sociologies taught and studied in agricultural and land grant colleges, denominational colleges, State universities, and white and Negro institutions.

When sociology entered the curriculum of colleges and universities it became subject to the laws of academic inheritance. A professor, like everyone else, likes to express his individuality by differing from his colleagues about this or that, but all in all professors are a rather tradition-bound group and have great respect for university and subject precedents. Like well brought up children they do not like to depart too far from their training, and in some academic fields the lines of training lead far back into the past. Our professors were trained by their professors who in turn were trained by other professors.

We are just beginning to get a generation of sociologists in the South who were trained in southern institutions. Their teachers in these institutions were trained in European and northern universities. This northern trained generation of teachers of sociology in southern institutions studied and carried out graduate research under some of sociology's great architects and system builders. These men were such inspiring teachers and such wise counselors that their students became loyal and devoted disciples. When their students came to the South or returned to the South they turned the methods and points of view

---

[11] Fred Lewis Pattee, *American Literature Since 1870* (New York: The Century Co., 1916), pp. 264–65.

[12] L. L. Bernard, "The Historic Pattern of Sociology in the South," *Social Forces*, XVI (October 1937), 10–12; also Bernard, "The Teaching of Sociology in Southern Colleges and Universities," *American Journal of Sociology*, XXIII (January 1918), 491–515.

of their mentors in the direction of a sounder and more rewarding study of southern society than this society had ever before received.[13] They have advanced the sociology of the South and things southern to the status of a respectable body of knowledge and for this the rest of us will ever be indebted to them.

But the fact seems to be that in the process of passing sociology along from one generation to another some of us have inherited a conception of sociology as a dialectic to be advanced by criticism of the concepts of the various "schools." Preoccupations with such logicisms may make us very sharp and brilliant but it lands us in a vicious circle from which there is no escape. The consequence is a sort of sociological scholasticism. Immersed in such scholasticism we can discuss almost any of the problems of sociology without once looking to see what concretely we have in the problem. We refer rather to what the authors of textbooks, i.e., the authorities, have said about it.

Another result, apparently, of academic inheritance is the fact that much of the procedure of sociological research in the South as elsewhere falls in the domain of custom, and too often the methods used are only survivals of older ones or blind imitations of the methods of others. This seems particularly true of statistics, a procedure so "objective" as to have a minimum use for the facts of experience. Professor R. E. Park has illuminated us upon the subject of rote learning.[14] We need also to consider the subject of rote teaching but of more immediate interest to us is the matter of rote research. Rote research is manifest by the extent to which we flounder around in the rituals and mysteries of methodology, that mouth-filling word we sociologists love so well. It appears that many of us become so much concerned with methodology that the thing to be studied comes to seem unimportant. Perhaps we have committed to memory the steps to be taken in "correct" scientific procedure. We have defined the problem and ascertained the sources of data. We have formulated a hypothesis and we have read the literature. We have consulted the statistician and he has told us just what questions we must ask in the questionnaire in order to treat the returns statistically. And finally we have decided whom to interview and we think we had better collect some cases. The only trouble is we are not particularly interested in the matter we have decided to study.

Speaking of a disposition to follow too closely the procedures of the masters rather than their spirit of inquiry, Dr. W. I. Thomas wrote in a letter, "You will remember that the chemist Ostwald followed the careers of all his students and that in his *Grosse Männer* he said that all his students who attended his lectures regularly and were attentive failed to amount to anything while all those who neglected the lectures became distinguished. My aversion to the formal attention to methodology is just here—that it is not only unfruitful but it tends to a fixation of habits and sterility."[15] One of the almost inevitable consequences of inheritance of any kind is a tendency toward formalism, and to combat this in the field of sociology it is necessary for us to wage continuous battle against rote teaching and rote research.

The obsession with fact gathering as an end in itself, an obsession which places some of us at the opposite extreme from the scholastics, is perhaps a result of the cult of formal objectivity. The fact gatherer proceeds under the assumption that the facts need only be gathered and allowed "to speak for themselves." His conclusions are his opinions concerning what the facts say. Perhaps the investigations of the fact gatherer are really in the nature of surveys. They are not ordinarily related to hypotheses and there is a minimum utilization of available theory. Ordinarily the facts are gathered and organized under common sense concepts. Many if not most of these investigations are carried out to aid in the formulation of policies or as instruments of reform. As such they are useful and effective. When reform is needed there is no gainsaying the value of a shovelful of facts to help it along. And there certainly is no quarrel with any sociologist who has a healthy respect for those compulsory ex-

---

[13] One of the first of these was Dr. W. E. B. Du Bois who in 1896 went to Atlanta University and there undertook "what was perhaps the first real sociological research in the South." Guy B. Johnson, "Negro Race Movements and Leadership in the United States," *American Journal of Sociology* XLIII (July 1937), 65.

[14] "A Memorandum on Rote Learning," *American Journal of Sociology*, XLIII (July 1937), 23–36.

[15] Quoted in Louis Wirth, "Criteria and Objectives of Research in the Social Sciences," Conference of Representatives of University Social Science Research Organizations held at the Faculty Club, Cambridge, Mass., November 1937, p. 60.

periences we call facts. Most of us would profit if we paid more attention to the facts and many of us would do well if we left our offices and campuses more often to get closer to the grass roots. But the mere fact gatherer is far from being a man of science. As John Dewey has said, "No amount of mere fact finding develops science nor the scientific attitude in either physics or social affairs. Facts merely amassed and piled up are dead; a burden which only adds to confusion. When ideas, hypotheses, begin the play upon facts, when they are methods for experimental use in action, then light dawns; then it becomes possible to discriminate significant from trivial facts, and relations begin to take the place of intellectual scraps."

It may be suggested that while the thing studied, that is, the South, is now somewhat better understood, the sociology of the South has not appreciably advanced the fundamental body of sociological theory. There has not yet come out of the South, I believe, a volume comparable to *Folkways, The Theory of the Leisure Class, Human Nature and the Social Order,* or *The Polish Peasant.* If the value of sociology or any other science is to be tested by the question, Does it yield a better understanding and control than can be had by common sense? and if the answer is yes, then the science in its existing state of theory is, of course, valuable. It follows, however, that advances in social theory are an indispensable desideratum for advances in understanding and control. Research and theory should react upon each other and develop each other. The point is that southern sociological research is obligated to advance our knowledge of the South but it also is under obligation to advance the science of sociology. Shall southern sociologists continue to leave to sociologists in other parts of the world the formulation of newer viewpoints as a guide to research, or will they use the rich resources of southern experience to help advance the body of sociological theory themselves? Is it sufficient to mark out the South as historians mark it out that is, as an area to be studied as an end in itself, for its own sake alone, or is it not also a part of our business to use the South as a field of observation for the study of human nature and society generally?

It has been charged that the South has been on the defensive so long that its people have lost the art of self-examination, and Lambert Davis asserted that "Southerners have made surprisingly few discoveries about the South chiefly because they assumed they already knew it."[16] Perhaps we have not made the discoveries about the South we ought to have made and perhaps our passion for self-discovery has not been commensurate with our opportunity. If so, it is a challenge to advance the sociology of the South. But the real question goes much deeper than this and becomes: Have southern sociologists made the discoveries about the nature of social organization and social processes we ought to have made and how great is our interest in utilizing the southern situation to make such discoveries? To the extent we are concerning ourselves with this fundamental question we have sociology in the South.

SOCIOLOGY IN THE SOUTH

The sociology of the South at its extreme is the sociology of self-conscious intellectuals who minimize the facts of their own experience and the life experiences of the people in the community around them. It is the sociology of the career or office sociologist, the sociologist of the book. It is rather paradoxical that sociology, the science which, more than any other, is charged with the study and understanding of the simply human, should itself stand in need of humanizing. Sociology requires devotees who like people and who find people interesting, all kinds and conditions of people, people as they are, the good and the bad, the white and the black alike. To the sociologist in a special sort of way nothing human is alien.

Now the South is a land of sprawling diversity and great contrasts, and the people in it have combined and recombined to effect all sorts of relationships and types. Regardless of what its partisans or its enemies may think of this land, the South is full of the matter of sheer human interest. In the 1880's when American writers were discovering provincial types, dialects, and customs they found in the South, more than in any other section, the sort of literary material demanded. The human nature resources of the region were exploited so thoroughly that Professor Pattee called the period "The Era of Southern Themes and Writers." "Nowhere else," said he, exaggerating a bit perhaps, "were to be found such a variety of picturesque types of humanity: Negroes, crackers, creoles, mountaineers, moonshiners, and

[16] In the *Saturday Review of Literature* XVIII (July 16, 1938), 5.

all those incongruous elements that had resulted from the great social upheaval of 1861–65. Behind it in an increasingly romantic perspective lay the old regime destroyed by the war; nearer was the war itself, most heroic of struggles; and still nearer was the tragedy of reconstruction with its carpetbagger, its freed slaves, and its Ku Klux terror. Nowhere in America, not even in California, had there been such richness of literary material."[17] The literary interest in the South, it might be added, is perhaps even stronger today than it was in the 1880's.

Not only are the materials for a great literature present in the South but also for a great sociological renaissance. Recently two southerners, Jonathan Daniels, white, and J. Saunders Redding, Negro, took to their automobiles and travelled around the South to see what was going on and to talk to hitchhikers, filling station operators, waitresses, farm laborers, TVA officials, miners, planters, textile workers, and State officials.[18] Readers who viewed the panorama of southern life through the eyes of these two writers could hardly have failed to be deeply impressed by the stirring human drama being enacted in this section of the nation. In another book, edited by W. T. Couch, entitled *These Are Our Lives*, these same types of people are permitted to speak up for themselves, and we were surprised to find that, in spite of the apparent drabness of their lives, they had interesting and human stories to tell. All around the South social experiments are going on, some planned and some just happening. The people are talking and asking questions, more concerned about the future than southern folk usually are thought of as being. In short, the South is a region where human nature and social processes can be observed and studied somewhat as a naturalist studies vital behavior in the field and where the student possesses some special advantages for observation. And when such an authority as Wesley Mitchell tells us that "the most urgent item of unfinished business is to increase our knowledge of human behavior," such study assumes greater significance than the mere expression of idle curiosity.

Not that there is anything wrong with having idle curiosity. Quite the contrary. Scientific research does not begin with data nor with method but with an individual who ardently wants to find out something, and who is not deterred by the difficulties he encounters in his search for the answer. Most people possess some native curiosity which is, however, dissipated when difficulties are encountered. But there are a few sociological Galileos and Pasteurs and Darwins whose appetite for knowledge is simply whetted by the difficulties and who drive ahead. They seek facts that are relevant to the questions that trouble them, construct hypotheses in imagination, and then test the hypotheses by pitting the facts against them. They become concerned with methodological problems after they have discovered an interest. They have questions to ask of the data and they devise their own methods for getting answers or choose intelligently from existing methods. There is no substitute in any kind of scientific research for the curious and inquiring mind. Much more important than the methods of science is the spirit of science, and this spirit, says Charles R. Stockard, "is a fleeting and tenuous affair. It never exists where time and routine are important. It disappears with an eight-hour day or a six-day week or a nine-month year. The atmosphere is inspiring only where all time belongs to the spirit of science."[19]

A genuine spirit of scientific research in sociology is certainly not absent in southern sociology. In at least two southern universities—at the University of North Carolina under Dr. Howard W. Odum and at Fisk University under Dr. Charles S. Johnson—it can be seen in action, and its results are distinguished throughout the whole sociological fraternity.

A few years ago I visited a meeting of Alpha Kappa Delta, at the University of North Carolina, and during the course of the program a member read a list of the studies being carried on by the students and faculty. The list was very interesting. The studies were concerned almost entirely with problems in southern, mostly North Carolina, counties, or with aspects of southern state or regional life and welfare. It happened that shortly before I had visited Fisk University and there attended a meeting held by Dr. Johnson and his graduate students. It was a sort of acquaintance meeting, and each student was asked to state the problem upon which he was working. These

---

[17] *Op. cit.*, pp. 295–96.

[18] Jonathan Daniels, *A Southerner Discovers the South* (New York; Macmillan, 1938); J. Saunders Redding, *No Day of Triumph* (New York: Harper, 1942).

[19] "The Spirit of the Laboratory," *Science*, LXXXV (April 9, 1937), 346.

studies ranged the world; students were writing theses on aspects of society in Brazil, South Africa, the Philippines, and some of the islands of the Pacific and of the West Indies. The contrast between the character of the studies announced at these two meetings was striking, but at both institutions one felt the presence of enthusiasm and life. The important thing at each university was not the number of the students and faculty engaged in research, nor the nature of their projects, but the spirit of the place. Spirit is a hazy thing to describe but it is all-important, nevertheless, and when it is absent no amount of money available for research, no amount of personnel or distinguished talent, no amount of equipment and convenience will carry research very far or learn very much beyond mere formal knowledge about the world in which we live.

The impression gained of the work of the sociologists at the University of North Carolina is that they frankly are interested first and foremost in immediate social welfare and social control. Their view, apparently, is that the way to build up a knowledge of social facts in their significant relations is by the pragmatic device of entering upon a course of social planning and experimentation, that science does not precede but follows efforts at control. The University of North Carolina sociologists have concerned themselves particularly with the so-called Negro problem as the focal point in the complex of southern social problems, but they have taught us to see all our problems in their interrelations and in the context of southern life as a whole. They pursue investigations along this line under the rubric of regionalism.

The sociologists at Fisk University also have studied and are studying immediate aspects of southern life, but they seem to be much more interested in the comparative use of nonsouthern experience in the analysis of southern society. Their studies are not confined to southern horizons or to southern historical levels. They seek to wrench analysis clear of the particularistic assumptions of a single culture and to put the phenomena of southern life in a wider context of relationship and meaning. Especially are they concerned to make a contribution to the comparative study of race relations. It might be fair to say that the sociologists at the University of North Carolina are interested primarily in *conditions* while those at Fisk University are more interested in *processes*.

Men probing for solutions to the social problems of their day often end up by discovering society.

They sometimes rise above place and time through the paradox of putting themselves more intensely into their place and time. At this point there is a tendency for interest in social problems to at least make room for an interest in sociological problems and for the pursuit of a kind of knowledge which does not promise to be immediately useful but without which rational control in the practical affairs of life may never be gained. This requires comparative study. The South as a unique historical society cannot be compared with anything, but regions and sections, not only in the United States but throughout the world, are subject to comparative study. So is the plantation, and so are race and race relations.

There is, of course, no reason why southern sociologists should not turn their attention to the study of any segment of social life in which they may be interested. Southern sociology would be the poorer if interest in the family, population, crime, et cetera, were not strongly represented here. But a review of the history of southern sociology suggests that the lines along which it may make its greatest contribution, not only to an understanding of the South and its problems, but to the progress of science generally already have been marked out for it. The relations between the races is the axis upon which southern life has turned for a hundred years or more. Southern sociology began with it, developed with it, and must continue with it. In the midst of wide diversity of economic interests and social backgrounds there still is just one South because of the Negro problem. More than anything else it has defined the section. More than anything else it has defined and influenced southern sociology. To be sure the race problem is no longer a sectional or even a national problem. It now is a world problem. This means that the scope of comparative study has been widened immeasurably and it also means that southern studies in race relations have value and meaning in an ever-widening circle of social science. It is in the field of race relations, perhaps, that southern sociologists have their finest opportunity to contribute to the science of sociology itself.

It is probable that the South will feel the impact of the changes to follow the present world war more acutely than any other region of the nation. As Southern sociology adjusts to these changes, and attempts to study and control them, it may undergo profound change itself.

SOUTHERN CHILDREN AND FAMILY SECURITY[1]

T. J. WOOFTER

CHILDREN occupy a much more important place in southern families than in other regions (Table 1). In absolute numbers more than one-third of the nation's children are in southern homes. In later life migration distributes many of these children throughout the country, emphasizing the national stake in their development.

Western States average only about 0.9 of a child per family as against nearly 1.5 in Southern States. The Northeast and North Central States average almost exactly 1 child per family. The average children per family is about the same for whites and Negroes within the urban and farm population, but the Negro total is higher because they are more rural. On the other hand, nonfarm family wage or salary incomes in the South ($965) are only about two-thirds of the national average ($1,380). The support of a child population one-third larger than that of other regions by family incomes which are one-third smaller raises many problems of family economics and has its effect both upon the level of living of the parents and of the children. These problems constitute a challenge not only to families but also to the planners and legislators of States and communities and students of social policy who are concerned with the maximum equalization of opportunity.

The "American" standard of living is not always maintained by the earnings of a single wage earner who provides the sole support of a family. The inadequacy of the individual earnings of many workers for the full satisfaction of the needs of

their family is indicated by the number of supplementary earners in families—wives, sons, daughters, and other relatives who contribute to the common budget. The proportion of families with supplementary earners and the differential incomes of such families is shown in Table 2.

The South as a whole has a higher proportion of families with more than one earner than the national proportion, and within the South 42 percent of the Negro families have more than one earner as against 31 percent of the white families. When all wage or salary workers, farm and nonfarm, are classified by relationship to the family head, the distribution is: head of family 57 percent; wives 10 percent; and other relatives of the family head 33 percent.

The social consequences of the need for the earnings of members of the family other than the head are of very wide significance. To mention only the most obvious implications: Child labor with its lack of educational opportunity results. Families with working wives usually have few children, and when wives or widows with young children do work, the home life of the children is often neglected. Adult offspring, who remain to contribute to family support, usually delay their marriages and start their own families later.

The analyses presented herewith deal with family income (as of 1939) based upon the Census enumeration of 1940. Only occasionally in recent years has information been available as to the family incomes of a sufficiently large segment of the population to warrant safe generalizations. These occasions were the Consumer Purchase Study of 1935–36, The National Health Survey of 1935, and the Census enumeration of 1940.[2] The latter is more comprehensive in coverage and lends itself to more accurate relation of the family income to family composition; that is, the census data can be more accurately reduced to per capita incomes for the various types of families. A serious deficiency of the census figures, however, is that they include only wage or salary income and, therefore, exclude farm incomes and the incomes from business enterprises, professional fees,

[1] In this analysis the States included in the southern region are those included by the Census of 1940 in its regional division of the country. These analyses were computed from the following volumes of the U. S. Census of 1940: Population—Characteristics by Age; Population—Families—Wage or Salary Income, 1939; Population—The Labor Force—Wage or Salary Income, 1939; Population and Housing—Families—General Characteristics; Population—Families—Types of Family; Population—Families—Sizes of Family and Age of Head. For a fuller discussion and methods of computation, see T. J. Woofter, "A Method of Analysis of Family Composition and Income," *Journal of the American Statistical Association*, December 1944.

[2] It is probable that another cross section will be provided by the special census of 1945.

investments, and income in kind. Therefore, the families which are subject to clear-cut analysis on the basis of census data are the nonfarm families whose incomes are derived from wages or salaries only. This group comprises about 42 percent of all families in the United States.

In the South almost half the children are in farm families, and while clear-cut analysis of farm incomes in relation to family size is not possible from census figures, it is known that farm incomes

are lower and farm families are larger than those of nonfarm areas. In Table 1 it was indicated that for the country as a whole there were 1.6 children per family in the farm population as against 0.9 of a child in the urban population. The average number of adults is likewise somewhat larger in farm families. If, therefore, it had been possible to include the farm families in the following analysis, the discrepancy between the incomes of families with children and the incomes of

TABLE 1

PRIVATE FAMILIES AND PERSONS IN FAMILIES, BY AGE, COLOR, RESIDENCE, AND REGIONS, 1940

	FAMILIES (IN THOUSANDS)	PERSONS (IN THOUSANDS)*		AVERAGE PER FAMILY		MEDIAN NON-FARM WAGE OR SALARY INCOME
		18 yrs. old and over	Under 18 yrs. old	18 yrs. old and over	Under 18 yrs. old	
United States:						
Total....................	34,949	83,578	39,353	2.390	1.126	
White................	31,680	76,206	34,673	2.406	1.094	
Nonwhite..............	3,269	7,372	4,680	2.255	1.440	
Urban................	20,649	49,336	19,219	2.380	.931⎱	$1,380
Rural nonfarm.........	7,226	16,451	8,730	2.277	1.208⎰	
Rural farm.............	7,074	17,791	11,404	2.515	1.613	
Northeast................	9,503	23,750	9,589	2.499	1.009	1,575
North Central............	10,989	26,086	11,452	2.372	1.044	1,441
South (Total)............	10,305	24,475	14,567	2.400	1.414	965
White.................	7,895	19,168	10,895	2.429	1.380	1,228
Nonwhite..............	2,410	5,577	3,672	2.314	1.523	505
West....................	4,152	8,997	3,745	2.168	.901	1,454

* Persons under 18 years of age who were heads of families or wives of heads were classified as over 18 years of age. In subsequent references "adults" means persons over 18 years of age and heads and wives under 18, "children" means persons under 18 years of age exclusive of family heads and wives.

TABLE 2

PERCENTAGE OF URBAN FAMILIES BY NUMBER OF WORKERS AND MEDIAN FAMILY INCOME, FAMILIES WITH WAGE OR SALARY INCOME ONLY,* SOUTHERN REGION

	ONE EARNER	TWO EARNERS	THREE OR MORE EARNERS
White:			
Percent of families.....	68.4	24.7	6.9
Median income.......	$1,234	$1,621	$2,140
Nonwhite:			
Percent of families....	57.6	32.4	10.0
Median income.......	$420	$692	$1,038

* Excluding families with no earnings or not reported.

families without children would be even more pronounced than in the nonfarm population. From this point on, the statements, except Table 4, relate to nonfarm families with wage or salary income only.

Within the South, as in other regions, the great majority of the children are cared for by families with relatively low income. The concentration of children at the lower end of the income scale is shown by Table 3 and Figure 1, in which the average number of children per family decreases from 1.37 in families with incomes from $500 to $1,000 to 0.97 in families with incomes of $5,000 and over. The slight rise from the $1 to $500 group to the $500 to $1,000 group is attributable to the association of low wages with youth of the family head.

TABLE 3

CHILDREN IN NONFARM WAGE OR SALARY FAMILIES, BY FAMILY INCOME, SOUTHERN REGION

FAMILY INCOME	CHILDREN UNDER 18		FAMILIES (IN THOUSANDS)
	Per family	Total (in thousands)	
Total	1.261	4,717	3,730
$1– 499	1.291	1,230	953
500– 999	1.367	1,324	980
1,000–1,499	1.319	886	671
1,500–1,999	1.225	594	483
2,000–2,499	1.159	327	282
2,500–2,999	1.067	149	140
3,000–4,999	.932	168	181
5,000 and over	.970	39	40

than elsewhere, the average age of father at birth of first child (about 27 years) being nearly a year younger than the national average. This indicates that the support of the first child is an item in the family budget from the time the father is

TABLE 4

EDUCATION OF HEAD OF FAMILY, BY NUMBER OF CHILDREN, ALL FAMILIES, SOUTHERN REGION

TYPE OF FAMILY	MEDIAN SCHOOL GRADES COMPLETED
No child	7.7
One child	8.0
Two children	7.7
Three or more children	6.4

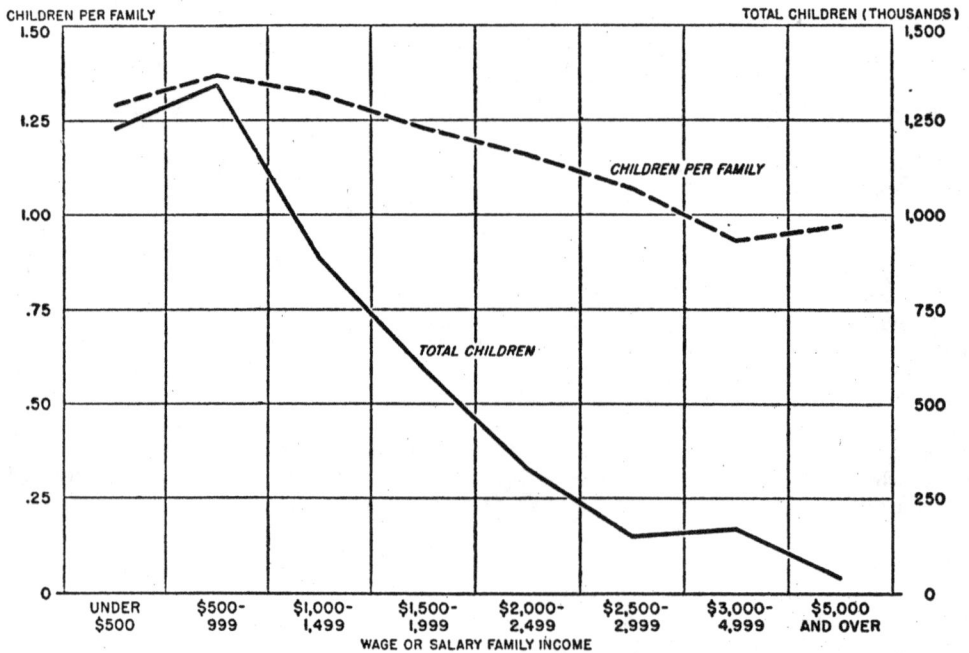

FIG. 1. CHILDREN PER FAMILY AND TOTAL CHILDREN IN FAMILIES BY WAGE OR SALARY FAMILY INCOME, NONFARM FAMILIES, SOUTHERN REGION, 1939

Ignorance and improvidence account for part. but not all of this excess size of low income families. The reverse relationship between education and family size is indicated by Table 4.

Another factor which tends to concentrate children where incomes are lower is the relatively younger age at which families have their maximum family responsibility. This age is younger than that at which the maximum earning capacity is reached. Families in the South are started earlier

about 27 until he is about 45 years old. On the other hand, the average father's earning capacity continues to increase until he is nearly 50, considerably after the time when most of his children have become self-supporting.[3] (Figure 2)

The extent to which the burden of child support

[3] For a fuller discussion of the relationship of age to size of family and income, cf. T. J. Woofter, "Family Size in Relation to Income and Age of Family Head," *American Sociological Review*, December 1944.

is heavier in the younger years of the family when incomes are below the lifetime peak is shown in Figure 2. On the left of this figure the top line indicates the constant rise of the unit income of families without children up to the time when the head is age 45 and the maintenance of a relatively high level up to age 55. The average family, on the other hand, has a lower unit income after the

two-child family is better off financially at 30 than at any subsequent time up to age 50, and the father of a four-child family never attains the unit income which he enjoyed in his 20's.

The concentration of the majority of children in the larger families (Table 5) (Figure 3) causes a very unequal distribution of responsibility for children.

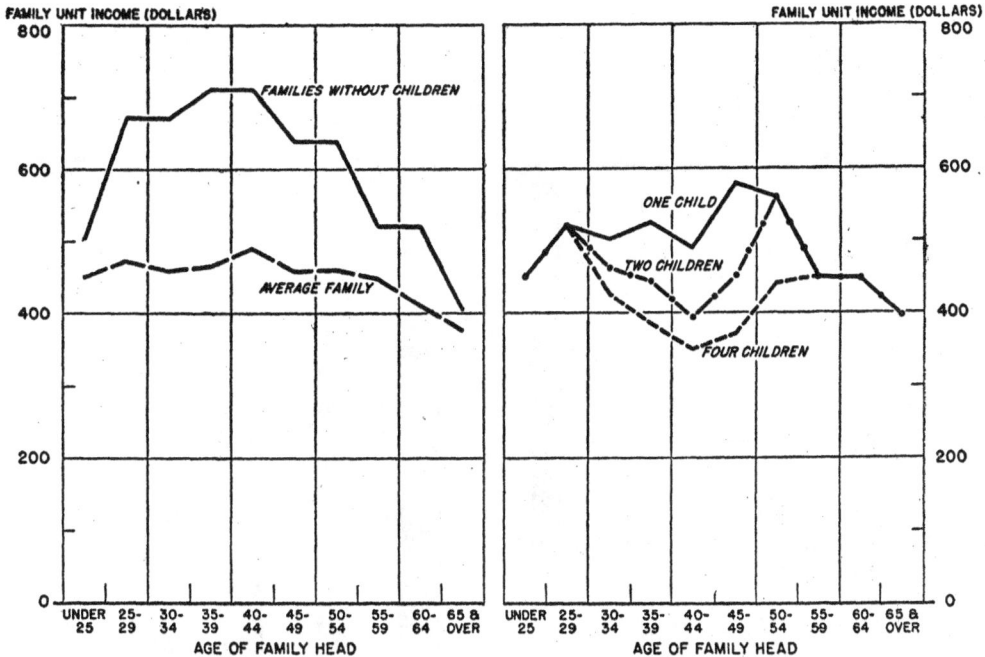

FIG. 2. FAMILY UNIT INCOMES OF FAMILIES HEADED BY MAN WITH WIFE PRESENT, VARYING NUMBER OF CHILDREN

TABLE 5

UNIT INCOME AND NUMBER OF CHILDREN, BY TYPE OF FAMILY, THE SOUTH URBAN AND RURAL NONFARM
(FAMILIES WITH MALE HEAD AND WIFE PRESENT)

TYPE OF FAMILY	NUMBER OF FAMILIES	NUMBER OF CHILDREN	PERCENT OF ALL CHILDREN	PERCENT OF ALL FAMILIES	MEDIAN FAMILY INCOME	MEDIAN UNIT INCOME
No children..............	1,140,960	0	0	37	$1,144	$473
One child................	804,960	804,960	19	26	1,164	400
Two children............	546,160	1,092,320	25	17	1,133	331
Three or more children....	616,940	2,448,100	56	20	885	201

head is age 25 until the children begin to reach the self-sustaining age. The right-hand portion of Figure 2 shows what happens to the average family income of man and wife families when one child is added when the head is age 28, another when he is age 30, and two others before he is age 35. In the one child family the increase of family income with age about keeps pace with the increase in child expense. The father of a

While more families have one and two children, a smaller proportion of the children is included in these small families than is to be found in the families of three or more children. In the South 37 percent of the families have no children, and the 20 percent of the families with 3 or more children have responsibility for 57 percent of the children.

The relative supporting capacity of family incomes is more accurately measured when they are reduced to a *per capita* basis than when *total* family incomes are compared. In reducing family incomes to a per capita or family unit[4] basis, this analysis uses the crude device of counting adults over 18 as a full family unit and children under 18[5] as a half unit. On this basis the median family unit income in the South is $330 as against $474 in the United States. Figure 4 shows the difference in family unit income between the averages of families of various types in the country as a whole and in the southern region. There is a sharp differential in income among families with varying

three or more children (averaging four) have unit incomes of only $107 as against a United States general average of $474 and a United States average for families without children of $635.

The discrepancy in family unit incomes between the families with children and those without children is particularly striking (cf. Table 5, Figures 3 and 4). The families with no children have a unit income of $473, while those with three or more children have a unit income of $201, or considerably less than one-half that of the childless familis. This taken in conjunction with the previous point that 56 percent of the children

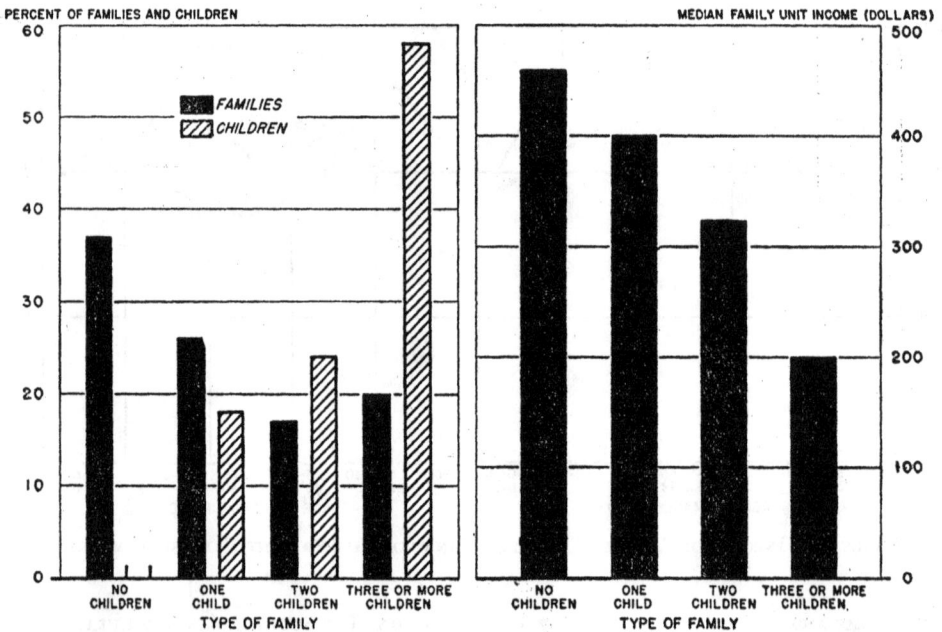

FIG. 3. PERCENTAGE OF FAMILIES AND CHILDREN, AND INCOME FROM SALARY OR WAGES, BY TYPE OF FAMILY NONFARM POPULATION, SOUTHERN REGION, 1939

numbers of children, but the inadequacy of the incomes of families headed by women is particularly striking. Such families in the South with

[4] The complex considerations involved in the proper weighting of individuals of varying sexes and ages in respect to their consumer needs are too detailed to be included in this article. For a discussion of the merits and shortcomings of the procedure used here, see an article by the author, "A Method of Analysis of Family Composition and Income," *Journal of the American Statistical Association*, December 1944.

[5] Children under 18 include only those who are not themselves heads of families or the wives of heads of families. These heads and wives who are under 18 years of age are classified with the adults.

are included in the three or more child families indicates that a considerable majority are concentrated in families where the income is not adequate to provide fully for family needs.

The same story is told in a different way in Table 6 (Figure 5) which distributes all families regardless of type by the unit family income. Here, again, it will be noted that 78 percent of the southern children are in families with unit incomes below $450 or less than the national family unit average of $474.

Examination of the nonfarm incomes and family composition by States in Table 7 reveals that the inclusion of the border States in the South substantially increases the regional average family unit income. The deep South States from North Carolina to Arkansas generally have larger num-

fluenced by the large proportion of miners, mill workers, and other recent migrants from the farm.

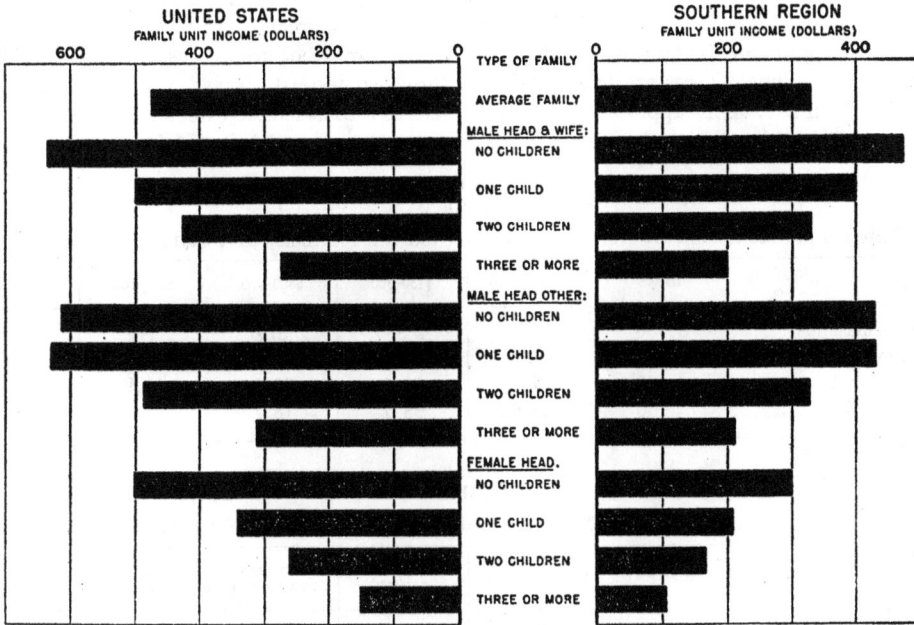

FIG. 4. FAMILY UNIT INCOMES OF WAGE OR SALARY FAMILIES BY TYPE OF FAMILY, NONFARM FAMILIES, U. S. AND SOUTHERN REGION, 1939

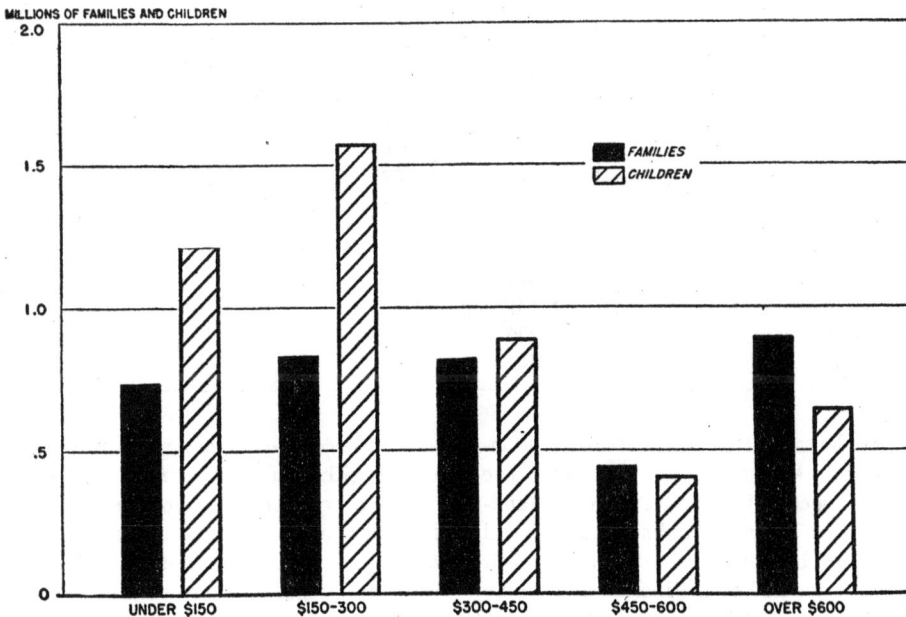

FIG. 5. NONFARM WAGE OR SALARY FAMILIES, AND CHILDREN, BY FAMILY UNIT INCOME, SOUTHERN REGION

bers of children and smaller family incomes than the States of the upper South. The composition of wage earning families in these States is in-

This factor also tends to keep the wage level below that in the States which were industrialized earlier.

The extent to which the family incomes described above are adequate for the support of children involves a number of difficult judgments. The use of the term "adequacy" assumes some agreement upon a yardstick which measures the minimum or optimum budget of goods and services which are judged necessary to maintain a family of a given size. This approach, evidently, involves a considerable amount of subjective judg-

difficulty that many families have appreciable amounts of noncash income which are not included in the census incomes treated in this article. The most common items of noncash remuneration in the farm labor group consists of room and board furnished instead of cash wages. In this group and to a considerable extent in the rural nonfarm group, home production of food also renders de-

TABLE 6

FAMILIES AND CHILDREN IN NONFARM WAGE OR SALARY FAMILIES, BY FAMILY UNIT INCOME

	TOTAL	UNDER $150	$150–300	$300–450	$450–600	OVER $600
Families (thousands)......	3,730	736	835	819	444	895
Children (thousands)......	4,717	1,217	1,570	883	404	643
Percent of families........	100	19.7	22.4	22.0	11.9	24.0
Percent of children........	100	25.8	33.2	18.7	8.5	13.8

TABLE 7

FAMILY INCOME AND COMPOSITION OF NONFARM WAGE OR SALARY INCOME FAMILIES, SOUTHERN STATES

STATE	FAMILY INCOME	ADULTS PER FAMILY	CHILDREN PER FAMILY	UNITS PER FAMILY	FAMILY UNIT INCOME
Alabama...........................	$799	2.28	1.39	2.98	$268
Arkansas...........................	677	2.17	1.20	2.77	244
Delaware...........................	1,497	2.37	1.05	2.90	516
Dist. of Columbia....................	1,907	2.28	.85	2.71	704
Florida.............................	867	2.26	1.06	2.79	311
Georgia............................	817	2.30	1.28	2.94	278
Kentucky..........................	955	2.33	1.32	2.99	320
Louisiana..........................	846	2.32	1.28	2.96	286
Maryland..........................	1,431	2.42	1.10	2.97	482
Mississippi.........................	606	2.18	1.21	2.78	218
North Carolina......................	973	2.39	1.53	3.16	308
Oklahoma..........................	1,031	2.16	1.20	2.76	374
South Carolina......................	820	2.28	1.49	3.03	271
Tennessee..........................	921	2.34	1.38	3.03	304
Texas..............................	982	2.25	1.21	2.85	345
Virginia............................	1,161	2.39	1.34	3.06	380
West Virginia.......................	1,206	2.39	1.58	3.18	379
Southern Region....................	966	2.28	1.28	2.92	330

ment in the determination of the items to be included in the so-called adequate budget. The comparison of specific incomes with such a standard requires that the goods and services included in the adequate budget be priced and that their total cost be compared to the income of a family or group of families. This involves tedious pricing from time to time and place to place.

The comparison of cash family incomes with the cost of standard budgets also encounters the

ceptive the comparison of retail prices of standard budgets with available income.

From a practical viewpoint the use of the cost of standard or theoretical budgets as a measure of adequacy is often unacceptable for the reason that such budgets, even when restricted to minimum standards in many areas, cost more than the median family income available.

This may be illustrated by the use of the WPA maintenance budget which provides a level of living including those goods and services which represent normal or average minimum requirements for industrial service or other manual workers. This budget originally priced by the WPA in 1935 was subsequently priced in a number of cities by the Bureau of Labor Statistics with some modification in the food requirements. The price of this budget in the first quarter of 1940 may be used as representing levels fairly comparable to the year 1939 when the incomes were reported to the census. General comparison between the unit cost of the maintenance budget and the median unit income and lower 25

TABLE 8
UNIT COSTS OF MAINTENANCE BUDGET AND MEDIAN FAMILY UNIT INCOMES, SOUTHERN CITIES*

	UNIT COST MAINTENANCE LEVEL	MEDIAN UNIT INCOME	LOWER 25 PERCENT UNIT INCOME
Atlanta, Georgia.....	$412	$381	$213
Baltimore, Maryland.	408	505	321
Birmingham, Alabama.........	392	349	188
Houston, Texas......	401	488	263
Jacksonville, Florida.	398	412	222
Memphis, Tennessee.	399	309	179
New Orleans, Louisiana........	393	355	198
Richmond, Virginia...	408	484	253

* The unit costs were obtained by dividing the cost of the maintenance budget by 3.25, since this is the factor representing the unit size of family which the budget is designed to support. Median and quartile family unit incomes obtained by dividing median and quartile family income of city by unit composition of nonfarm families of the State.

percentile unit income in southern cities is shown in Table 8.

These comparisons indicate that in the lower wage cities the unit cost of the maintenance budget is considerably above the median unit income, or, expressed in another way, more than 50 percent of the families in these cities were living below the level represented by the maintenance budget. In the higher income cities— Baltimore, Houston, Jacksonville, and Richmond —the income available to the median family is above the cost of the maintenance budget. The income of the lower 25 percent of the families, however, is considerably below this level. This

would indicate that even in the higher income cities, 30 to 40 percent of the families have incomes below the maintenance level.

Special significance of this comparison for families with children is evident from the previous figures which indicate that in the family with 3 or more children the median unit income was only $200 as against the regional average of $330. The other heavily disadvantaged class which is to be found in all cities regardless of general wage level is represented by the families with female heads. Their unit incomes even without children average less than the regional average of all families, while those with 3 or more children have a unit income which is less than one-third of the regional average.

In measuring adequacy, therefore, the use of the average unit income available to families of a given type or in a given region may be considered as an alternative to pricing a theoretical budget. The application of this method may be made as follows: In Table 7 it was pointed out that the median nonfarm family unit income in North Carolina was $308. It is possible to compare insurance benefits and relief grants prevailing in the State at approximately the same time and similarly reduced to family units. These grants and benefits so reduced to a unit basis per annum are shown in Figure 6. If it is assumed that this is the only source of support for such families then the survivors benefits under Old Age and Survivors Insurance approach adequacy, unemployment compensation is only about one-third adequate, and the grants which were made to families receiving aid to dependent children and general assistance are considerably less than one-third of adequacy. The wide gap between payments under all of these programs and the level of adequacy as measured by the income on which the average family actually lives should dispel any notion that these security measures are pampering the poor or encouraging idleness. This gap likewise indicates the extent to which benefits and grants could be increased before adequacy is approximated. It emphasizes the special disadvantages of children who are living in these families.

The striking disadvantage of families with children in their ability to maintain a level of living anywhere near as high as that of families without children and the concentration of such a large proportion of the children in a small proportion of the families provides the unanswerable justification for public tax-supported programs for child development. It is largely through such use of tax funds that society safeguards its future and equalizes the all important responsibility for bringing up children.

The wide disparity between the level of living which can be attained by families with children and by families without children at the same income level is also undoubtedly a major factor in the tendency towards the limitation of size of family which has set in so strongly in the last few decades. The conditions back of these statistics of dis-

would be in the improvement of the quality of the future population. Measures which are designed to insure the security of larger families and assist in the development of their children would also tend to insure a full opportunity for the physical and intellectual development of the children. There is not space in this article for a detailed examination of the measures which should be included in a population policy or broad social policy with regard to the families with children. It should be said, however, that it is a question of such sweeping importance that it should be taken

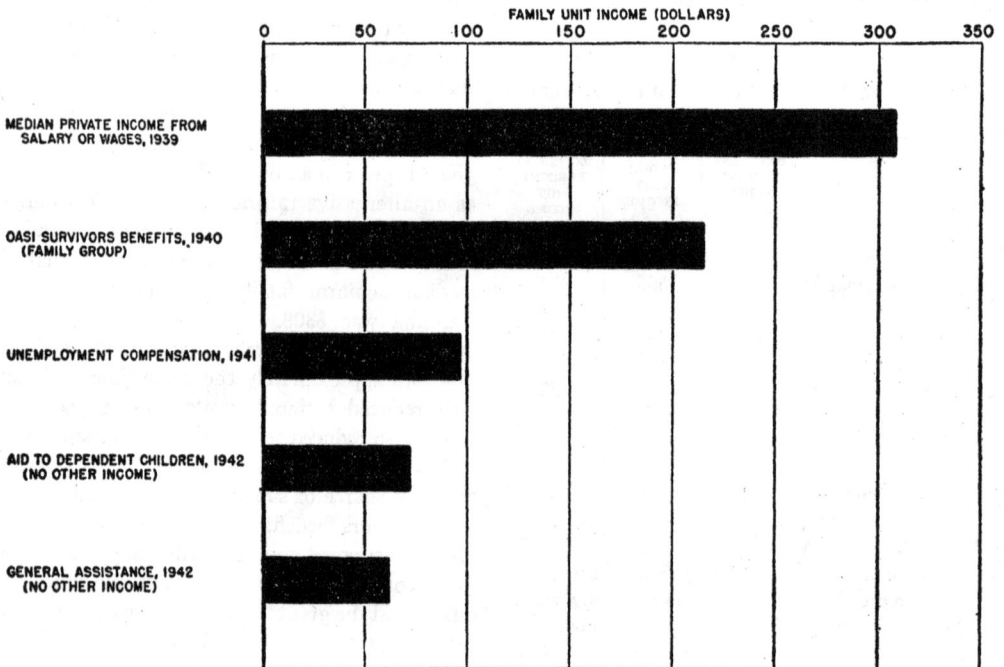

Fig. 6. Private Income from Salary or Wages, and Benefits and Grants Supplementing Private Income (1940 Purchasing Power), North Carolina

crepancies in per capita income are, of course, known in a general way by married couples, and they balance realistically the satisfaction of a family with children against the sacrifices which are inevitable if additional needs are included in the family budget.

The implications of this maladjustment between family income and the needs of large families point up the importance of a more coherent policy or set of policies which will underpin the security and stability of the families with more than one child.

The birth rate might to some extent be increased by such policies, but the more important effects

under careful consideration in the administrative and planning agencies of the State and local governments and of private organizations throughout the country. The broad provisions of such policies should include:

1. Measures to insure the security of family income.

2. Supplementation of the incomes of larger families in cases where the opportunities of the children for development are limited by the lack of income.

3. More systematic development of the services

for children which are supported by tax funds and more widespread availability of these services for the health, education, and cultural development of all dependent children.

A NORTHERNER VIEWS THE SOUTH*

RUTH LANDES

RECENTLY in Louisiana a distinguished sugar planter observed to me, "The South is the disease of the United States." We were discussing the poverty and backwardness of his area, and its chronically disaffected relations with the "East." His comment referred specifically to the South's one-party political system whose operations drew, he thought, a circle of black magic around the region, precluding the play of free competition and blacking out the light of modern thought. But I answered that he seemed to be concentrating on a symptom of the disease rather than on its cause.

To Northerners also, particularly to those whose thinking like my own is conditioned by the currents of life in large cities, the South is the problem of our commonwealth. As the war years move on, she draws just such issues within our borders as we are already facing in battle overseas. Why is she the only American area to disallow free political expression? Do her sectional quarrels mean that she is still chafing against the bonds of political union? What is the significance of the unruly positions her representatives take in the sphere of race relations?

We Northerners possess few facts about the South, and do not understand her. We imagine that she fell out of step with the Nation after 1865, and that she then turned in upon herself. Her subsequent internal developments have been a mystery to us. We have no inkling of the motives that drive her people, of the logic that supports their judgments.

A northern child's, and many an adult's first awareness of the Southland comes from meeting occasional migrant Negroes who work in our kitchens and live in our ghettos. The reaction is a confused one. There are uneasiness and fear,

and we seldom clarify our relations with individual Negroes. The Civil War and Reconstruction years are so presented to us in the schools that we can make no dynamic connection between those times and upheavals and the presence and status of Negroes in our northern cities; no philosophy of interracial conduct has been presented for our use. Films and best sellers, on the other hand, provide us with a definite if special outlook. They offer beguiling picturizations of the antebellum South as some country of Cockaigne where men were chivalrous and ladies glamorous, and their former slaves were attached to them by silken bonds. Yet the creed of the North contains a fierce repudiation of slavery in any form, and the schools do teach us that this principle was sanctified by our blood in 1865. Thus the faery-tale South looms also as a menacing sinner. We condemn her on the anti-slavery principle alone, not knowing more about her, and unaware of the extent to which she has actually influenced us in our own unfair treatment of Negroes. The economic and other necessities of the southern slave period are unimportant to us, interesting though they may be. We view the defunct institution of slavery and the present unhappy state of race relations by themselves, ripped from any context. They are an absolute evil, blamable on the South.

And yet there remains an ineradicable feeling of appreciation for the South. So vividly do we recall the tremendous contributions her great men made to the young Republic that today she still carries prestige, even after secession and crushing defeat, despite the horrible disorganization of the Reconstruction and the chronic disaffection she has shown ever since. The careful hearings she receives, from the halls of Congress to jive sessions in Tin Pan alley, are often gilded with some sentimentality. This accolade is rendered even in the Negro world. We northerners play at adopting southern nicknames and accents and tones of speech, we dream of warm, magnolia-scented nights

* Submitted March 1944 and delayed publication for use in this issue agreed upon by the author.—*Editors.*

and sing songs about Basin street, and the poetry of bayous we have never seen.

But the stresses of war now rouse all our sleeping mistrust of the South. We see that race relations are worsening, conflicts becoming widespread by contagion, and overt. Southern spokesmen refuse to honor federal regulation of an increasingly intolerable situation. They caution their supporters against the "carpet-bag" and "bureaucratic" agencies of the Federal Government that allegedly threaten to demolish the democratic processes of the land. We wonder how they mean their words, how they view their own oligarchical methods of control, their unfairly applied literacy clauses, their poll tax system, their controlled primaries and other methods of assuring favored elections. We wonder why southern spokesmen reiterate the language of democracy when they are eager to withhold the vote from even their own relatives in uniform in order to exclude uniformed Negroes from southern ballot boxes, all being done in the name of the doctrine of States' rights. We wonder at the devious southern mind.

Some southerners have tried to tell us about themselves. We hear lone voices protest as do our own against injustices to both black and white but we realize that they are not representative. In a voluminous and varied literature we are told a great deal about the mind of the Negro, but his is not the mind of the dominant or representative South. Others have tried to explain the region's special institutional abuses, like farm tenancy, even apologizing for them. One of the most sympathetic of these accounts is by that charming poet and humanitarian philosopher, William Alexander Percy.

Southern apologists speak however within a peculiar universe of thought. They refer to unenunciated realities that all southerners have grown up with, but of which we of the North are unaware. My own experience taught me that one must live a while in the South, with southerners, in order to learn the key words and what they mean. Thus, one hears a familiar vocabulary, but the timbre echoes differently. To sense the implications, one must follow tones of the voice, gather the things that are left unsaid, hear the eloquent silences, note the special actions. In very truth, these words serve another style of living. At times I felt like a psychiatrist observing a patient.

We in the North, for example, outlaw the word "nigger," considering it respectful to use instead the word "Negro." South of the line however, "nigger" can have intimate connotations, notably in the address of benevolent whites, and "colored" is in vastly greater repute as an indicator of respect than is "Negro." One finds exactly these southern distinctions in French and in new world Portuguese where "Negro" is considered brusque and is therefore confined to scientific discussions while a kindlier word meaning "black" serves ordinary purposes.

"Kindness" is another key term connoting noncomparable values in New York and in Louisiana. In the North it has the simple meaning of a generally considerate attitude to everyone. In Louisiana, however, it is tremendously elaborated in the practices of upper-class whites to connote deep emotions and many significant relationships. "We are kind to Negroes," these southerners say, even if they have just explained the necessity of lynching Negroes, or that before the war they would never have dreamed of paying them wages. "How do you mean, kind?" I ask, wondering at the stress. They answer, "Well, we *like* them. We take care of the darkies who work for us as if they were our kin. They know that while we live, they'll never want for anything. They come to us for any money they need, whether it's for a birth in their family, or a marriage or sickness or death, or just that they're lonesome to visit somebody somewhere. They know we won't refuse, that we'll give them more than they asked for, and will never bother them to repay us. They trust us and they like us. You couldn't get one of our darkies to leave us. They wouldn't know what to do without us—and we wouldn't know what to do without them! We have had generations of the same family serving us. We bail them out of jail. And they are good to us. I'll trust a darky any time, and with large amounts of money where I wouldn't trust a white man. But I wouldn't think of giving him a wage for domestic work! And in fact he makes out better this way, childlike as he is! Now you people up East don't like darkies, and they know it, and they don't like you no matter how much equality you give them."

This institutional "kindness" flows from a thoroughgoing personalness in the aristocratic style of living in the South, and does not exist in the North anythwere. It cannot exist in the North because it rests on bygone feudalistic economic and social institutions. The southern white man of the upper class, operating like some squire or lord, is kind and patronizing to his colored dependents, and in return they are expected to show him unlimited devotion. It is a ragged kind of feudalism compared with European prototypes, but its true character emerges clearly against the contrasting industrialized, free life of the North. Such personal relationships in the South serve both to reassure and to enslave, have an equal hold on white master and black man, and are the emotional heart of the feudalistic way of life. Possibly this patterned behavior survives most vigorously in south Louisiana where Latin peoples and traditions predominate. I felt the same social bonds in the communities in north Brazil whose history and social organization largely parallel those of our South. An expression of this behavior that disconcerts a northerner used to meeting numbers of persons is the intimate individualization of people. Regardless of race or social position, everyone is recognized and called by his first name, preferably by a nickname, and prefaced by some title of courtesy. This is as true in Louisiana as in Brazil.

Since individuals matter so, anything that anyone does is intensely important, and people are watched closely. Nobody is casual about anything. This attitude results in the accumulation of considerable high feeling that can break out in violence. It also results in double lives, and skeletons left lying in closets until it is deemed necessary to pull them out for political battles. A delightful safety valve in Louisiana is a peculiar type of humor that I will call gallic: it is dry, good-humored, and stresses the ridiculous. It can be understood then how departures from established behavior are of tremendous moment. Mr. Thomas, for example, paid white and colored workers in his fish canning plant equal wages because federal wage and hour regulations required him to do so. He grew furious with a competitor, however, not because this man was paying his colored help less, as he was, but because he allowed employees of both races to eat, sleep, and work together unsegregated on fishing boats in the gulf. It was interesting that the Negroes understood Mr. Thomas' position and preferred to work for him. He was upper-class and "kind," and these facts were more important to them than the money in which indeed they were not much interested. But employment with Mr. Thomas gave them prestige in their own eyes. The other was an aberrant and, though a rich man, was "trash," a stranger to the tradition of "kindness."

This personalized mechanism holds in its grip whites of the so-called upper class. With Negro help, this class carries on the southern tradition, although since the Civil War it has been reinforced by sons of "trash" stock that has grown wealthy. Poor whites or "trash" are the real disinherited of the South. Hating both the blacks and the white aristocrats, for these together keep southern institutions alive, they in turn are scorned by both groups. Their revenge on the aristocracy is to be vicious to Negroes. Caste-like feeling runs high in the area, and from earliest days aristocratic children are trained to separate their interests and personalities from those of inferior classes, while they are trained to identify them with individuals of their own class. In Louisiana an interesting class distinction is made between "American" families who settled after 1803, the year of the Purchase, and "French" families living there since colonial times; the former is richer and more broadly cultivated, the latter is French-speaking, Catholic, and proudly provincial. This creates a kind of duplicated upper class, each group looking askance at the other. Members of the upper class are expected to be loyal to one another, and to be gracious and hospitable. It is astonishing to what lengths this obligation can be carried. Many Louisiana households can tell of the guest who arrived to stay a month and remained years until claimed by the grave. I myself met a woman who remained eighteen years. And I visited for four months, in consequence of a week-end invitation.

When this obligation is ruptured, a feud results. And feuds are common. There are families of the same standing who exhaust one another through the rivalrous behavior called for by the feud. As someone observed of Louisiana, this "is not a shooting State, like Texas. It battles with words, no matter how muddy," and so the feuds there seldom involve physical violence. Feuding is commonly expressed by spending large amounts of money in purely wasteful ways. In one instance a rupture developed between two men who were partners in a multi-million dollar business, and one of them, trying to embarrass the other by large spending, actually paid his way into bankruptcy competing with the other for the favor of buyers and workers. Sons of other feuding families went to the same college but would not talk to one another, told malicious stories about each other, and cheered for opposing football teams with the usual consequences. It is said that children of feuding families who chance to marry each other are expelled from both families, being adjudged guilty of violating primary ties of loyalty. Hence, friendship with an individual prevents one from establishing pleasant relationships with the hereditary enemy, or so it is said. The origins of feuds are seldom clear, being temperamental and private, although everyone agrees that they give enormous zest to an otherwise unbearable monotony.

This great graciousness and this great hate are complementary aspects of the aristocratic tradition. Likewise it can be said that Negroes are one face of that class coin whose other face is the white aristocracy.

This class feels deeply that Negroes "belong" to it, are a dear part of its civilization. Negroes associated with this class feel the same way, and in south Louisiana consider themselves "Creole" and are proud of speaking French. Whites are so certain of the loyal devotion of their Negroes that accusations of restiveness are seldom laid to their door but are laid instead at the door of northern agitators. The Great Agitator of course is Mrs. Roosevelt and with her southerners have entered into a deep feuding relationship where reasonable arguments and facts have no place. Poor whites align themselves with aristocracy in this quarrel. The alleged "Eleanor Clubs" justify the feud, ghostly though their reality may seem to outsiders. At least this situation channels harsh white feelings away from Negroes.

Hence it is also understandable why personalities are far more powerful in southern politics than are political or other ideological issues. This was a factor in the complaint of my planter friend about the one-party system. Class obligations and feuds operate in this sphere, too, resulting in the extraordinary spectacle of multiple factions within the southern Democratic party. The situation is extreme in Louisiana. It obscures real issues, keeping the air stormy with clouds of individual hates and loves.

In this setting of a relatively simple, unmechanized, stable agricultural world dominated completely by small numbers of interested people, changes are sponsored by single personalities. No point, especially an unaccustomed one, carries weight unless a known individual brings it forward. The point comes to life through him; by itself it is meaningless. Elsewhere in our country, a person's fortune can be made by the social significance of his words. But here, words acquire value because the speaker is a man of power, usually a white of the upper class. This behavior cannot be fought against: it is the way social control is exercised in the deep South.

Since personalities direct general behavior and thinking, it follows that the lot of Negroes is peculiarly insecure. Southerners regard outside criticism of their race relations as an unpardonable invasion of their sovereign privacy, called in other spheres "States' rights." Such comment is a challenge to feud. A southerner cannot understand disinterested criticism, since everything is interpreted personally. This reaction has unpredictable consequences because of the great passion behind it. A southerner is either your friend or your enemy. Hence the South feuds now with the Administration and threatens to split off as a faction of the national Democratic party. She feuds traditionally with the "Yankee" North over economic and racial issues, warning of imaginary tattered banners of the Reconstruction, despite the fact that now her congressional representatives are allied with the Republican party. And as in the Civil War, the Negro is somewhat of a third party while the South tramples on him in efforts to pound the "Yankees." Yet the country cannot ignore the fact that there is a difference, that the Negro has been a free citizen for eighty years, and is now more united and desperate than ever before in his struggle for civil liberties.

The South has not fully realized this, possibly is less awake to it now than it was in 1865 when confronted with ex-slaves and Union soldiers carrying guns. The contemporary white South of all classes lulls herself with day dreams that look backward to shattered or imagined antebellum glories; and southern Negroes, as William Alexander Percy said, having the most exquisitely amiable manners in the world, do not care to disturb the precarious peace. As in the great days landed families deplored slavery and sometimes practiced manumission, so now upper-class families admit the need of helping Negroes to a higher social status. But they want to do it by the benevolent methods of the southern tradition. They protest that they "know how to handle Negroes," and that Negroes, as southerners, should be advanced by southern ininstrumentalities. The poor whites have not fashioned a progressive program for relations with either Negroes or aristocrats.

What will black and white southerners do? How will they adjust to the divergent social trends in the rest of the United States, and indeed in the world? What is their future?

It must be recognized that the South is a land of yesterday. That is the cause of her hostile and anachronistic behavior. Her institutions, her responses, her goals are outmoded, out of rhythm, irrelevant to the national trends. Her sectional feeling, so vehement as to all but differentiate her into another nation, her violent devices for social control, like her graceful hospitality are survivals of an age long since left behind by the North. That is why the regions cannot understand each other. The habits of both frontier and plantation days are still real along the Mississippi, but the North has forgotten their compulsives. Mechanization and mass production, high standards of living without discrimination for all the millions of the giant cities, the extension of democratic privileges and responsibilities to every anonymous citizen—these northern ways are as yet impossible to the rural, isolated, pre-industrial South, inconceivable to her and repugnant. Of all the United States, the South is most trapped by poverty and disease, illiteracy, political corruption, and a deep want of ambition. She holds no prevailing social convictions newer than those of the Reconstruction years. She is unable to participate in modern American democracy. In conflict with our times, she is a demoralizing influence.

But this condition cannot last. Her very wartime conflicts with other regions, echoing in explosions within her own area, bring her into closer contact with the Nation than she has been for generations. Even now she is in transit to the twentieth century. War-contract factories have been springing up, and the countryside must become mechanized and urbanized. As economic interests proliferate, and technological developments move ahead, and her ways and goals of living adjust in conformity, her thought and language must acquire meanings closer to those in more advanced parts of the country. The regal, dangerous personalness of southern living will become more like the egalitarian impersonalness of northern living. The sectional and racial differences that can survive as paramount in an isolated, pre-industrial world necessarily become minimized in an industrial civilization. Social energy has to flow away from them to the wider world. As this development comes upon her, although even now foreshadowed by varied and violent clashes, the South must grasp the wider orientations of the balance of the country. Through changes in her own interests, in her economic structures and objectives, her class and race and regional conflicts must alter their present patterns and begin to resolve themselves. The South cannot be eyed apart from the rest of the country, nor should she be. Her future is inseparable from that of the entire United States.

A DEMOGRAPHIC STUDY OF THE AMERICAN NEGRO*

T. LYNN SMITH

THIS paper is a summary of the data concerning the demographic situation and trends among the American Negro population. After a brief section treating the validity of the data, the exposition is confined to three major topics: (1) the composition of the population, and particularly the distinguishing features of the age profile, the sex distribution, and the marital status of the Negro population; (2) the growth of population and the factors having to do with mortality and reproduction, which are responsible for the natural increase; and (3) internal migration. Most of the information presented has been secured from census sources. But these data would have little

* This is Paper Number 1, Journal Series, Institute of Population Research, Louisiana State University.

meaning were it not for the many excellent studies that have recently been made in the fast developing study of population. Data for the white population are included only when they are useful for comparative purposes.

THE VALIDITY OF THE DATA

The United States has had one hundred and fifty years of experience in the taking and tabulating of census materials, but the data concerning the Negro population still leave a great deal to be desired. Large numbers of Negroes are missed in the census enumerations, and the proportion of Negroes omitted is larger than that of white people. These omissions are not merely interesting, but they have far-reaching consequences. For example, there is a tendency to apportion State and federal funds for education, agriculture, welfare, etc., on a per capita basis. Since any equitable distribution of tax money must rely heavily upon the population factor, each person interested in the education and welfare of the Negro population should make every effort to reduce the percentage of omissions.

Not only are high proportions of the Negro population missed in the taking of the census, but the data that are secured are less reliable than those for other race and nativity groupings. A few specific cases will help demonstrate this proposition. Of all the data secured in the decennial enumeration, those pertaining to the age of the population are probably the most significant. But few of us who hastily reply to or parry the census enumerator's questions on age realize the importance that these basic data have for the social security program, the life insurance business, and a long list of other highly important private and public activities. Yet it can easily be demonstrated that age data are full of errors, and the material for the Negro population is particularly deficient.

Most obvious of all discrepancies in census data is the tendency for ages to cluster in the even years, in the numbers ending with five, and especially in the ages ending with zero. On the other hand, there is always a deficiency in ages not exactly divisible by two or by five. The existence and nature of these discrepancies are readily revealed by charting the reported ages according to single years. The United States Census regularly does this by means of the age and sex pyramid.[1]

Ellsworth Huntington has advanced the proposition that the extent of the discrepancies in the reported ages below 25 is the best measure of the "general intelligence" of a population, and has presented a series of charts designed to show the nature of the variations as between the sexes, the regions, and the principal race and nativity groups.[2] Huntington mentions the use of index numbers as

---

[1] See, for example, *Sixteenth Census of the United States, 1940*, Population, Volume IV, "Characteristics by Age, Marital Status, Relationship, Education, and Citizenship," Part 1, United States Summary (Washington: Government Printing Office, 1943), pp. 9–11.

[2] Cf. his contribution "Society and Its Physical Environment," in Jerome Davis and Harry Elmer Barnes (eds.), *An Introduction to Sociology* (Rev. Ed., Boston: D. C. Heath and Company, 1931), pp. 272–276.

a device for gauging the relative amount of error in the reported ages and he indicates that his indexes vary from zero in Minnesota and North Dakota to 300 in Mississippi. This makes it obvious that the situation in Minnesota and North Dakota is regarded as perfect and that the others are judged in relation to these norms, but we are not informed as to the manner in which the indexes were constructed.

This methodological point is raised not merely because conclusions are usually only as good as the techniques employed, but also because it is very important to have an accurate device for gauging the amount of error that is present in a given age distribution. This should be constructed so as to permit the formation of a judgment about the accuracy of age reporting in Minnesota and North Dakota as well as a means of judging their relative position in comparison with other States. Considerable experimentation leads to the suggestion of the method described below and utilized in the calculations presented in this discussion.

The United States Census and those of many other countries present age distributions for single years beginning with under one and ending with 99, or a total of 100 one-year age periods. Omitting the persons whose ages are unknown and those 100 years of age and over, approximately 10 percent of the remainder normally should be of an age exactly divisible by ten, another 10 percent in other ages exactly divisible by five, 40 percent in the other even number ages, and the remaining 40 percent in the odd number ages other than those ending in five. The effects of each of the known concentrations, i.e., on even years, years ending in 5, and years ending in 0, is to reduce the proportion of the population in the odd-number ages other than those ending in 5. Consequently the ratio of the percentage of the population reporting ages 1, 3, 7, 9, 11, 13, 17, 19, etc., to 40 percent is a fairly reliable gauge of the accuracy of the reported ages. By expressing the observed percentages in these odd-number ages as a percentage of 40 gives an easily understood and useful index number. On such a scale perfect reporting would give a score of 100; and any tendency for the reported ages to concentrate in the even years and in the ages ending with 5 or 0 would reduce the rating.

In an exploratory manner a considerable number of calculations have been made and it is interesting to observe the results. For the year 1940 the population of the United States taken as a whole made a score of 95.5 out of the possible 100, indicating that there is considerable error in the data. This was substantial improvement over the 94 registered for 1930. Minnesota and North Dakota are by no means perfect as far as correctly reporting ages is concerned, the score for the former being 97.6, for the latter, 97.4. However, Mississippi rates only 90.6. This represents considerable improvement in Mississippi, for in 1930 the corresponding index was only 88.5.

There are also considerable differences among the various categories into which the population may be divided. Interestingly enough, in the United States, males make a slightly better showing than females as is indicated by the score of 96 for the former and 95.5 for the latter. Despite the fact that they contain relatively small proportions of Negroes, for whom the index is very low, urban areas fail to make as good a showing as rural areas, the scores being 95.5, 96.2, and 95 for the urban, rural-nonfarm, and rural-farm areas, respectively. But the racial difference is the pronounced one with the white population scoring 96.1, the non-white only 90.1. For 1930 for which more detailed racial breakdowns are possible, the native whites of native parentage rated 95.8 and the Negroes only 87.3. Rural-farm nonwhites score lowest of all, 88.5, although urban nonwhites rate only 91.3. Among whites, on the other hand, the rural-farm index (96.3) is slightly higher than the urban score (95.9).

Another highly significant discrepancy in the age data grows out of the female's "instinct" to appear younger than the chronological reality. The female of the species, of all races, is prone to understate her age, but in this respect the Negro females seem to be much more successful than their white sisters. For example, computations made by one of my colleagues and me indicate that the average understatement of age by native white women aged 30 to 34, inclusive, amounts to 1.6 years, while for the comparable Negro group the average is 4.2 years.[3] In other words, the group of Negro women reported in the census as aged 30 to 34 actually consists almost entirely of those aged 35 to 39.

The discrepancies in our basic population data are not confined to errors in number of persons, nor to the inaccurate reporting of ages. There is con-

vincing evidence that serious errors are introduced through erroneous reporting of the sex of Negro children.[4] For example, birth registration figures indicate a sex ratio at birth among Negroes of approximately 103.3 males to every 100 females; but the census consistently reports more Negro females than males in the first year of life. There seems little doubt that the census ratio is in error, a fact which reflects extreme carelessness in the enumeration of infant Negroes.

There are also many improvements possible in the data relative to various other characteristics of the Negro population, such as marital status, literacy, and occupation; in the recording of births, deaths, marriages; and especially on the records of the migration of the Negro population.

THE COMPOSITION OF THE POPULATION

To analyze adequately each aspect of the composition of the Negro population would be a long and involved process. Therefore, only three of the more important elements of population make-up are considered here: age, sex, and marital status.

Age. The distinctive features of the age distribution of the Negro population are brought out by comparing the age profile of Negroes with that of the native whites. This comparison, allowing for all of the known discrepancies in the age data, discloses that the age pyramid for Negroes is comparatively squat. People under 45 are relatively more numerous in the Negro than in the white population, and there is a marked scarcity of Negroes above the age of 45. This deficiency increases progressively until the age of 75 has been attained. In the age distribution of Negroes the group 70–74, inclusive, has only slightly more than one-half the relative importance that it has in the age distribution of native whites. Such a squat shaped age pyramid is characteristic of a population whose birth rates and death rates are both comparatively high.

Negroes also differ somewhat from native whites in the extent to which various age groups concentrate in the cities, in the villages, and on the farms of the Nation. In general, urban populations contain very low proportions of children, exceedingly high percentages of persons in the working and childbearing ages, and relatively few old persons.

[3] T. Lynn Smith and Homer L. Hitt, "The Misstatement of Women's Ages and the Vital Indexes," *Metron*, XIII (1939), 106.

[4] T. Lynn Smith, "Errors in the Sex Classification of Negro Children in the United States Census," *Congres International de la Population*, V (Paris 1938), 97–106.

Aged females, however, are found in cities in larger proportions than aged males. The typical age concomitants of urbanity, the scarcity of children, the concentration of persons in the ages 15 to 45, and scarcity of oldsters are more pronounced among urban Negroes than in any of the other race and nativity groupings. Similarly, the tendency for the city to retain aged females is more pronounced in the case of Negroes than it is among whites. Thus we may say that the urban age characteristics are best exemplified among the Negroes who dwell in cities.

The village and suburban population is grouped together in the extremely heterogeneous catch-all category which the census calls rural-nonfarm. It is distinguished by a relatively large proportion of children, a scarcity of persons at the working ages, and most important of all, an exceedingly high percentage of persons in the advanced ages. Rural-nonfarm Negroes generally have a less pronounced deficiency of persons in the working ages and a less marked concentration of oldsters than is true of rural-nonfarm population. In other words, the typical age characteristics of rural-nonfarm areas are less pronounced among Negroes than among whites. This is largely because rural-nonfarm Negroes are concentrated in the South where many villages of less than 2,500 represent a relatively high degree of urbanization for the area in which they are located.

The farm population generally contains exceedingly large proportions of children, a very marked scarcity of persons of the productive and working ages, and a relatively large proportion of old people. Among these oldsters, the concentration of men is much more pronounced than that of women. In this respect also there are some significant differences between Negroes and whites. The concentration of children is about the same in each racial group, but the scarcity of persons in the producing ages is much more pronounced among the former than the latter. However, a larger proportion of Negroes than of whites of both sexes live out the last years of their lives on the farms.

Sex. The very low proportion of males, or the high proportion of females, in the Negro population is another demographic characteristic of considerable significance. The sex ratio among Negroes has been low ever since the importation of slaves was prohibited and it has been less than 100 at every census since that of 1830. In 1940 there were in the native Negro population of all ages only 94.9 males per 100 females compared with 100.1 among native whites. Considering only persons of 15 years of age and over, the sex ratio in 1940 was only 93.4 for Negroes compared with 99.1 for native whites.

This low sex ratio among the Negro population is a highly significant phenomenon. For the most part, it rests upon the low sex ratio at birth (approximately 103 as compared with 106 among whites); in turn the low sex ratio at birth probably has as one of its chief determinants the high proportion of stillborn births among Negroes. Among all conceptions the sex ratio probably is about 110, while for stillbirths it varies between 120 and 170.[5] Therefore, because of the high proportion of males among the foetuses who are dead at birth, a high proportion of stillbirths among all pregnancies should reduce the sex ratio among live births.

That this low sex ratio at birth, whatever its cause, is the major factor in the femininity of the Negro population seems evident from the following analysis. Among all Negroes, foreign-born as well as natives, the sex ratio in 1940 was only 95. Eliminating the foreign-born Negroes, the sex ratio among natives was only 94.9, as stated above. Very few Negroes leave the United States. Therefore, immigration and emigration have no significant influence upon the Negro sex ratio in this country. The other significant factor, namely the length of the expectation of life, exerts a buoying rather than a depressing effect upon the sex ratio among Negroes. This may be indicated from the data in the life tables (1939–1941) for whites and Negroes in the United States. If the sex ratios at birth among whites and Negroes were 100 in each case, the population of each race were stationary, and if no factors other than differences in life expectation were influencing the sex ratios, then there would be only 93.7 males per 100 females among whites as compared with 94.2 among Negroes. Thus the prevailing low sex ratios among Negroes would be even lower than they are were it not for the short life span of this colored race. Because neither migration nor life expectation contributes to explain the scarcity of males among the Negro race, the low sex ratio at birth remains as the single factor to which the phenomenon may be attributed.

The effects of this low proportion of males in the

[5] Cf. Sanford Winston, "The Influence of Social Factors Upon the Sex-Ratio at Birth," *American Journal of Sociology*, XXXVII (July, 1931), pp. 11–12.

Negro population is accentuated by the maldistribution of the sexes in the various regions of the country. As is true of all long-distance migration, the flood tide of northward migration of Negroes has carried away excessive proportions of males from the South. The result is that the northern Negro population is excessively masculine, that of the South excessively feminine. For example, according to the 1940 Census, in Atlanta there were only 76.2 Negro males for every 100 females, while in St. Paul, Minnesota, the corresponding ratio was 136.2. Thus, great regional imbalances still further accentuate the problems arising from the excessive femininity of the Negro population.

Marital Status. Undoubtedly the data relating to the marital status of Negroes are among the least reliable of the materials published in the Census. Nevertheless, it is possible to make some fairly dependable observations concerning this aspect of the Negro population. In the first place, it appears certain that Negroes mate earlier than the native white population and that a smaller proportion of Negroes than native whites live out their lives without mating. In the population 15 years of age and over the census of 1940 reported only 32.9 percent of the native Negro males as single as compared with 36.8 percent of the native white males; and only 24.8 percent of the native Negro females as single in comparison with 29.4 percent of the native white females. Furthermore, for each of the sexes in every age group the proportion of single persons was smaller for Negroes than for native whites.

That Negroes mate at an earlier age than native whites seems to be established by the data showing the proportions married according to age. Negroes between 15 and 30 years of age of both sexes are reported as married in larger proportions than are native whites. In the older age groups, however, after death and divorce have had time to play significant rôles, the contrary is true. For the population of all ages 15 years and over taken collectively, native Negro males have a slightly higher proportion (60.6 percent) married than native white males (59.5 percent), and Negro females a slightly lower proportion (56.4 percent) than native white females (60.2 percent). All in all it would appear that the extent to which the population is living in the married state is approximately equal for the two races.

The low proportion of single Negroes finds its counterpart in high proportions of persons reported as widowed and divorced. In fact the proportion of widowed is more than half again as high among native Negroes as native whites, the percentages in the population 15 years of age and over being 5.6 percent among Negro males and only 3.6 percent among native white males, and 16 percent among Negro females compared with 9.7 percent among native white females. Furthermore, at all ages the percentages widowed among Negroes are considerably above those for native whites. In 1930 the situation was similar among those reported as divorced. But in 1940 only 1 percent of the native Negro males aged 15 years and over were classed in this category as compared with 1.3 percent of the native whites; and 1.7 percent of native Negro females were reported to the census enumerator in comparison with 1.8 percent of the native white females.

THE GROWTH OF POPULATION

Numbers and growth are the aspects of population study in which it has been possible to arouse the greatest interest. Thanks to Malthus and his successors, including such moderns as East and Ross, men have long lived under the fear of overpopulation. Quick to catch the popular fancy have been the alarmist doctrines that population tends to outrun the food supply, that mankind is already well along the crossroad leading to poverty and misery due to excessive numbers of people, and that we are in imminent danger of having to hang out the sign "Standing Room Only." At the very time our reproductive springs were becoming too dry to produce enough offspring to meet replacement needs, these popular delusions enjoyed widespread acceptance even among the educated classes. That human gullibility and the compound interest curve have been sufficient to limit most university study of population matters to the "problems" of growth is merely an indication of our obsession with numbers.

A comparable obsession has to do with the relative rates of growth of the Negro and white populations. For decades one of the most widespread popular fancies in the United States has been the belief that Negroes were increasing at a rate far exceeding the one at which the white population was growing. That there has been no factual basis for such a belief is readily established. At every decade from 1790 to 1930, the rate of increase among the white population exceeded that of the Negro. Negroes constituted one out of five persons when the new

American nation was founded; in 1930 and in 1940 they constituted less than one in ten. Nor has this relative loss been because of the tidal waves of immigration to our shores. Every decade since 1850, when the white population was first classified according to nativity, the native white population has increased more rapidly than the Negro.

However, events may intervene to give validity to this widespread belief. Although the increase of the white population has exceeded that of the Negro population in the past, there is little to warrant the assumption that it will continue to do so. In fact the years between 1930 and 1940 probably saw a reversal of the relative positions of whites and Negroes in regard to rates of increase, and it is extremely likely that Negroes will actually increase more rapidly than whites in the decades immediately ahead of us. This appears to be a certain eventuality unless a great loosening of the immigration restrictions occurs, or unless Negroes flock to the cities at an even more rapid rate than they are now doing. As will be indicated below, real race suicide results from urban residence. My own prediction is that the proportions of Negroes in the 1950 population of the United States will be about 10.5 percent.

For the analysis of the growth of population it is necessary to consider two factors: (1) natural increase; and (2) migration. Natural increase in turn refers to the balance between births and deaths and in order to analyze it we must first have information relative both to the fertility and the mortality of the population. For many decades migration has had little bearing on the total number of Negroes in the United States. Even though there has been some influx of Negroes from Puerto Rico and the West Indies, in 1940 there were in the whole United States only 83,941 Negroes who were not born in this country; in 1930 the number was 98,620; and in 1920 the figure was only 73,803. Nor do many Negroes leave our shores for other lands. Thus fertility and mortality, the components of natural increase, are the factors to analyze in examining the growth of the Negro population.

Fertility. Because they have been concentrated largely in the most rural portions of the most rural regions in the United States, Negroes have produced offspring more rapidly than the white population. In 1870 their rate of reproduction was 113 percent of that of the native white population, in

1900 it was 114, and in 1940 it was 114.[6] In all probability a similar differential prevailed in the years before 1870. In any case it seems to be a fact that the fertility of the Negro population has been somewhat greater than that of the native whites.

In view of the facts that the Negro population has long been predominantly rural, but that it is now concentrating into urban areas more rapidly than the white population, it is interesting to consider how the fertility of the Negro holds up in the urban environment. On the basis of the available data the conclusion seems inevitable that urban life dries up the reproductive springs of the Negro population even more rapidly than it leads to race suicide among whites. Fertility rates among urban Negroes are consistently below those of urban whites, and the differential between rural and urban fertility is much more pronounced among the former than among the latter. Thus in 1940 the fertility ratio[7] (a fairly accurate measure of the speed of reproduction) for rural farm whites was 180 percent of the urban; while the comparable percentage for Negroes was 238.[8] Furthermore, the differentials in 1930, 1920, and 1910 were comparable and pointed to the same conclusion.[9]

Mortality. That the mortality of Negroes is considerably above that of whites is well known. The following data are presented merely to assist in gauging more accurately the magnitude of the differential. According to the latest life tables prepared in the Bureau of the Census and relating to the years 1939–1941, the life expectation of Negro males at birth was 52.26 years, as compared with 62.81 for white males; for Negro females the life expectation at birth was only 55.56, as compared with 67.29 for white females. Comparable differentials prevailed throughout the life span until the age of 64, after which the superiority is

[6] Based on the number of children under 5 per 1,000 women aged 15–44, inclusive. See also National Resources Committee, *Population Statistics: 1. National Data* (Washington: Government Printing Office, 1937), p. 40.

[7] The fertility ratio is computed as follows:
$$\frac{\text{number of children under 5}}{\text{number of women 15–44}} \times 1000$$

[8] Data for the computation taken from the *Sixteenth Census of the United States.*

[9] For the data, see National Resources Committee, *op. cit.*, p. 40.

with the Negroes. At age 50 the life expecta-
tions of Negro and white males were 19.06 and
21.96 years, respectively, and that for Negro and
white females was 20.95 and 24.72, respectively.[10]
Thus the more rapid reproduction of Negroes is
offset by the fact that members of the Negro race
also die at a more rapid rate than the white
population.

Lest these observations create a misunderstanding it should be emphasized that only in a very
few of the nations of the world does the life expectation of the population anywhere nearly approach
that of the Negroes in the United States. In other
words, North American Negroes have not yet
acquired as much in the way of health services and
the knowledge of healthful living, especially those
associated with the care and feeding of infants,
as their white fellows; but if compared with the
great mass of the world's population, even the
peoples of most prewar European states, in these
respects the Negroes occupy a very enviable
position.

The Rate of Natural Increase. The number of
births minus the number of deaths gives the natural increase of a population. Were it not for emigration and immigration, this figure would also
give the growth or decrease of population. Unfortunately it is impossible to compute the rate of
natural increase in this country because the registration of births is too incomplete. For example,
as late as 1939, according to tests made by the
Bureau of the Census, there were 23 counties in
Mississippi in which less than 90 percent of the
births were registered.[11] Registration of Negro
births is particularly deficient,[12] and a much
smaller proportion of rural than urban births is
registered.[13] Fortunately, students of population
have devised methods for measuring more accurately the speed of reproduction by means of the
fertility ratio (i.e., a ratio of children under 5 to
women of childbearing age), and this has made it
possible to balance the fertility of the population

[10] *Vital Statistics—Special Reports*, Vol. 19, No. 4
(1944), pp. 38–45.

[11] *Vital Statistics—Special Reports*, Vol. 9, No. 10
(1940), p. 53.

[12] Cf. P. K. Whelpton, "The Completeness of Birth
Registration in the United States," *Journal of the
American Statistical Association*, XXIX (1934), 15–17.

[13] T. Lynn Smith, "Rural-Urban Differences in the
Completeness of Birth Registration," *Social Forces*,
XIV (March 1936), 368–372.

against the mortality. Based on such data the
Bureau of the Census introduced for the first time
into its 1940 reports calculations of the net reproduction rate, a refined measure of natural increase.
At this time they also calculated and presented
comparable indexes for the year 1930. The results
are very interesting. In 1930 the net reproduction
of the whites and the nonwhites (largely Negro—
further subdivisions are not available) was approximately equal. That for the whites was 111 and
that for the nonwhites 110. In other words with
mortality and reproduction at their 1930 levels
and ignoring the effects of migration, in the course
of a generation the white population would increase
by 11 percent, the nonwhite by 10 percent. Actually the rate of increase of the two exactly kept pace
with one another between 1930 and 1940; the proportion of nonwhites in the population was 10.2
percent in 1930 and it was the same in 1940.
(Most of this total, 9.7 in 1930, is Negro.) But in
the meantime the net reproduction rates rapidly
drew apart. That for the nonwhites fell, but only
to 107, a level considerably above that necessary
to meet replacement needs. But that for the white
population fell to only 94, a level six percent below
that necessary to produce enough children to
replace the persons who die.

In view of the rapidity with which the proportion
of Negroes resident in urban areas is approaching
that of the whites, it is interesting to consider the
net reproduction rates of the whites and nonwhites
with the data further divided according to residence. Significantly enough for 1940 the net reproduction rate of urban Negroes (nonwhites) is 74,
the same as that of whites. Such a rate is of
course far below that needed to keep up the population. In rural areas, on the other hand, the rate
was 140 for whites and 160 for nonwhites.[14] Rural
Negroes continue to be concentrated in the most
rural parts of the Nation. I believe that this is the
fundamental element in the differentials. Every
refinement introduced into the study of the net
reproduction rate in the United States tends to
emphasize the importance of the rural-urban differential in fertility and to minimize the racial and
regional differences in reproduction rates.

INTERNAL MIGRATION

As previously indicated, immigration and emigration have played minor rôles in the demographic

[14] These data are from a release by the Bureau of the
Census, *Series P. 5*, No. 13 (August 23, 1941).

processes of the American Negro. But the same cannot be said about internal migration. Some of the more important of the Nation's migratory currents past and present are the flight of the Negro from the land, the flood tide of movement from the South to the North, and the annual movement of hundreds of thousands of rural Negroes from one farm or plantation to another. The data relative to these important constituents of internal migration will be summarized under the headings: (1) rural-urban migration; (2) State-to-State migration; and (3) farm-to-farm movements.[15] Although these three do not exhaust all the aspects of the internal migration of Negroes, they do include the residential shifts that have been of major importance.

Rural-Urban Migration. Already indicated are the facts that city people, both white and Negro, fail to produce enough offspring to maintain the population, and that the deficit is approximately equal in the two races. Therefore, to show that the Negro population is urbanizing at a more rapid rate than the white population is to give evidence that the migration of Negroes from farms to cities is more rapid than that of whites. This proposition, in turn, is easily established. In 1910 only about one out of four (27.3 percent) Negroes lived in urban centers, while nearly one-half (48.2 percent) of the white population resided in towns and cities of 2,500 or more inhabitants. By 1940 nearly one-half (48.7 percent) of the Negro population of the United States were urban residents, while the percentage of urbanites among the white population had increased to only 57.8. In other words this is evidence that the urbanization of the Negro population is fast approaching that of the white. A more rapid flow of Negroes from the farms to the cities is the factor responsible for the change.

State-to-State Migration. Judged on the basis of residence in a State or census division different from the State or census division of birth, native Negroes are more migratory than native whites. In 1930, 82.8 percent of the native Negroes were living in the census division in which they were born; among native whites the corresponding percentage is 84.3. Also according to the data for 1930, 25.3 percent of the native Negroes were living in a State other than the one in which they had

been born, while for the native whites the corresponding percentage is 23.4. Furthermore, in only nine of the forty-eight States was the proportion of native Negroes who were residing in the State of birth below the corresponding percentage among native whites. The nine exceptions are all States in the South that have been exporting large numbers of Negroes to other areas, namely Virginia, South Carolina, Georgia, Florida, Alabama, Mississippi, Louisiana, Texas, and Oklahoma. To a considerable extent the migrations that involve the crossing of State lines are also a cityward movement, but in either case the data mean that the Negro of the present is living amid social and cultural surroundings to which he is stranger to a greater extent than his native white contemporary. Prior to the last two decades this was not true.

Farm-to-Farm Migration. Literally hundreds of thousands of American farm families shift from one farm or plantation to another in the course of a year, mainly in the interval between harvest and the preparation of the soil for the new crop. Some of this movement forms a necessary element in the climbing of the agricultural ladder and thus is highly beneficial. But a very large share of the movements is confined to areas where large-scale agricultural operations are indicative of the fact that the agricultural ladder is not operating, and where it is extremely doubtful if the majority of the moves are beneficial to anyone concerned. This aimless and socially and economically pernicious milling around of the farm population is most acute in the South. In the popular mind it is also associated with the Negro race; and not infrequently the Negro is endowed with some kind of "migratory instinct" in order to account for the frequency with which sharecroppers shift from one plantation to another.

Interestingly enough the facts do not bear out the popular supposition that Negro agriculturists move about more than whites. Consider some of the data. In order to make valid comparisons it is best to limit the analysis to the southern States, in which category the census includes three divisions (South Atlantic, East South Central, and West South Central). This group includes along with the 13 States more usually included in the South the States of Delaware, Maryland, and West Virginia. In 1940 in the southern States taken collectively, 22 percent of the white owner operators and only 18 percent of the Negro owner operators had been less than five years on the farms

---

[15] These are not, of course, mutually exclusive categories.

which they were occupying.[16] Similar differentials prevailed in each of the three divisions. On the other hand only 41 percent of the southern white owner operators had been on their farms for 15 years or more, while the comparable percentage for Negroes is 46. These data indicate definitely that those Negro farmers who have attained the status of owner operator are considerably less migratory than their fellows of the white race.

Similar are the racial differentials among tenants other than "share croppers." In the entire South 62 percent of the whites and only 49 percent of the Negroes had been less than five years on the farms they were occupying in 1940. On the other hand, only 7 percent of the white and 14 percent of the Negro tenants had been on their farms for 15 years or more.

But it is the Negro sharecropper who is generally

[16] These data and those to follow were compiled from the *U. S. Census of Agriculture: 1940*, Vol. III (Washington: Government Printing Office, 1942).

thought to be excessively mobile. That he moves about a great deal is indisputable: 64 percent of all southern Negro share croppers in 1940 had been less than five years in the locations they were then occupying. However, the corresponding percentage for members of the white race was much higher, 72 percent. In this case also the differential prevailed in all three of the census divisions. Furthermore, in the southern States 5 percent of the Negro sharecroppers had been on the places they were occupying for 15 years or more, while such a degree of stability was exhibited by only 3 percent of the white sharecroppers. Again, this very marked differential was of approximately the same magnitude in each of the divisions. Thus the evidence reveals that even those Negroes who fall into that great category of farm laborers called share croppers are actually a great deal less migratory than whites of similar status.

The conclusion to be drawn from these comparisons is that farm Negroes are definitely less migratory than whites of comparable tenure classes.

ORGANIZATION FOR REGIONAL PLANNING

C. HERMAN PRITCHETT

CHARLES E. Merriam has defined planning as the process of "looking backward at what we can learn from experience, looking around at what we can learn from observation, and looking forward to see where we are going."[1] At the present time no one disputes that government must participate in this process. When Congress abolished the National Resources Planning Board, it did not intend that there should be an end of federal planning. Indeed, it promptly set up planning committees of its own. While there are lively disputes as to how far planning processes should be extended, that area of contention is irrelevant to the present discussion, once the need for at least some governmental planning is admitted.

In this process of looking backward, forward, and around, it is clear that federal, State, and local units must participate, according to their capacities, their opportunities, and prevailing notions as

[1] "The Possibilities of Planning" *American Journal of Sociology*, 49 (March 1944), p. 399.

to division of functions among levels of government. But there is another level at which planning should also proceed, one which has up to the present been largely unrecognized so far as the establishment of governmental institutions is concerned—the regional level. There is no need, for present purposes, to define with attempted precision the fields in which the region appears to be the most desirable planning area, or the size and nature of the regions that should be recognized for various planning purposes. It is enough to agree that there are subjects which are not large enough necessarily to demand national treatment, yet too extensive for effective State action. For purposes of suggestion only, and not delimitation, it may be assumed that the regional rôle may most appropriately include major segments of the planning responsibilities for wise use of physical resources— water, land, forests, and minerals.

Regional planning, however, must meet a problem that does not exist at the other levels, namely, the absence of governmental implementation of a regional character. For national, for State, for local planning we have existing establishments on which planning responsibilities can be placed, and which must plan if their normal activities are to be carried on successfully. But planning in regional terms must be more inventive. It must either evolve new regional units, or turn the attention of existing federal units into regional channels, or build up States and State units into agencies with regional consciousness. All of these things can happen, and to a limited extent have happened during the past decade or two. But they require some experimentation, some taking of thought. For that reason it may be of value to review and analyze the experience that has accumulated with respect to organizational development for regional planning.

II

Four major types of regional planning organization have been utilized. First of all, regional planning functions can be performed, and are being performed, by the ordinary federal departments, bureaus, boards, and commissions. Many of the regular federal agencies, and practically all of those having to do with resource development, are engaged in regional planning in the sense that they are working out special programs for, or adapting regular procedures to, the needs of the various sections of the country. Some agencies are of course more aware of the regional concept and of regional differences than others. The Bureau of Reclamation, with jurisdiction over the entire western section of the country, carries out its program of conservation of water resources in terms of plans developed for the various waterway systems. The Soil Conservation Service plans its demonstrations of practical soil-conserving measures for selected watersheds. The National Resources Planning Board issued a notable series of regional planning reports for the principal regions of the Nation.

The use of regular federal agencies, which customarily operate in a restricted subject-matter field, but with Nation-wide jurisdiction, for regional planning purposes has certain advantages. They have expert staffs which can bring all there is to be known on a particular subject to the formulation of plans for the different regions. They can employ or develop specialists in a way that would not be possible for agencies of smaller size or more diverse responsibilities. What is learned on one project is carried over by the agency to all of its

subsequent projects. A basic uniformity in policy or design or administration tends to result. Thus the Bureau of Reclamation is able to accumulate experience in water control and irrigation projects on all the western watersheds, to develop by wide practice the best forms of water and power contracts, to acquire comparative knowledge of various types of dry land farming, and so on.

But there are also disadvantages. The central department or bureau is usually isolated in Washington, a long way from the region concerned. It may try, more or less successfully, to overcome this handicap by regional offices, such as those the NRPB set up, or by extensive field contacts. But there is also the fact of the agency's specialization in a single field, which often leads it to overemphasize that particular angle, and to develop a sense of possession and proprietorship of the field. It may consequently ignore the contributions that other agencies are in a position to make and resent suggestions for a cooperative approach. One may hope that this type of reaction is gradually yielding to an improved spirit and a greater sense of professionalism in the public service, but it still occurs all too frequently.

Discussion of the regular federal agency as used for regional planning purposes must also take into account the extent to which planning and action responsibilities are combined in the same organization. Where the agency has no operating functions, problems of the sort just suggested are less serious. The National Resources Planning Board furnished a good example of such a situation. Since it had no direct responsibilities for effectuating the plans it prepared, it had no vested interests which its plans had to protect or which would hamper it in making recommendations for allocation of the projects planned. Moreover, the Board had no problem of working out operating relationships with the States and local government units in the various regions for which it planned. The Bureau of Agricultural Economics is another case of a federal agency whose planning responsibilities do not extend into the action field. When this Bureau was reorganized in 1938, it was purposely stripped of its operating functions so that it could be free to concentrate attention upon its planning duties for the Department of Agriculture.[2]

Where the federal agency has both planning and

[2] John M. Gaus and Leon O. Wolcott, *Public Administration and the United States Department of Agriculture* (Chicago: Public Administration Service, 1940), pp. 311–312.

action responsibilities, as is usually the case, the situation is more complicated. Under those conditions the tendencies toward centralized control and over-specialization inherent in a federal limited-purpose bureau require special attention if they are not to undermine any successful regional approach. The bureau may maintain officers in the region who appreciate its special problems and who seek to adapt the general national policies of the bureau to its needs, but they are responsible to a bureau chief in Washington, and he takes orders from his department head, so that final decisions may be made on the basis of paper knowledge and by officials motivated principally by a desire to maintain nationally uniform procedures. How this system of departmental responsibility works out in the case of the Interior Department's control over the Grand Coulee irrigation project has been described as follows:

Sole responsibility rests in the Secretary himself. In theory he stakes every acre, picks every settler, signs every contract, constructs barns, fences, houses, collects interest or rent ... But alas, Mr. Ickes has a million other duties. The actual work will inevitably be done by officials many times removed, whose sole personal responsibility will be to carry out regulations devised on E Street.[3]

A centralized federal bureau is also going to have to fight inherited routines and patterns of thought if it makes significant use of other federal agencies and local governmental institutions in the various regional programs which it administers. If there is absence of cooperation between a federal agency and local units in its regional program, it may not, of course, be the federal agency that is at fault. It may be local somnolence or incompetence or political dislike of the national agency. But whatever the reason, the gap between a centralized federal bureau and local government institutions is too often unbridged, and where that is the case it can scarcely be said that the federal program is operating on a truly regional basis.

III

A second device for performing regional planning functions is one which brings together, on a more or less formal and regularized basis, a number of federal agencies concerned with a particular region or regional problem. This method is admirably adapted to correcting the over-specialization and

possessiveness just noted as likely to characterize regional planning by separate federal agencies. Perhaps the best example of this technique is found in the Columbia Basin Joint Investigations, organized by the Bureau of Reclamation to provide a plan and program for the settlement and development of the Columbia Basin irrigation project.

Realizing the dangers involved in unsound exploitation and unwise development of the lands to be opened up by the project, and appreciating the complexity and magnitude of the investigations needed to answer the questions that had to be answered, the Bureau of Reclamation sought the assistance of many agencies and organizations—public and private, federal, State, and local—on matters falling within the domains of their special interest and competence. The Bureau posed 28 specific questions on which it wished information. The first problem, for example, was formulated as follows:

On other northwestern irrigation projects where basic conditions are similar to those which will be encountered on the earlier units of the Columbia Basin project, what types of farm economy (including crops and crop programs) have been successful? Most successful? Unsuccessful, if any?

To each problem investigators were assigned who were experts on the particular subject. Often advisers were designated to work with them.

To hold together the work of the many persons engaged in the Joint Investigations, the Bureau of Reclamation relied chiefly upon a field coordinator, with headquarters in the region. His principal duty was to facilitate in all practicable ways close cooperation among the members of particular investigation groups and among the leaders of different groups concerned with interdependent problems. He was available at group and intergroup conferences. He circulated information and memoranda of general interest and utility to participants in the investigations. He helped to furnish information to the public of the region, through the information officer of the project, on the nature and progress of the investigations.[4]

In addition, the Department of Agriculture, which was the other federal agency most concerned with the problem, designated a member of its staff to act as field representative of that Department for the Joint Investigations, with the general re-

[3] Catherine Bauer, "Columbia Basin: Test for Planning," *New Republic*, 107 (1942), p. 280.

[4] See U. S. Department of the Interior, Bureau of Reclamation, *Columbia Basin Joint Investigations: Character and Scope* (Washington, 1941).

sponsibility of coordinating the phases of the work assigned to the bureaus of that Department. Finally, it was contemplated that in the later stages of the investigations a board of review would be appointed by the Bureau of Reclamation to appraise plans of settlement and development based on the reports, and to recommend appropriate action programs for carrying out accepted proposals. Probably there has never been another federal interdepartmental planning project worked out with greater care or appreciation of the problems involved. Catherine Bauer has commented that "as a concrete effort in coordinated regional planning it is a long step beyond even the TVA."[5]

The value of such a cooperative planning program is obvious, and it demonstrates how far some government agencies are willing to go in making regional planning a joint venture. The limitations must not be overlooked, however. A group of experts called together from various agencies and fields can turn up data and supply answers to questions, but their role is essentially supplementary to that of a permanent organization which knows what questions the experts should be asked, and which has continuous responsibility for the full development and integration of plans, and for their modification in the light of actual experience. Periodic commissions of expert inquirers cannot take the place of, though they can greatly assist, a permanent planning staff.

Moreover, an organization set up on such a co-operative and temporary basis is obviously not adapted to the performance of operating functions. In this particular case, the Bureau of Reclamation retained full responsibility for carrying out the action programs which were to result from the joint investigation. However, it would be possible to create a permanent operating organization representing two or more federal agencies, if such a step was considered desirable. When the Federal

Government first undertook a measure of responsibility for flood control on the Mississippi River, a device somewhat along those lines was employed. The Mississippi River Commission was created in 1879, composed of three members appointed by the President from the Corps of Engineers, one from the Coast and Geodetic Survey, and three additional members from private life, two of whom were required to be civil engineers. The staff of the Commission was to be secured by detail of officers and employees from the Corps of Engineers and the Coast and Geodetic Survey. This form of organization has persisted, in spite of considerable dissatisfaction with the Commission. It has been able to cooperate fairly effectively with the States and local levee districts. Its plans and surveys are submitted to Congress through the Secretary of War, and actually the Commission is usually effectively controlled by the Corps of Engineers. The Commission does not undertake directly construction operations; the Secretary of War details any required number of engineers to supervise the work of private contractors on Commission projects.[6] There is little in the Mississippi Valley Commission plan of organization to recommend it for consideration.

IV

The third possible type of regional planning organization is a federal regional agency, autonomous and completely outside the regular departmental system. The Tennessee Valley Authority is so far the only example of this type. The special regional characteristics of the TVA are so well understood as to need no detailed description here.[7] Regular federal agencies characteristically function in a fairly limited subject matter field, but with jurisdiction over the entire country, or at least a major portion of it. The TVA reverses this situation, having a wide planning responsibility for a limited geographical area. One should not, of course, picture the Authority's planning powers as broader than they are. The TVA has no re-

---

[5] *Op. cit.* The National Resources Planning Board has employed much the same technique in certain of its regional planning projects. To report on the Pecos River valley, for example, the Board set up the Pecos River Joint Investigation, involving study by the Weather Bureau of climatic characteristics and data of the region, by the Geological Survey of water resources, by four bureaus in the Department of Agriculture of water utilization, by the Park Service, the Fish and Wildlife Service, and the Forest Service of recreational and wildlife values, and by the Corps of Engineers of flood control. See *The Pecos River Joint Investigation* (Washington: Government Printing Office, 1942).

[6] Arthur D. Frank, *The Development of the Federal Program of Flood Control on the Mississippi River* (New York: Columbia University Press, 1930).

[7] See David E. Lilienthal, *TVA: Democracy on the March* (New York: Harper, 1944); Herman Finer, *The T.V.A.: Lessons for International Application* (Montreal: International Labour Office, 1944); C. H. Pritchett, *The Tennessee Valley Authority: A Study in Public Administration* (Chapel Hill: University of North Carolina Press, 1943).

sponsibility for planning public works in the region, except for its own program. It has no part in the field of housing, except for its own projects. Its role in industrial and transportation planning is quite limited. But in spite of such gaps and restrictions, its statutory powers (derived through presidential delegation) to make "surveys of and general plans for" the Tennessee basin area which will be useful to Congress and the states "in guiding and controlling the extent, sequence, and nature of development that may be equitably and economically advanced through the expenditure of public funds . . . for the general purpose of fostering an orderly and proper physical, economic, and social development of said areas" give it a remarkably wide area for the performance of planning functions.

The great advantages of the TVA type of regional agency lie in its closeness to the area for which it is planning and the breadth of its jurisdiction within the area. Instead of land and water and forests and minerals and transportation being split up among separate agencies, each jealous of its own domain, the TVA can include and interrelate all these elements in its planning approach. Thus the TVA avoids and ignores the lines which regular federal departments must draw. Nor is it concerned with State boundaries or other jurisdictional lines except where nature has drawn them.

The regional agency plan of organization does of course create some difficult problems. One has to do with the relationship between the regional body and the planning work of the regular federal agencies which continue to operate in the regional area. The Department of Agriculture and the Army Engineers and the Forest Service and the Geological Survey were not excluded from the Tennessee Valley when the TVA was created. They continued to function in that region with their regular Nation-wide programs. The TVA, coming into existence with multiple-purpose planning responsibilities which included agriculture and dam building and forestry and mapping, might easily have run afoul of these single-purpose agencies. Actually this did not happen, or at least it happened very seldom, for the TVA dedicated itself to a settled policy of cooperation with other federal agencies. It entered into agreements, contracts, and memoranda of understanding with them. In some cases it turned over its property or facilities to them. It supplemented their programs by supplying additional personnel; some-

times it subsidized them by adding its own funds to their appropriations.

The TVA showed equal wisdom and skill in integrating the agencies of State and local government into its development program.[8] Because it was an inhabitant of the Valley, it appreciated in a way that a Washington bureau could hardly have realized, the necessity of proceeding so far as possible through the governmental institutions closest to the people. So it has consistently sought to narrow the area in which it would operate directly, and to encourage and stimulate the role of State and local agencies in regional development. The result has been that this incursion of a federal agency into the Tennessee Valley has had the effect of strengthening, not weakening, the region's own governmental institutions and resources. Thus experience demonstrates that the most serious problems posed by the regional agency type of organization can, with goodwill and care, be solved, and even turned into positive advantages.

The planning activities of the TVA have been deeply affected by reason of the fact that it was also engaged in a tremendous action program. In fact, officials of the TVA would deny that there is any real possibility of drawing a line between their planning and their action responsibilities. As Chairman Lilienthal has recently written:

The TVA idea of planning sees action and planning not as things separate and apart, but as one single and continuous process . . . If TVA had been a "planning agency" in the sense that its responsibility had been limited to the making of plans—the usual meaning of the term—those plans would probably have met the fate of so many other plans: brochures decorating bookshelves, adornments of the bibliography of a sterile learning.[9]

While the results of combining planning and action in the TVA program are certainly a strong justification for such a merger, it need not be assumed that consideration of federal regional agencies limited to planning functions is precluded. Several suggestions for the establishment of agencies of this kind have been made, most notably in President Roosevelt's 1937 proposal for the creation of a number of so-called "conservation

---

[8] See Lawrence L. Durisch, "Local Government and the T.V.A. Program," *Public Administration Review*, 1 (1941), pp. 326–334.

[9] *Op. cit.*, pp. 199–200.

authorities."[10] These organizations were referred to at the time as "little TVAs," but the program outlined by the President would have given them almost none of the action responsibilities of the TVA. He indicated that the work of these regional bodies would consist chiefly in developing integrated plans to conserve and safeguard the prudent use of waters, water power, soils, forests, and other resources of the areas. Projected programs would be reported by the regional bodies annually to Congress through the President after he had had the projects checked and revised in the light of national budgetary considerations and of national planning policies. Projects authorized to be undertaken by Congress could then be carried out by those departments of the government best equipped for the purpose. Only in unusual cases did the plan contemplate that the regional authorities themselves would undertake the development projects. The proposal was not adopted by Congress.

V

The fourth possibility is that of building a regional planning organization on the basis of the States in a given regional area. A successful example of this form has been the Pacific Northwest Regional Planning Commission, including the States of Washington, Oregon, Idaho, and Montana. So long as the National Resources Planning Board was in existence, that agency was in a position to aid and activate such regional organizations, so that they were in effect joint federal-state agencies. On this basis they were able to do some important work. Without the assistance of an agency like the NRPB, however, multi-state planning organizations face a difficult future. The need for the work they can do remains as great as ever, but they will suffer from the absence of a single point of contact with the Federal Government and a center of federal interest in their activities. There is also the possibility that they will be easier prey to the pressures of strong local interest groups who have a stake in the kind of planning recommendations made.

A form of interstate planning tied somewhat less to federal support is that represented by the Interstate Commission on the Delaware River Basin, popularly known as Incodel. This Commission was set up with four members—a senator, a representative, an administrative official, and a member of the planning board—from each of the four States in the basin. The Commission was in effect a joint governmental agency of those States, financed by their appropriations, and concerned with the problem of conservation, development, and control of the natural resources of the basin.[11]

Neither in the case of Incodel nor the Pacific Northwest Commission were any operating responsibilities given the regional organizations. Effectuation of the plans prepared remained for the individual States or interested federal agencies. It would be possible, of course, for a group of States to join in regional administration of their plans, but they would have to create for this purpose a regional agency with the requisite legal and corporate powers. The device of the interstate compact is readily available to the States for this purpose, but they have shown no eagerness to use it for the creation of regional operating agencies.[12] The Port of New York Authority, now over twenty years old, continues to be the only important example of an interstate development organization.

VI

In reviewing these various forms of regional planning organization, perhaps the most puzzling aspect is why the federal regional type of agency, having proved so successful in the case of the TVA, should not have been employed in any other instance. The absence of imitators has not been because of lack of interest or suggestions. The number of bills which have been introduced in Congress since 1933 providing for the establishment of regional authorities on various watersheds probably runs over a hundred. While many of these proposals did not suggest a complete duplication of the TVA, they were all affected in some degree by its example.

One explanation for the failure of such efforts has been the opposition of regular federal departments and agencies, which, however well rationalized, has been founded on jealous fear of loss of some of their functions to the new agencies. This conflict was seen very clearly in the Columbia River prob-

[10] See "Creation of Conservation Authorities," Hearings before the Senate Committee on Agriculture and Forestry on S. 2555, 75th Cong., 1st sess. (1937).

[11] David W. Robinson, "Voluntary Regionalism in the Control of Water Resources," *The Annals*, 207 (1940), pp. 116–123.

[12] See C. H. Pritchett, "Regional Authorities through Interstate Compacts," *Social Forces*, 14 (1935), pp. 200–210.

lem. Grand Coulee was a Bureau of Reclamation project, and Bonneville was constructed by the Corps of Engineers. Neither proposed to lose control to a regional development agency, such as was proposed for the area. Disposition of the power generated at the two dams clearly required administration by a single agency, but the Department of the Interior was able to forestall the establishment of an independent regional agency for this purpose by securing instead the creation of a new bureau, the Bonneville Power Administration, in the Department of the Interior.[13] While the Department of Agriculture has had less occasion to take part in such controversies, its single-purpose units, such as the Forest Service and the Soil Conservation Service, would also oppose loss of some of their functions to regional development organizations.

The case against regional authorities, however, is not founded solely on departmental jealousies. Many persons who have no identifications of this sort still feel doubts about the wisdom of dismantling existing departmental programs for distribution among decentralized regional authorities. The Pacific Northwest Regional Planning Commission, for instance, reported in 1936 its belief that a federal regional authority should be set up for that area, but with important restrictions. The Commission did not see why the regional agency could handle soil erosion control better than the Soil Conservation Service was doing it. They came to similar conclusions concerning the work of the Forest Service, the Bureau of Reclamation, the Resettlement Administration, and the Rural Electrification Administration in the area. So they ended up by recommending that the proposed authority have only power functions. As already noted, President Roosevelt's notion in 1937 was that the plans made by the conservation authorities he recommended would be turned over to the regular departments for administration. One of the bills in Congress proposing an Arkansas Valley Authority would have made the organization a regional unit in the Department of the Interior, while another one made it clear that any agricultural program worked out by the proposed authority would be administered by the Department of Agriculture. Other instances of the same type of reaction could be given.

On the other hand, Lilienthal's recent book offers a strong defense for regional decentralization of the TVA type. The chairman of the TVA feels that the formula required by present conditions is decentralized administration of centralized authority, and that a practical way to secure this goal is by creation of additional regional agencies embodying the essential characteristics of the TVA.[14] As to the pattern of relationships and division of responsibilities that would exist between a nation-wide set of regional authorities and the regular federal departments, he assumes that the good relations built up between the TVA and the Washington agencies can be duplicated in other regions. He also feels that there will be no difficulty in coordinating the various regional agencies, preventing them from competing with each other by offering lower power rates, for example. His view is that Congress will lay down the broad policies they must follow, and that the opportunity which each authority will have to adopt diverse operating methods within the limits of those policies is one of the great advantages of decentralization.

These arguments may be more accurately appraised in the context of an immediate situation such as is furnished by the current interest in establishing a Missouri Valley Authority.[15] Unfortunately this valley furnishes an almost classic example of how federal departmental jealousies and local vested interests can prevent any unified consideration of the problems of water control and utilization. The up-river States are interested in irrigation, and the Department of the Interior is their instrument; the down-river States want navigation and flood control, and support the Army Engineers. Clearly nothing short of an autonomous valley-wide authority can resolve these conflicts in the general interest and determine upon a unified plan of multiple-purpose development such as the TVA has put into effect.

[14] Lilienthal states the three essentials of the TVA idea as "a federal autonomous agency, with authority to make its decisions in the region; responsibility to deal with resources, as a unified whole, clearly fixed in the regional agency, not divided among several centralized federal agencies; a policy, fixed by law, that the federal regional agency work co-operatively with and through local and state agencies." *Op. cit.*, p. 153.

[15] Ralph and Jean L. Coghlan, "For A Missouri Valley Authority," *New Republic* (September 4, 1944), pp. 266–268. See S. 2089, 78th Cong., 2d sess., introduced by Senator Murray.

[13] C. H. Pritchett, "Administration of Federal Power Projects," *Journal of Land and Public Utility Economics*, 18 (1942), pp. 379–390.

Even in a spectacular case of this sort, however, it will be difficult to secure a combination of interests and forces strong enough to break the hold of established mechanisms and habits. It is certain that most regional planning is going to continue to be performed by governmental agencies of the traditional type. Under those circumstances hope for progress lies in a vigorous promotion of the regional concept and a continuing attack on departmental centralization and compartmentalization.

REGIONALLY PLANNING THE FAR EAST

ELIZABETH GREEN AND CRAIGHILL HANDY

INTRODUCTION

POLITICALLY and commercially China has been for the U. S. A., internationally speaking, a distinct "region" from the days of our earliest continuous intercourse.[1] This commenced with American penetration of Far Eastern waters in pursuit of trade in tea and other Oriental goods in our infant Nation's earliest days before 1800, and continued with the sandalwood trade to China out of Hawaii and other Pacific islands coincident with our whaling era in the Pacific in the early nineteenth century. It was strengthened during the succeeding era of our "China Clippers," sailing in competition with the "East Indiamen" from London, in that most picturesque of all maritime eras from 1830 to 1870.

The direct outgrowths of the earlier phase of trade with China were, first, the pioneering missionary enterprise of Samuel Wells Williams and his confreres in South China from 1833 onward, next the official trade and treaty missions from 1844 onward, and finally our formal recognition of the Chinese Imperial government when Anson Burlingame (under Secretary of State Seward) was sent by President Lincoln to serve as first Minister at the Court of Peking, in 1861.

Our dealings were always specifically with China, not with "the Far East" or "the Indies." Independent, and each of a different order, were Commodore Perry's and Townsend Harris' negoti-

[1] For England the traditional relationship has been quite different, as China, Southeast Asia, and the East Indies were originally and for over 200 years regarded as parts of the commercial field in which the charter of the East India Company granted monopoly rights. In other words, China was and has remained for the British Empire not primarily a "country" but an area that is part of the Far Eastern sphere of commercial enterprise.

ations with Japan, and Admiral Dewey's *coup* in the Philippines. Activity within the rest of Asia and the East Indies we were content to leave to the Portuguese, Dutch, British, and French. To Americans, the Far East has always meant primarily and particularly China.

Likewise, for Americans, from the earliest settlement of Virginia and New England, the "New World" was of course a distinct region. The inability of the reactionary elements in England to realize this was a fundamental cause of our Revolution and Declaration of Independence. By 1823 the new Nation was in a position to give weight to its views, and our concept of the entire western hemisphere as a great regional entity or "sphere" in international politics was crystallized in President Monroe's Declaration.

Thus, it was during the first half of the nineteenth century that the United States and China emerged in each other's view as nations and as neighboring regional political spheres. From Anson Burlingame's time there has existed uninterrupted between them the tradition and sentiment of mutual interest, understanding, and interdependence. Generally it is assumed that this understanding is entirely the consequence of the historical, economic, and political factors operative within the last century and a half. We believe that it rests upon affinities implicit in China and America by reason of the effect and control of specific, basic environmental factors common to both these neighboring areas. What we hope here to demonstrate is (1) that this mutual understanding and interdependence results from fundamental geographic, ethnic, and cultural parallelisms between the East Atlantic and North American regions, and (2) that these similarities and the resultant interdependence, if recognized for what they are, should lead to cooperation and planning on a basis of common principles that, for the future, must extend beyond the exigencies of profitable and stable commercial and political relations. These premises, if valid, make incumbent on us as a nation in these times a peculiar and particular responsibility as collaborator with and adviser to the Chinese nation in its East Asiatic sphere and role.

I. AREAS AND REGIONS OF EAST AND SOUTHEAST ASIA AND NORTH AND MIDDLE AMERICA

Sociologists and others who are concerned with the development of scientific regional planning as projected in the school of thought led by Professor Howard W. Odum and his colleagues will find it interesting to compare the rough general tabulation of geographic regions in China which is indicated in Table 1 with the careful delineation of regions in terms of economic factors presented by Cheng Ch'eng-k'un in his important article entitled "Regionalism in China's Postwar Reconstruction," published in *Social Forces*, vol. 22, no. 1, October 1943, pp. 1–20. We purposely have not based our geographic regions on those delineated by Dr. Cheng because by doing so we would have involved in the discussion of general geographic equivalences, which is the subject of this paper, a great deal of detail about and comparison of economic resources, similarities, and differences which are immaterial to the thesis we seek to expound. For example, the existence in China and the U. S. A. alike of a great midland river system wherein intensive agriculture, compact population, and communication by inland water transport have become highly developed is a highly significant factor in the past social evolution and the destiny of the two peoples; whereas points as to whether the agriculture practiced, the types of transport used, and nature of rural and urban culture, etc. resemble each other, are secondary. Such points may be raised *ad infinitum* if one attempts to enter into a minute examination of Dr. Cheng's economic regions of China in comparison with economic regions of America. That study and comparison will be most fruitful. It is, however, not the subject of this paper, beyond the general geographic considerations indicated in the notes following Table 2. We prefer to leave such a comparison to scholars and scientists better qualified than ourselves to discuss scientific socio-economic regionalism.

Nevertheless it is significant to note, without here entering into detailed comparison, that our geographic regions not only do not conflict with, but, taking an overall view, accord with Dr. Cheng's economic regions, except that a single geographic region in our table may include several of his economic regions. His twelve economic regions are: 1. Kiangsu-Chekiang, 2. Hopei-Shantung-Honan, 3. Kwangtung-Fukien, 4. Liaoning - Kirin - Heilungkiang - Jehol, 5. Shansi-Chahar-Suiyuan, 6. Yunnan-Kweichow-Kwangsi, 7. Shensi-Kansu-Ninghsia-Chinghai, 8. Sinkiang, 9. Hupeh-Hunan-Kwangsi-Anhwei, 10. Szechuan-Sikang, 11. Mongolia, 12. Tibet.

Climate[2]

The temperature range in China and the United States is approximately the same, with South China slightly warmer in summer and northwestern U. S. A. somewhat colder in winter. This may be seen by following isotherms through the two countries on any temperature map (Bartholemew, Pl. 2). An annual minimum of 50°F. in Hainan Island (off the southernmost coast of China) and Formosa, finds its counterpart in southern California, Mexico, and southern Florida. The Yangtze Valley and Chekiang (the province directly below Shanghai), with a minimum of 32°F. corresponds roughly with upper southern California, Texas, and northern Florida, while Shantung and Korea with temperature ranging to −10°F. in winter correspond to the Middle West and mid-Atlantic States. Manchuria can be as cold as northern New York or New England. In the summer, with maximum temperature of 95°F. along the southeastern coast of China and up to Korea, we have the equivalent of our West and

[2] Goode's *School Atlas*, (Rand McNally, 1925) by J. Paul Goode; Bartholemew's *Physical Atlas*, vol. III Meteorology (Edinburg, 1899); Bos-Niermeyer's *Schoolatlas der Geheele Aarde* (The Hague, 1929).

Equivalent Regions. Study of the larger regions which make up Greater China and the U. S. A. respectively, reveals the existence of significant equivalences. The regional equivalents are 1) east and southeast coastal areas; 2) old (geologically) eroded mountain chains flanking these areas; 3) midland dominant great-river zones; 4) great plains; 5) recent (geologically) major mountain systems westward; 6) plateaux, and 7) great basin areas that are parts of these systems. In Table I an attempt is made to define similarities, a) *geographic*, b) *climatic*, c) *historic*, and d) *functional* in some detail in Columns I and II. Significant divergences are noted in a footnote to the table.

TABLE 1

EQUIVALENT REGIONS

	I THE UNITED STATES	II GREATER CHINA
1. *East to South-east* COASTAL	a. *Geographic.* Rivers, harbors, bays; Gulf Stream offshore. b. *Climatic.* Alternating oceanic-tropical (warm, wet) and temperate-continental (cool, dry) controls. c. *Historic.* Foreign contacts, cosmopolitanism, race mixture. d. *Functional.* Fishing, coastal and overseas trade, ship-building, and industries associated with shipping and ports.	a. Rivers, bays, harbors; Japan Current offshore. b. Oceanic-tropical "monsoon" (warm, wet) alternating with continental (cool, dry). c. Foreign contacts, cosmopolitanism race mixture. d. Fishing, coastal and overseas trade, ship-building, and industries associated with shipping and ports.
2. *East to South-east* RANGES	a. Old eroded ranges of low altitude, valleys, piedmont and upland habitable areas. b. Oceanic and continental controls alternating. c. Small communities settled by infiltration. d. Farming, grazing, local commerce and industry *regional.*	a. Old eroded ranges of low altitude, valleys, piedmont and upland habitable areas. b. Oceanic and continental controls alternating. c. Small communities settled by infiltration. d. Farming, grazing, local commerce and crafts *regional.*
3. *Midland* RIVER BASIN	a. Mississippi River system, flood-plain and delta. b. Continental controls predominate northward. c. Settled in second great phase of national expansion. d. Intensive agriculture, inland waterways, large trading cities, *inter-regional* commerce, compact distribution of population.	a. Yangtze River system, flood-plain and delta. b. Continental controls predominate northward. c. Settled in second great phase of national expansion. d. Intensive agriculture, inland waterways, large trading cities, *inter-regional* commerce, compact distribution of population.
4. PLAINS	a. "The Great Plains," central north and northwest areas. b. Continental, hot in summer, cold in winter. c. See footnote 4-c below. d. Grazing, grain, overland commerce, sparser settlement.	a. The plains of China, central, north and northwest. b. Continental, hot in summer, cold in winter. c. See footnote 4-c below. d. Grazing, grain, overland commerce, sparser settlement.
5. *Great Western* MOUNTAIN AREA	a. Geologically recent western mountain systems with great altitudes, deep gorges, rugged environment, lowlands habitable. b. Montane climate. c. Recent settlement. Aborigines survive. d. Agriculture, grazing, trade, cultural isolation, mineral resources, rugged spirit and physique.	a. Geologically recent western mountain systems with great altitudes, deep gorges, rugged environment, lowlands habitable. b. Montane climate. c. Late settlement. Aborigines survive. d. Agriculture, grazing, trade, cultural isolation, mineral resources, rugged spirit and physique.
6. PLATEAU	a. See footnote 6-a below. b. Hot to cold. c. Settled recently. d. See 5-d above.	a. See footnote 6-a below. b. Hot to cold. c. Settled late. d. See 5-d above.
7. GREAT BASIN	a. "Great Basin Area" within the heart of the western mountains. b. Montane climate. c. Recent settlement. d. Grain, grazing, overland trade, cities and towns, isolation.	a. "Red Basin" of Szechuan within the heart of the western mountains. b. Montane climate. c. See note 7-c below. d. Grain, grazing, overland trade, cities and towns, isolation.

TABLE 1—*Concluded*

Divergences. 1-b. The climate of East Asia is not dominated by the influence of circumpolar cyclonic storms as is that of North America. On the other hand with respect to tropical cyclonic storms affecting the coastal areas there is a definite, though not exact, parallel. Caribbean and South Atlantic hurricanes are larger in scope than their counterparts, called typhoons, which sweep the coasts of China from south to east. The effects, both physical and cultural, are similar.

1-c. With respect to the time scale of history we may take it to be roughtly 1 to 10. *Viz.* One century of American history is equivalent to a millenium of Chinese. In the matter of the settlement of the east and south coastal areas there is an interesting contrast: In America this area was the first settled and the source of subsequent settlement inland, whereas in China settlement progressed from inland seaward.

2-a. The ranges flanking the China coast are lower than those in North America. They are now thoroughly deforested, though formerly they supported timber, and someday may be expected to be reforested.

3-a. The Mississippi, of course, contrasts with the Yangtze in running North to South instead of West to East, but this geographical fact has little significance in relation to our thesis.

3-c. An important fact not to be overlooked is this, that although these rich midland regions were settled in the second major phases of expansion of America and China respectively, in America it was the overseas and early East-coastal civilization that set the pattern for our culture, whereas in China it was the inland civilization of the midland with its background of North and West which set the pattern for Chinese culture.

4-c. The Plains were settled late in America, early in China.

6-a. The American Plateau Area is a "plateau" in the sense in which the word is popularly used, whereas the plateau region of southwest China is a plateau in the geological sense, consisting of ridges and valleys deeply eroded, with little flat land, at high elevation. This area in China also has far more rainfall and warmer climate than our plateau area.

7-b. The temperature in the Red Basin is warmer than that of our Great Basin, and rainfall is ample for all-year-round rice cultivation.

7-c. While Szechuan was settled very early (the old wall of Chungking is dated 320 B.C.) its isolation has retarded the introduction of advances both in Chinese and modern civilization.

East Coasts and Texas; whereas on the Plains, both of China and the United States, where summer heat is untempered by the ocean, maximum temperatures run well above 100°F.

Mean annual rainfall is as follows (Bartholemew, Pl. 18):

China		*U. S. A.*
Under 10″	Mongolia	Southwest, Great Basin, Plateau, Western Plains
10″–20″	Northwest China	Middle Great Plains
20″–40″	Manchuria, Chihli (Hopei), Szechuan	Eastern Great Plains
40″–60″	Yangtze Valley	Mississippi Valley Eastward
60″–80″	All of South China	—

Note: The greater rainfall in South China accounts for its richer vegetation and the high humidity which make South China seem more tropical than our Southeast.

Prevailing winds also correspond (Bartholemew, Pl. 14). In January and February these blow south and southeastward from Siberia, swinging to east and southeast along the coast, while in the U. S. A. the prevailing winter winds are blowing southeast and eastward over the country. July and August see the moisture-laden monsoon winds blowing north and northeastward from the China Sea and the equatorial Pacific, while the rain-bearing winds of our summer come northward from the Gulf and northeastward from the South Atlantic.

We can here indicate only in barest outline the interesting climatic equivalences. Maps alone, showing temperature, rainfall, winds (Bartholemew), cyclonic storms (Goode, map 12) and ocean currents (Bos-Niermeyer, Pl. 3), can convey the full weight of evidence and sense of its significance from an environmental point of view.

The cyclonic storms of the Caribbean and Gulf regions in our own hemisphere (which sometimes reach "hurricane" proportions), and those in the China Sea area (which when reaching "hurricane" proportions are termed "typhoons") affecting southeastern China, Korea, and Japan (Goode's Atlas, map 12) have both parallel origins, meteorologically, and parallel effects and influence on the land, peoples, and cultures respectively of southeastern and eastern United States and southeastern and eastern China, Korea, and Japan. These tropical cyclonic storms produce humidity and rain over wide areas for extended periods; they affect shipping, fisheries, ports, agriculture, com-

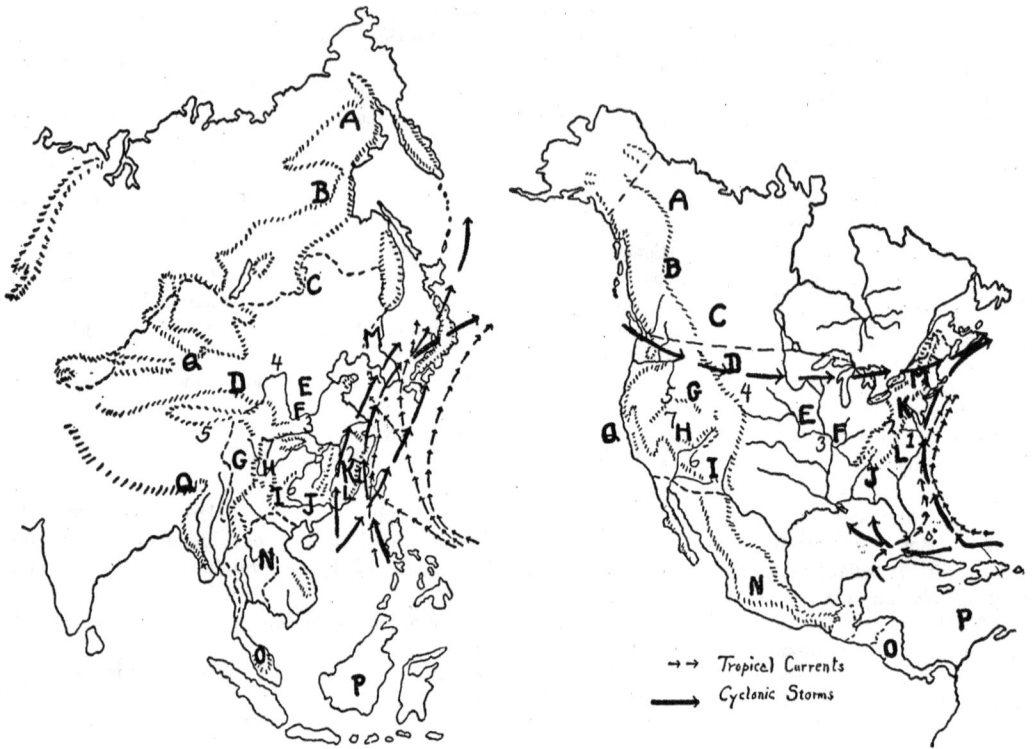

FIG. 1

TABLE 2

EQUIVALENT AREAS OF NORTH AND MIDDLE AMERICA, AND EAST AND SOUTHEAST ASIA

(Capital letters refer to figure 1)

North and Middle America		*East and Southeast Asia*
Northwest Canada and Alaska	A	Northeast Siberia and Kamchatka
Northwest Territories of Canada	B	Eastern Siberia
Alberta, Saskatchewan, Manitoba	C	Mongolia, N. Manchuria
Northwestern States east of Rockies	D	Kokonor, Sinkiang, Kansu, Shensi
The Great Plains	E	The Plains of So. Manchuria, Mongolia, Chihli (Hopei), Shensi, Honan and Shantung
Mississippi Flood Plains, Tributaries and Delta	F	Yangtze Flood Plains, Tributaries and Delta
Rocky Mountain States	G	Western Szechuan, Tibet
Great Basin	H	Red Basin of Szechuan
Plateau and Southwest	I	Eastern Szechuan, Yunnan, Kweichow, Kwangsi
Gulf States	J	So. Kwangsi, Kwangtung, Tonking
Appalachian Mountains	K	Southeastern Mountains
Middle and South East Coasts, Coastal Plains and Piedmont	L	Kiangsu, Chekiang, Fukien
New York and New England	M	E. Shantung, Korea, N. Japan and Hokkaido
Mexico and Guatemala	N	French Indo-China and Siam
Central America	O	Malaya
Caribbean (Islands, Columbia, Venezuela, Guiana)	P	Island Asia (East Indies and Philippines)
West Coastal and Pacific Barrier	Q	Himalayan and Desert Barriers

munications; influence settlement, building practices and structural principles; furthermore, barometric pressure, temperature, humidity, etc., which reflect the conditions producing these storms, affect all biological processes directly and profoundly.

East Asia is *not* subject to the procession of circumpolar cyclonic storms which harass and control the winter climate of the middle northern belt of our continent, crossing southern Canada, the Great Lakes, and northern States. These circumpolar storm tracks arising out of the meeting of warm and cold air over the North Atlantic and North Pacific respectively, fade out across Siberia by reason of the vast land mass of Eur-Asia. Consequently northern China, though experiencing cold weather from Arctic continental sources in the winter, does not have great winter storms and snows such as affect North America and Europe. Climatically, China is in this important feature less comparable to North America than is Europe. Leaving aside for the moment racial differences, the lack of winter cyclonic storms in China may have something to do with the more placid temperament of the north Chinese as compared with north Europeans and Americans of the northern States.

Referring to Table 2, we note: **A.** Arctic, subarctic. **B.** Coasts, forest and mountains (in Asia less rugged). **C.** Tundra to plains (in Asia more arid). **D.** Mountains and plains (in Asia, arid). **E.** Great plains (in Asia more arid). **F.** The midland river region in China has less diversity of climate, due to west-to-east course; piedmont and valley zones less fertile and with fewer resources. **G.** The potentialities of Tibet cannot be weighed against those of our Rocky Mountain States, for Tibet is yet to be explored by scientists and engineers. **H.** Mineral resources rank first in America's, agricultural in China's warmer, wetter great basin. **I.** Our Plateau and Southwest is arid and temperate, while China's is wet and subtropical. **J.** Southernmost China bordering the China Sea is more tropical than our Gulf States, which are agriculturally superior. **K.** Our southeastern mountains are higher and richer in mining, forest, and agricultural resources, water power, soil, and range of climate. **L.** In harbors and fisheries, in forests, agriculture, waterways and waterpower, this area in the U. S. A. is superior to its equivalent in China. **M.** This area in Asia is less rich in mineral, agricultural, and forest resources. This zone's deciduous forests are strikingly like our northeastern forests. **N.** The Southern area is more tropical, perhaps potentially superior to its equivalent in America—unless we use irrigation on a vast scale. **O.** With rubber and tin as primary resources, and Singapore as the greatest Far Eastern port, Malaya outranks Middle America. But Middle America is relatively less developed. **P.** The East Indies and the Philippines potentially far outweigh the Caribbean in human, mineral, agricultural, and forest resources. **Q.** Westward from America is ocean, the vast island-studded Pacific, with Island Asia, Southeast, and East Asia beyond. Westward from China are the Himalayan walls extending northward and westward from Burma across northern India; and in the north and northwest, the Gobi and Mongolian deserts; beyond these lie south and west Asia, Europe and Africa. There appears to be little if any geographic parallelism here. And yet from the point of view of conditioning environmental influence and activation, America's westward ocean barrier and China's westward mountain-desert barrier *are* equivalent. Both have served as (1) *isolating* barriers. Both also have been (2) mediums and means of slow but continuous communication and trade: on the Pacific, overseas (a) to the islands and (b) Asiatic mainland in Central Asia, overland via the ancient routes, connecting (a) Southwest China with India via Burma and Assam, (b) Western China via Tibet with Northern India, (c) Northwest and Northern China via Sinkiang with Afghanistan and Northwest India, Persia, Southwest Asia, Europe and Africa.

Against the factors of topography, soil, resources, and climate, it is necessary in evaluating overall potentials to weigh the factors of human resources: demographic (population distribution), ethnic and genetic (quality and race), and such imponderables as heritage of culture, character, aptitude, inventiveness, etc. It would be rash to make any summary of potential resources, material and human. Against American superior material resources and technical skill, for example, must be weighed China's numerical population and its reproductive powers, and Chinese stability, patience, persistence, endurance, and capacity for sustained effort and survival with a minimum of food and material.

The parallelism may be extended in an overall analogy, as between the Western and Far Eastern "hemispheres," as follows:

America	*East Asia*
Canada	Siberia
U. S. A.	China
Mexico	Southeast Asia
Middle America— Caribbean	Malaya and Island Asia

Careful examination of the continental areas under consideration demonstrates two facts: (1) Nowhere else on our globe can be found another continental area that resembles these two (Eastern and Southeastern Asia and North and Middle America) and offers so many parallels and equivalences; and (2) between no other continental areas (Middle, Southern or Western Asia, Europe, Africa, South America) can such a table of overall corresponding areas and regions be drawn up. In other words, these two great spheres are not only neighbors, but are unique in the world in their geographic affinity, and consequently can and should enjoy an intimate association, on the human plane, in working out a concordant destiny based upon common interests and principles, mutual understanding and joint effort.

II. MILITARY CONSIDERATIONS

There is nothing in the problem of future military arrangements and strategy which conflicts with the conceptions we are advocating, namely intimate neighborly collaboration on a grand scale between the two pivotal great powers, the United States and China, in their respective spheres of North America and East Asia.

Professor George B. Cressey,[3] of Syracuse University, has summarized so well and so simply the military aspect of the future Pacific and Far Eastern set-up from the point of view of American security and interests, that we avail ourselves of his statement as expressing our views precisely. Cressey, as a geographer having long and intimate first-hand acquaintance with China, and representing a practical American humanitarian point of view, sees the problem of the relation of our country to the Pacific and the Far East with the extended vision and perspective of the social, economic, and political evolutionist, rather than that of the academic geopolitician like Nicholas Spykman.[4] Cressey writes:

[3] *Asia's Lands and Peoples* (New York: Whittlesey House, 1944), p. 10.

[4] Spykman's *The Geography of the Peace* (New York: Harcourt, Brace & Co., 1944) represents a third stage of extension of the Eur-Asiatic world picture originated by Mackinder in 1904, taken up and utilized as a political instrument and philosophy by Haushofer. We believe that the regional parallelism and cooperation to which we point offer a better guarantee of peace than the strategy of Rimland-Heartland geopolitical principles of power politics which the U. S. A. has always avoided. While recognizing Spykman's work

Dutch Harbor, Pearl Harbor, and Panama are the Pacific fortresses for the defense of continental United States. Beyond them are the outposts of Kiska, Midway, Samoa, and other small islands. These form a natural American sphere. To go farther is to lengthen supply lines and enter areas where there are thousands of islands. To control Guam it is necessary to have all of the Marshall, Caroline, and Mariana groups. To enter the South Pacific there is no stopping till one reaches Australia and Singapore. Thus Japan took Korea to protect her islands, then Manchuria to protect Korea, later on Inner Mongolia to protect Manchuria, and she wants Eastern Siberia to protect the whole. One should beware that the appetite does not grow with the eating and exceed the capacity of the digestion.

The only possible trans-Pacific enemies of the United States for a century to come are the Soviet Union, China, and Japan. Australia and Southeastern Asia are too weak. The United States might have disagreements with a free Philippines, but the latter could scarcely attack. Whatever the future possessions of European powers in the Pacific, the United States should easily enjoy superior advantages. China will be busy with internal development for decades and has never had conspicuous maritime interests; if imperialistic her interests will turn southward. Climate and topography make it unlikely that the Soviet Union can ever be a major Pacific power, and any war would be via Alaska rather than the broad Pacific. Only Japan promises to be a future threat, and if her outer island territories are removed, she will be without offensive striking power. Hence the Dutch Harbor-Pearl Harbor defense line appears reasonably adequate.

With this view of our natural inner and outer Pacific defense zones we concur completely. Beyond this it should be the part of the U. S. A., in a military sense, simply (1) to stand by and sustain China as preserver of law and order in East Asia, and (2) to cooperate with the British, Dutch, and Chinese in neutralizing the Micronesian-Melanesian island fringe which was used by Japan in launching this present war southward and eastward; but direct military responsibility in East Asian waters or territory, after victory, is literally "out of our sphere." Thus military considerations not only do not conflict with the geographic and political factors but add their weight to these in demarking Eastern Asia and Island Asia as a distinct sphere in which China is the logical leader,

as a masterly analysis and contribution, we should certainly deplore its influencing American policy too heavily. Its motivating conceptions and reasoning are not, in our opinion, genuinely American in principle or spirit.

exactly as these same considerations (military security) have demarked the Western "Hemisphere" as a distinct sphere in which the U. S. A. is the pivotal great power.

III. POLITICAL AND ECONOMIC CONCEPTS

A. Retrospect

The uninterrupted tradition and sentiment of mutual understanding between the United States and China, of which we spoke at the outset, is popularly assumed in this century to have been the direct if not exclusive outgrowth of the celebrated "Open Door Policy"[5] enunciated by our Secretary of State John Hay in 1899 at a time when the carving up of China into zones of exclusive interest by the several European Powers was underway and its consummation imminent. In reality, the actual founding and nurture of this tradition dates back, officially to the first United States Commercial Commission to China in 1844 under Caleb Cushing, and back of that to the early missionary scholars who served it and its successors as Secretary-Interpreters and who strongly influenced its policies in direct contrast to the prevailing diplomacy of the day.

Most notable of these is the famous Dr. Samuel Wells Williams,[6] second American to go direct to the China mission field (in 1833), whose 43 years of residence in China were devoted equally to Christian service, Chinese scholarship, and official diplomacy. In the course of 15 years of diplomatic service his influence in the direction of fairness and moderation *toward* China and of extended Christian opportunities *in* China was marked.

The other most notable impress upon Chinese-American relations and upon the American China policy, antedating the era of "The Open Door," was made by our first Minister of Legation at the Court of Peking, Anson Burlingame, who went out to establish that Legation in the turbulent year of 1861. An exceptionally broad-visioned and warm-spirited man, with a political background of service in the Congressional Committee on Foreign Affairs, Burlingame's name became associated with that (for the times) startling new "Doctrine" of international procedure (the recognition of Chinese territorial and civil integrity)

which became official American policy at a moment in history electric with potential disaster for China, and which, more than any other event of that age, saved China from outright partition and set the tone for a growing Chinese-American sympathy and friendship.

In strong contrast to the "Burlingame Doctrine" which took cognizance of the sovereign rights of a nation and a people and sought to build on a reciprocal basis of benefits bestowed and concessions gained,[7] the prevalent tone of "diplomatic" dealings with the already decadent Manchu Government was that of harsh "realism," as exemplified in the so-called "Gunboat policy" of Britain and France and later, before the close of the nineteenth century, zealously copied and improved upon by Germany and Japan in China. American official abstinence from participation in the fruits of bayonet-enforced treaties and territorial concessions, certain specific modifications of aggressive policy on the part of European Powers achieved through the influence of American diplomacy, and the actual averting of partition may be directly traced to the Burlingame Doctrine of "fair and open policy." These facts, together with the traditional cultivation of good will through a century of religious, educational, and medical missionary endeavor, have built up a relationship of confidence between the American and Chinese peoples which is as definitely an obligation as it is an asset on the part of both to foster and continue.

At the close of World War I the United States, pursuant to its century-old Far Eastern policy of

---

[5] Samuel Flagg Bemis, *A Diplomatic History of the United States* (New York: Henry Holt, 1942), pp. 482–502.

[6] Frederick W. Williams (ed.) *Life and Letters of S. Wells Williams* (New York: Putnam, 1889).

[7] "We seek for China that equality without which nations and men are degraded. We seek not only the good of China, but we seek your good and the good of all mankind. We do this in no sentimental sense. We would be practical as the toiling millions whom we represent. We invite you to a broader trade. We invite you to a more intimate examination of the structure of Chinese civilization. We invite you to a better appreciation of the manners of that people . . . and we shall ask for them, from you, modern science . . . and the holy doctrines of our Christian Faith." This when Burlingame had resigned his diplomatic post to accept a mission on behalf of the Chinese Court to the Western nations, and had arrived in America with his Chinese colleagues and their entourage on the first lap of their world tour. After fruitful months in England and less success in Germany and France, he died of pneumonia in St. Petersburg in 1867 before the completion of the mission. See Frederick W. Williams, *Anson Burlingame and the First Chinese Mission to Foreign Powers* (New York: Scribner's, 1912).

supporting an independent China, took the initiative in calling the Washington Conference to consider limitation of armament and the grave problems confronting China vis-a-vis "The Powers." A primary purpose was the strengthening of that revolution-torn nation and her release from the foreign strictures (specifically Japanese) made upon her sovereignty and territory during four years of world conflict. In the course of World War II this major American objective in Asia has remained to the fore. It has not always been easy for our State Department to reconcile this objective with the quite other policies and objectives in Asia of our associates and allies, notably France and Britain, and it is not proving to be easy at the present time. Nor has each and every American Administration in the past been equally undeviating or uncompromising in the pursuit of our traditional State policy in this field. But, as Walter Lippmann has said,[8] the chief Far Eastern commitment of the United States has ever been that of "opposing the dismemberment of China into spheres of imperialist influence" and of fostering what is today unmistakably "the objective of the Pacific war and its most notable consequence—the emergence of China as a new great power in the modern world."[9]

Mr. Lippmann in his later book[10] dealing with war objectives states that this emergent China, in "the shape of things to come," will demonstrate the inevitability of his contention that if the problem of *world order* is capable of solution at all it will be only in an order "composed of the great regional constellations of states which are the homelands, not of one nation alone but of the historic civilized communities." Such a regional system will naturally (and, we add, *inevitably, by reason of historical, geographic, cultural, and ethnic compulsions*) "form around China," and "that it will in time encompass not only the Chinese dependencies in the North but also the whole or the greater part of the mainland of Southeast Asia

[8] *U. S. Foreign Policy: Shield of the Republic* (Boston: Atlantic, 1943), p. 156. See also: Samuel Flagg Bemis, (ed.), *The American Secretaries of State and Their Diplomacy* (New York: Knopf, 1929), X, 240–249.

[9] What Mr. Lippmann does not stress is the point that for China this is a *re-*emergence, historically logical in view of her age-long position as *the* great power in the Asiatic ancient world.

[10] *U. S. War Aims* (Boston: Atlantic, 1944), pp. 87, 92–95.

is probable."[11] We believe that ultimately this is destined to encompass Island Asia (the East Indies and the Philippines) also.

B. REGIONALISM

This concept of a Far Eastern Sphere (or several spheres) is not of course original with Mr. Lippmann, though his grasp of the essential nature of such a concept in the future world frame is new and vigorous. Nathaniel Peffer, J. B. Condliffe, Bruno Lasker, W. L. Holland, P. E. Corbett (to name but a few students of the Far East) have been dealing with these concepts for years; these men are thinking regionally, but are not proposing "blueprints" for regional organization.[12] Others, such as S. R. Chow and Raymond Kennedy, have definite plans to offer.

Professor S. R. Chow not only thinks regionally but builds an elaborate plan for regional organiza-

[11] This sound analysis and prognosis *in re* Far Eastern regionalism is of quite another order than the blueprint drawn by Ely Culbertson in his "World Territorial Table," in *A System to Win This War and Win the Peace to Come* (privately printed, 1943). Mr. Culbertson grasped the essential importance of a regional substructure for world organization, but his schematic table consists simply of a convenient jig-saw patterning of the hemispheric maps and is not based either upon wide knowledge of current history or considerations of racial, political or economic geography.

[12] In his article on "Regionalism and Plans for Post-War Reconstruction", Vol. 21, No. 4 of *Social Forces*, James T. Watkins dismisses these writers along with numerous others from any serious consideration, with the coverall statement: "It must be stated at the outset that so far as can be discovered from the works under review scientific regionalism plays no part in the thinking of any of the peace planners"; and "we look in vain, therefore, if we look for an approach to the problems of post-war reconstruction which is grounded solidly upon the science of the region" (p. 381). What Professor Watkins means, if we understand him aright, is that the principles of "regionalism" exemplifying sociological and ecological research, have not as yet been applied to the Far Eastern sphere. Using the word "science" with a larger meaning, we would consider that actually "the science of the region" is prominent in the thinking of such men as Condliffe, Holland, Lasker, for their conceptions are grounded in the first place in thorough scientific training and discipline, and secondly in a long experience and practical knowledge of the geographic, economic, and social factors in the particular area under discussion.

tion, basing it upon the necessity of a closer-knit harmony of interests, and of the machinery for safeguarding them, than is possible within a single world organization.[13] But he talks in terms of "the Pacific," and "the Pacific" is not a region: it is too vast, too diverse—and mostly water! Although it has been useful as a geographical-political concept in past decades of preliminary cooperative endeavor around the great ocean, the phrase in reality connotes simply a communicating medium between regions. Therefore, it seems to us that despite its carefully wrought scheme and its many valuable details, for which potential planners must be grateful, Professor Chow's community of association, like the Pacific concept, is too vast, too diverse, and too widely separated in distance and in all but the most basic of security interests, to be practical.

True regions are born, not made. Not only must a truly functional region have geographic-demographic unity, but to achieve political permanence it should be geared to a firmly established, responsible nation of the first order which will act as stabilizer and pivot, or core. This, in our view, is a *sine qua non* of functional success. Such a condition exists in the Western Hemisphere in the leadership of the U. S. A., in Australasia in that of Australia; it will in time re-demonstrate its existence in China's sphere, as it has in the past.[14] If Professor Chow had been less the

internationalist—more the true "scientific regionalist"—he would, we believe, have constructed a more workable plan than the one which Dr. Hu criticizes on the very grounds of its "regional" character. He would have shown himself more acutely aware of the historic and potential position of China as pivotal great nation in the East Asian region; while at the same time his internationalist viewpoint would have convinced him of the inescapable dependence of the region upon this regained leadership, for any durable peace and security.[15]

The inevitability of this regained leadership as the basis for any durable peace and security in the East Asiatic sphere we believe we have demonstrated conclusively (if briefly) on historic, cultural, and geographic grounds in an article dealing mainly with China's place in the last stages of the Japanese war and the initial phases of the peace—namely invasion and negotiation. In this same article we dealt in general terms with the need for a regional union[16] in the Far Eastern sphere,

[13] S. R. Chow, *Winning the Peace in the Pacific* (New York: Macmillan, 1944). In a preface to Prof. Chow's book Dr. Hu Shih, the seasoned internationalist, expresses disagreement with the desirability of regionalism vs. world organization. We do not believe the problem to be one of *alternatives*, or that Prof. Chow so presents it. He conceives of regional organization as a *facility* within the world mechanism. Perhaps Pearl Buck correctly estimates Dr. Hu's objection when in a book review (*Asia and the Americas*, New York, Feb. 1944) she suggests that he "believes that the problems of Asia are not so different from those of other parts of the world as to need a regional government under a world organization." This reaction would be quite understandable if regional organization were conceived of as being so restricted, but regionalism as a universal principle within a world federation or association has come to be the chief concern of all those who think in terms of regions or "spheres," and does not, it seems to us, present an obstacle or a danger to world union as such.

[14] India, and her surrounding territories, constitute another true region in the sense defined above, one of

potential magnitude so great in itself that it will be unfortunate indeed if either nationalistic aspirations of the moment or interests of any sort succeed in tacking it as an appendage onto a Far Eastern organization, or in throwing it into an international discard, or leaving it shamelessly in the status of colonial annex. This is not the place to enter into a discussion of India in the Asiatic or world picture, but it is undeniable that India's status and role, though cast on a different stage and within another orbit, are intimately bound up with those of China.

[15] In this particular his countryman T. S. Chien, writing in *Foreign Affairs*, New York, July, 1943, on China's peace aims, shows himself to be more realistic. Keenly aware of the regional viewpoint and of his country's intense concern with the shape of the East Asiatic future, he lists as of equal importance with 1) the technical mechanisms of security, 2) restoration of lost territories, and 3) opportunity for national economic development, a much less tangible factor, namely the *unhindered resumption of China's traditional "position of dignity"* among the smaller Asiatic nations—an ancient position lost only during the last 150 years of Manchu decadence, foreign imperialism, and domestic revolution.

[16] Elizabeth Green and Craighill Handy, "China First," *Asia and the Americas* (New York: January, 1944). "In stressing this conviction of China's destined leadership we are not advocating any application of the Führer principle which General Chiang so vigorously repudiates in his own delineation of 'China's After-War Aims'; nor are we suggesting that China

operating within the frame of world association. In a subsequent (uncompleted) study we developed in some detail a tentative plan for such a union, based fundamentally on functional regional cooperation of interests and endeavors rather than on purely political conceptions and mechanisms. This plan (A Proposed Union of States of East Asia) conceived of China as pivot in a naturally motivated grouping of her immediate mainland neighbors, plus Japan, plus Indonesia—both of which are tied by many long-range factors, past and future, to the coasts of the Asiatic mainland facing them.[17]

Our present conception, looking at the map of East and Southeast Asia in terms of the most rigorous postwar realism, is modified by the inescapable fact that China, materially weakened though morally and (in terms of nationhood) psychologically greatly strengthened by the war, will emerge from her ordeal in no condition to meet any immediate test of strength or challenge to her authority in her sphere. As contrasted with American leadership in the Western Hemisphere, Chinese power will not for some time to come be sufficient, unaided, to enforce or guarantee an equivalent "Monroe Doctrine" in the East Asiatic

_____

'replace western imperialism in Asia with an oriental imperialism'; but quite simply that China must be willing to assume, in the modern world, the responsibility of leadership which was anciently hers within her historic sphere ... The western Pacific is, in war and in peace, a true region. It has an historic background of regionalism which must be understood, and an aspiration toward regional freedom of action which must be facilitated, not obstructed, if it—or the world—is ever to know peace."

[17] Dr. Raymond Kennedy of the Yale Graduate School, foremost American expert on Indonesia, has offered a plan for Indonesian union which conceives ultimately of a "State" which shall unite the insular Indies, the Philippines and peninsular Malaya in a single, gradually achieved, autonomy. This Indonesian State would cooperate regionally with a mainland federated state comprising China, Tibet, Thailand, Indo-China, Korea. See the final chapter of his book, *The Ageless Indies* (New York: John Day, 1942), and contrast with Panikkar, *The Future of Southeast Asia* (New York: Macmillan, 1943), and Lasker, *Peoples of Southeast Asia* (New York: Knopf, 1944), for this area.

region. This situation exists by reason of the long-established vested interests of other Powers, Asiatic and non-Asiastic, in that area—interests which the exigencies of the present war will not by any means have liquidated completely by the war's end. Hence the picture must be recognized as, peripherally, one of overlapping areas of influence, responsibility and interest; while at the center of her mainland orbit Chinese autonomy operates unchallenged. From this center her influence will naturally extend outward (northeast, southeast, and south) to those fringes of her sphere where other interests and influences overlap— there to join in cooperative regional responsibility with the Russian in Mongolia, Dutch in Indonesia, French in Indo-China and Thailand, British in Thailand, Malaya, and Burma.

In this regional picture America's responsible share is also clear. By then our territorial (though not our protective) commitments in the Philippines will have been resolved; but by reason of this very negligibility of our territorial claims and interests in the area, ours will most fittingly be the role of chief friend and guarantor to China during the period of her national recuperation. It will be during this same period that two other processes will normally and coincidentally take place: (1) the consolidation of China's natural regional leadership (leadership, *not* domination), and (2) the gradual achievement of native autonomy and relinquishment of foreign authority in the various dependencies adjacent to China proper. When this latter process is complete, the region which we (and before us, history!) denominated as China's natural sphere will have "come of age" as a potent factor for peace and stability in the modern world.

So, in a word, as the important military considerations affecting our own security and obligations to other nations not only do not conflict with but definitely *accord* with our scheme for Far Eastern regionalism, so equally do the political and economic factors add their weight to our thesis that China and America have unique and intimately related backgrounds and destinies and owe it to each other and the world to act as partners in the important business of domestic planning and cooperation with other nations and regions.

www.ingramcontent.com/pod-product-compliance
Lightning Source LLC
Chambersburg PA
CBHW080424270326
41929CB00018B/3147